03950

MYSTICAL THEOLOGY

The sweet and living knowledge that she says he
taught her is mystical theology, the secret knowledge of God that spiritual persons call contemplation. This knowledge is very delightful because it is
knowledge through love. Love is the master of this
knowledge and what makes it wholly agreeable.

The principal property involved in calling contemplation a 'ladder' is its being a science of love, which
. . . is an infused, loving knowledge, that both illumines and enamours the soul, elevating it step by
step unto God its creator.

St John of the Cross

For Heinrich Dumoulin

BOOKS BY WILLIAM JOHNSTON

The Mysticism of 'The Cloud of Unknowing'
The Still Point
Christian Zen
Silent Music
The Inner Eye of Love
The Mirror Mind
The Wounded Stag
Being in Love
Letters to Contemplatives

TRANSLATIONS
From the Japanese

Silence by Shusaku Endo
The Bells of Nagasaki by Takashi Nagai
Meeting God through Science by Mutsuo Yanase
Call to Meditation by Kakichi Kadowaki

Mystical Theology

*

THE SCIENCE OF LOVE

William Johnston

HarperCollins*Publishers*

Fount Paperbacks is an Imprint of
HarperCollins*Religious*
Part of HarperCollins*Publishers*
77–85 Fulham Palace Road, London W6 8JB

First published in 1995 by HarperCollins*Publishers*
This edition published
in 1996 by Fount Paperbacks

1 3 5 7 9 10 8 6 4 2

Copyright © 1995 William Johnston

William Johnston asserts the moral right to be
identified as the author of this work

A catalogue record for this book is
available from the British Library

0 00 628 0021

Printed and bound in Great Britain by
Caledonian International Book Manufacturing, Glasgow

CONDITIONS OF SALE

This book is sold subject to the condition that it
shall not, by way of trade or otherwise, be lent, re-sold,
hired out or otherwise circulated without the publisher's
prior consent in any form of binding or cover other
than that in which it is published and without a
similar condition including this condition being
imposed on the subsequent purchaser.

All rights reserved. No part of this publication may be
reproduced, stored in a retrieval system, or transmitted,
in any form or by any means, electronic, mechanical,
photocopying, recording or otherwise, without the prior
permission of the publishers.

CONTENTS

————— ✳ —————

PART II DIALOGUE

PART III THE MYSTICAL JOURNEY TODAY

INTRODUCTION

---*---

The twentieth century has witnessed an upsurge of interest in mysticism. Academic studies of mystics East and West appear in great numbers, as perceptive scholars realize that mysticism is one of the most important religious experiences in human life. But even more important than the academic studies is the number of modern people who are practising meditation and find themselves drawn into the deeper states of consciousness that are ordinarily called mystical. Beginning with the repetition of a mantra, or awareness of the breathing, or the savouring of a phrase from sacred Scripture, they feel drawn beyond thinking and reasoning to a unitive consciousness wherein they rest silently in the presence of the great mystery that envelops the whole universe.

When people enter into deep states of consciousness they need guidance and help. Such is the teaching of all the great mystical traditions, for the journey into the mystery that lies at the heart of things is fraught with peril. Without a safe guide one can wander in illusion or get lost in the tempests or simply come to a standstill, making no progress.

Fortunately, from the early centuries of our era there has existed within Christianity a science of mystical theology which aims at teaching people to pray, guiding them through the dark night to the summit of the mountain. The first known treatise on mystical theology was written at the end of the fourth or the beginning of the fifth century by an anonymous Syrian monk with heavy Neo-Platonic influence, who affixed the name of Dionysius the Areopagite to his work. His *Mystical Theology* is written in the form of a letter to a disciple, giving practical instruction on how to ascend the mountain of prayer. It leads the disciple beyond imaging, reasoning and thinking into a cloud of unknowing where, like Moses, he meets God in impenetrable darkness.

At the same time, the desert fathers in Egypt were guiding their disciples in the ways of contemplative prayer, teaching them to enter into wordless silence where they would encounter God. Their teaching profoundly influenced Eastern Christianity where mystical theology flourished, as the hesychasts taught the Jesus prayer and led their disciples to the heights of contemplation.[1] The desert fathers also influenced Western monasticism where contemplation put down roots that remain to this day.

The fourteenth century saw a galaxy of mystics in the Rhineland, in Flanders and in England. These mystics were also teachers and spiritual guides. The English author of *The Cloud of Unknowing*, who also translated the *Mystical Theology* of Dionysius, writes letters to a disciple, giving instruction on how to enter the cloud, how to avoid the pitfalls, how to weather the storms. A similar movement appears in sixteenth-century Spain where the Carmelites teach an ecstatic mysticism centred on the cross of Jesus and the renunciation of all things for love. They guide contemplatives through the dark night of the soul to the summit of Mount Carmel or through the mansions to the centre of the interior castle.

In the first half of the twentieth century mystical theology — sometimes called ascetical and mystical theology — was taught in Catholic seminaries and faculties of theology throughout the world. Again, it was a practical or pastoral discipline which taught the students to pray and to guide the contemplatives they would meet in their future ministry. Textbooks, written by some outstanding mystical theologians, spoke of acquired and infused or mystical contemplation.[2] The former was acquired by the ordinary process of knowing, aided by divine grace. Infused or mystical contemplation, on the other hand, was pure gift, infused by God: it could in no way be merited. It begins with what St Teresa called the prayer of quiet wherein one rests silently in the presence of God, paying no attention to the wandering distractions of the restless mind; then one passes through the dwelling places of the interior castle until one reaches the goal which is the spiritual marriage. One subject of controversy concerned the frequency of mystical contemplation. Some authors spoke of the universal call to mysticism, claiming that infused contemplation was an ordinary development of the Christian life and that it was included in the grace of baptism. Others held that mystical contemplation was a charismatic gift granted to a few privileged people.

After the Second Vatican Council mystical theology ceased to be taught in Catholic seminaries and departments of theology. The changed circumstances in the whole world seemed to render it irrelevant. But what about the future?

The present writer believes that the time has come to rewrite mystical theology for the men and women of the twenty-first century. The time has come to restore it to its honoured place in the curriculum of theological studies. However, it cannot be taught to the twenty-first century just as it was taught to the fourth and to the sixteenth centuries. It must be renewed and updated; it must be made relevant. The challenge confronting us is to be true to the Gospel and tradition while facing the unique problems that have arisen in the twentieth century.

In the precise understanding of mystical theology this book follows St John of the Cross, making the adaptations and changes that seem necessary in our time.

In his prose writings St John of the Cross is primarily a teacher and a guide, who leads his reader to the summit of the mountain or the centre of the soul where supreme wisdom dwells. At the beginning of *The Ascent of Mount Carmel* he laments that many good people fail to make the progress they should: 'And so it is sad to see them continue in their lowly method of communion with God because they do not want to know how to advance or because they receive no direction on breaking away from the method of beginners.' Confident that his own doctrine is sound and trustworthy he writes:

> With God's help, then, we will propose doctrine and counsel for beginners and proficients that they may understand or at least know how to practise abandonment to God's guidance when they want to advance.[3]

The first lesson, then, is abandonment to God. Alas, the contemplative kicks and screams like the child who refuses to be carried by its mother. St John of the Cross is a skilful spiritual guide who teaches the child to surrender to its mother: he teaches the contemplative to open her heart to the inflow of love that comes from God. He has at his disposal a body of doctrine derived from sacred Scripture, from mystical tradition, from his own experience and from the experience of those who have opened their hearts to him. Well versed in the ways of prayer and spiritual direction, he is the mystical doctor par excellence.

However, when he comes to define mystical theology he follows an ancient tradition according to which theology means wisdom. He makes no distinction between mystical theology and mystical wisdom or mystical prayer. He even equates mystical theology with contemplation, writing that 'contemplation is mystical theology which theologians call secret wisdom and which St Thomas says is communicated into the soul through love'.[4]

This present book, however, understands the word theology in a more modern sense. That is to say, it takes mystical theology not just as the secret wisdom that comes through love but as *the science that reflects on, and teaches, the secret wisdom that comes through love*. In order to develop such a science it is necessary to consider what is this secret wisdom that comes from love, what is this secret and loving knowledge.

In his great poem *The Spiritual Canticle* where he sings of the love of bride and bridegroom, St John of the Cross tells us that the bridegroom gives his breast to the bride and teaches her a sweet and living knowledge. This sweet and living knowledge, he explains, is contemplation or mystical theology:

> The sweet and living knowledge that she says he taught her is mystical theology, the secret knowledge of God that spiritual persons call contemplation. This knowledge is very delightful because it is knowledge through love. Love is the master of this knowledge and what makes it wholly agreeable.[5]

Here two words call for explanation: one is *love* and the other is *secret*. When St John of the Cross says that mystical wisdom comes through love he means not our love for God but God's love for us. 'We love because God first loved us' writes St John; and St Paul says that the love of God is poured into our hearts by the Holy Spirit who is given to us. The mystical life begins with a deep experience of this infusion of divine love.

In the early stages of the contemplative life one may enjoy a gentle and consoling sense of God's presence. But as time goes on (perhaps after the suffering of the dark night) the infused love of God lights a fire in the depths of one's being. This inner fire is the central phenomenon of the Christian mystical experience. The English author of *The Cloud* calls it 'the blind stirring of love'. The hesychasts speak constantly of the divine fire.

At first this fire may not seem like fire. It is, in the paradoxical words of St John of the Cross, a dark fire. This is because it is doing work of purification:

> In the beginning of the spiritual purgation, the divine fire spends itself in drying out and preparing the wood — that is, the soul — rather than heating it. Yet as time passes and the fire begins to give off heat, the soul usually experiences the burning of love.[6]

Smoke belches out. Then the log catches fire. Eventually it shoots forth flames, becoming a living flame of love that wounds the soul in its deepest centre. This living flame of love is the Holy Spirit.

The second word that calls for explanation is *secret*. Secret knowledge is mystical knowledge — it is obscure, dark, formless knowledge in a cloud of unknowing. It is knowledge that is experienced as nothingness or emptiness or the void. The poor contemplative, unable to understand what is happening, cries out in anguish. St John of the Cross explains the secrecy of God's communications:

> This communication is secret and dark to the work of the intellect and other faculties. Insofar as these faculties do not acquire it but the Holy Spirit infuses it and puts it in order in the soul, as the bride says in The Song of Songs (Song of Songs 2:4), the soul neither knows nor understands how this comes to pass and thus calls it secret.[7]

There are two kinds of knowledge. One is the distinct, particular knowledge that is acquired through the ordinary process of knowing and is used in ordinary life, in science and in scholarship. But there is another knowledge that is vague, dark, formless, general and loving. This is secret, mystical wisdom.

Then comes the paradox. This vague, dark and secret knowledge is light. It is the light of God which in its intensity blinds the soul, plunging it into darkness and causing great torment. The inner light, like the inner fire, is the centre and core of Christian mystical experience. The fire and the light are inseparable.

And the light, like the fire, is gift. No one can arouse it by human effort. God is the teacher; and St John of the Cross delicately describes the divine pedagogy:

> In contemplation God teaches the soul very quietly and secretly, without its knowing how, without the sound of words, and without the help of any bodily or spiritual faculty, in silence and quietude, in darkness to all sensory and natural things. Some spiritual persons call this contemplation knowing by unknowing.[8]

Knowing by unknowing! These words echo through the apophatic tradition from the time of Dionysius. They mean that in order to know with divine wisdom one must abandon ordinary knowing. One must enter the cloud. One must un-know.

Such is mystical theology as explained by St John of the Cross. However, as has already been said, his writings expound a whole science of this secret and loving wisdom. They reflect on it and teach it to others. In doing this they make use of sacred Scripture and scholastic theology.

The interpretation of sacred Scripture is one of the great challenges confronting mystical theology today. No one can neglect the wealth of biblical scholarship that has graced the twentieth century. No one can neglect the literary criticism, the form criticism, the redaction criticism and the growth in knowledge about historicity, about authorship and about literary genres. And growth continues. Scholars come to see that there are many ways of interpreting the

Scriptures: those who limit themselves to one approach are greatly impoverished. What, then, about the mystical approach?

St John of the Cross states clearly that he will not rely on science or on experience but on sacred Scripture:

> In discussing this dark night, therefore, I will not rely on experience or on science, for these can fail and deceive us. Although I will not neglect whatever possible use I can make of them, my help will be sacred Scripture. Taking Scripture as our guide we do not err, since the Holy Spirit speaks to us through it.[9]

The Holy Spirit speaks to us through it. This is the key to the mystics' interpretation of the Scriptures. God is the author. The Second Vatican Council stated this traditional belief clearly and went on to say: 'The sacred Scriptures contain the word of God and, since they are inspired, really are the word of God; and so the study of the sacred page is, as it were, the soul of sacred theology.'[10] The Council further quoted the words of St Ambrose that 'we speak to Him when we pray; we hear Him when we read the divine sayings'.[11] Most important of all is the Council's contention that there is a presence of Christ in the Scriptures. There are two tables, the table of the Word and the table of the Eucharist. Christ is present in both.

Now there are two ways of studying the sacred page. One can take the scholarly and critical approach, asking about authorship, historicity, literary genres and so on. This is completely necessary for a correct understanding of the Scriptures. Yet the student of mystical theology who limits himself or herself to such an approach will not find the secret wisdom that comes through love. Such a person will not find the presence of Christ. Such a person is eating the outer rind without relishing the delicious inner fruit.

The second approach is contemplative or mystical. It does not neglect scholarship, but it puts more emphasis on savouring and relishing the sacred page with faith. One may repeat a phrase from any of the sacred books, opening one's heart to the guidance of the Holy Spirit, the Divine Teacher, who dwells in the sacred books and in the human heart. In this way one is open to receive the secret wisdom that comes from love.

St John of the Cross, who listens to the Spirit while reading the Scriptures, is aware that those who do not share his faith will regard his interpretations as absurdities. This is particularly true of his reading of The Song of Songs:

> If these similitudes are not read with the simplicity of the spirit of knowledge and love they contain, they will seem to be absurdities rather than reasonable utterances, as will those comparisons of the divine Song of Solomon and other books of sacred Scripture where the Holy Spirit, unable to express the fullness of his meaning in ordinary words, utters mysteries in strange figures and likenesses.[12]

The secret wisdom that comes through love may seem like foolishness.

In this century some scholars have distinguished between the prophetic experience of the Semitic religions and the mystical experience of the Asian religions. Such a thesis, however, is out of keeping with the Christian mystical tradition. In the writings of St John of the Cross, Isaiah, Jeremiah, Ezekiel are consummate mystics, and Elijah has a particularly privileged place in mystical literature. For one who believes in divine authorship the secret wisdom that comes through love is found in every page of the Bible.

From the fourteenth century mystical theology in the Latin church was profoundly influenced by scholasticism. Nor was St John of the Cross an exception. In the prologue of *The Spiritual Canticle* he distinguishes between scholastic theology which is speculative and mystical theology which is experienced. Clearly he believes that scholastic theology is not really necessary. To Mother Ana de Jesus he writes:

> I hope that although some scholastic theology is used here in reference to the soul's interior converse with God, it will not prove vain to speak in such a manner to the pure of spirit. Even though Your Reverence lacks training in scholastic theology, through which divine truths are understood, you are not wanting in mystical theology, which is known through love and

by which these truths are not only known but at the same time experienced.[13]

The distinction between understanding and experiencing through love is significant.

Yet the sanjuanist prose is penetrated with a scholasticism that makes difficult reading for many modern people. The saint distinguishes between sense and spirit, as when he speaks of the superficial night of sense and the terrible night of spirit. In explaining union with God he speaks of the three powers of the soul, saying that there is faith in the intellect, hope in the memory and love in the will. Again he tells us that knowledge and light are in the intellect, while love and fire are in the will. The interplay between the two faculties of intellect and will is an important aspect of his doctrine.

This book describes the scholastic background to the traditional mystical theology. However, when it comes to propose a mystical theology for our day it follows the theology of the Second Vatican Council. Furthermore, instead of speaking of the faculties of the soul, it talks of levels of consciousness. Here the methodology of Bernard Lonergan has proved very helpful.

After describing the ordinary process of knowing — which is experiencing, understanding and judging — Lonergan speaks of another kind of knowledge that comes from the gift of God's love. This would seem to be mystical wisdom. Again, in saying that through religious conversion one's being becomes being-in-love, he uses a language that reminds one of The Song of Songs and the living flame of love. His work could be of great value in the formation of a renewed mystical theology.[14]

Authentic Christian mysticism is nothing but a living of the Gospel at a deep level of consciousness. It is death with Jesus and resurrection with Jesus in accordance with the burning words of a great mystic, 'For if we have been united with him in a death like his, we will certainly be united with him in a resurrection like his' (Romans 6:5). Death and resurrection are lived out in the Eucharist which commemorates the great mystical experience of Jesus himself. And in this context one opens one's heart to the Holy Spirit who is the blind stirring of love, the living flame of love, the inner light, the cloud of unknowing, the dark night of the soul, the secret and loving wisdom.

The task of a modern mystical theology is to convince the world that death and resurrection with Jesus, far from being irrelevant, is the ultimate solution to our overwhelming problems. It is not an easy message. Mystical theology besides being the science of love is, in the words of the Jewish martyr Edith Stein, the science of the cross. Following the Gospel, it proclaims that the cross is not terrible. Paul glories in the cross; and the Russian pilgrim who recited the Jesus prayer was filled with joy.

In attempting to write a renewed mystical theology the author has been faced with a number of challenging questions.

The first concerns renewal. Traditional mystical theology was written almost exclusively for monks and nuns and professionally religious people whose life style was geared to the pursuit of wisdom and the search for God. Celibate people, they could devote long hours to prayer, to liturgy and (if they lived in monasteries) to silent work in the fields. But the scenario has changed. This is the age of the laity. Now married people who live a busy life in factory or classroom or office or laboratory aspire to a life of meditation and mysticism. A renewed mystical theology must ask about the role of the living flame of love in the secular activity of such people. Nor can it neglect marriage. It must ask about the role of sexuality in the mystical life.

A second question stems from the fact that Asian religions are assuming a growing importance in the lives of men and women throughout the world. Dialogue between Buddhism, Hinduism and Christianity is beginning to flourish. Now everyone knows that Asian religions are profoundly contemplative. Asia has given the world mystics filled with secret and hidden wisdom, mystics who have experienced the emptiness, the nothingness, the darkness and the void, mystics who have known the *Lama Sabachthani*. The only kind of theology that talks to them is a mystical theology that is highly experiential, a mystical theology created by people who, having lived the death and resurrection of Jesus, experience the burning love of the Holy Spirit.

Again, dialogue with Asia has already taught the world much

about meditation. Asian meditation is holistic. It stresses the role of the body and teaches us how to sit, how to breathe, how to eat, how to fast, how to sleep, how to watch and how to relax. Those who teach mystical theology to modern people cannot neglect the role of the body.

Then there is the phenomenon of modern science. It is no secret that the world view of modern people has been conditioned by the discoveries of great scientists like Galileo, Newton and Einstein. In the twentieth century relativity and quantum theory have shocked scientists to the roots. Astonished at the seeming irrationality of things in a chaotic universe, some scientists have turned to the outrageous paradoxes of Eastern mysticism. The only Christian theology that will talk to them is a mystical theology that recognizes paradox — a mystical theology that has few words and much experience.

Another problem stems from the fact that modern Christians see social concern as an integral part of their vision. They feel obliged to fight against evil structures that oppress the poor and destroy the environment. A modern mystical theology cannot ignore the social agony of our world. It must demonstrate that the same living flame of love which drives mystics to the solitude of the desert can drive mystics to the hurlyburly of life and to social involvement. Indeed, society is revolutionized by mystics who are inspired by this living flame of love.

This book, then, is a modest attempt to do for the twenty-first century what St John of the Cross did for the sixteenth century. That is to say, its aim is to teach contemplative prayer to men and women who are thirsting for the living water. The author writes primarily for Christians but he dares to hope that the book will say something to others who are united with us in the search for truth. At the beginning of his academic life he wrote a somewhat scholastic book on mystical theology entitled *The Mysticism of 'The Cloud of Unknowing'*. Now, after thirty years of experience, he approaches the same subject. As the shadows lengthen, he realizes that the mystery can never be adequately expressed; he resonates with the words of the dying Hamlet: 'The rest is silence.'

NOTES

1. See *The Mystical Theology of the Eastern Church*, Vladimir Lossky, St Vladimir's Seminary Press, New York 1976.
2. Réginald Garrigou-Lagrange (1877–1964), Adolphe Alfred Tanquerey (1854–1932), Joseph de Guibert (1877–1942), Juan González Arintero (1860–1928) and others.
3. *The Ascent of Mount Carmel*, Prologue 4. (From now *The Ascent*.)
4. *The Dark Night*, 2.17.2. St John of the Cross calls mystical theology 'the science of love'. See *The Dark Night* 2.17.6 and 2.18.5.
5. *The Spiritual Canticle*, 27.5.
6. *The Dark Night*, 2.12.5.
7. Ibid., 2.17.2.
8. *The Spiritual Canticle*, 39.12.
9. *The Ascent*, Prologue 2.
10. *Dei Verbum*, 24.
11. Ibid., 25.
12. *The Spiritual Canticle*, Prologue 1.
13. Ibid., Prologue 3.
14. The writer met Bernard Lonergan in Boston a few years before his death in 1984 and told him that his method culminates in mystical experience. Lonergan smiled and said, 'Yes, yes . . .!'

PART I

The Christian Tradition

ONE

✳

Background (I)

THE NEW TESTAMENT

From the earliest times the Christian community found it necessary to teach prayer. The disciples had asked Jesus how to pray as John the Baptist had taught his disciples; and in response Jesus told them to say 'Our Father . . .' Besides this he taught them by example. Luke. in particular, paints a picture of Jesus climbing the mountain or retiring to the desert, spending the whole night in prayer. Jesus was very busy at times. People were milling around, asking to be healed. 'But he retired to the wilderness and prayed' (Luke 5:16).

And there were mystical experiences of Jesus. There was his baptism in the Jordan when the Spirit descended like a dove and the voice of the Father was heard. There was his transfiguration on the mountain — a scene that fired the imagination of the Byzantine church — when his clothes became dazzling white and there appeared to him Moses and Elijah speaking of his departure (his ἔξοδος) which he was to accomplish at Jerusalem. There was his prayer at the Last Supper when he gave them his body and blood. There was his dark night of agony in Gethsemane when he sweated blood; and there was his prayer on the cross when he forgave his enemies and with the psalmist cried out: '*Lama Sabachthani*.'

The New Testament is filled with prayer. Of special importance is the fourth gospel which soars like the eagle to the highest heavens. Throughout its pages we meet the Risen Jesus who, outside space and time, says: 'I am.' And then there is the last discourse. The message of love and trust that reverberates through those chapters — from the washing of the feet to the prayer for unity — has nourished the contemplative life of millions from the beginning of

15

Christianity to this very day. For whoever reads this gospel is the disciple whom Jesus loved.

And then the apostle to the Gentiles. Paul gives instructions to the Corinthians about how they should conduct themselves during their prayer meetings when some spoke in tongues and others prophesied. He speaks about the eucharistic assembly, urging his beloved ones to be reverent and to discern the body of the Lord. In his letters he prays that they will grow in wisdom, that they will be rooted in love. Paul was constantly praying for the children he had begotten in Christ. And in addition to this there was Pauline prayer that we would now call mystical. Paul knew a man, in the body or out of the body he did not know, God knows. And this man was raised to the third heaven and heard voices that humans do not hear. This was indeed a mysterious experience. Paul himself was baffled.

And then Peter went up on the roof to pray and fell into a trance. He had a vision of a huge sheet containing all kinds of animals and he, too, heard a voice. Ananias saw visions and heard voices; so also did Cornelius the centurion. The spirit of mystical prayer runs through The Acts of the Apostles.

Nor did these experiences end with the last page of the New Testament. Prayer flourished; mystical prayer went on. Martyrdom was the great grace. Conversation with God — διάλεξις it was called — and liturgical, eucharistic prayer were the food of Christians.

Now when prayer becomes deep, when it enters into new states of consciousness (to use the modern jargon) people need help and direction, for the path of prayer can be steep and stony. One can easily be deceived. 'Even Satan disguises himself as an angel of light,' writes Paul (2 Corinthians 11:14) and there are all kinds of pitfalls. Or people can get discouraged and give up the struggle. That is why it is necessary to elaborate a theology of prayer — including a theology of mystical prayer — that will guide and protect and encourage those who would climb the mountain of God.

ORIGEN AND THE SONG OF SONGS

As Christianity moved into the Greek world, the early Christians were faced with problems of adaptation and inculturation. New ways of thinking and praying arose. And there also arose outstanding teachers and theologians, though at that time the teacher of prayer and the teacher of theology were not clearly distinguished.

Pre-eminent among the theologians and spiritual masters was Origen of Alexandria (185–254) who was to exert incalculable influence on the whole Christian world for many centuries. For Origen the great religious experience was martyrdom in which the disciple laid down his life for his flock and for his enemies, as Jesus laid down his life for humankind. Origen also wrote about prayer; he commented on the Our Father; he wrote extensive commentaries on sacred Scripture. For him scriptural exegesis was an important religious experience.

The Origenist treatise, however, which most influenced mystical theology was the commentary on The Song of Songs. This is a masterpiece of which Jerome (347–420) was to write to Pope Damasus that while Origen surpassed all writers in his other books, in his The Song of Songs he surpassed himself. 'And this exposition of his is so splendid and so clear,' Jerome continues, 'that it seems to me that the words "The King brought me into his chamber" have found their fulfilment in him.'[1] Small wonder that a modern scholar speaks of this commentary as 'the first great work of Christian mysticism'.[2]

The Song of Songs has always been a controversial book. Some have taken it as no more than a voluptuous Middle-Eastern love song and have wondered how it could ever have come into the Bible. Others have considered it a profoundly holy book, speaking of the union between Yahweh and Israel. A beautiful story is told of Rabbi Aquiba in the second century. Replying to a Jewish leader who denied that The Song of Songs was part of Scripture he said: 'All the ages are not worth the day on which The Song of Songs was given to Israel. For all the writings are holy but The Song of Songs is the holy of holies.'[3]

Controversy is unnecessary. The Song is at the same time erotic and holy, symbolizing the love of God for humanity. That is why human lovers and mystics alike resonate with its archetypal rhythms.

The great contribution of Origen was to apply this love song to the union of the individual person with the Word Incarnate, while retaining its communitarian dimension. At the beginning of the commentary he describes The Song of Songs as 'a marriage-song which Solomon wrote in the form of a drama and sang under the figure of the bride, about to wed and burning with heavenly love toward her bridegroom who is the Word of God'. Then he continues: 'And deeply indeed did she love him, whether we take her as the soul made in his image, or as the Church.'[4]

The fact that Origen kept the ecclesial dimension of this love is of the greatest significance. It means that for him what we now call mystical prayer is not an activity of the small, isolated, separate ego but part of the great symphony in which the whole Church sings its song of praise to Christ the Bridegroom, loving him deeply and being loved by him.

And Origen, like thousands of commentators after him, struggled with the love of The Song of Songs. What is its nature? How do we explain it?

Origen is at pains to tell us that The Song of Songs is no eulogy of carnal love. Referring to Plato's *Symposium* he tells us that even among the wise and learned Greeks there were some who did not understand the true meaning of love and rushed into carnal sin. 'Wherefore we also . . . earnestly beg the hearers of these things to mortify their carnal senses. They must not take anything of what has been said with reference to bodily functions, but rather employ them for grasping those divine senses of the inner man.'[5] But what are these divine senses of the inner man?

Considerable research has been done on Origen's spiritual senses. Karl Rahner maintains that they are an entirely new set of five senses in the spiritual realm. He maintains, moreover, that Origen found evidence for the existence of these senses in sacred Scripture — in Moses, the prophets, John and Paul.[6] Be that as it may, the notion of interior senses is taken up by other mystics, notably St Teresa of Avila who speaks of seeing but not with these eyes, hearing but not with these ears, smelling but not with these nostrils and so on. It seems impossible to explain mystical experience without some such psychology. And studies in this area continue today.

Origen's commentary on The Song of Songs was widely read in the Middle Ages in the Latin translation of Rufinus. His mystical interpretation was to establish a tradition in Christian mysticism which has never died. Bernard of Clairvaux composed ecstatic homilies on The Song of Songs. Ruysbroeck writes mystically about spiritual espousals. The unemotional author of *The Cloud of Unknowing* writes about the marriage betwixt God and the soul, as also does the English Richard Rolle. And the bride-bridegroom theme is at the heart of the teaching of the sixteenth-century Spanish Carmelites.

St John of the Cross knew The Song of Songs by heart. It was his favourite scriptural text. On his deathbed, we are told, when the surrounding monks were reciting the penitential psalms, he graciously stopped them and asked that The Song of Songs be read. This story becomes credible when one reflects that, in the sanjuanist vision, death is the moment when the spiritual marriage is consummated and the soul enters into glory.

Yet the great achievement of Origen is not precisely that he commented on The Song of Songs but that he saw love as the core and centre of Christian prayer. With him, mystical theology (though that terminology was not yet used) became a theology of love. And so it remains and will remain.

THEOLOGY OF NEGATION

The fourth century gave birth to three eminent Greek theologians — the Cappadocian fathers they are called — whose doctrine on the incomprehensibility of God was to reverberate through all subsequent mystical theology. The brothers Basil of Caesarea and Gregory of Nyssa together with their common friend, Gregory of Nazianzus, knew from their profound prayer and contemplative reading of sacred Scripture that God is the mystery of mysteries who dwells in light inaccessible or darkness impenetrable. No one has seen God. No one will ever see God. In his awe-inspiring presence we put our finger to our lips like Job.

And Gregory of Nyssa in his *Life of Moses* appeals to the example of the great Hebrew lawgiver climbing the mountain and entering the cloud of darkness. Moses left everything, even thinking, to enter into the unknowing and to meet God. And there is no other way in which the human can meet the divine.

From the Cappadocians stems the theology of negation (known also as *apophatic theology* from the Greek) which reaches a climax at the end of the fifth century with the divine darkness of Dionysius, also known as Pseudo-Dionysius. He it was who introduced into Christianity the terminology mystical theology with his famous treatise entitled *Concerning Mystical Theology*:

$$\Pi\epsilon\rho\grave{\iota}\ \mu\upsilon\sigma\tau\iota\kappa\tilde{\eta}\varsigma\ \theta\epsilon\text{o}\lambda\text{o}\gamma\acute{\iota}\alpha\varsigma$$

For Dionysius the word theology means wisdom, the highest wisdom, while the word mystical derives from 'mystery'. He teaches a path which is mystical in the sense that it is secret, hidden, formless, dark, ineffable. It cannot be expressed in clear-cut images and concepts. It is the wisdom of Moses on the mountain of God.

Dionysius himself has always been a controversial figure. His identity is controversial and his orthodoxy has been questioned. What we know is that someone in the ancient world affixed to his writings the name of Dionysius the Areopagite, the disciple of St Paul.[7] Though questions of authenticity did arise, the Dionysian writings became extremely influential throughout the Eastern world; and they were greeted with enthusiasm in the West after the ninth century when the Irishman, John the Scot, known as Erigena, translated them into Latin. Bonaventura calls Dionysius the prince of mystics; Thomas Aquinas quotes him some seventeen hundred times; Dante sings the praises of the Areopagite. His *Mystical Theology* strongly influenced the apophatic mystical tradition from Eckhart and Tauler to St John of the Cross and on to this very day. The author of *The Cloud of Unknowing* considered him so important that he made a free translation — it may well be called an adaptation — entitled

Deonise Hid Divinite

And his works were influential not simply because they came from the pen of one who was allegedly close to St Paul but also because of their intrinsic worth. He may not be the prince of mystics but he is a towering figure in the mystical world.

Serious questions about Dionysius were raised by Erasmus and the reformers in the sixteenth century. In our day, studies of his writings keep appearing. What we now conjecture is that he was a Syrian monk, a Christian Neo-Platonist influenced by Proclus, who flourished at the end of the fifth or the beginning of the sixth century. His writings are clearly the work of a committed Christian who had deep religious experience.

After the Cappadocians and Dionysius, the theology of negation flowed into the main stream of theology. The Fourth Lateran Council, held in November 1215, declared that 'between creator and creature no similarity can be noted without a greater dissimilarity being noted'.[8] And the First Vatican Council (1869–70) added that 'the divine mysteries so exceed the created intellect that, even when given in revelation and received by faith, they remain covered over by the veil of faith itself'.[9] Moreover this theology of negation assumes even greater importance today as Christianity opens windows to the mystical breeze that blows from Asia, for it is primarily mystical theology, together with the living experience of the mystics, that reminds us of the awful mystery of existence — that eye has not seen nor ear heard neither has it entered into the human heart to conceive the things of God.

At the same time it is important to remember that mystical theology has its own unique and practical negative methodology. The tradition that stems from Dionysius tells the would-be mystic to stop thinking. It insists that God is not this, not this, not this and it urges him or her to tread all things beneath a cloud of forgetting in order to enter the silent mystery of God. Obviously such a methodology has its dangers which the wise mystical theologian will squarely face.

And there is one more important point. While negative theology is a precious and integral part of the Christian tradition it would be a tragic error if, blinded and fascinated by negation, we were to overlook the theology of affirmation, otherwise known as *cataphatic theology*. The great Cappadocians did not do this. They were above all theologians of the Blessed Trinity. Furthermore, for Gregory of Nyssa, the Moses who ascends into darkness enters into the mystery of Christ (for Gregory is above all Christocentric) and God speaks to him face to face as to a friend. Yes, God is the great unknown yet we dare to raise our voices and say: 'Our Father'. And so the Cappadocians and the mystical tradition that flows from them blend the apophatic and cataphatic into a single paradoxical experience.

For the great paradox of all theology, but particularly of mystical theology, is that we know God and we do not know God. While the theme of unknowing and ignorance flows through the mystics, we also find that they talk constantly about God as an intimate friend whom they know very well. Again, while mystical theology from Gregory of Nyssa to John of the Cross keeps harping on the theme of darkness, we suddenly realize that the darkness is light. How do we explain such paradox? How do we explain that at the same time we know God and do not know God?

The Eastern theologians, particularly Gregory Palamas (1296–1359), taught that we know God according to his uncreated and loving energies but his essence is completely unknowable. They quote Basil: 'For his (God's) energies descend to us while his essence remains inaccessible.'[10] In a later chapter this will be more fully developed.

The Latin mystical tradition, moulded by Aquinas, claimed that while we do not know what God is by reasoning we can know him by love. By love we can, as it were, touch the very essence of God. The author of *The Cloud* puts it well. We human beings, he claims, have a knowing power and a loving power. To the knowing power God is completely incomprehensible but, marvel of marvels, God can be grasped directly by the loving power. And then, in his inimitable and charming way, he draws the practical conclusion: 'And therefore I would leave all that thing that I can think, and choose to my love that thing that I cannot think. For why, he may well be loved, but not thought. By love he may be gotten and holden; but by thought neither.'[11] St John of the Cross is in the same tradition, but he speaks more scholastically in terms of intellect and will. Even his darkest pages of unknowing are filled with talk of 'loving knowledge'.

So much for the tradition that flows from the Cappadocians and Dionysius. Mystical theology is still a theology of love but now it is also a theology of mystery. More will be said about Dionysius as this book progresses. Now let us glance at another movement which was to shape the course of mystical theology East and West.

THE DESERT FATHERS AND MONASTICISM

Mystical theology owes an incalculable debt to the holy cenobites and hermits who, in the third and fourth centuries, retired to the Egyptian desert to pray, for from them stems the monastic movement which was to nourish prayer, mystical prayer, for almost two millennia throughout the Christian world. The desert fathers were not academics nor were they scholars. They have left no subtle treatises on theology; but they were stalwart ascetics of deep faith and they lived to the full the life of Christian prayer. Moreover they bequeathed to posterity a fund of humorous stories, paradoxical sayings and shrewd counsels which are vibrantly alive today. Indeed their sayings have assumed special relevance in the twentieth century. Thomas Merton was quick to observe that the desert fathers talk like Zen masters. They shock and startle with outrageous riddles that knock unsuspecting disciples into enlightenment and lead them to peaks of wisdom. In the desert spiritual direction is alive.

And to the desert came two wise men who will for ever merit the title of mystical theologian.

The first was Evagrius of Pontus (345–399). A learned Greek with strong Origenist influence, Evagrius studied with the Cappadocians before coming to the solitude of the desert. His writings issue less from his assiduous study than from his silent prayer. Evagrius it was who said that the theologian is one who prays and the one who prays is a theologian. Prayer, not study, was the key to theology; for in prayer one receives from God true knowledge about God; that is *theognosis*.[12]

Of special significance for mystical theology is Evagrius' doctrine of pure prayer:

$$\text{Προσε υχὴ καθαρά}$$

This is prayer of no-thinking. It is prayer without images or ideas of any kind. We hear Evagrius say that 'prayer is the suppression of every concept' and: 'In your longing to see the face of the Father in heaven, never try to see any shape or form when you are praying.' Or again: 'Blessed is the mind which has acquired a total absence of form at the moment of prayer.'

All this is a practical application of the theology of negation and recalls the Moses of Gregory of Nyssa. But let us not forget that, like his Cappadocian teachers, Evagrius is strongly cataphatic and Trinitarian. His doctrine is profoundly scriptural.[13]

And a second learned man came to the desert, this time from the West. John Cassian (365–435) born in the modern Romania was an outstanding teacher of prayer.[14] He followed Evagrius closely while creating his own terminology. Where Evagrius spoke of passionlessness (*apatheia*), John Cassian spoke of purity of heart, a biblical term that has been used ever since. Again, following Evagrius, he taught the prayer of repetition which later flourished in the East as hesychasm. He also taught silent, imageless prayer of no-thinking, claiming that face to face with God one needs no words.

From the desert Cassian returned to the West where he founded two monasteries at Marseilles. His writings were to influence St Benedict who states in his rules that Cassian's *Institutes* and *Conferences* should be read regularly. They *were* read regularly and Cassian made his mark on the whole monastic movement in the West.

And it was precisely in the monasteries that the tiny seed of prayer was sown in the soil of Europe. It grew into a mighty tree which bore fruit in mystical experience and mystical theology. The great achievement of the monastery was that it brought together liturgy and silent prayer according to the beautiful monastic saying:

Semper in ore psalmus
Semper in corde Christus

Always a psalm on the lips: always Christ in the heart. In the monasteries mystical prayer can never be separated from liturgy: it is constantly nourished by Scripture and by Eucharist.

Moreover, in the monasteries mystical theology was the science of spiritual direction. Some theologians held, and still hold, that mystical prayer — the dark cloud of Gregory, the pure prayer of Evagrius, the wordless prayer of John Cassian — was no more than the normal development of ordinary meditation and conversation with God. One begins with words and enters into silence in accordance with the teaching of the poet who said that words after speech pass into silence. And all theologians agreed that it was primarily the liturgy that gave birth to such prayer in the Christian heart and that wordless prayer is a silent entering into the mystery of Christ, the mystery of the Trinity.

It is indeed interesting to note that so much spiritual wealth, including monasticism itself, came to Western Europe from the East. The Second Vatican Council pays tribute to the enormous contribution of Eastern Christianity. After speaking about the beauty of Eastern liturgy it goes on:

> Moreover, in the East are to be found the riches of those spiritual traditions to which monasticism gives special expression. From the glorious days of the holy Fathers, there flourished in the East that monastic spirituality which later flowed over into the Western world, and there provided a source from which Latin monastic life took its rise and has often drawn fresh vigour ever since. Therefore Catholics are strongly urged to avail themselves more often of these spiritual riches of the Eastern Fathers, riches which lift up the whole person to the contemplation of divine mysteries.[15]

To lift up the whole person to the contemplation of divine mysteries has always been the ideal of mystical theology.

But what about the West?

No mystical theology can neglect Augustine.

CONTEMPLATION IN THE WEST

In an excellent book entitled *Western Mysticism* and published in the first part of this century, Cuthbert Butler selects three mystical giants to represent the West.[16] They are Augustine of Hippo (354–430), Gregory the Great (540–604), and Bernard of Clairvaux (1090–1153).

In his prologue Butler points out that the word *mystical* comes from Dionysius and was not current in the West until the late Middle

Ages, while *mysticism* is quite a modern word. 'Consequently,' he goes on, 'contemplation is the word that will be met with in St Augustine, St Gregory and St Bernard, to designate what is now commonly called "mystical experience".'[17]

The Latin word *contemplatio*, the ordinary translation of the Greek *theoria* is more frequently used in monasteries and convents in the West even today. Contemplative prayer is a common phenomenon. It is quiet or simple prayer in a cloud of unknowing. That is to say, it is prayer without reasoning or thinking. One remains silent in the presence of God or uses a few words that are repeated, as in the Jesus prayer. The important thing, as St Teresa of Avila said so well, is not to think much but to love much. And from this basic, quiet contemplation there may, as time goes on, arise moments of enlightenment or ecstasy or awakening. Or the simple sense of presence may grow to a fire of love or a night of darkness.

Such contemplative or mystical experience is found in Butler's three mystics. Here, however, it will be sufficient to consider briefly one who stood at the crossroads of Western civilization when Rome collapsed and barbarian hordes pillaged the crumbling empire. Augustine of Hippo, mystic and prophet, was to enlighten the Christian world for almost two thousand years with profound wisdom that arose from his prayer, his study and his experience of life.

While other aspects of Augustine's thought have been studied and re-studied his mystical theology has been somewhat neglected. Some theologians have even questioned the reality of his mystical experience. Yet to one who reads the *Confessions* with an open mind it is difficult to deny that the poetic sentences come from the pen of one who was at once a consummate mystic and powerful thinker. 'My mind in the flash of trembling glance came to that which is.'[18] What an enlightenment is here! Or again, the great scene at Ostia where the mother and the son together rose to ecstatic heights of contemplation. And then the profound pathos of that cry: 'Late have I loved you . . . And behold, you were within me and I was outside . . . you were with me, and I was not with you.'[19]

When it comes to mystical theology, however, the great contribution of Augustine is in the area of grace. Convinced of the radical insufficiency of human nature he can pray: 'Give what you command, and command what you will.'[20]

While this doctrine of grace is central to the whole of human life, it is particularly important in mystical theology. All is gift. Authentic mystics are aware that human effort is useless — unless it is human effort given by God. One must never forget the prior love of God. 'We love because he first loved us' (1 John 4:19). 'You have not chosen me but I have chosen you' (John 15:16). The call is a gift. Progress is a gift. One must always wait on God. One must not awaken love before its time. Methods and techniques that savour of Pelagius are a constant danger. And over against this the Augustinian doctrine of grace flows into the mystical tradition and must for ever remain.

CONCLUSION

We have seen that a mystical theology slowly developed over the first five centuries of Christian history. With Origen it is a theology of love. With the Cappadocians and Dionysius it is also a theology of mystery. With the desert fathers it is a pastoral science of spiritual direction. With monasticism it is wedded to liturgy — to Word and to Eucharist. With Augustine the dimension of grace is underlined.

And now there arises the question of sources. On what sources is this mystical theology based? Is it a product of Christian revelation alone? Or has the Hellenistic world made its contribution to the rich contemplative experience of the early Christians?

This problem must be faced in the next chapter.

NOTES

1. Origen, *Commentary on The Song of Songs*, R. P. Lawson ed., (Westminster: MD: 1957) p. 265. All future references are to this edition and will be designated *Commentary*.
2. *Commentary*, p. 6.
3. See *Christ in the Psalms*, Brian McNeill, Dublin Veritas 1988, p. 88.
4. *Commentary*, p. 21.
5. *Commentary*, p. 79.
6. See Karl Rahner 'Experience of the Spirit: Source of Theology' in *Theological Investigations*, trans. David Moreland, New York, Crossroads 1983.

7. 'At that point Paul left them. But some of them joined him and became believers, including Dionysius the Areopagite . . .' (Acts 17:34).

8. *Enchiridion Symbolorum, Definitionum et Declarationum de Rebus Fidei et Morum*, compiled by H. Densinger, 806.

9. Ibid. 3016.

10. *Patrologia Graeca*, ed. J. B. Migne, Paris, 32, 869.

11. *The Cloud of Unknowing*, C. 4.

12. See *God's Exploding Love*, George Maloney, Alba House, New York 1987, p. 17.

13. During his lifetime Evagrius enjoyed a prestige equal to that of the church fathers but after his death his writings came under suspicion — not his teaching on prayer but his *Problemata Gnostika* where he develops philosophical and cosmological thought in an Origenist way. This work was used for his condemnation at the Second Council of Constantinople in 553.

14. See *John Cassian: Conferences*, trans. Colm Luibheid, Paulist Press, New York 1987.

15. *Unitatis Redintegratio*, III.15.

16. *Western Mysticism*, Cuthbert Butler, Constable, London 1922, (Third edition 1967).

17. Ibid. p. 4.

18. '(Mens mea) pervenit ad Id quod est in ictu trepidantis aspectus' (*Confessions*, VII.23).

19. *Confessions*, X.27.

20. 'Da quod jubes, et jube quod vis' *Confessions*, X.29, 40.

TWO

Background (II)

If the Christian community gradually elaborated what was later called a mystical theology, we must ask about sources. Where did the Church Fathers learn about prayer? And where did they learn what we now call mystical prayer?

SCRIPTURAL SOURCES

From what has been said it will be clear that the chief source was sacred Scripture. Even a superficial glance at the writings of the Fathers shows how they read and reread the Scriptures, meditated on the Scriptures, lived the Scriptures, so much so that their writings can be taken as nothing less than commentaries on the Scriptures against the background of their times.

And certain texts that are of special value for a mystical theology keep recurring like a refrain. One such text is the Our Father. Commentaries on the Lord's prayer are written by Tertullian, Cyprian, Origen, Gregory of Nyssa, Peter Chrysologus. Later, St Teresa of Avila is to follow in this tradition in her *Way of Perfection*. It is as though the two words 'Our Father' contain all mystical theology — the immense love of God and the trusting human response — and the one who recites them will eventually be carried beyond words and thoughts into the mystery of mysteries which is a cloud of unknowing.

Then there is Magdalene sitting at the feet of Jesus. Here is the supreme model of contemplation. So great is her ecstatic love that she is carried beyond words and concepts into the immense silence which is the divinity of Jesus.

Again, there are important texts in St Paul. 'I live, now not I, but

Christ lives in me' (Galatians 2:20) is the experience of one who has lost the little ego to turn toward God and cry out: 'Abba, Father.' And there is that text in Corinthians where Paul says that 'anyone united to the Lord becomes one spirit with him' (1 Corinthians 6:17).

Mention has already been made of the patristic focus on the Transfiguration and on Moses climbing the mountain. These are scenes that passed into the Christian mystical tradition where they remain to this very day. Yet there are other scenes even more important.

The early Christians gathered around the table of the Lord for the breaking of bread and to recite the mysterious words in remembrance of him: 'This is my body which will be given up for you.' 'This is the cup of my blood, the blood of the new and everlasting covenant. It will be shed for you and for all so that sins may be forgiven. Do this in memory of me.' For the early Christians these words, recited at the liturgy, were the most significant words in the whole Bible. They enshrine the mystery of the faith: the death and resurrection of Jesus. And so the central religious experience of the Christian — the experience to which all mystical theology finally points — is to die and rise with Jesus who died and rose. This is the experience of Paul who prayed to know Christ and share his suffering — 'becoming like him in his death, if somehow I may attain the resurrection of the dead' (Philippians 3:10, 11). This death and resurrection is lived out in the Eucharist.

It should be noted that the patristic approach to the Scriptures was quite different from the historical critical approach that has dominated the twentieth century. For the Fathers, reading the Scriptures was a religious experience. They believed that, as they read, they were guided and taught by the one whom Augustine called the *magister internus*, the inner teacher without whose guidance no one could understand anything. The Holy Spirit, guiding the community into all truth as the fourth gospel had promised, was the prime teacher of all theology.

But while the Spirit acts through sacred Scripture, we must still ask if the same Spirit acts in other ways. We must ask about the non-scriptural sources of patristic mystical theology. And here we find ourselves in a storm of controversy.

HELLENISM

The end of the nineteenth and the beginning of the twentieth century witnessed extensive research into the origins of Christianity. Most influential among the historians of that period was the liberal Protestant theologian Adolf von Harnack (1851–1930) whose critical and profound scholarship dominated the academic world for many decades. Harnack was impressed, and dismayed, by the progressive Hellenization of Christianity. The introduction of Hellenistic culture together with pre-Christian and non-Christian ideas had contaminated the pure spring water of the Gospel. It had found its way into dogmas which disfigured the true countenance of Jesus of Nazareth. And so the task of Christianity was to purify itself so as to recover the true unadulterated essence of the Gospel; and this could only be done by the historical critical method. Harnack claimed that he was simply continuing the work of the sixteenth-century reformers; and indeed he is a true successor of Martin Luther who, at the end of his life could say to his students: 'I have taught you Christ, purely, simply and without adulteration.'

And this way of thinking inevitably influenced attitudes towards mystical theology which, it was assumed, was one more manifestation of the pagan leprosy that had infected Christianity. Particularly pernicious, it was said, were the writings of Pseudo-Dionysius. After all, were not these the work of the Neo-Platonist, masquerading as a Christian, using the language of the Greek mystery religions to introduce into Christianity a Plotinian ecstasy that was foreign to the true biblical spirit? Had not Luther himself said that Dionysius was pernicious in that he Platonizes more than he Christianizes? 'I admonish you,' said Luther, 'to shun like the plague that "Mystical Theology" of Dionysius and similar books which contain such idle talk.'[1] How convincingly it could be argued that Hellenism was obscuring the true features of Jesus of Nazareth!

And while Catholicism was much more positive in its attitude towards Hellenism, certain Catholic theologians had grave reservations about the apophatic mystical theology that stems from Gregory of Nyssa and Dionysius. One could mention, for example, an eminent Platonic scholar who was a French Dominican. A. J.

Festugière maintained strongly that in their mystical theology the Fathers were Platonizing. For Festugière the authentic Christian spirit appears in the evangelists, in Ignatius, Irenaeus, the martyrs and the monastic tradition. But there was another much less Christian movement: 'It is the Alexandrine school, Clement and Origen. And the links in the chain can be easily discerned: in the East they are all the teachers of contemplation, Evagrius, Gregory of Nyssa, Diadochus of Photice, Pseudo-Denys; and in the West, Augustine and (to the extent that he follows Augustine) Gregory the Great.'[2]

Assuredly, Festugière did not regard Hellenism as a dangerous cancer (he loved the Greeks too much for that) but for him it was something independent of, and parallel to, the authentic Christian spirit. Nor is he alone. Some Catholic theologians today have misgivings about the dark Dionysian tradition that flows through the Rhineland mystics, *The Cloud of Unknowing*, St John of the Cross and still lives in the writings of the early Merton, T. S. Eliot and many Carmelite writers. This tradition, they claim, has yet to be purged and cleansed from Neo-Platonic impurities that disfigure the beautiful countenance of authentic Christian spirituality.

The writings of Harnack and Festugière and others sparked off sharp controversy and stimulated further scholarship. Of particular interest for the present work is the research into the use of the words 'mystery' and 'mystical' in the ancient world.

'MYSTERY' IN THE NEW TESTAMENT

The word 'mystery' and the plural 'mysteries' are found in the New Testament with rich meaning. In the Gospel 'mystery' is used in connection with the parables. 'To you has been given the mystery of the kingdom of God, but for those outside, everything comes in parables . . .' (Mark 4:11). And, 'To you it has been given to know the mysteries of the kingdom of heaven, but to them it has not been given' (Matthew 13:11). What are these mysteries? What is the secret that the disciples alone can understand?

The mystery is the kingdom of God:

μυστήριον τῆς βασιλείας τοῦ θεοῦ

And one commentator does not hesitate to say that the mystery revealed to the disciples is 'Jesus himself as Messiah'.[3]

But it is in the Pauline letters that the notion of mystery is most fully developed. In the First Epistle to the Corinthians Paul speaks of the mystery of God:

τὸ μυστήριον τοῦ θεοῦ

This mystery Paul did not teach in lofty words or wisdom — 'for I decided to know nothing among you except Jesus Christ, and him crucified' (1 Corinthians 2:2). Paul, borrowing the Gnostic terminology of his adversaries, insists that the real wisdom and the real mystery is the cross. This is a stumbling block to Jews and foolishness to Gentiles but to those who are called, both Jews and Greeks, it is Christ the power of God and the wisdom of God. In short, the mystery is Jesus crucified.

Again, in the captivity epistles, the notion of mystery is at the centre of Paul's message.[4] Here he speaks of the mystery hidden throughout ages and generations and now revealed to the saints. This is 'Christ in you, the hope of glory' (Colossians 1:27). And later in the same letter he goes on to speak of God's mystery which is Christ himself in whom are hidden all the treasures of wisdom and knowledge. Again, in Ephesians he speaks of the mystery of Christ, hidden for ages in God and made known to him by revelation; and he prays that they may know the love of Christ that surpasses knowledge. Great is the mystery. Overwhelming is the mystery. Awful is the mystery. It is the mystery of the marriage of Christ to the church:

τὸ μυστήριον τοῦτο μέγα ἐστιν

'This is a great mystery and I am applying it to Christ and the Church' (Ephesians 5:32). Small wonder that Paul earnestly begs his beloved ones to pray that he may open his mouth with confidence to make known the mystery of the Gospel.

And the First Epistle to Timothy, quoting apparently from a

hymn used in the early church, proclaims that 'without any doubt the mystery of our religion is great':

μέγα ἐστιν τὸ τῆς εὐσεβείας μυστήριον

It then elaborates on the mystery:

> He was revealed in the flesh,
> vindicated in the Spirit,
> seen by angels,
> proclaimed among the Gentiles,
> believed in throughout the world,
> taken up in glory (1 Timothy 3:16).

It is hardly necessary to develop here the use of the word *mysterion* in other parts of the New Testament as in Revelation. Enough to say that the mystery of the New Testament 'betrays no relation to the mystery cults'.[5] Bouyer can write of the Pauline mystery that 'its context is to be sought not in the Greek mysteries . . . but in the Jewish sapiential literature and apocalypses, that is to say, free from any Greek influence'.[6]

The mystery, then, that came to the Church Fathers from the New Testament was the mystery of Christ who died and rose and will come again. It is the mystery of Christ who reveals the Father, the mystery of Christ who redeems the world. It is the mystery enshrined in the central question of the Gospel:

> Who do you say that I am? (Mark 8:29).

Peter was able to reply, not because he had learned the answer from flesh and blood but because he had received a revelation from the Father.

Such is the New Testament mystery of Christ.

'MYSTERY' AND 'MYSTICAL'
IN THE CHURCH FATHERS

It must be remembered that the Church Fathers were born in the Graeco-Roman world with its sophisticated and highly developed culture. Most of them were intelligent and educated people who could not, and did not wish to, deny their cultural birthright when they embraced this new, Semitic religion. Hellenism was in the air they breathed, the water they drank, the language they spoke. And so they took words like mystery and mystical from the surrounding world, using them as vehicles to express the teaching of the New Testament. But they could not totally deny the meaning these words already had. That would be impossible.

It is true that the word 'mystery', probably rooted in the Greek *muein* meaning to close the mouth, was used in connection with the ceremonies of the mystery religions, ceremonies which had to be kept secret. However, Louis Bouyer goes to great pains to prove that the Fathers used the word 'mystery' in their own way — in a liturgical and scriptural context where 'it is quite certain that it owed nothing at all to Hellenism, but everything to that flowering, in Christ and in the new-born church, of the divine seeds already planted in Judaism'.[7]

Bouyer maintains that the adjective 'mystical' is used by the Fathers in three contexts. The first is when they speak of sacred Scripture. The Scriptures are mystical because they enshrine the Pauline mystery of Christ, and the mystical interpretation is one that discerns the mystery. The second concerns the Eucharist which is the mystery of faith. And so the word is used in a liturgical context relating to the great mystery later formulated in the chant: 'Christ has died; Christ has risen; Christ will come again.' The third use of mystical is in connection with a religious experience: a spiritual, as opposed to a carnal, experience is called mystical. Probably Origen was the first to use mystical in this third sense.

Bouyer cites an impressive number of patristic texts and then, as though confronting Harnack and Festugière, he concludes:

It seems to us that after reading all these texts it has become impossible to present Christian mysticism as an element imported from Neo-Platonism.[8]

As for Dionysius, his Neo-Platonic background is undeniable, but he is clearly rooted in the same patristic tradition. His *Mystical Theology* must be taken in conjunction with his other extant works: *The Divine Names*, *The Celestial Hierarchy*, *The Ecclesiastical Hierarchy*, and *The Letters*. Then one sees that Dionysius was not all darkness, that his theology of negation is carefully balanced by a theology of affirmation, that his whole approach is scriptural, liturgical and ecclesial. While the framework is Neo-Platonic and the probability that he was a disciple of Proclus remains, he never explicitly quotes any pagan source (though reading between the lines one can find allusions to the *Timaeus* and the *Symposium* of Plato and to the Neo-Platonists) and for him the Greeks are not authoritative teachers. Bouyer concludes that, while the connection of Dionysius with Neo-Platonism is undeniable, 'his mystical theology, as he understands it himself, is his manner of recognizing the Christ at the breaking of bread in all the Scriptures'.[9]

If the conclusion of Bouyer is correct, it is of the greatest significance not only for the understanding of the patristic mystical tradition but also for the understanding of a renewed mystical theology today.

With this in mind we can glance briefly at the first *Mystical Theology*.

THE FIRST *MYSTICAL THEOLOGY*

The first *Mystical Theology* is a work of spiritual direction. Dionysius, the master, gives instruction to his disciple Timothy, telling him how to enter the silence, the void, the nothingness, the emptiness. He must imitate Moses (and here we find the influence of Gregory of Nyssa) who climbed the mountain and entered the cloud but did not see God — since no one has ever seen God — but only the place where God dwells.

Dionysius, then, is interested in directing his disciple rather than elaborating a theology of negation; and it might be added that this is a characteristic of mystical theology that has never changed. To this very day mystical theology is pastoral. It is oriented to guidance, to helping people on their way to God.

Dionysius opens his treatise with a prayer to the triune God:

> O Trinity
> Beyond Being
> Beyond Divinity
> Beyond Goodness
> Guide of Christians in wisdom divine
> Direct us to the mystical heights . . .[10]

In this prayer we see a judicious blending of the apophatic and the cataphatic. On the one hand God is the mystery of mysteries beyond anything we can know. On the other hand we know by faith that God is triune and that he gives us grace and help in the journey of life. In this way knowing and unknowing are combined in prayer.

After the prayer, the master turns to his disciple with practical advice:

> And you, dear Timothy,
> in the sincere exercise of
> mystical contemplation, abandon
> all sensation and all intellectual activities,
> all that is sensed and intelligible,
> all being and non-being.[11]

Here is a message of total renunciation. Timothy is to give up all thinking, all reasoning, all sensing. He does so to enter the ecstatic darkness beyond all being:

> By the undivided and absolute ecstasy
> of yourself and of all,
> absolved from all, and
> freed from all,
> you will be purely raised up
> to the ray of divine darkness
> beyond being.[12]

Here is the ecstasy, the going forth from all things, the abandonment of all thought to enter the divine darkness of supreme wisdom.

Many commentators have compared these passages with the Neo-Platonic ecstasy. Vladimir Lossky, for example, remarks that if we compare the Dionysian ecstasy with the Sixth Ennead of Plotinus we are bound to record some striking resemblances; but he then goes on to show that the two ecstasies are in fact quite different.[13]

Even more interesting and important are the comments of the author of *The Cloud of Unknowing*. In his English translation of this work he makes some significant changes in the text (in the fourteenth century this was not unethical) by having Dionysius tell Timothy that he will be drawn above mind *in love*, by urging him to enter into the darkness *with love*, and by saying that Moses was called by *an extraordinary love*.[14] And this makes all the difference, for in place of a cold, philosophical, Neo-Platonic Moses who separates himself from matter to enter a world of pure spirit, the English author gives us a Moses all ablaze with love for God, climbing the mountain and separating himself from all things in the utmost poverty of the spirit.

In writing this, the author of *The Cloud* follows the medieval mystical tradition. But is he really faithful to the thought of Dionysius?

Perhaps he is, for elsewhere, in *The Divine Names*, Dionysius speaks powerfully about the ecstasy of St Paul which is an ecstasy of rapturous love:

So also the great Paul, caught up in rapture by divine love and seized by its ecstatic power, said with words inspired, 'I live, now not I, but Christ lives in me.' As a true lover rapt out of self into God, he lives not his own life, but that life for which he yearned, the life of his beloved.[15]

Without a doubt this vibrant passage reveals a Dionysius keenly aware of the role of love in the mystical ascent.

And so the Dionysian ecstasy entered the Christian mystical tradition and occupied therein a central position. In the works of Christian mystics it becomes a going forth from self in the abandonment of all things understood in the context of the gospel exhortation to abandon everything for the love of Jesus. It is the path of one who joyfully abandons everything to find the treasure hidden in the field or to buy the pearl of great price. What is distinctive about the mystical tradition is that one abandons not only material possessions but also thinking, reasoning, conceptualization, forms and all securities. And, as the mystical tradition develops particularly in St John of the Cross, one abandons all sensible and spiritual consolation, all visions, all voices, all natural and supernatural clinging. Nothing, nothing, nothing, and even on the mountain, nothing.

One abandons all for love and for wisdom — or, more correctly one abandons all for loving wisdom. St John of the Cross, speaking of the dark, supraconceptual knowledge refers to Dionysius. 'This knowledge', he writes, 'is general and dark to the intellect because it is contemplative knowledge, which is a ray of darkness for the intellect, as St Dionysius teaches.'[16] He also says that the obscure, dark or general knowledge of contemplation is pure faith.

And as the mystical tradition develops, it understands the Dionysian ecstasy in the context of The Song of Songs: the bride going forth to meet the bridegroom who is the Word Incarnate. This going forth reaches a climax with the spiritual marriage which is the gateway to eternal life where is enacted the eternal marriage, the marriage in glory between God and the soul.

One more point in Dionysius must be mentioned. From the very beginning he issues a warning that the Christian tradition did not overlook. 'See to it', he writes to Timothy, 'that none of this comes to the ears of those who are not ready.'[17]

The prudent teachers and guides in the monasteries came to know well that this rigorous ascent in the abandonment of all is not for everyone. It is for those who are called. Woe to the person who abandons all before the time has come:

Do not stir or awaken love
until it is ready (Song of Songs 3:5).

And so, acutely aware of the dangers of a premature kenosis, the wise mystical tradition worked out certain signs by which one may know that the time has come to hearken to the voice of the bridegroom to climb the mountain of total renunciation in the company of Moses and the mystics. Do not awaken love until it is ready!

Mystical theology was written and re-written as generations moved on and new cultures were born. The teaching of Dionysius was purified, corrected, developed; but the basic pattern of human, mystical experience remains remarkably similar. As one reads Dionysius, *The Cloud of Unknowing*, Meister Eckhart, John of the Cross, Thérèse of Lisieux, Edith Stein, one is conscious that the same spirit is at work in all. Needless to say, there are variations according to personality and culture and education and charismatic gift, but all are leaving everything, even discursive knowledge, to enter into the mystery of mysteries where they find the highest wisdom that comes from love.

THE FIRST GREAT DIALOGUE

Mystical theology, it has been said, came to birth when Hebrew Christianity flowed into the Mediterranean world and encountered the culture of the Greeks. That was a momentous meeting, the consequences of which are still to be evaluated.

Yet today we are in a position, as never before, to understand what happened. For we Christians of the twentieth century find ourselves in a remarkably similar situation. Faced with a cultural revolution that is causing a spiritual upheaval of unparalleled magnitude, Christianity is in the process of extracting itself from one culture and putting down roots in another. African Christians are aware that they are Africans. Asian Christians are aware that they are Asians. Postmodern western Christians are aware that they are postmodern people. All love and treasure a cultural heritage which they will not, and cannot, deny. All are faced with problems of inculturation — of translating the message of Jesus Christ and the person of Jesus Christ into a new world. All realize that this calls for dialogue; and all know that dialogue is hard work.

Now the early Christians were like us in many ways. They loved the Gospel of Jesus Christ and were willing to die for it as they gathered around the table of the Lord for the breaking of bread. But they also loved the world in which they lived and to which they proclaimed the good news. And so, like us, they were faced with problems of inculturation and dialogue, even though they did not use the terminology we use today.

And the gigantic task of inculturation began with Paul of Tarsus. A diaspora Jew, fluent in Greek, a citizen of no mean city, a disciple of Gamaliel and a mystic to boot — Paul, the apostle to the uncircumcised, was sufficiently cosmopolitan to see that the Gentiles must be Gentiles: there was no question of making them live like Jews. When Cephas at Antioch drew back from eating with the Gentiles, Paul opposed him to his face, because he stood self-condemned: 'If you, though a Jew, live like a Gentile and not like a Jew, how can you compel the Gentiles to live like Jews?' (Galatians 2:14).

And Paul's way of thinking won the day. The Spirit descended abundantly on the Gentiles; Peter saw a vision and heard a voice telling him that nothing was unclean; and the Council of Jerusalem decided to impose no further burdens on the Gentiles than the essentials: that they abstain from what had been sacrificed to idols and from blood and from what was strangled and from fornication.

As for Paul, when his own people would not listen he shook the dust off his feet and carried the good news to the Gentiles in Asia Minor and Rome and perhaps as far as Spain.

Yet Paul was keenly aware of the enormous difficulties inherent in his vocation. The wisdom of Jesus Christ was foolishness to the Greeks, but he must teach it — and woe to him if he did not! He was encountering people who were enemies of the cross of Jesus — whose end was destruction, whose god was their belly and whose glory was in their shame. Again, he was aware of the weird Gnostic and syncretic ideas floating around in the Mediterranean world. He saw many, many things that were incompatible with the Gospel of Jesus Christ. Nevertheless, the Gentiles must be Gentiles. They must love and appreciate the world they lived in.

The policies of Paul almost tore the infant Church asunder; but in the long run they bore fruit. Clement, Origen, Evagrius, Augustine and the rest were born into, and moulded by, a Graeco-Roman world that they appreciated and loved even when they saw its evils. Their task was to introduce into that culture the wisdom of Jesus crucified.

And so they elaborated a theology which helped them see the Spirit at work in the whole world before the coming of Jesus. Before the call of Abraham there was a revelation to the whole human race, a revelation that still remains. Particularly important was the text of the fourth gospel telling us that the Word enlightens everyone coming into the world. To this Word Justin Martyr attributes all the truths of non-Christian religions. Such theology opened the way to dialogue with the Greek world.

Of course the early Christians made mistakes. Origen, Evagrius, Tertullian held ideas that the community could not reconcile with the Gospel. And even Augustine nods. But no one doubts that the essentials were maintained in all their purity. Jesus was the Word Incarnate. His mother was the mother of God (*theotokos*) so that it can be truly said that Jesus is God and man. The scandal of the cross was not questioned. The foolishness of the Gospel was proclaimed.

And the work of inculturation was profoundly creative. The Council Fathers at Nicaea (325) and Ephesus (431) and Chalcedon (451) saw aspects of Jesus that Hebrew Christianity had not seen. From within another culture they faced with new creativity the key question of the Gospel: 'Who do men say that I am?' (Mark 8:29).

And this was something that Harnack and his disciples, limiting themselves to the historical critical method, did not see. In their search for the historical Jesus as 'the real Jesus' they failed to realize that through the historical process and the work of inculturation where the Spirit is active, men and women of living faith, far from disfiguring the face of Jesus, see more and more deeply into its essential beauty.

And one more point is of the greatest significance for mystical theology. The Greeks had a different approach to the great mystery of life — they had a different religious experience and a different way of praying. This will be clear to anyone who reads Plato or Plotinus or Proclus. And so the Moses of Gregory of Nyssa and Dionysius had to be different from the Moses of Exodus and Deuteronomy. The Gentiles had to pray like Gentiles and not like Jews.

One is tempted to think that neither Harnack nor Bouyer understood the process of dialogue and inculturation. Both were wary of Greek influence. Harnack thought it was pernicious; Bouyer tried to minimize it, as though it was peripheral. The truth is that in those early days a cultural marriage took place between Jew and Gentile, Hebrew and Greek.

And today, as Christianity faces the new world, may we await another marriage and welcome its offspring, a new mystical theology?

NOTES

1. Quoted by Karlfried Froehlich in 'Pseudo-Dionysius and the Reformation of the Sixteenth Century' in *Pseudo-Dionysius: The Complete Works*, trans Colm Luibheid, Paulist Press, New York 1987, p. 44.
2. *L'Enfant d'Agrigente* by A. J. Festugière, Paris 1950, p. 141. The thesis of Festugière is discussed by Andrew Louth in *The Origins of the Christian Mystical Tradition*, Oxford 1981.
3. G. Bornkamm, 'Mysterion' in *Theological Dictionary of the New Testament*, ed. Gerhard Kittel, Eerdmans Publishing Co., 1967, p. 819.
4. It is not certain that Ephesians and Colossians were written by Paul; but here the question of authorship is not important.
5. G. Bornkam, Op. supra cit., p. 824.
6. 'Mysterion' by Louis Bouyer in *Mystery and Mysticism*, The Philosophical Library, New York 1956.
7. *A History of Christian Spirituality Vol. 1: The Spirituality of the New Testament and the Fathers*, Louis Bouyer, Burns and Oates, 1968, p. 525. For further discussion of this problem see: *Neoplatonism and Christian Thought*, ed. Dominic J. O'Meara, State University of New York Press, Albany 1982.
8. 'Mysticism: An essay on the History of a Word' in *Mystery and Mysticism*, The Philosophical Library, New York, 1956, p. 137.
9. Ibid. See Also: *Denys the Areopagite*, Andrew Louth, Morehouse-Barlow CT 1968, p. 21.
10. *Mystical Theology*, C. 1.
11. Ibid.
12. Ibid.
13. See *The Mystical Theology of the Eastern Church*, Vladimir Lossky, St Vladimir's Seminary Press, New York 1976, p. 29.
14. See *The Mysticism of 'The Cloud of Unknowing'*, William Johnston, Source Books, Trabuco Canyon, California and Anthony Clarke, Wheathampstead, Herts. Reprinted 1992. p. 34ff.
15. *The Divine Names*, IV, 13.
16. *Living Flame*, 3:49.
17. *Mystical Theology*, C. 2.

✳

THREE

Reason versus Mysticism

TOWARDS SYSTEMIZATION

Christianity in its origins is not systematic. The gospels consist of parables and stories and sayings of Jesus, reaching a climax in the great drama of his death and resurrection. All is aimed at bringing the reader or hearer to *metanoia* or conversion of heart. The author of the fourth gospels says explicitly that he writes in order that the reader may believe, and believing have life in the name of Jesus.

Some attempts at systematization were made by the Greek Fathers and were formulated in dogmas at Nicaea (325), Ephesus (431) and Chalcedon (451). However, the great movement towards a systematic theology took place in the Middle Ages, extending over the years that separated Anselm of Canterbury (1033–1109) from Thomas Aquinas (1225–74). This was a time of intense and feverish intellectual activity when the theologians of the medieval universities tried to put order and coherence into the Scriptures, the patristic writings, the materials of the Councils and all that goes by the name of tradition. They were attempting to find an overall systematic view of the Christian message.

And at the beginning of this mighty effort that was to bear fruit in the monumental achievement called scholasticism, there took place a historical and significant dispute between a brilliant, if tragic, philosopher and a fervent, if uncompromising, mystic. Peter Abelard (1079–1142) and Bernard of Clairvaux (1090–1153) clashed on a problem that is central to mystical theology.

BERNARD AND ABELARD

Peter Abelard was acutely aware of the paradoxes and apparent contradictions in Christian teaching. Always something of an *enfant terrible*, he wrote his *Sic et Non* to show how one hundred and fifty-eight propositions can at the same time be proved and disproved by arguments drawn from the Scriptures, the Fathers, the Councils and reason. Convinced of the enormous power of human reason and filled with admiration for the Greek philosophers (though he could not have read them extensively) he composed a theological work on the Blessed Trinity which was condemned by the Council of Soissons in 1121 and committed ignominiously to the flames. Yet he continued perseveringly with his intellectual work.

Viewed from the twentieth century, Abelard's intentions were praiseworthy. He wanted to find a rational basis for Christianity; and modern scholars see him as an important forerunner of the great thirteenth-century synthesis between faith and reason that was normative in Catholic theology until the Second Vatican Council. Moreover he never wanted to separate himself from Christ, saying in his inimitable way that, in the event of an insoluble conflict, he would reject Aristotle rather than St Paul.

But to Bernard, educated in a monastic tradition where theology was a meditation and a prayer, Abelard was robbing Christianity of its mystery with a thoroughgoing rationalism. God (as the Greek Fathers had said so well) is a mystery — above all concepts and reasoning. To go to God one leaves all rationalization and enters into wordless silence, for no one has ever seen God. Consequently, to circumscribe God, to put God into categories or formulae, to put God into a conceptual framework is to demean God and borders on blasphemy. This is particularly the case when one speaks of the Trinity, which is the mystery of mysteries. Abelard, wrote Bernard, believes that he sees nothing through a glass darkly, but beholds all things face to face.[1]

And so they clashed. Bernard wrote to Pope Innocent II and to many bishops, denouncing Abelard who was condemned without a hearing at the Council of Sens in 1141 and died in the following year. Yet the vehemence with which Bernard pursued his unfortunate adversary is both puzzling and painful. Is this the Bernard who wrote so ecstatically about the love of God and commented eloquently on The Song of Songs?[2]

The dispute between Bernard and Abelard — between mysticism

and rationalism — runs through medieval theology and continues to this very day. The agony of the mystic finds medieval expression in those lugubrious passages where the holy à Kempis sighs that he would feign have compunction than know its definition, and asks what value is there in disputing about the Trinity if you are displeasing the Trinity.

Yet before à Kempis wrote his *Imitation*, the thirteenth century had given birth to a genius who was at once a consummate mystic and a brilliant dialectician. Thomas Aquinas (1225–74) combined within himself the mystical role of Bernard and the dialectical role of Abelard. In the angelic doctor, as he came to be called, reason and mysticism met and were reconciled.

AQUINAS THE MYSTIC

Thomas Aquinas was a special kind of mystic. We know that he spent long hours in prayer and long hours in study. There are stories of his deep absorption from which he would suddenly awaken to propound some doctrine of faith with the self-confidence of one who had had an earth-shaking enlightenment. A Dominican friar, his ideal was to give to others the fruit of contemplation:

Contemplata aliis Tradere

There can be no doubt that his profound teaching and writing came not only from intense study but also from a heart that was on fire with the love of God and with love for the sacred texts that he expounded. We get glimpses of his tender devotion in his lyrical poetry:

Pie Pelicane, Jesu Domine,
Munda me immundum
Tuo Sanguine

Particularly impressive is his love for the Eucharist, again expressing itself in poetry that describes the sacred banquet with tender devo-

tion and theological accuracy. He was a true Dom__
life was oriented toward teaching. As it is better for the
light than just to burn, he said, so it is better to give to ot__
of contemplation than just to contemplate.

THOMISTIC METAPHYSICS

In his effort to create a systematic substructure for the Christian message, Thomas turned to the Greeks, especially to Aristotle whose newly translated works were pouring into contemporary Europe.

The central problem of Greek philosophy — as it is the central problem of *mystical theology* — was the celebrated paradox of *the one and the many*. It is the ordinary experience of human beings that we are surrounded by many things: men and women, plants and animals, stones and stars. But it is the experience of philosophers and poets — and also of mystics — that there is only one thing. For there are times when these endowed people stand at zero point or the still point and see that all is one. How do we reconcile the experience of unity with the experience of multiplicity?

Closely associated with this is the problem of the reconciliation of opposites. We are surrounded by opposites — heat and cold, black and white, up and down, first and last, life and death, heaven and earth, all and nothing. And most of us know mystics and enlightened people who blandly ignore all this diversity and talk in outrageous paradox as if opposites did not exist.

And then there is God. The great problem is the distinction, if any, between God and the universe. On the one hand, we raise our eyes to heaven and say: 'Our Father'. On the other hand, God is the great reality in which we live and move and have our being. So we are one with God and not one with God. This paradox is writ large in mystics who have got themselves into trouble for seemingly saying that they were God.

Following Aristotle, Aquinas resolves this conflict with his theory of essence and existence. All things are one by reason of their existence — they are one in *that they are*; and all things are different by reason of their essence — in *what they are*. When I look out on the rld and see only existence I see unity, with myself as part of the totality. When I see essences, I am aware of multiplicity.

In God, however, essence and existence are identical. *What God is* and *that God is* are the same. For God is being in the full sense of the word. Indeed, it can be said that God is the only Being, and all other beings participate in his existence. When he comes to state the most appropriate name for God, Thomas selects *Qui Est*, the one who is, and he appeals to Exodus where God says to Moses:

Ego Sum
I am

While this interpretation of Exodus may not give joy to the hearts of scriptural exegetes, it is sound metaphysics.[3]

All things, then, participate in the being of God. The mystics frequently appeal to the Second Epistle of Peter where it is said that we 'may become participants of the divine nature' (2 Peter 1:4). And Thomas explains this with his doctrine of analogy.

The notion of existence is not univocal — for if it were, all existences would be the same and the result would be pantheism. The notion of existence is not equivocal — for if it were, we would be completely different from God and the result would be agnosticism or dualism. But the notion of existence is analogous. That is to say, the same and different. When we say that the universe exists and that God exists we are using the word *existence* analogously.

Practically, we can speak of God by affirmation, negation and pre-eminence.[4]

via affirmativa — God is
via negativa — God is not (as creatures are)
via eminentiae — God is (in a pre-eminent way)

From this we can see how Thomas differs from Dionysius who, fascinated by the mysterious darkness, places God beyond existence. Thomas, on the other hand, keeps the paradox. God does exist. This is the way of affirmation. But (and here is the mystery and the paradox) God's existence is so different from all other existences that we can say that God does not exist. Alas, some well-intentioned mystics have come to grief in saying that God does not 'exist'; and they might have been saved by an understanding of the Thomistic doctrine that existence is an analogous concept — and God exists in a pre-eminent way.

All this may sound like idle speculation; but it is made eminently practical and pastoral by one of the great mystical theologians of the fourteenth century. The author of *The Cloud of Unknowing* counsels his disciple to eschew all essences and to concentrate his attention on existence. Do not think about *what you are* or about *what God is*, he says. Only concentrate on *that you are* and *that God is*. In this way you will enter into a great oneness (for contemplation is a one-ing exercise) and forgetfulness of self. Here are his words:

> And therefore think of God in his work as thou dost on God: that he is as he is and thou art as thou art.[5]

This is a theme that runs all through the mystical teaching of this English author. Unite your blind being to the blind being of God. Here *blind* means without thought of what you are or what God is. Moreover he justifies this teaching with a careful Thomistic metaphysics:

> For he is thy being, and in him thou art what thou art, not only by cause and by being, but also he is in thee both thy cause and thy being . . . evermore saving this difference betwixt thee and him, that he is thy being and thou not his.[6]

This last statement that 'he is thy being and thou not his' is a carefully accurate statement of Thomistic analogy.

Furthermore, this same author justifies his prayer of pure existence by stating that existence is an all-inclusive notion. Whatever you say about God is contained in the little word 'is'. So do not bother about essences, he says, since all you need is included in existence:

> For if thou say: 'Good' or 'Fair Lord' or 'sweet', 'merciful' or

'righteous', 'wise' or 'all-witting', 'mighty' or 'almighty', 'wit' or 'wisdom', 'might' or 'strength', 'love' or 'charity', or whatever other such thing thou say of God, all it is hid and contained in this little word 'is' . . . and if thou add a hundred such sweet words as these: good, fair and all that other, yet went thou not from this little word 'is'. And if thou say them all, thou addest not to it. And if thou say right none, thou takest not from it.[7]

Elsewhere the author counsels his disciple to bury all essences beneath a cloud of forgetting so as to be aware only of existence. All this is a practical application of the doctrine of Thomas Aquinas.

However, to understand the mystical prayer of this English author one must also recall his teaching on love. When the mind is empty and devoid of essences, there arises a movement of love which he calls 'a naked intent' of the will:

And look that nothing remain in thy working mind but a naked intent stretching unto God, not clothed in any special thought of God, in himself, how he is in himself, or in any of his works, but only that he is as he is.[8]

This love is all-important. To grasp it we must consider the two ways of knowing in Thomas Aquinas.

KNOWLEDGE THROUGH CONNATURALITY

In the *Summa Theologica*, Aquinas speaks of two kinds of knowledge. There is knowledge that comes from scientific enquiry or the perfect use of reason. And there is another kind of knowledge through 'connaturality'. Here one 'co-natures' with the object which is, so to speak, embodied in oneself. Thomas uses the word inclination — one judges *per inclinationem*. This is a knowledge that comes from love and from union.

Such knowledge by connaturality is particularly valuable in the area of morality. While the professor who reasons and thinks and elaborates a moral theology may have no virtue whatever, the person who possesses the virtue knows intuitively and with a remarkable surety — because he or she is 'co-natured' with the virtue and is living it. Speaking about the two kinds of knowledge, Thomas illustrates his point by referring to chastity:

> Now rectitude of judgment is twofold: first on account of perfect use of reason, secondly on account of a certain connaturality with the matter about which one has to judge. Thus, about matters of chastity, a person after enquiring with reason forms a right judgement, if he or she has learned the science of morals, while the one who has the habit of chastity judges of such matters by a kind of connaturality.[9]

Here a distinction is made between the person who has mastered the science of morals (and such a one could conceivably be quite an immoral person) and the person who has the habit. The latter person possesses the virtue of chastity — is united with it, loves it, lives it and, in consequence, knows it in an intuitive way. Such a person may not write learned books, but his or her 'connatural' knowledge is sound and reliable.

Thomas here makes no claim to originality. This doctrine he says, is found in Aristotle, to whose writings he appeals: 'Hence in the *Nichomachean Ethics X* it is said that the virtuous person is the measure and rule of human acts.'[10] Indeed a basic notion in Aristotelian ethics is: if you want to know what virtue is, look at the virtuous person, for such a one really knows.

It could be added (if a brief digression is permissible) that this knowledge through connaturality is found all through Sino-Japanese culture and is particularly evident in Buddhism. In the tea ceremony, the flower arrangement, calligraphy and the martial arts — all the so-called 'ways' — one identifies with the object and with the surroundings. In this way one enters into the state known as 'no-mind' or 'non-self'. This is not, as is sometimes said, a denial of the self but an attempt to describe a state of consciousness whereby one identifies with the surroundings so closely that the separated self is lost. And all this leads to a supraconceptual knowledge which is powerfully holistic and deeply human. Such knowledge or wisdom is the very core of Zen.[11]

KNOWLEDGE THROUGH LOVE

Knowledge through connaturality is of special importance when we come to speak about God. For the one who loves knows God, the one who does not love does not know God. For God is love.

At the beginning of the *Summa Theologica*, Thomas Aquinas, asking if sacred doctrine is truly wisdom, asserts that it is indeed wisdom above all human wisdom. He then goes on to distinguish two kinds of wisdom. The first and most important wisdom is that which is a gift of the Holy Spirit. Only after speaking about this does the angelic doctor go on to speak about study. Here are his words:

> The first manner of judging divine things belongs to that wisdom which is set down among the gifts of the Holy Spirit. 'The spiritual person judges all things' (1 Corinthians 2:13). And Dionysius says (*Div. Nom.* 11) Hierotheus is taught not by mere learning, but by experience of divine things.[12]

The highest wisdom, then is a gift of God. The love of God is poured into our hearts by the Holy Spirit who is given to us. With this doctrine of connaturality and wisdom as a gift of the Holy Spirit, Thomas lays the foundations for subsequent mystical theology.

The person who possesses the Spirit, then, judges all things. As for Hierotheus, yes he did study and learn; but more importantly he was taught by experiencing divine things. The Latin is:

patiens divina

This seems to mean experiencing (literally 'suffering') the mysteries of Christ in prayer, in recitation of the divine office, in participation in the eucharistic liturgy. In all this *patiens divina* Hierotheus is filled with a new spirit of loving wisdom that overflows in understanding, counsel, fortitude, piety, knowledge and the fear of the Lord. This is quite different from the mere learning he acquires through study.

And this wisdom comes from love. Not our love for God but God's love for us. Elsewhere in the *Summa* Thomas speaks of connaturality for divine things:

Now this sympathy or connaturality for divine things is the result of love, which unites us to God, according to 1 Corinthians 6:17: 'The one who is joined to the Lord is one spirit.'[13]

Obviously, as has already been said, this is very scriptural doctrine, for the First Epistle of St John tells us that the one who loves knows God and the one who does not love does not know God, for God is love. Sacred Scripture does not say that the one who studies theology knows God, but the one who loves.

The love of God, then, is poured into our hearts; we are united with God; we are one with God; and through this love comes the highest wisdom.

In his more technical passages Thomas makes use of Aristotelian psychology to speak of the interplay between love and wisdom — between will and intellect. Wisdom which is a gift 'has its cause in the will, which cause is charity, but it has its essence in the intellect, whose act is to judge aright'.[14] The two faculties of intellect and will are so closely related that true love in the will necessarily leads to knowledge:

> Both are rooted in the same substance of the soul, and since one is in a certain way the principle of the other, consequently what is in the will is, in a certain sense, also in the intellect.[15]

What is in the will is, in a certain sense, also in the intellect. This may sound abstract; but it plays an important and practical role in St John of the Cross (who was a convinced Thomist) when he says that a powerful experience of God's love in the will leads to a profound enlightenment in the intellect. Knowledge and love are closely intertwined: the Spanish mystic speaks constantly of loving wisdom.

But what is the nature of this connatural knowledge that comes from love? How do we experience it? Clearly it is not conceptual; it has nothing of the Cartesian clear and distinct idea.

And it is here that the apophatic dimension of Aquinas comes forcibly to the fore. God is known as unknown (*quasi ignotus cognoscitur*). God is known as mystery. 'In this life', Thomas writes, 'we cannot know what he is and thus we are united to him as to one unknown."[1]

Et sic ei tamquam ignoto conjungamur

This is indeed the experience of the apophatic mystics: to love and to be united with one whom they know not. Who or what they love they do not know. This is the obscure night. This is the cloud of unknowing.

Aquinas speaks further about this knowing through not-knowing when he asks the question: 'Whether ecstasy is an effect of love?' He quotes Dionysius to the effect that love does produce ecstasy; and then he proceeds to say that by ecstasy one is placed outside oneself and outside of ordinary knowledge. This is the situation of no-thinking. One is raised to a higher knowledge 'so as to comprehend things that surpass sense and reason'.[17]

And in Thomas the knowledge from connaturality and the knowledge from scientific enquiry were admirably blended and harmonized. He was a consummate mystic and a powerful thinker. But in the end it was the mystic who triumphed. After his great enlightenment he refused to write and spoke but little, saying that all he had written was like straw compared with what he had seen. The knowledge of connaturality had won the day. The knowledge from scientific enquiry was like straw.

CONNATURALITY WITH CHRIST

Knowledge through love and connaturality is of the greatest importance in one's relationship with Christ. Here there is no question of knowing Jesus in images and concepts, no question of what the author of *The Cloud* calls good and pious meditations on the passion. Rather is it a question of silent love and union, leading to supraconceptual wisdom.

Thomas speaks of this when he poses the question: 'Whether mutual indwelling is an effect of love?'[18] And he answers in the affirmative by quoting the Johannine text that 'those who abide in charity abide in God, and God in them' (1 John 4:16). Then he goes on: 'Now charity is the love of God. Therefore, for the same reason, every love makes the beloved to be in the lover, and vice versa.' And he further says that 'the beloved is contained in the lover, by being impressed on his heart and thus becoming the object of his complacency. On the other hand, the lover is contained in the beloved inasmuch as the lover penetrates, so to speak, into the beloved.'[19] Here Thomas comes remarkably close to The Song of Songs. His doctrine helps us understand the Pauline 'I live, now not I, but Christ lives in me' (Galatians 2:20) and the many passages about mutal indwelling in the fourth gospel.

When one grasps this knowledge of Jesus through love and connaturality, one can understand how thousands of mystics have spent hours with Jesus in Gethsemane or have knelt at the foot of the cross without thinking or reasoning, always remaining in the imageless silence of a cloud of unknowing.

Thomas, however, stresses that this imageless love penetrates to the person of Jesus, the Word Incarnate; and in some surprising passages he advises his readers not to be too attached to the sacred humanity — 'We ought not to rest in it as in an end in itself, but through it we should reach out to God.'[20] Christ, he tells us, took away his physical presence lest the hearts of the disciples be captivated by his purely human qualities. In the *Summa* he writes:

> Such is the weakness of the human mind that it needs a guide not only to the knowledge, but also to the love, of divine things by means of certain sensible objects known to us. Chief among these is the humanity of Christ . . . Accordingly, things relating to Christ's humanity are the chief incentive to devotion, leading us there as a guide, although devotion itself has for its principal object things that concern the Godhead.[21]

Following Thomas, Ruysbroeck says that 'never creature may be, or become, so holy that it loses its created being and becomes God'; and he adds: 'Even the soul of Our Lord Jesus Christ shall remain creature and other than God.'[22] Note that he says 'the soul of Our Lord Jesus Christ', not the person.

And the author of *The Cloud of Unknowing* advises his disciple to abandon pious meditations on the life and death of Jesus when the time comes to enter into the obscure silence of the cloud. Following a long mystical tradition, he describes Mary Magdalene sitting lovingly at the feet of Jesus and tells us that her gaze penetrated beyond his humanity to his divinity: 'she regarded the sovereignest wisdom of his Godhead lapped in the dark words of his Manhood'. At first his words sound like a Neo-Platonic rejection of matter but on closer scrutiny they appear as good Thomism.

This doctrine is very important for sound spiritual direction and is at the very centre of mystical theology. It does happen that people enter into the loving knowledge of connaturality — and then they fear that they have lost Jesus. Needless to say, they have not lost Jesus. They have found a different knowledge of Jesus. Yet on such occasions ignorant directors urge them to get to work and think about the Jesus of the gospels. Against such directors St John of the Cross inveighs vigorously, calling them blacksmiths who pound with a hammer and destroy the delicate work of God.[23] Some directors do not understand the knowledge of connaturality that comes from loving union.

And this doctrine is expressed with poetic beauty in the medieval lyric *Jesu Dulcis*. The poet begins by extolling the true joy that the memory of Jesus brings to the human heart:

Jesu Dulcis Memoria

This is the memory of Jesus with images and thoughts and deep feeling. But then the poem goes on to say that sweeter than honey and all things is the presence of Jesus:

Eius Dulcis Praesentia

Here is poetically described the transition from *memory* to *presence*, from *thought* to *contemplation*. One enters into the obscure knowledge of connaturality in which there are not pictures nor clear ideas of Jesus but only the sense of his presence. Rightly does Etienne Gilson declare that this poem 'describes the movement by which the soul rises from remembrance of the passion of Christ to mystic union'.[24]

It should be remembered, however, that union with Jesus, the Word Incarnate, is not the last stage in the mystic way. United with the Word and filled with the Spirit one calls out: 'Abba, Father.' In other words, one enters into the very heart of the Trinity and lives the very life of the Trinity.

All this throws invaluable light on apophatic mysticism. From the patristic era until our own day, sceptical theologians and puzzled spiritual directors have wondered how Jesus Christ fits into the Dionysian darkness. Where is Jesus in the cloud of unknowing into which the mystic enters in the abandonment of thought? And the answer is that Jesus is known through connaturality. That is to say, he is known *per inclinationem*; he is known by love; he is known by union. And through him and through his love the Father is also known, not in clear-cut images but as mystery. '. . . *et sic ei tamquam ignoto conjungamur*.' We are united with the one we do not know.

MYSTICAL THEOLOGY IN DECLINE

Thomas Aquinas dominated Catholic theology for six hundred years. He was a saint and a mystic. His doctrine of connaturality, of knowledge through love, of wisdom as a gift of the Holy Spirit issued from a mind and heart that were always united with the living God. His contemplative prayer and his love for the Eucharist were the very core of his life.

Now Aquinas was a man of his time and he belonged to the Order of Preachers. Like Abelard he was a brilliant dialectician who wanted to find a rational basis for the Christian message and to confront the enemies of his faith. For a systematic substructure he turned to Aristotle; but his theological doctrine came from revelation — from Scripture and tradition — and he created a magnificent synthesis of reason and faith. It was all the overflow of his mystical experience: *contemplata aliis tradere*.

Alas, the successors of Thomas, who taught energetically in the schools, paid little attention to the Master's teaching of connaturality and knowledge through love and the gift of the Holy Spirit. A decadent scholasticism was preoccupied with questions and syllogisms and rapier-like distinctions (the word *distinguo* echoed through the lecture halls) and it wanted to prove to the world that the system was reasonable. Abelard would have rubbed his hands with glee. Bernard would have wept: the scholastics were trying to see nothing through a glass darkly and to behold all things face to face. Where was the mysticism that had filled the writings of the Fathers?

While within the monasteries and religious houses of the West mystical prayer did quietly flourish, and while there was an extraordinary mystical awakening in sixteenth-century Spain, the Catholic establishment was wary about mysticism. The errors of the *alumbrados* and the quietists had made their mark.[25] Those who aspired to mystical prayer were regarded with suspicion; novices were warned about the dangers of false mysticism, pantheism, quietism, illusion and self-hypnosis.

In the Protestant tradition, from the time of the reformers, mystical theology was associated with Neo-Platonism, Gnosticism and the mystery religions of the Graeco-Roman world. Furthermore some eminent writers felt that mystical theology overlooked the prophetic and even the ethical dimension of sacred Scripture.[26] For this reason, mystical theology as such did not flourish in the Protestant tradition.

Today, however, we are face to face with a new world that is attracted by mysticism and is impatient of irrelevant and wordy speculation. Now we are entering into dialogue with the mystical religions of Asia, religions which live connaturality. In these circumstances a revival of Christian mysticism will certainly come. Indeed, it is already with us. Will the much neglected mystical theology become the centre of all theology? Surely this is the way of the future.

NOTES

1. See *The Mind of St Bernard of Clairvaux*, G. R. Evans, Oxford 1983.
2. See *The Mystical Theology of St Bernard*, Etienne Gilson, New York 1955. Also *Peter Abailard*, J. G. Sikes, New York 1965.
3. *Summa Theologica*, I, q. 13, a. 11, c. All future references to the *Summa Theologica* will be designated *S.T.*
4. *S.T.*, I, q. 13.
5. *The Book of Privy Counselling*, C. 1.
6. Ibid.
7. Ibid. C. 4.

8. Ibid. C. 1.
9. *S.T.*, II, II. q. 45, a. 2, c. See also 'On knowledge through connaturality' by Jacques Maritain in *The Review of Metaphysics*, June 1951, p. 473.
10. '. . . dicitur quod virtuosus est mensura et regula actuum humanorum', *S.T.*, I, q. 1, a. 7, ad 3.
11. See 'Ways of Knowing: a Buddhist-Thomist Dialogue', Kakichi Kadowaki in *The International Philosophical Quarterly*, Dec. 1966.
12. *S.T.* I, q. 1, a. 6, ad 3.
13. *S.T.*, II, II, q. 45, a. 2, c.
14. Ibid.
15. *S.T.*, I, q. 87, a. 4, ad 1.
16. *S.T.*, I, q. 12, a. 13, ad 1.
17. *S.T.*, I, II, q. 28, a. 3, c.
18. *S.T.*, I, II, q. 28, a. 2.
19. Ibid.
20. In Joann., 7, 32.
21. *S.T.*, II, II, q. 28, a. 3, ad 9.
22. *The Book of Supreme Truth*, C. II.
23. *The Living Flame*, 3.43.
24. Gilson, Etienne, Op. supra cit., p. 82.
25. Both the *alumbrados* in sixteenth-century Spain and the quietists in seventeenth-century Europe attached an exaggerated importance to passivity in mental prayer.
26. See *Agape and Eros* (Three volumes), A. Nygren, London 1932–9. Also *Word and Faith*, G. Ebeling, London 1963.

FOUR

Mysticism and Love

THE PRIMACY OF LOVE

Before the Second Vatican Council, when 'Ascetical and Mystical Theology' was part of the seminary curriculum, students were taught that Christian perfection consists in charity. Joseph de Guibert (1877-1942), one of the better known professors of the Gregorian University, formulated his thesis succinctly:

> Thesis 1. Charity is the principal norm for judging the perfection of the Christian life.[1]

This thesis was the cornerstone of the old ascetical and mystical theology.

As was customary in the theology of that time, de Guibert first lists his adversaries. There are the Gnostics who thought that perfection consists in knowledge and contemplation (*theoria*). There are the Montanists who sought perfection in gifts of prophecy and ecstasy. Then there are Messalians, Brethren of the Free Spirit, Beghards, Spanish *illuminati* and quietists, all of whom exaggerated in some way the role of prayer and contemplation in the Christian life.

Against these adversaries de Guibert quotes the great commandment to love God with one's whole heart and soul and mind and strength and to love one's neighbour as one's self. He also quotes the fourth gospel and gives us extensive quotations from St Paul. Then come the Church Fathers: Clement of Rome, Ignatius, Irenaeus, Gregory of Nyssa, Augustine, Cassian, Gregory the Great and Bernard of Clairvaux. And, of course, Thomas Aquinas is there. All with one voice, claims de Guibert, proclaim that love is the centre of the Christian life.

While modern scholars might say that de Guibert is oversimplified in his treatment of his adversaries, and less than critical in his biblical and patristic scholarship, his central thesis cannot easily be denied. And from it there springs an important corollary: mysticism that is not rooted and grounded in love cannot be called Christian. 'If I speak in the tongues of mortals and of angels but do not have love, I am a noisy gong and a clanging cymbal' (1 Corinthians 13:1).

BERNARD OF CLAIRVAUX

De Guibert quotes Bernard of Clairvaux (1090-1153) as an eminent example of one whose spiritual teaching is grounded in love. Likewise Etienne Gilson in *The Mystical Theology of St Bernard* insists that the mystical theology of Bernard is all centred on the fourth chapter of The First Epistle of St John where we read that God is love, that God first loved us and that one who loves knows God.[2] The mystical theology of the mellifluous doctor, as Bernard was called, begins and ends with this text.

That Bernard was a lover is clear from his homilies on The Song of Songs, from his treaties on the love of God, and from everything he wrote. 'The reason for loving God is God Himself', he says. 'The measure of loving God is to love without measure.' He describes stages of growth in love. At first our love for Christ is sensible or 'carnal' since it is directed to the sacred humanity of Jesus who lived in this world. Such love is a gift of God; and Bernard is noted for his tender love for the Jesus of the gospels and for that deep devotion to the Virgin Mary expressed in his immortal *Memorare*.

Yet one must go beyond such sensible love, he says, 'for it is carnal compared with the other love which is not so much related to the Word made flesh as to the Word as wisdom, the Word as truth, the Word as holiness'.[3] Such love leads to ecstasy (*excessus mentis*), to spiritual marriage with the Word, to union with God; for 'anyone united to the Lord becomes one spirit with him' (1 Corinthians 6:17).

Like Origen, Bernard follows The Song of Songs in speaking

about the embrace, the kiss, the ecstasy and the marriage. And again, like Origen, he sternly warns the reader about the danger of eroticism:

> Take heed that you bring chaste ears to this discourse of love; and when you think of these two lovers, always remember that not a man and a woman are to be thought of, but the Word of God and a soul.[4]

Such is Bernard's approach to carnal love. One wonders if he ever solved the problem of a love that is at the same time mystical and incarnational. While it is true, as Gilson says, that he was rooted in The First Epistle of St John, he was also well versed in the Church Fathers. For his doctrine of ecstasy and the divinization of the soul through love, he turned to Maximus the Confessor (580-662) in the translation of Scotus Erigena; and we know that Maximus was steeped in the Cappadocians and Dionysius. From them did the great Cistercian inherit some Neoplatonic dualism? Or was it simply his character and education that come through in his writing? Perhaps it was not his vocation to reconcile the carnal and the spiritual. Perhaps this challenging problem, so central to all mystical theology, still awaits solution in our day.[5]

Be that as it may, Bernard made an enormous impact on Western spirituality and continues to exert influence through Cistercian monasteries everywhere.

SCHOOLS OF SPIRITUALITY

The Middle Ages saw the rise of schools of spirituality associated with the great religious orders, and each of these schools had its own brand of mysticism. They can truly be called schools because they taught people to pray — and finally to pray mystically. Indeed, mystical experience was the crown and glory of each school.

The oldest school and, in some ways, the most venerable was the Benedictine with its roots in the rule of St Benedict (480-550). In this school were three important practices which nourished the spirit of all who entered.

The first was manual labour in the fields. The old monastic dictum that to work is to pray was profound and even mystical:

Laborare est Orare

Contact with the soil and the wind and the rain, contact with God in nature was a real religious experience. It is interesting to note that Buddhist monasticism values this same experience; and dialogue between Buddhist and Christian monasticism is beginning to flourish in our day.

The second important practice was the reading of sacred scripture known as

Lectio Divina

This was the practice of reading the Scriptures slowly and lovingly. One might take a phrase from the Bible (later other holy texts were used) and repeat it quietly, savouring its inner meaning, identifying with it or 'eating' it as the author of Revelation ate the scroll. This practice frequently led to a state of consciousness where one used no words at all, remaining silent in the presence of God. This Benedict, following the tradition of the desert fathers, called 'pure prayer'. It is indeed a gateway to wordless, mystical prayer in a cloud of unknowing.

The third important practice was liturgical — chanting the divine office and celebrating the Eucharist.

Let us remember that liturgical action can be a mystical experience. To understand this one need only reflect on what was said in the last chapter about connaturality. There it was said that there is a knowledge that comes through life, through love, and through union. One, as it were, *becomes* the object, thus acquiring an intuitive knowledge. Now this kind of knowledge comes to those who gather around the table of the Lord to celebrate the Eucharist with devotion. They *become* the body and blood of Christ. They *live* the death and Resurrection of Jesus as they chant: 'Christ has died: Christ has risen: Christ will come again.'

Christ has died
Christ is risen
Christ will come again

Indeed this is the basic Christian mystical experience: to die and rise with Christ and with him to enter into glory.

For the fact is that Christian mystical experience cannot be divorced from the Eucharist. In some ways it can even be called an extension of the eucharistic celebration. This is abundantly clear in *The Cloud of Unknowing* where the English author teaches his disciple a eucharistic prayer.

> That that I am and how that I am
> as in nature and in grace,
> all I have it of thee, Lord, and thou it art.
> And all I offer it unto thee
> principally to the praising of thee,
> for the help of all mine even Christians
> and of me.[6]

The author spells out this prayer in words but when existentially practised it is a silent offering of one's blind being to God together with Jesus who offered himself to the Father for the redemption of the world. Note that the author writes, 'and thou art it'. That is to say, God is his all; God is his very being. And so, in an extraordinary paradox, he offers his all to the Father who is his all and his very being. This is both mystical and eucharistic.

The great contribution of the Benedictine school was in the area of Scripture and liturgy. But other schools of spirituality arose, associated with the new religious orders that were coming to birth in the Middle Ages.

There was a Franciscan school inspired by the *poverello*, the stigmatist of Assisi who loved the birds and the flowers, who sang to brother sun and sister moon, who loved to have nothing and whose personal charm has captivated the whole world. The great scholastic theologian of the Franciscan school was Bonaventure (1221-74), the Seraphic doctor, who has been called the Thomas Aquinas of mystical theology. Like his beloved Francis he saw the Incarnation at the heart of the universe.

Then there were the Victorines of the Abbey of St Victor in Paris. Here lived the illustrious Hugh and his disciple Richard of St Victor, some of whose works were translated into English by the author of *The Cloud*. Richard began the systematic study of the spiritual life and is notable for his doctrine of ecstasy, of inner fire and of passionate love.

All these schools nourished mysticism, each in its own way. And while the monks and nuns aspired to the mystical life, the secular world was also searching for love.

THE SACRED AND THE SECULAR

While Bernard and Richard of St Victor and Bonaventure wrote ecstatically about the love of God, contemporary Europe was also wrestling with the problem of love. And the secular and the sacred necessarily influenced one another.

In France of the eleventh century the troubadours suddenly appeared, singing love songs to a mistress who was something of a goddess to be worshipped by men. This was also a time when the *Ars Amatoria* of Ovid was much in vogue. C. S. Lewis has pointed out that courtly love, as it was called, was adulterous and dishonourable; yet it contained beautiful elements of courtesy and devotion which made an enormous impact on European life and literature and religion.[7] Indeed, Western spirituality from that time has had a romantic dimension that distinguishes it from anything that has arisen in Asia and even from the devotion of the orthodox Christianity of Greece and Russia.

It is scarcely surprising, then, if courtly love influenced the interpretation of The Song of Songs. It is not surprising to hear that the young Francis of Assisi wrote love poetry and later became God's troubadour. Chivalrous love is a powerful force in the life of St Ignatius of Loyola. St John of the Cross is a romantic to the core.

And then (returning to the twelfth century) there was the love of Héloïse and Abelard, so widely known and discussed that Etienne Gilson can say that 'the passionate drama of Héloïse and Abelard, more fertile in ideas than one might suppose, riveted all eyes on the problem of love.'⁸ For Abelard wrote love poems for Héloïse; and she in turn wrote letters with reflections on pure and disinterested love. And all this led to theological debate about disinterested love of God and the possibility of embracing damnation for the love of God. More reasonable and commonsensical was the *De Amicitia* (On Friendship) of Cicero. Here was a beautiful and noble ideal of friendship which was to influence the Cistercian Aelred of Rievaulx (1109-67), known as the English Bernard, and through him the whole Cistercian tradition.

All in all, the spirit of the time flowed into religious life. All were searching for the true meaning of love.

THE FOURTEENTH-CENTURY MYSTICS

The fourteenth century witnessed a remarkable surge of mystical energy throughout Europe. In the far north, in Sweden, we find the visionary and prophetess Bridget (1302-73) who came to Rome and talked straight to popes and bishops and kings. In the south was Catherine of Siena, Dominican tertiary, also a prophetess and now a doctor of the church — who likewise talked to the rich and powerful and called a spade a spade. In Britain, amidst a galaxy of mystical writers we find the charming and deeply cultured Dame Juliana of Norwich and the practical, yet profound, anonymous author of *The Cloud of Unknowing*.

But it was in the Rhineland that the influential mystical writers flourished. Most powerful and creative was the great Dominican friar, Meister Eckhart (1260-1327) with his disciples John Tauler and Henry Suso. Their mystical and charismatic ideas spread to the Netherlands where John Ruysbroeck (1293-1381) spent decades in solitude and became a canon of St Augustine. He was great as mystic, theologian and writer.

Yet not all fourteenth-century mysticism was edifying. We have already seen how Joseph de Guibert quickly dismissed the Beghards and the Brethren of the Free Spirit. Modern scholasticism would be much more nuanced in its treatment of these movements. Nevertheless, it cannot be denied that there were enthusiasts who, in the name of pure spirit, composed mystical treatises on spiritual espousals and seraphic love that led to sexual extravagances. All in all there was profound mystical experience joined to distressing excesses. But through it all the Spirit was clearly at work.

It should be noted that all this took place in a period of history when Europe was one and could still be called Christendom. Educated people spoke a common language, Latin; and liturgical celebration was similar throughout the continent. It is not surprising, then, if we find remarkable similarities in Eckhart, *The Cloud of Unknowing* , Julian of Norwich, Ruysbroeck and the rest. All the more so, since at the heart of the mystical movement were Dominicans who held fast to the Christian tradition and revered St Thomas Aquinas.

Yet this was also a time of controversy.

Never let us forget that the wisdom of the mystics comes from life rather than from books. It is knowledge of connaturality, knowledge that is the fruit of love. Those who are writers and artists try to express their experience in theological treatises or in sermons and exhortations; and this was particularly true of men and women who belonged to active religious orders. They knew very well that words were inadequate to express what they experienced and they sometimes fell into error or were tragically misunderstood.

Saddest of all is the story of Eckhart.

Recent studies make it clear that Eckhart was a deeply committed Christian who never wavered in his loyalty to the Church. Richard Woods, himself a Dominican, quotes Hugo Rahner to the effect that the Meister was a loyal Catholic, completely orthodox in his teaching when it is viewed as a whole.[9] Similarly Karl G. Kertz asserts that his doctrine of the birth of God in the soul is 'perfectly sound Catholic doctrine'. Again, the American scholar Bernard McGinn maintains that when taken out of context much of Eckhart might seem to conflict with traditional teaching but it can all be interpreted in 'a fundamentally orthodox sense'.[10]

Why, then, was Eckhart condemned? Richard Woods maintains that it was not for unorthodox ideas; neither was he a victim of petty church politics. It was that Eckhart was an artist and his accusers were bureaucrats. 'It was the poetry they could not appreciate, the daring excesses of speech and flights of imagination by which the great scholar transcended the arid limitations of the learned disquisition and dispute, seeking to move his listeners by the art of preaching.'[11]

All of this is of the utmost importance in the twentieth century and will be even more important in the twenty-first. For the fact is that Eckhart is in the forefront of the Buddhist-Christian dialogue. Dr D.T. Suzuki found in Eckhart much that resonates with Zen Buddhism; but he believed that Eckhart's God was quite different from the God of the Christians. Again, Professor Shizuteru Ueda, the distinguished Kyoto professor, while he believes that Eckhart is authentically Christian, is not convinced that Eckhart's teaching is in harmony with the institutional Church. Since Eckhart was condemned by ecclesiastical authority and comes across as a kind of Galileo among the mystics, it is difficult to quote him as a spokesman for Christianity in the modern world. One can only hope that the Dominican proposal that the whole question of Eckhart be ecclesiastically re-examined will lead to his reinstatement as an orthodox spokesman for a mystical understanding of the Gospel of Jesus Christ.[12]

Yet all this controversy led to a significant theological development. It became clear that there was need for a mystical theology that would be a separate branch of the overall science of theology. Such a specialized, mystical theology was necessary for two reasons.

First, many mystics in the fourteenth century found themselves in a cloud of unknowing and were crying out for help. They needed solid guidance; their mystical experience called for a firm theological basis. Such a basis was not given by the ordinary scholastic theology taught in the schools.

Secondly, as already mentioned, there were all kinds of aberrations. It was necessary to make clear what is meant by union with God as opposed to pantheism and what is meant by contemplation as opposed to quietism, for the mystical path is full of pitfalls; and false prophets frequently deceive the people. Consequently, a new science of mystical theology had to emerge.

A NEW BRANCH OF THEOLOGY

From what has been said it will be clear that mystical prayer existed from the earliest times in the Christian community. However, in the Church Fathers mystical theology — that is to day, theological reflection on mystical experience — did not exist as a separate discipline. It was part of their general theology and it had, so to speak, to be extracted from their overall theology. When Etienne Gilson comes to write *The Mystical Theology of St Bernard*, he tells us that he is concerned with 'that part of his (Bernard's) theology on which his mysticism rests'. In other words Bernard wrote no formal mystical theology. And the same could be said about Augustine, Gregory of Nyssa, Bonaventure and Thomas.

To this, however, there is one notable exception. Dionysius did write his *Mystical Theology* as a specialized treatise on a very clear-cut subject. He wrote as a spiritual director guiding his disciple in a concrete way of prayer which can be called mystical or hidden. That is to say, it was a prayer that went beyond reasoning and thinking and images into the silence of a cloud of unknowing.

Now in the fourteenth century the treatise of Dionysius became the model for others who wanted to write precisely about this kind of religious experience. While they did follow Dionysius and appealed to his authority, they were reading a Dionysius who had been translated by Erigena, interpreted by Aquinas, purified, re-thought and thoroughly Christianized. How much of the original, Neo-Platonic Dionysius remained in the fourteenth century is a question that need not concern us here. What matters is that now, following his example, there arose specialized treatises that dealt with mystical theology as a distinct science, as a separate branch of theology.

Here of special importance as a mystical theologian is John Ruysbroeck who fought clearly and sternly against the mystical errors of his day. But even more important is the author of *The Cloud of Unknowing*, for this Englishman is not directly concerned with systematic or dogmatic or scriptural theology. He is interested in the theology of a path to God — a special path trod by those who know God by unknowing. Reading between the lines it is clear that he has a profound grasp of the doctrines of the Blessed Trinity, of the

Incarnation, of original sin and the rest; but he is primarily interested in these dogmas in so far as they are experienced by the mystic on the way to God. He is, moreover, a spiritual director who is aware of the pitfalls, the storms, the nights and all the psychological upheaval that is part and parcel of this privileged path. All in all, is he not a theologian of the way? And is not this new branch of mystical theology a theology of the way?

Yet another systematic mystical theologian is John Gerson of the University of Paris (1363-1429). Gerson wrote both speculative and mystical theology, insisting that the latter is the work of love. Mystical theology, he wrote, is 'experiential knowledge of God through the embrace of unitive love'.[13] Here the word *experiential* is important: mystical theology far from being abstract and speculative is experiential and holistic knowledge that guides the mystical pilgrim on the way of love.

TWO KINDS OF KNOWLEDGE: TWO KINDS OF PRAYER

And in this new branch of theology, as in every branch of theology, an enormously influential person was Thomas Aquinas. It will be remembered that Thomas spoke of two kinds of knowledge; and corresponding to these two kinds of knowledge mystical theology saw two kinds of prayer.

One kind of knowledge was *acquired* by the process of scientific inquiry. That is to say, it was acquired by experiencing, understanding and judging. Following Aristotle, Thomas had held that there is nothing in the intellect which was not previously in the senses.[4] Consequently knowledge came from the exterior senses to the interior senses and was conveyed to the intellect by what was called the *species impressa* or *species acquisita*.

The second kind of knowledge — more properly called wisdom was a gift of the Holy Spirit. It did not come from the exterior senses but was directly *infused*; for the love of God is poured into our hearts by the Holy Spirit who is given. And so the *species* were not *acquisita* but *infusa*. That is why the subsequent mystical tradition spoke of mystical prayer as *infused contemplation*.

God, says the author of *The Cloud*, works all by himself.[15] And Thomas Aquinas says that there are times when God works 'sine medio' — without the mediation of created things.[16] And this is the wonder of the mystical life: that God works directly on the human person, infusing into his or her heart knowledge and love. And the knowledge received in this way is not clear-cut and conceptual nor is it found in images and pictures. It is obscure knowledge in a cloud of unknowing or in a dark night. It can be painful knowledge because the human is not always ready to meet the divine and can be plunged into darkness by the excess of light. But it is what the author of *The Cloud* calls 'high ghostly wisdom' brighter than ordinary knowledge as the light of the sun is brighter than that of a candle.

And when this loving wisdom is infused into the human mind and heart one must abandon that other kind of knowledge that comes from scientific inquiry. In other words one must stop thinking. This is of the greatest importance, for at the outset, this infused contemplation may be very quiet and delicate. If one insists on thinking and reasoning and engaging in scientific inquiry, one may smother the tiny flame of love. And what a tragedy this is!

And so the advice at the beginning is: no thinking. Allow the inner flame to grow! Let the process take place! Do not fight against the spirit. In this way one embarks on the mystical path or, more correctly, one allows oneself to be drawn upward along the mystical path to God.

THEOLOGY OF LOVE

The love of God, then, is poured into our hearts by the Holy Spirit. The author of *The Cloud* speaks of 'the blind stirring of love'. It is a stirring because it is experiential; it is blind because it is love without thought. Again, he speaks of a 'naked intent of the will'. It is naked because not clothed in thought. Others speak of inner fire and inner light. This love, as has been said, is infused or poured into the heart, and St John of the Cross later speaks of 'an inflow of God into the soul'. However, one can also call it a welling up of God — as though God surfaces or is born. Yes, something new is born; and we know that birth can be bloody and painful both for the mother and the child.

The mystical life is the story of the birth of this love and its growth. From a tiny spark it becomes what St John of the Cross calls 'a living flame of love'. But what is this love?

St John of the Cross says clearly that the living flame of love is the Holy Spirit. Furthermore, following the Christian mystical tradition, he attaches great importance to the Pauline words: 'I live, now not I, but Christ lives in me' (Galatians 2:20). The Spirit is dwelling within; the Word is dwelling within; the Father is dwelling within. And so this love which is at the same time human and divine is quite different from what we ordinarily call love. We call it love by analogy.

Again, this love cannot be acquired by human effort nor is it the result of ascetical practices or sophisticated techniques. It is not merited. God gives it to whom he wills and when he wills. This is the constant teaching of the traditional mystical theology. One must wait until (as the author of *The Cloud* says) Jesus calls one to enter the sheepfold. Until this time comes, one must keep busy with good and pious reflections on the life and death of Jesus. One only enters the sheepfold in answer to a call.

CONCLUSION

Authentic Christian mysticism is based on love. About this there is no shadow of doubt in the Christian tradition. 'We love because he first loved us' (1 John 4:19).

However, when we come to speak concretely and philosophically about the nature of this love, enormous problems arise. The medieval world, both religious and secular, grappled with this problem of love with varying degrees of success. Then in the fourteenth century a remarkable flowering of mystical experience made it necessary to elaborate a specialized theology of mystical experience to guide devout people in their life of prayer, to protect them from error, to distinguish the true from the false, to separate the sheep from the goats. Since this mystical theology is aimed at studying the experience of love rather than analysing its nature, it can be called a theology of the way.

While this mystical theology owed a great debt to a thoroughly Christianized Dionysius, it was shaped above all by the teaching of

Thomas Aquinas. Moreover, while it was developed and enriched by the Spanish Carmelites of the sixteenth century, it remained basically unchanged from the fourteenth century until the Second Vatican Council.

But now it is necessary to consider another rich, Christian mystical experience that developed without any influence from Thomas and the scholastics. In the next chapter we will look to the mystical experience of Eastern Christianity.

NOTES

1. *Theologia spiritualis ascetica et mystica*, Joseph de Guibert S. J., Rome, 1946, II.II.
2. *The Mystical Theology of St Bernard*, Etienne Gilson, (Reprinted) London 1955, p.21.
3. *In Cantica*, PL 183.
4. Quoted by Cuthbert Butler in *Western Mysticism*, p.67.
5. Gilson writes: 'There can be no hesitation about the object and nature of mystical love as conceived by St Bernard. It was a spiritual love, in sharp opposition to every kind of carnal love. His doctrine is too uncompromising on this point to leave any room for doubt. In a sense it was the whole of his doctrine. Carnal love, wherever it spring from concupiscence, is something that has to be extirpated, and even when it occurs in the spiritual order it is something to be surpassed.' (Op. supra cit, p.172.) Such an approach scarcely solves the problems of modern people.
6. See *The Mysticism of 'The Cloud of Unknowing'*, William Johnston, Source Books, California and Anthony Clarke, Wheathampstead, Herts (Reprint) 1992, p.235.
7. See *The Allegory of Love*, C. S. Lewis, Oxford 1958. See also *Agape and Eros*, Anders Nygren, 1932 (Reprint), University of Chicago Press, 1982.
8. Op. supra cit. p.13.
9. *Eckhart's Way*, Richard Woods O. P., Michael Glazier, Delaware 1986, p.212, 213.
10. Ibid. p.215.
11. The Dominican General Chapter at Walberg in 1980 proposed that the whole process by which Eckhart was condemned be re-examined.
12. Op. supra cit. p.VII.
13. '*Theologia mystica est experimentalis cognitio habita de Deo per amoris unitivi complexum.*'
14. '*Nihil est in intellectu quod non fuit prius in sensu.*'
15. *The Cloud of Unknowing*, C.26.
16. Thomas Aquinas says that out first parents, before the fall, knew God 'without mean': '*sine medio*' — '*non per medium argumentationis ex creaturibus sensibilibus. . .*' (II Sent., d. 223, q.2. art 1, ad 1). For Thomas our first parents in the state of original justice were contemplative.

FIVE

✳

Eastern Christianity

THE GREAT SCHISM

For the first millennium of the Christian era the Greek Church of the East and the Latin Church of the West shared a common religious heritage and enjoyed a common faith. Inevitably there was sporadic tension between Rome and Constantinople; but there was no major break. In his well-known book *The Mystical Theology of the Eastern Church*, Vladimir Lossky writes about the 'indivisible treasure' both Churches shared; and he goes on to say with ecumenical grace: 'The Orthodox Church would not be what it is, if it had not had St Cyprian, St Augustine and St Gregory the Great. No more could the Roman Catholic Church do without St Athanasius, St Basil or St Cyril of Alexandria.'[1] In spite of disputes and quarrels the two Christian traditions formed the one body of Christ.[2]

The year of the tragic rupture between East and West is usually set at 1054. Then it was that the papal legate Humbert in the name of Pope Leo IX (who was already dead) hurled on the altar of Hagia Sophia in Constantinople a document excommunicating the Patriarch Michael Cerularius, who responded by excommunicating the papal delegation. Neither Rome nor Constantinople excommunicated the other's followers; but violent language was used and a point of no return was reached.

In the ensuing years the two branches of Christianity grew apart not only in terms of dogma and church government but also in terms of theology. We have already seen how Latin theology came to be dominated by a scholasticism which was unable to guide people in the path of mystical prayer so that a separate branch of theology — mystical theology — was elaborated. This new theology arose in the mystical climate of the fourteenth century, was developed magnificently by the Spanish Carmelites in sixteenth-century Spain, and was taught in Catholic seminaries throughout the world until the Second Vatican Council.

On the Eastern Church, however, scholasticism made little impact. Thomas Aquinas, it is true, was translated into Greek in the fourteenth century and had some Byzantine admirers; but mainstream Eastern theology stayed with the Church Fathers and was proud to carry on the patristic tradition. Eastern Christianity, moreover, found no need to create a separate discipline called 'mystical theology' since mystical theology remained the centre of all theology. This point is stressed by Lossky who says that there is no theology without mysticism and goes on, 'Mysticism is accordingly treated in the present work as the perfection and crown of all theology: as theology *par excellence*.'[3] In short, all authentic theology comes out of prayer and, above all, out of mystical prayer.

The mysticism of the Orthodox Church shines forth splendidly in its beautiful liturgy, particularly in its celebration of the Eucharist, and in its exquisite iconography. But it is above all in hesychasm that we find the deep mystical experience that speaks powerfully to the modern world.

HESYCHASM

Hesychasm is the quiet prayer in which one recites the name of Jesus with faith and love. The word itself comes from the Greek *hesychia* meaning quiet.

$$ἡσυχία$$

Hesychasm flourished, and continues to flourish, at the holy mountain in Northern Greece where monks from many parts of the world spend a life of prayer and fasting. Mount Athos, one of the great monastic centres of all time, was particularly alive in the fourteenth century. That was the time when Gregory Palamas (1296–1359), mystical theologian and saint of the Orthodox Church, spoke to the world in defence of this venerable way of prayer.[4] But the roots of hesychasm go far back in Christian tradition. Already in the sixth century St John Climacus wrote about 'the memory of Jesus' united with the breathing:

> Unite the memory of Jesus with your breathing; then you will find the true value of hesychia.[5]

In fact the prayer of the heart, as it was called, goes back to the desert fathers. Gregory traces it back even further. His mystical theology was accompanied by a tender devotion so that he could write: 'Mary is the perfect hesychast, introduced at the age of three into the Holy of Holies of the Jewish temple to give herself up to ήσυχία, to silent contemplation, or better, the subject par excellence of deifying power.'[6]

So hesychasm goes back to Mary.

The main characteristics of hesychasm can be enumerated as follows:

1) Entering into a state of quiet without reading or thinking or reasoning or imagining. In this stage hesychasm resembles St Teresa's prayer of quiet and the early contemplative states described by many mystics.

2) Repeating the Jesus prayer. There are several formulas, one of the most common being, 'Lord Jesus, Son of God, have mercy on me a sinner.' What matters is the name of Jesus which, when recited with faith and love, has power to move heaven and earth.

3) Regulating the breathing so that it becomes rhythmical and at the same time fixing one's gaze on the heart, the stomach or the navel. The aim is 'to let the mind go back into the heart', a process which is called *omphaloscopia* from the Greek word *omphalos* meaning navel.

ὀμφαλοσκοπία

4) Feeling inner warmth which may become like a fire within. Or one may have a vision of divine light, sometimes called 'the light of Tabor'.

5) The aim of all is deification or *theosis*.

θέωσις

Here a key text is The Second Letter of Peter which speaks of 'participants of the divine nature' (2 Peter 1:4).

THE RUSSIAN PILGRIM

For a practical and vivid description of this prayer one can do no better than read the charming account of the anonymous pilgrim who in the nineteenth century walked through Russia and Siberia reciting the name of Jesus. His deep religious experience is preserved in the classical little book *The Way of a Pilgrim*.[7]

The pilgrim had heard the New Testament injunction to pray without ceasing, and he kept asking what it meant and how it could be put into practice. Then he met an old monk who urged him to call upon the divine name of Jesus with lips and with heart at all times and in all places, even during sleep. He was to say, 'Lord Jesus Christ, have mercy on me'; and the monk assured him that this prayer would bring deep consolation — and would eventually repeat itself without effort on his part. For practical advice he quoted St Symeon the New Theologian:

> Sit down alone and in silence. Lower your head, shut your eyes, breathe out gently and imagine yourself looking into your own heart. Carry your mind to your heart. As you breathe out say, 'Lord Jesus Christ, have mercy on me.' Say it moving your lips gently or simply say it in your mind. Try to put all other thoughts aside. Be calm, be patient and repeat the process very frequently.[8]

The old monk quickly became his *starets* or spiritual father and gave him a rosary, telling him to recite the prayer three thousand times each day, then six thousand times, then twelve thousand times — whether standing or sitting or lying down. And soon, as his *starets* had predicted, he found that the prayer was reciting itself without effort on his part. 'It was as though my lips and my tongue pronounced the words entirely of themselves without any urging from me.'⁹ Then, alas, his *starets* died. For a couple of roubles he bought an old, worn copy of the *Philokalia*, put it in his breast pocket with his Bible and went on his way, always reciting the name of Jesus.¹⁰

And then a new development took place. The prayer entered his very body. 'It seemed as though my heart . . . began to say the words of the prayer with every beat . . . I gave up saying the prayer with my lips. I simply listened carefully to what my heart was saying. It seemed as though my eyes looked right down into it.'¹¹

He felt some pain in his heart and a great love for Jesus. There further came into his heart 'a gracious warmth' which spread through his whole breast. And all the time he retained his relationship with his beloved, departed *starets* who even appeared to him in a dream, giving him light and guidance.

In this way the Jesus prayer became his whole life, giving him joy and consolation while alone and filling him with love and compassion for all whom he met on his way.

FIRE

Reading the story of the pilgrim and other Eastern mystics, one has to be impressed by their incarnational dimension. All is focused on Jesus of the Gospel who is also the Word made flesh. And as the body of Jesus is important so also is our body. Symeon, as we have seen, tells us to carry our mind and thoughts from the head to the heart. This surely strikes a chord with modern people who constantly hear from psychology that they must 'get out of the head and into the body'. Moreover, hesychasm emphasizes posture and breathing and body-awareness. Like Zen and yoga it reminds us that the abdominal area — the region of the navel — is a centre of energy. All in all this is very Christian and very Asian.

Then there is the fire in the body. Again it is Symeon who speaks most eloquently about this inner fire. Nor is his fire a mere metaphor. There is something very real in the agony and the ecstasy he describes when he writes:

Among those in whom this fire is burning the fire arises with a great flame and reaches up to heaven, not allowing the one who is embraced any pause or repose. And this is not in an unconscious manner . . . but possesses full feeling and knowledge and having in the beginning an unsupportable suffering, for the soul is endowed with feeling and reason.[12]

From this one can understand how Symeon is the implacable enemy of abstract, speculative theology that abandons feeling. The true Christian, he claims, experiences the grace of God as a mother experiences the movement of a child within her womb. Only the experience of grace is like fire, in fulfilment of the words of Jesus, 'I came to cast fire upon the earth and how I wish it were already kindled' (Luke 12:49).

What is the fire that Jesus brought? Is it not the deep mystical experience that every Christian can enjoy? Indeed, one who talks about God must have experienced God. 'They have not seen the divine light within them', he laments, 'yet they dare to discuss the intricate mysteries of the Trinity.'[13] As one reads Symeon one understands Lossky's contention that every dogmatic work has at its roots mystical experience. One also understands that the East calls Symeon the new theologian not because he read a lot of books but because he experienced God and was consumed by the fire.

And this fire fills the spiritual tradition of the East. Of special value is the writing of a great Russian mystic of the nineteenth century. Theophan the Recluse (1815–94) retired from the episcopate to live in solitude where he devoted himself to prayer and to writing letters of spiritual direction. His writings on 'the burning of the spirit' remind one of St John of the Cross. The Jesus prayer, writes Theophan, enkindles in the heart a fire of love. And just as physical fire applied to a damp log causes ugly smoke to belch forth, so the fire of the love of God at first causes suffering because of the impurity of the human person. But when the impurities are burned out, the whole person is set on fire with love. After speaking about the log, he writes:

So it happens with human beings. They receive the fire and begin to burn — and how much smoke and crackling there is only those who have experienced it can know. When the fire is properly alight the smoke and crackling cease, and within reigns only light.[14]

This is the process of purification. The ugly smoke that pours forth from the damp log causes what St John of the Cross calls the dark night.

LIGHT

Closely related to the experience of fire is that of light. Here again the witness of Symeon the New Theologian is very important. As a young man he had an extraordinary experience of light:

> One evening, when he was praying and saying in spirit, 'God have mercy on me a sinner,' a divine light suddenly shone on him from above and filled the room. The young man no longer knew whether he was in the house or under a roof, for on all sides he saw nothing but light: he was not even aware of being on earth . . . He was one with this divine light and it seemed to him that he himself had become light and left the world altogether. He was filled with tears and unspeakable joy.[15]

This experience was to transform the life of the young Symeon. Later he is to say that the light never leaves him day or night, whether he eats or drinks, not even in his sleep or moving from place to place. Always he is united with the light.

Gregory Palamas was in the same tradition. More must be said about him now.

CONTROVERSY

The practice of the hesychasts on Mount Athos led to bitter controversy when Barlaam of Calabria (1290–1350), a learned Greek from Southern Italy, raised his voice in protest. Barlaam ridiculed the bodily techniques of the hesychasts. The monks were navel-gazers, men who thought their souls were in their navel. As for the light, this was a purely natural phenomenon. More than that, he accused the hesychasts of being trapped in Messalianism, the heresy which said that one can have a material vision of God and was roundly condemned by the Byzantine Church in the fourth and fifth centuries.

It was the iconoclastic attacks of Barlaam that occasioned the rise of the mystical theologian of towering stature that we have already spoken of. Gregory Palamas stands to Orthodoxy as Thomas Aquinas stands to Catholicism. Now he emerged from Mount Athos to defend his fellow monks and the Eastern mystical tradition which he loved. Gregory made no claims to profound scholarship of the modern kind. 'When, after two decades of ascetic seclusion,' writes Kallistos Ware, 'he (Gregory) became drawn into controversy with Barlaam, it was as a spokesman for his fellow-monks. He did not claim to be in any way an expert in the philosophy of Plato, Aristotle or Proclus, but sought to defend the *living experience* of the holy hesychasts of the past and of his own day.'[16] Kallistos Ware then goes on to make a statement which is of the utmost importance for mystical theology:

> This emphasis on living experience is the key to any just assessment of Palamism . . . Those who approach Palamism from an exclusively philosophical viewpoint, treating it as a metaphysical theory . . . will inevitably miss the true meaning of what Palamas is trying to say.[17]

In other words, one must understand the literary genre of the writings of Palamas.

In answer to Barlaam's ridicule of the bodily dimension of hesychasm, Gregory replied that the physical techniques were not essential to the practice and then went on to stress the surpassing dignity of the human body. Not only the soul but also the body is made in the image of God and shows forth the glory and beauty of God. Furthermore, divinization or *theosis*, the climax of the hesychast practice, transforms both soul and body. For one whose background was deeply influenced by Neo-Platonism this was a great breakthrough.[18]

Yet Gregory's great achievement was to elaborate a theology of light which is still central to all Orthodox thinking.

THEOLOGY OF LIGHT

Innumerable texts of sacred Scripture speak of the light. There are the Johannine writings which tell us that the true light that enlightens everyone was coming into the world. Then there is the blinding light, brighter than the noonday sun, that shattered Paul on the road to Damascus. Again there is the light on the face of Moses, so dazzling that he covered his face with a veil. But most important for Gregory Palamas and the theology that stems from him is the great event called the Transfiguration.

With Peter, James and John, Jesus ascends the mountain and is transfigured before them. Intense light shines from his body and through his clothing, enveloping the disciples so that they share in the light and see his glory. 'Lord, it is good for us to be here!' (Luke 9:33). This is divine light. Ordinarily the divinity hides itself but now in a wonderful way it shines forth; and the disciples share in the mystical experience of Jesus.

Now the Orthodox tradition that stems from Palamas claims that many of the saints also share this mystical experience. Like Jesus they are filled with a light that shines forth from their whole person; or like the apostles they see the light of Jesus within or around. There was no change in Jesus, this tradition says. Jesus was always filled with light and was always radiating light to the world. The change took place in the apostles who were now able to see something to which they were previously blind. And similarly we Christians may at times find that we are awakened, that our eyes are opened to see Jesus as the light of the world. Then we see light of another order, brighter than anything we could imagine.

Yet the question of the nature of this light was, and still remains, a thorny issue. Hesychast texts indicate that the saints see the light with their bodily eyes, just as the disciples saw the light of the transfigured Jesus with their bodily eyes, and it was this that prompted Barlaam to liken the hesychasts to Messalians. How can we explain the role of the body in this vision of light?

The *Tomus Hagioriticus*, a Palamite profession of faith dating from about 1340 and signed by all the *hegumenoi* of the Holy Mountain faces this problem. It distinguishes three kinds of light:

sensible light
intellectual light
uncreated light

The *Tomus Hagioriticus* then makes an important comment: 'Nevertheless when those who are worthy receive this grace and this spiritual and supernatural power, they perceive both with the senses and the intellect what is above all sense and all intellect . . . in a way that is known only to God and to those who have experienced this grace.'[19] Here the senses and the intellect share in something that transcends both sense and intellect. Yet all is a mystery, known only to God.

And later, in sixteenth-century Spain, St John of the Cross comes up with a somewhat similar explanation. He speaks constantly of light — of a spiritual light which *overflows* on the senses causing sometimes great joy and sometimes great pain. Such is the unity of the human person that spiritual experiences must inevitably influence the body. Indeed, it is in this way that St John of the Cross explains the stigmata. A deep spiritual wound overflows on the body and causes physical wounds.

Yet another doctrine of Gregory that was to disturb the scholastics and cause endless controversy was his distinction between the divine essence and the divine energies. This is closely related to his theology of light; for the uncreated energies are energies of light and of love.

UNCREATED ENERGIES

The problem facing Gregory is central to all mystical theology. We know God; and we do not know God. God is the mystery of mysteries; we know *that* he is, but we do not know *what* he is. No one has seen God who dwells in inaccessible light which is impenetrable darkness. And yet we *do* know God. We can be very intimate with God who spoke to Moses as one might speak to a friend. Friendship with God is the great privilege and joy of the one who believes; it is the consolation of the mystic. Is there any solution to the paradox?

Gregory asserts that we cannot know the essence of God but we can know the divine energies.

Now this distinction fits the experience of many mystics who tell us that while God is like night to the soul they experience him as fire, as light, as overwhelming energy. Mystics East and West speak of a flood of energy that sweeps through their whole being causing rapturous ecstasy or agonizing depression. There can be no doubt that the energy unleashed in mystical experience can be very terrible and can shake the human person to the depths. St John of the Cross maintains that this energy would kill us if God did not intervene in his loving mercy.

And so Palamas speaks of the divine energy, of the uncreated energy, and all the time he is thinking of mystical experience. His is a magnificent insight, of great value today when Christianity faces the surge of mystical energy that flows through the mystics of Asia. Not that Gregory is an innovator or an original thinker in this area. Orthodox theologians insist that his doctrine of uncreated energies goes back to the Greek Fathers, and that Gregory simply developed and made precise something which was already in the Christian mystical tradition.

Yet from the metaphysical viewpoint it remains controversial. In answer to scholastic objections that this distinction argued against the divine simplicity, Palamite theologians said that the uncreated energies are God just as the divine essence is God. There is no question of dividing God or denying his simplicity. Again, the divine energies are not attributed to one person; they are the energies of the Blessed Trinity — Father, Son and Holy Spirit. Furthermore, they maintained that this distinction helps us to explain *theosis* or deification without falling into pantheism.[20]

Before the Second Vatican Council, scholastics who studied Orthodoxy were baffled and dismayed by this distinction. It just did not fit into the scholastic framework. Yet some Benedictine scholars were quietly sympathetic. Dom Clement Lialine quotes Lossky to the effect that every dogmatic work has at its root a mystical experience; and he continues, 'This is especially true in the case of Gregory Palamas, for all who know him be they Catholic or Orthodox, are once more in agreement in their opinion that all his theology tends towards one end, the explanation and justification of a mystical experience.'[21]

At the Council of Constantinople in 1353 the Orthodox Church accepted the Palamite teaching while anathematizing all who would deny it. Gregory died in 1359 and was canonized in 1368. His doctrine is so central to Orthodox theology that Kallistos Ware, reacting to the criticisms of some Catholic theologians, can write that 'the Palamite distinction between essence and energies in God is not simply a private and personal speculation of some fourteenth-century Byzantine thinkers, but it possesses conciliar authority for the Orthodox Church, since it has been confirmed by councils which Orthodoxy accepts as ecumenical in their significance. For us Orthodox, the Palamite teaching has become part of Holy Tradition.'[22]

MYSTICAL LIGHT IN THE WEST

Many Western mystics, like their Eastern counterparts, have had experience of intense light. Here it will be sufficient to speak of three outstanding mystics of light.

The first is the great Bishop of Hippo.

In the *Confessions* Augustine relates, how, entering into the very depths of his being under the guidance of God, he came to see the immutable light that is above all lights, a light that cannot be grasped by the eyes of the senses nor by the eye of the spirit:

On entering into myself I saw, as it were with the eye of the soul, what was beyond the eye of the soul, beyond my spirit: your immutable light. It was not the ordinary light perceptible to all flesh, nor was it merely something of greater magnitude but still essentially akin, shining more clearly and diffusing itself everywhere by its intensity. No, it was something entirely distinct, something altogether different from all these things; and it did not rest above my mind as oil on the surface of water, nor was it above me as heaven is above the earth.[23]

Such was the light in the depths of Augustine's being and in the depths of all creation. He goes on to speak of this as uncreated light:

> The light was above me because it had made me; it was below
> because I was created by it.[24]

And Augustine makes a statement that would have delighted the heart of Symeon the New Theologian: 'One who has come to know the truth knows the light.'

So much for Augustine.

A second mystic of light was an eminent theologian, artist and poetess, besides being the abbess of a large and flourishing Benedictine abbey. Hildegaard of Bingen (1098–1179), in the foreword to her *Scivias*, writes about the great light that poured into the very depths of her being:

> In the year 1141 of the incarnation of Jesus Christ, the Word of
> God, when I was forty-two years and seven months old, a
> burning light of extraordinary brightness coming from heaven
> poured into my entire mind. Like a flame that does not burn but
> fires, it inflamed my entire heart and entire breast, just like the
> sun that warms an object with its rays.[25]

Hildegaard goes on to say that this light enabled her to understand clearly the whole Bible without scholarly knowledge of grammar and texts.

The third mystic of light is Teresa of Avila (1515–82) who speaks eloquently of a light that is totally different from the light we ordinarily see. Modern people might say that it is totally different from the light that travels from outer space to our planet through millions of light years. She writes of 'another region from this in which we live, where there is shown another light so different from earth's light that if one were to spend one's whole life trying to imagine that, one would be unable to do so'.[26]

What is this light? Is it the light seen by the hesychasts?

Teresa associates this light with the glorified body of Jesus and the bodies of the saints in glory. She does not, it is true, speak explicitly of the Transfiguration but from the context she seems to have in mind a light similar to that which shone from the transfigured body of Jesus. And she writes:

> It is a light so different from earthly light that the sun's brightness that we see appears very tarnished in comparison with that brightness and light represented to the sight, and so different that afterwards you would not want to open your eyes.[27]

> This light seems like natural light while the light of the sun seems artificial, for it is a light that never ends and has no night.[28]

And this light is operative not only in her relationship with Jesus but also in her relationship with other humans. Here again she is at one with the hesychasts.

One night she was very distressed because Father Gratian was ill; and then suddenly he appeared to her:

> A light appeared in the interior of my soul, and I beheld him coming along the road with a white countenance. Although by reason of the light by which I saw, he had to have a white countenance, it seems to me that so do all those who are in heaven. And I wondered if the light and brilliance of our Lord makes them white.[29]

Here the key to understanding the vision is the glorified body of Jesus which lends a whiteness to all others who are in glory. And Father Gratian seemed to share in this glory.

Now the light experience of these mystics may resemble those of the hesychasts; but the reaction of Western theologians was quite different from that of Palamas. The scholastics felt no obligation to defend the mystics against their critics. They did not attempt to build a theology on their experiences. For them mystical experience had little theological significance. And this was true of the mystical theologians of this century like Joseph de Guibert, Garrigou-Lagrange, Alphonse Tanqueray and the rest. They revered mystics but they drew no theological conclusions from what they wrote and said.

The East, as has been said, was quite different. Living experience was of the greatest theological value. Let us listen again to Kallistos Ware: 'But there is one thing, so Gregory believed, that is always decisive: the experience of the saints. The true aim of theology is not rational certainty through abstract argument, but personal communion with God through prayer.'[30] In other words, the contention of Evagrius that the theologian is one who prays and the one who prays is a theologian never died in Eastern theology.

TWO THEOLOGIES

In the middle of the twentieth century, when Orthodoxy and Catholicism began to dialogue, the problem of two opposing theologies arose; and sincere efforts at reconciliation were made. There is, however, more than a hint of condescension in the words with which the French theologian, Martin Jugie, sums up the Palamite controversy:

> Two methods or two ways for arriving at knowledge of God met and faced one another; one, a scientific method drawing its principles both from a sound philosophy and from the sources of revelation interpreted by the ancient doctors, and clinging to these principles; the other a mystical method directed towards the experience of contemplatives devoted to the hesychastic life.[31]

Jugie had no doubt that his scientific method was superior to the mystical method of the East.

Then came the Second Vatican Council. Pope Paul VI in Rome and Patriarch Athenagoras in Constantinople made profoundly Christian gestures of reconciliation. On 7 December 1965, in solemn ceremonies at St Peter's and at the Patriarch's cathedral in Istanbul the excommunications and anathemas that had lasted for nine centuries were withdrawn. Meanwhile, the Council Fathers with characteristic wisdom had faced the theological problem:

> In the investigation of revealed truth, East and West have used

different methods and approaches in understanding and proclaiming divine things. It is hardly surprising, then, if sometimes one tradition has come nearer than the other to an apt appreciation of certain aspects of a revealed mystery, or has expressed them in a clearer manner. As a result, these various theological formulations are often to be considered as complementary rather than conflicting.[32]

The Council goes on to pay tribute to the authentic theological traditions of the Orientals which are directed towards a full contemplation of Christian truth.

After the Second Vatican Council, scholasticism collapsed. New theological methods arose. No one can question the value of the historical critical approach to Scripture and patristics that is now in vogue; no one can deny the immense value of modern, scientific scholarship and research. Yet the West has to learn an important lesson from the Orthodox tradition: the value of prayer and mystical experience for theology. Profound wisdom comes not only from scientific research but also from contemplation. This is the doctrine of Thomas Aquinas who speaks of connaturality and knowledge that comes from love. Such wisdom will be all the more necessary as Christianity enters into dialogue with the mystical religions of Asia. Symeon the New Theologian and Gregory Palamas have a message for today.

NOTES

1. *The Mystical Theology of the Eastern Church*, Vladimir Lossky, St Vladimir's Seminary Press, New York (Reprint) 1976, p. 12.
2. There were, of course, heresies in the universal Church. Nestorians after the Council of Ephesus (431), and Monophysites after the Council of Chalcedon (451), broke away. But there was no major break between East and West.
3. Op. supra cit., p. 9.
4. See *A Study of Gregory Palamas*, John Meyendorff, London 1964.
5. Quoted by Louis Bouyer in *A History of Christian Spirituality*, Vol II, London 1968, p. 557.
6. Quoted by Dom Bede Winslow in *The Eastern Churches Quarterly*, Nov. 1954, Preface.
7. *The Way of a Pilgrim*, translated from the Russian by R. M. French, The Seabury Press, New York 1965.

8. Ibid., p. 10.
9. Ibid., p. 14.
10. *The Philokalia* meaning 'the love of beauty' is a collection of ascetical and mystical writings of the Fathers of the Eastern Church over a period of eleven centuries. It was translated into Russian by Bishop Theophan the Recluse.
11. Op. supra cit., p. 19, 20.
12. *The Mystic of Fire and Light: St Symeon the New Theologian*, George Maloney, Dimension books, New Jersey 1975, p. 80.
13. Ibid., p. 33.
14. *The Art of Prayer: an Orthodox Anthology*, Compiled by Igumen Chariton, trans. E. Kadloubovsky and E. M. Palmer, Faber and Faber, London 1966, p. 156.
15. Louis Bouyer, Op supra cit., p. 562.
16. 'The Debate about Palamism', Archimandrite Kallistos Ware in *The Eastern Churches Review*, Oxford, Vol. IX no. 1–2, 1977, p. 58.
17. Ibid.
18. See 'The Hesychast method of prayer and the transformation of the body' in *Gregory Palamas: The Triads*, ed. John Meyendorff, Paulist Press, New York 1983.
19. Quoted by Vladimir Lossky in *In The Image in Likeness of God*, St Vladimir's Seminary Press, 1974, p. 58.
20. 'The idea of deification must always be understood in the light of the distinction between God's essence and his energies . . . The Orthodox Church, while speaking of deification and union, rejects all forms of pantheism.' Kallistos Ware, *The Orthodox Church*, Penguin Books, Middlesex, 1983, p. 237.
21. 'The Theological Teaching of Gregory Palamas, Dom Clement Lialine in *The Eastern Churches Quarterly*, Jan. 1946.
22. 'The Debate about Palamism' p. 54.
23. *Confessions*, 7.10.16.
24. Ibid.
25. *Scivias*, 1.
26. *The Interior Castle*, VI.5.7.
27. *Life*, 28.5.
28. Ibid.
29. *Spiritual Testimonies*, 54.
30. 'The Debate about Palamism', p. 63.
31. *Theologia Dogmatica Christianorum Orientalium*, II, p. 57.
32. *Unitatis Redintegratio*, III.17.

SIX

Wisdom Through Love

TOWARDS THE SPANISH CARMELITES

We have seen that Thomas Aquinas speaks of two kinds of knowledge: one that comes through scientific inquiry and the other that comes through love. He himself developed at great length the knowledge of scientific inquiry in the *Summa Theologica* and his other writings; and the scholastics who came after him carried on this study with rigorous devotion. But it was left to the mystical theologians to probe deeply into the knowledge that comes through love. And particularly in the fourteenth century there arose theologians — many of them Dominicans and disciples of Thomas — who reflected on this loving knowledge or wisdom and created a separate branch of theology that we now call mystical theology.

The wisdom that comes through love, Thomas had said, is a gift of the Holy Spirit. It is the response to the call of one who first loved us. 'We love because he first loved us' (1 John 4:19). It is infused wisdom and love; for the love of God is poured into our hearts by the Holy Spirit who is given to us. Since it is infused it does not come through the senses; it does not bring clear-cut, conceptual knowledge nor is it linked to images and pictures. It is obscure knowledge in a cloud of unknowing.

Ordinarily this love and the accompanying wisdom arise in the context of prayer. One may begin to pray using the faculties as one uses them in the process of scientific inquiry (this came to be called discursive prayer) or one may begin by reflecting on a scene from the Gospel. But, if one is drawn to contemplation, the time comes when the infused gift of the Spirit is so powerful that it impedes thinking. One is unable to think or, at any rate, one has considerable difficulty in doing so. Now is the time to abandon discursive prayer for quiet contemplation in a cloud of unknowing. This is the first stage of a mystical ascent that goes on and on and on. The tiny spark of love becomes a raging fire that envelops the whole personality giving great joy and great suffering.

Now the mystical theology that came to birth as a separate discipline in the fourteenth century was carried forward with extraordinary mystical insight and vigour by the Spanish Carmelites in sixteenth-century Spain. St Teresa of Avila (1515-82), more correctly known as Teresa of Jesus, and her collaborator and friend, St John of the Cross (1542-91), both mystics and doctors of the church, left a rich mystical heritage that has nourished the spiritual life of Christians everywhere from the sixteenth century to this very day.

First let us consider Teresa.

TERESA AS MYSTICAL THEOLOGIAN

That Teresa was a consummate mystic no one doubts. But was she also a mystical theologian?

Assuredly she was not a scholastic theologian, though she did learn some scholastic theology from her directors. But if by mystical theologian we mean one who reflects theologically on mystical experience, then we cannot easily refuse the title of mystical theologian to Teresa. For she was constantly reflecting on mystical experience, both her own and that of others; and she wrote prolifically about it. She herself says that it is one thing to have a mystical experience; it is another thing to understand it; and it is yet another thing to explain it. Here are her words:

> For it is one grace to receive the Lord's favour; another to understand it; it is yet another thing to express this understanding in words.[1]

And then she goes on to say that the grace of understanding is of immense value:

> And although no more than the first grace seems necessary, it is

a great advantage and a gift for the soul that it also understand the favour so as not to go about confused and afraid, and so that it may be courageous in following the path of the Lord.[2]

Teresa, then, can be called a mystical theologian because she had great insight into the mystical process and was able to articulate it in writings of extraordinary power. She always had great esteem for learned theologians who knew about the ways of prayer, partly because she herself had suffered greviously from pious men who knew nothing about mysticism. Not that she belittled experience. For her the ideal was the combination of mystical experience and mystical theology. This she found in Peter of Alcantara, John of the Cross and Balthasar Alvarez.

Her mystical theology is a theology of love, love of God and love of neighbour. In prayer, she said, it is necessary to love much, not to think much. Her classical work *The Interior Castle* describes the stages of love, culminating in the spiritual marriage between the bride and bridegroom. Here she described with literary power and theological accuracy Christian non-dualism as a unitive love in total self-forgetfulness.

Yet without any doubt her great and unique contribution to mystical theology is found in her teaching on the Incarnation.

TERESA AND INCARNATION

Teresa's mystical teaching focuses on Jesus, the Word made flesh. She is famous for her insistence that one must remain with the human Jesus. This is all the more remarkable when one reflects on her raptures and ecstasies and flights of the spirit which seemed to bring her into a different world. Moreover she was familiar with the *nada, nada, nada*, of her saintly collaborator, St John of the Cross. Like him she experienced the void and the emptiness and the dark nights. But Jesus was always there and she insisted that it must be that way. But where, we may bluntly ask, was Jesus in the void? How does she fit Jesus into the imageless darkness?

Certainly she is not thinking of an image or picture of Jesus; she does not mean that one should always contemplate visually a scene from the Gospel. It was rather that she had a strong sense of the presence of Jesus through interior senses or through some deeper layer of consciousness. She had, moreover, a sense of the glorified body, particularly of the glorified body of Jesus which is outside space and time. In other words she had a sense of what Teilhard de Chardin later called the Christ of the universe or the cosmic Christ. Of this Jesus we can have no adequate image. But whatever way one explains it, the Word Incarnate was always present to Teresa; her spiritual marriage is not a union with the imageless Godhead but with the Word made flesh.

And together with this stress on love for the Word Incarnate was a very practical down-to-earth stress on love for one's neighbour. Like most mystical theologians, she was a spiritual guide; and the burden of her teaching, following The First Epistle of St John, was that we cannot be sure that we love God but we can be sure that we love, or do not love, our neighbour. This is the test of progress in prayer; this is the supreme norm of discernment.

How interesting is Teresa! At one moment she is rapt to the third heaven and hears voices that no human ears can hear, and the next moment with both feet firmly on the ground she is laughing at the foibles of her beloved sisters.

SANJUANIST MYSTICAL THEOLOGY

St John of the Cross was primarily a poet; and his theme is love. He has been called the doctor of nothing — *doctor de la nada* — and his dark night has become proverbial; but those who know him call him doctor and poet of divine love. He is the bride of The Canticle, wounded and passionate, abandoning all things in search of the one she loves. 'Where have you hidden, beloved . . .?"

> *¿Adonde te escondiste,*
> *Amado, y me dejaste con gemido?*

The bride abandons all for love. If one offered for love all the wealth of his house it would be utterly scorned.

Besides being a poet John of the Cross was a theologian of considerable stature, steeped in Aquinas and familiar with the fourteenth-century mystical tradition.[4] His mystical theology is a theology of love. Indeed he defined mystical theology as *the secret wisdom that comes from love*. Let us consider one passage from *The Spiritual Canticle*.

In the great poem which he began to write in the Toledo prison, the saint takes on himself the role of the bride and sings ecstatically of the immense love of the bridegroom, son of God. 'There he gave me his breast; there he taught me a delicious knowledge.'[5]

> *Allí me dió su pecho*
> *Allí me enseño ciencia muy sabrosa*

And in his prose commentary he gives a somewhat sober explanation of these enigmatic words, saying:

> The secret and delicious knowledge he taught her is mystical theology which spiritual persons call contemplation. This knowledge is very delightful because it is knowledge through love.[6]

Here the poet identifies mystical theology with mystical experience whereas today we would speak of mystical theology as *reflection on* mystical experience. But that is not important. What matters is that this knowledge is very delicious (*muy sabrosa*) and delightful. It is not the abstract or speculative knowledge of the bespectacled academic but the experimental, passionate, holistic knowledge that pervades every fibre of the mystic's being. It is the vibrating wisdom of one who is filled with sacred energy and all-consuming love. It is a wisdom that transforms mind and body, giving ecstatic joy and intense suffering. Possessed by this love, men and women will dance with joy and weep with pain; they will write lyrical poetry or paint great works of art. Possessed by this love and wisdom, people may act like fools. For finally mystics are foolish lovers. Is there not some similarity between the mystic and the lover and the madman?

In another passage St John of the Cross identifies mystical theology with contemplation and the dark night. He writes:

This dark night is an inflow of God into the soul, which purges it of its habitual ignorances and imperfections, natural and spiritual, which the contemplatives call contemplation or mystical theology.[7]

Here the saint describes the dark night as an inflow of God into the soul; but one who reads his work carefully sees that not only the dark night but the whole mystical process is an inflow of God into the soul. Mystical theology is an inflow of God into the soul. Sometimes this inflow causes the agony of the dark night: at other times it brings the overwhelming joy of enlightenment. In either case he writes that through it 'God teaches the soul secretly and instructs it in the perfection of love without its doing anything or understanding how this happens.'[8]

Mystical theology, then, is an inflow of God, teaching the soul the perfection of love.

But more must be said about the sanjuanist mystical love.

THE LIVING FLAME OF LOVE

In his exquisite little poem that describes the summit of the mystical life, St John of the Cross sings: 'O Living Flame of Love. . .'

¡oh llama de amor viva. . !

The living flame of love, he tells us, is the Holy Spirit who dwells within like an immense fire, shooting out flames of love. 'This flame of love is the Spirit of its bridegroom, which is the Holy Spirit. The soul feels the Spirit within itself not only as a fire which has consumed and transformed it, but as a fire that burns and flares within it . . .'[9] Small wonder if this flame wounds and finally kills.

When he writes this poem, he experiences God vividly and tastes God with a sweetness and an agony which is the delightful wound of the lover. But this flame was not always delightful. At the beginning it was a tiny spark, a loving movement in the depths of his being. Then it developed into a cruel fire that attacked and assailed him, causing intolerable grief and suffering and bringing on the oppressive, dark night. But now while the suffering remains, the oppressive darkness has gone. 'O sweet cautery, O delightful wound!'

¡Oh cauterio suave!
¡Oh regalada llaga!

Can we say anything about this love?

At the beginning it was love for the crucified Jesus; for John of the Cross was *of the cross*. And then love for Jesus crucified leads to *identification* with Jesus in accordance with the Pauline words, 'I live, now not I, but Christ lives in me'. Commenting on these words John of the Cross writes: 'In saying, I live, now not I he meant that, even though he had life it was not his, because he was transformed in Christ, and it was divine more than human. . . we can say that his life and Christ's were one life through union of love.'[10] Like Paul, John of the Cross is now so united with Christ that the love that burns within is both human and divine. It is the love of Jesus and his own love. Now it is non-objective love, radiating towards everyone and everything. Such is the living flame of love.

And this love leads to wisdom — to a supreme enlightenment or awakening which will reach its climax when, through death, he enters eternal life to enjoy the vision of God. 'How gently and lovingly you wake in my heart!'[10]

¡Cuán manso y amoroso
recuerdas en mi seno!

The knowledge obtained through love, the real mystical theology, is so wonderful 'that it seems to her that her previous knowledge, and even all the knowledge of the world, in comparison with this knowledge is pure ignorance'.[11]

He tries to describe this awakening but it cannot be put into words 'for this awakening . . . is a movement of the Word in the substance of the soul, containing such grandeur, dominion and glory, and intimate sweetness that it seems to the soul that all the balsams and fragrant spices and flowers of the world are commingled, stirred and shaken so as to yield their sweet odour, and that all the kingdoms and dominions of the world and all the powers and virtues of heaven are moved; and . . . all the virtues and substances and perfections and graces of every created thing glow and make the same movement all at once'.[12]

Such is the soul-stirring enlightenment to which love leads. It is an earth-shaking experience; but it is no more than a tiny foretaste of what is to come when through death we pass into eternity and see God face to face.

Yet St John of the Cross insists that in this life the greatest wisdom is *secret*. What does he mean by this word *secret*?

SECRET WISDOM

The word 'secret' is very important in mystical theology. To understand it we must first go back to Dionysius whose mystical is translated as secret or hidden. Secret or mystical knowledge, then, is knowledge that goes beyond reasoning and thinking, beyond clear and distinct ideas. Such knowledge is formless knowledge in a cloud of unknowing. It is to this knowledge that Dionysuis leads his disciple Timothy. It is to this knowledge that the author of *The Cloud* leads his disciple, telling him to keep his knowledge secret — another way of telling him to eschew thoughts and concepts and images and clear-cut ideas.

Again, mystical knowledge is secret because one does not understand it. 'Contemplation', writes St John of the Cross, 'by which intellect has a higher knowledge of God is called mystical theology, meaning secret wisdom of God. For this wisdom is secret to the very intellect that receives it.'[13] Here, then, we have yet another definition of mystical theology: secret wisdom of God. And the intellect which receives it does not understand. Indeed, the inability to understand is one of the greatest sufferings of the mystical life. 'What is happening to me?' is the anguished cry of the mystic in the dark night. 'I do not understand!' And John of the Cross replies that the dark night is secret: it is mystery. Do not try to understand! Wait upon God! Surrender! Trust in his mercy and love!

Again, God is secret. He is a hidden God: *Deus Absconditus*. He is the mystery of mysteries. He is like night to the soul. Only at the summit does God awaken in those hidden depths where he dwells secretly and alone:

Donde secretámente solo moras

And so St John of the Cross goes out in secret when no one sees him:

En secreto, que nadie me veía

He climbs the secret ladder — *la secreta escala* — that leads to 'where he waited for me, him I know so well, in a place where no one else appeared'.[14]

In all this, John of the Cross follows Aquinas. He finds two kinds of knowledge: the knowledge of scientific inquiry and the formless, secret knowledge that comes from love. It is the latter that guides him more surely than the light of noon.

MYSTICAL KNOWLEDGE AND THE BIBLE

It is clear, then, that in the medieval tradition that culminates in the writings of the Spanish Carmelites, mystical theology is the secret wisdom that comes from love. But one may legitimately ask if such wisdom can be found in sacred Scripture, and if so, where.

And to this St John of the Cross would answer that this sublime wisdom is in every line of the Bible. He finds it in The Song of Songs, in the psalms, in the writings of the prophets, in the gospels, in St Paul — everywhere in sacred Scripture. Perhaps, then, it would be of value to select one passage where Paul speaks powerfully of the secret wisdom that comes from love. It is a passage to which John of the Cross turns several times.

In The First Epistle to the Corinthians Paul has been speaking about the folly of the cross and the folly of his teaching. And then he pauses, as though with second thoughts, and says:

Yet among the mature we do speak wisdom though it is not a wisdom of this age . . . (1 Corinthians 2:6)

And he goes on to speak about God's secret and hidden wisdom:

$$\sigma o \Phi ί α ν \ \grave{ε} ν \ μ υ σ τ η ρ ί \dot{ω}$$

This is mystical wisdom — secret, formless, obscure, in a cloud of unknowing. Paul states clearly that he is talking about a knowledge that goes beyond images and concepts: 'What no eye has seen, nor ear heard, nor the human heart conceived, what God has prepared for those who love him' (1 Corinthians 2:9).

And this wisdom, the only wisdom that Paul claims to have, comes from the love of Jesus crucified — both his love for Paul and Paul's love for him. 'He loved me and gave himself for me' (Galatians 2:20), Paul had cried; and now he writes to the Corinthians that he decided to know nothing among them except Jesus Christ and him crucified. Paul's wisdom, his secret and foolish wisdom, came from love. It is a stumbling block to Jews and folly to Gentiles but to those who are called, both Jew and Gentile, it is Christ the power of God and the wisdom of God.

How full of paradox is the wisdom that comes from love! If you want to be wise, Paul says, you had better become a fool — a foolish lover. 'For God's foolishness is wiser than human wisdom, and God's weakness is stronger than human strength' (1 Corinthians 1:25).

Such is the wisdom of Teresa and John. It comes from a deep realization of the love of the crucified and a response of foolish love that finds expression in the passionate lines of The Song of Songs. And compared with this wisdom 'the knowledge of human beings and of the whole world is pure ignorance and unworthy of being known'.[15] Where can we find greater paradox?

MYSTICAL THEOLOGY TODAY

Before the Second Vatican Council mystical theology was taught in Catholic seminaries throughout the world. It was not an important subject (the centre of the stage was occupied by dogmatic and moral theology) but it had some distinguished theologians who spoke wisely to the people of that time. The French Dominican Réginald Garrigou-Lagrange wrote extensively about Aquinas and St John of the Cross. The Jesuits Joseph de Guibert and Auguste Poulain were practical directors of considerable stature. The textbooks of Adolphe Tanquerey were read and re-read by seminarians everywhere. All in all, mystical theology had its place in the curriculum of studies.

This mystical theology, however, was much broader in scope than the traditional version that spoke of 'the secret wisdom that comes from love'. De Guibert tells us that 'the term *mystical theology* came to indicate broadly the whole theological study of the spiritual life considered as a preparation for union with God in contemplation'.[16] Such mystical theology was also called ascetical and mystical theology or spiritual theology. While it did treat of infused contemplation following the great Spaniards, its principal aim was to teach the future priests how to pray and how to guide others in the way of prayer.

With the Second Vatican Council and the ensuing theological revolution it became clear that the mystical theology taught in the seminaries could no longer speak to the new people and the new world. The Council had opened the way to dialogue with the modern world and with the mystical religions of Asia. We were faced — and are still faced — with a world that is greatly interested in mystical experience and even looks to mystical wisdom for an answer to its many agonizing dilemmas and problems.

This means that mystical theology has to be re-written; and this book is a modest attempt to re-write mystical theology for the new era. Following the Christian tradition it understands mystical theology as *theological reflection on the secret wisdom that comes from love*, and it attempts to develop this tradition in dialogue with the modern world. The next part of the book, then, will reflect on the dialogue and its consequences for a new mystical theology.

NOTES

1. *Life*, 17.5.
2. Ibid.
3. *The Spiritual Canticle*, 1.
4. Apart from extensive references to Scripture, St John of the Cross refers explicitly to Augustine, Dionysius, Boetius, Gregory the Great, Aquinas, Aristotle and Ovid. He certainly was familiar with Bernard of Clairvaux, Hugh

of St Victor and *The Imitation of Christ*. His Spanish biographer, Crysogono, claims that apart from the Bible the greatest influence came from the medieval mystics, particularly from Ruysbroeck, Tauler and Suso. Did he know *The Cloud of Unknowing*? The similarity between the two is remarkable. We know that a Latin translation of *The Cloud* was circulating on the European continent. John of the Cross could have read it.

5. *The Spiritual Canticle*, 18.
6. *The Spiritual Canticle*, 27.5.
7. *The Dark Night*, 2.5.1.
8. Ibid.
9. *The Living Flame of Love*, 1.3.
10. *The Spiritual Canticle*, 12.8.
11. *The Living Flame*, 4.
12. *The Living Flame*, 4. 4.
13. *The Ascent*, 2.8.6.
14. *The Dark Night*, 4.
15. *The Spiritual Canticle*, 26.13. It should be noted, however, that St John of the Cross was a poet and often uses the language of hyperbole. Here he seems to despise the knowledge of scientific inquiry; but elsewhere he shows esteem for it. 'It should not be thought that because she remains in this unknowing that she loses there her acquired knowledge of the sciences; rather these habits are perfected by the more perfect habit of supernatural wisdom infused into her' (*The Spiritual Canticle*, 26.16).
16. *Theologia spiritualis ascetica et mystica*, I.II.3.

PART II

Dialogue

———— ✳ ————

SEVEN

Science and Mystical Theology

PHYSICS AND MYSTICISM

In an interesting book entitled *The Tao of Physics* and published in the 1970s, the American physicist Fritjof Capra declared that a number of modern scientists have become interested in mysticism.[1] Their research, he claimed, has led them to conclusions that are remarkably similar to the teachings of Hinduism, Buddhism and Taoism. Capra maintained that a great revolution had taken place in physics thanks to the two great discoveries of relativity and quantum mechanics. Physicists could no longer accept the mechanistic tenets of Newtonian physics according to which the universe is composed of dead matter and isolated particles; nor could they accept the dualistic and alienating Cartesian distinction between *res extensa* and *res cogitans*. Instead, they saw a world in which everything was interconnected, in which there were no separate existences or isolated entities. They were coming to a vision of unity like that of the mystics.

Capra's book, then, is a dialogue in which scientists and oriental mystics talk about the unity of all things, space-time, the reconciliation of opposites, complementarity, the yin and yang, the zen koan, the Kegon Sutra and the cosmic dance. Notions of the void, the nothingness, the emptiness — *mu* and *ku* in Japanese — are no longer foreign to the physicist. Capra quotes eminent scientists like Werner Heisenberg and Niels Bohr who felt that their study of physics was leading them into a new world or a new state of consciousness where the ordinary laws of logic no longer applied. 'Can nature possibly be so absurd as it seemed to us in these atomic experiments?' asked Heisenberg.[2] The seeming absurdity was leading them to the mystics. No longer could they talk glibly about the incompatibility of science and religion.

Capra begins with a description of his own quasi-mystical experience. While sitting beside the ocean watching the waves and breathing rhythmically, he suddenly became aware that the surrounding world was engaged in an immense cosmic dance of energy and that cascades of particles were coming down from outer space. He promptly told himself that this was the dance of Shiva. The Hindu vision and the scientific vision fitted together.

Needless to say, such a book engendered criticism, opposition and even ridicule. Nevertheless it gave incentive to a much needed dialogue between science and religion and inspired considerable debate throughout the world. It has been particularly influential in the New Age Movement and continues to make its impact everywhere.

While Capra writes extensively about Hinduism, Buddhism and Taoism, he says almost nothing about the mysticism of Judaism, Islam and Christianity. His alleged reason is that whereas mystical schools constitute the mainstream of Eastern religion and philosophy, they play only a marginal role in the West. This is a valid reason. Nevertheless there may be another unexpressed, yet more formidable, reason. The mystics of the monotheistic religions, while they believe in an immanent God present in the world and giving existence and unity to all things, believe also in a transcendent God, Creator of heaven and earth, to whom they cry out, 'Abba, Father!'

Is this belief in a transcendent God like an insuperable barrier separating the monotheistic mystics from the scientist and the Buddhist? Probably not, for while the monotheistic mystic believes in a transcendent God, he or she does not see a transcendent God. 'No one has ever seen God' (John 1:18) echoes through all mystical traditions. And so the Jewish, Islamic and Christian mystics experience in their own way the void, the nothingness, the cloud of unknowing and the unity of all things. In short, Capra's thesis may have validity for mystics of all religions, who come to an experience of the highest wisdom in emptiness.

MYSTIC OF SCIENCE

Several decades before Capra wrote his *Tao of Physics* a Christian mystic had faced similar problems. The life of the French Jesuit, Pierre Teilhard de Chardin (1881–1955), was nothing other than an interior dialogue between science and religion, culminating in a loving marriage between the two.

In a remarkable essay called 'How I believe' that might equally well have been called 'How I pray', Teilhard speaks about the growth of his inner life.[3] Asserting that he is by upbringing and intellectual training a child of heaven but by temperament and professional studies a child of earth, he says that he has allowed the two worlds to mingle and flow into one another in his mind and heart, until after thirty years devoted to the pursuit of inner unity 'I have a feeling that a synthesis has been effected naturally between the two currents that claim my allegiance'.[4] This is surely a fine description of his prayer: Jesuit contemplative prayer that was filled with the presence of God while never excluding the things of the world.

For Teilhard was a Jesuit, educated in a kind of contemplation that was peculiar to the Society of Jesus. St Ignatius of Loyola, founder of the Jesuits, wanted his sons to be constantly in dialogue with the world in which they lived. Himself a consummate mystic who spent many hours in silent contemplative prayer, he nevertheless loved the mighty cities; and he raised Cain when any would-be mystic expressed the desire to spend years in total solitude. Jesuit mysticism, he claimed, must be in the hurly-burly of the world; and he concluded his *Spiritual Exercises* with *The Contemplation for Obtaining Divine Love* which is a vision of a world penetrated with the presence of God — God present in all, working in all, giving himself in all — and Ignatius asks his retreatant to respond with a total offering of self.

Now Teilhard's inner life was formed by *The Spiritual Exercises*. Taking the contemplation for obtaining divine love from its sixteenth-century setting, he expressed it anew in the evolutionary context of the twentieth century. And in this way he came to see the world as holy ground, as a divine milieu: he saw an evolutionary process moving towards a point of convergence which he called

Omega. And as the inner dialogue continued he identified Omega with Jesus Christ at the second coming. Thus the two currents came together and formed a synthesis.

As Ignatius loved the mighty cities, so Teilhard loved the limitless cosmos. This is his most remarkable trait. While his contemporaries trembled with cosmic angst at the millions of light years that separated them from the nearest star, Teilhard with radiant optimism displayed unshakable faith in the cosmic process and the human enterprise. Indeed, in a daring statement that shocked the orthodox, he declared that if as a result of some interior revolution he were to lose faith in Christ, in a personal God and in spirit, he would continue to believe invincibly in the world.

But he did not lose his faith in Christ, in a personal God and in spirit. True to the Ignatian *Exercises* he never lost his deep love for the Jesus of the gospels who through his Resurrection became the Christ of the universe, outside space and time, standing at the point of convergence which is the parousia. Indeed, his passionate love for matter gave him a profound sense of the Incarnation and an almost childlike love for the Eucharist.

In an essay 'The Mass of the World' which Julian Huxley described as poetical, mystical, realistic, religious and philosophical, Teilhard sees the whole world as an altar and calls out to the Lord: 'I, your priest, will make the whole earth my altar and on it will offer to you all the labours and sufferings of the world.'[5] What a sense of the eucharistic sacrifice! And then there is his moving vision while praying before the monstrance. It is as though the round, white host becomes bigger and bigger until it envelops the whole cosmos. Then it recedes and returns to its insignificant place in the monstrance. For Teilhard this speaks of a cosmos divinized through the bread of life.

And as Teilhard loved the cosmos so he believed in human love as the highest form of energy. Totally committed to celibacy he yet believed in a deep man–woman love that transcends erotic desire and leads to a mutual indwelling that is a high point of intimacy. Nor was this empty theory. His life was enriched with remarkable friendships with men and women, friendships which constantly inspired his mystical vision.

If, following St John of the Cross, we define mystical theology as 'the secret wisdom that comes from love',[6] then we cannot easily deny that Teilhard was a thoroughgoing mystic and a mystical theologian, for in the last analysis he was a lover. His love for the cosmos, for humanity and for God dominated everything he said and did. And his wisdom was 'secret' in that it was formless and filled with mystery, inexpressible. Teilhard more than anyone knew that all he wrote could never express what he saw.

And the significant thing is that his inner mystical life was nourished not only by sacred Scripture and tradition but also by scientific data and the fruits of his scientific enquiry. In this he was a true Jesuit, faithful to the vision of Ignatius who wanted his sons to see God in all things — not in some things but in all things.

Teilhard's mysticism was only possible in the twentieth century. After him, mystical theology can never be the same.

LONERGAN, SCIENCE AND GOD

Teilhard was a visionary. Another Jesuit, this time a Canadian of Irish extraction, faced the scientific challenge in a more methodical way. Bernard Lonergan (1904–84) devoted his life to the study of method — What do I do when I know? — and his work came to a climax with *Method in Theology*.[7]

Lonergan saw clearly that the astounding success of modern science stemmed from its methodology, a new methodology that came to birth in the seventeenth century. The so-called scientific revolution which began with Galileo Galilei (1564–1642) and reached perfection with Isaac Newton (1642–1727) was a revolt against a deeply entrenched Aristotelian methodology used alike by scientists, philosophers and theologians. Based on first principles, particularly the principle of causality, this methodology led the scientist to secondary causes and the theologian to the first cause, the prime mover whom the scholastics, following Aquinas, identified with God. There was no conflict between physics and metaphysics, between science and religion. Since all used the same methodology, monks could be scientists and scientists could be monks, engaged in a common search for truth.

Then came the scientific revolution. 'What occurred toward the

end of the seventeenth century', writes Lonergan, 'was the beginning not merely of much better science but basically of a notion of
science quite different from the notion worked out by Aristotle and
taken for granted by his followers.'⁸ For the new method began with
experimentation (for Galileo, looking through his telescope was
more important than reading books) and ended with verification in
the laboratory. The Royal Society excluded from consideration
questions that could not be settled by an appeal to observation or
experiment.

And this method was powerful. It has achieved extraordinary
things and continues to dazzle men and women throughout the
world with its mind-boggling achievements. For it is ongoing. As
more and more data accumulates, further experiments are made,
new insights arise, new theories are formulated. Moreover scholarly
research has adopted a similar method, always looking for new data
and formulating new theories. The result is that an enormous explosion of knowledge has taken place and no one knows how or where
to store it all.

But what about God?

On this point Lonergan is clear. While the new methodology is
superior to anything that went before and while its pioneers were
often deeply religious people, the methodology itself does not, and
cannot, lead to God. After describing the methods of modern
science he goes on:

> For modern science is an empirical science. Whether it studies
> nature or man . . . it begins from data, it descerns intelligible
> unities and relationships within data, and it is subject to the
> check of verification, to the correction and revision to be
> effected by confrontation with further relevant data. Now such
> procedures cannot lead one beyond this world. The divine is
> not a datum to be observed by sense or to be uncovered by
> introspection. Precisely because modern science is specialized
> knowledge of man and of nature, it cannot include knowledge
> of God. God is neither man nor nature.⁹

He concludes with a radical statement:

It would only be the idolatry of identifying God with man or with nature if one attempted to know God through the methods of modern science.[10]

In this way Lonergan finds an immense gap between religion and modern science. We can conclude that if Teilhard de Chardin speaks about God, or if Fritjof Capra talks about wisdom in emptiness, they are no more than extrapolating, going beyond the rigorous, empirical methodology of orthodox science. Hard-headed science, preoccupied with this world alone, has no place for mystical vision.

Now in the opinion of the present writer this Lonerganian position is very questionable; it is not even true to Lonergan's own most basic thesis. However, before looking at it more carefully it is necessary to ask another fundamental question: If the scientific method does not lead us to God, how do we get to God? By what process do we come to know God?

Lonergan does not deny the metaphysical path to God. Faithful to the First Vatican Council he asserts that the human mind is *capable* of knowing God. However, he asserts that in concrete human living no one comes to know God without grace. 'I do not think that in this life people arrive at natural knowledge of God without God's grace, but what I do not doubt is that the knowledge they so attain is natural.'[11]

God's grace is God's love that is poured into our hearts by the Holy Spirit. The royal road to God, then, is the road of love. And for Lonergan love is the crown and climax of the method that he calls transcendental.

TRANSCENDENTAL METHOD

Lonergan's aim was to find a method so in conformity with the dynamic thrust of the human spirit that it would be valid for all men and women at all times and in all places and would be valid in all the sciences. This was transcendental method, a unifying force in the human world of knowing and loving.

Transcendental method is a way of being human and authentic. And since to be fully human one must transcend oneself, it is a way to self-transcendence.

To be true to the deepest thrust of the human spirit one must obey certain transcendental precepts of which the first are

Be attentive
Be intelligent
Be reasonable

Fidelity to these precepts leads to intellectual self-transcendence and intellectual conversion. One comes to realize that knowing is not just a process of having a look at something 'out there' but is a process of experiencing, understanding and judging.

Now the outstanding success of the scientific method is due to its fidelity to these precepts. The good scientist is attentive to the data, understands it intelligently, and formulates it reasonably. The pioneers of the scientific revolution acted according to these precepts. They did not, of course, reflect on their method (for this is the world of philosophers) but they did use it to achieve great things.

But to be human and authentic it is not enough to be intelligent and reasonable; one must also be moral. One must transcend self ethically; and this is done through obedience to another precept:

Be responsible

Fidelity to this precept leads to ethical conversion whereby one makes decisions not for personal satisfaction but from commitment to the objective good. Such ethical conversion is of the greatest importance for the scientist who would use his research responsibly. For example, the scientist working with nuclear energy must be concerned about how his or her research will be used.

But in the thrust towards authenticity the crowning precept is concerned with love. It is nothing other than the great command-ment to love with one's whole heart and soul and mind and strength. This leads to actual self-transcendence and to full humanity. It is religious conversion.

And so the transcendental precepts reach their climax with

Be in love

Lonergan treats of this at some length in *Method in Theology*.

BEING-IN-LOVE

When he comes to speak about love Lonergan, usually so dry, uses the passionate language of the mystics. He speaks of woman falling in love with man, and man falling in love with woman. One is reminded of The Song of Songs — 'You have ravished my heart, my sister, my bride' — or of the sanjuanist bride going forth ardently in search of her love. 'When someone transcendent is my beloved', writes Lonergan, 'he is in my heart, real to me from within me.'[12] And he speaks of the radical nature of being in love with God: 'All love is self-surrender, but being in love with God is being in love without limits or qualifications or conditions or reservations.'[13]

Love of God, then, is total commitment and, like man-woman love, it demands outward expression:

When a man and a woman love each other but do not avow their love, they are not yet in love. Their very silence means that their love has not reached the point of self-surrender and self-donation. It is the love that each freely and fully reveals to the other that brings about the radically new situation of being in love and that begins the unfolding of its lifelong implications . . . What holds true for the love of a man and a woman, also holds in its own way for the love of God and man.[14]

Then there is self-transcendence. The capacity for self-transcendence 'becomes an actuality when one falls in love. Then one's being becomes being-in-love . . . once it has blossomed forth and as long as it lasts, it takes over. It is the first principle. From it flow one's desires and fears, one's joys and sorrows, one's discernment of values, one's decisions and deeds.'[15]

In other words, one is completely possessed by an all-embracing love that dwells at the core of one's being or at the *apex animae*. How much is contained in the statement that one's being becomes being-in-love! Since God alone is Being-in-love in the fullest sense of these words, the creature who becomes being-in-love participates in the divine nature and is divinized. This is the doctrine of the mystics.

And it is important to remember that this love is not acquired by human effort. One does not sit down at a desk and coldly decide to fall in love. Love is a gift — in the old terminology it is sanctifying grace — poured into our hearts by the Holy Spirit and radiating to everyone and everything around. We love because he first loved us. Primarily gift, it is only secondarily a precept. It is a love that is at the same time human and divine.

Furthermore love leads to the most sublime wisdom, the wisdom of the mystics. This is a point that Lonergan does not develop but it flows from what he says. The wisdom that comes from love is not found in clear-cut images and concepts. It is formless, obscure, empty knowledge in a cloud of unknowing. It is true *sapientia*, a wisdom that surpasses scientific knowledge as the resplendent light of the sun surpasses the dim light of a tiny candle. But (and this is important) while it surpasses scientific knowledge it does not suppress or contradict it. The two can, and do, coexist in the one person.

From all this it will be clear that Lonergan's thinking is in conformity with traditional mystical theology which has always stressed that God can be loved but cannot be known. The author of *The Cloud of Unknowing* puts it picturesquely when he says: 'For why, he may well be loved, but not thought. By love may he be gotten and holden; but by thought neither.'[16] And then St John of the Cross speaks of mystical theology as the secret wisdom that comes from love, a love that is an inflow of God into the soul. Such love, after burning out defects and imperfections in the dark night, divinizes the soul, setting it on fire. O living flame of love!

Now the original and almost shocking thing in Lonergan is that he looks on mystical love as the goal and climax of human living. This love is the peak-point of that thrust towards self-transcendence and authenticity that is rooted in the minds and hearts of all human beings. There is nothing elitist about it. It is not a gift offered to Christians alone. It is not offered to religious people alone. It is offered to all men and women who would be fully human. Can we not conclude that for Lonergan there is a universal call to mysticism?

Yet the problem arises when he speaks about the scientific method. To this it is now time to return.

SCIENCE AND LOVE

Lonergan has said that science is methodologically geared to this world, that it begins with experiment and ends with verification, that it would be idolatry to say that one can come to God by the methods of modern science. In this way he excludes love and grace from the scientific methodology. And this is the Achilles' heel of the great Canadian theologian.

For the fact is that the grace of God is actively at work in the heart of anyone who seeks the truth with a humble heart. This is the clearly expressed teaching of the Second Vatican Council which, asserting that earthly matters and the concerns of faith derive from the same God, goes on:

> Indeed, whoever labours to penetrate the secrets of reality with a humble and steady mind, is even unawares, being led by the hand of God, who holds all things in existence, and gives them identity.[17]

Reading these simple words it is easy to believe that Isaac Newton, Albert Einstein, Niels Bohr were led by the hand of God in their scientific enquiry. And the same holds true for all committed scientists who search for the truth with unrestricted love.

Furthermore, when the Second Vatican Council came to an end in 1965, the Council Fathers sent messages to various groups of people throughout the world. And they spoke to scientists — to men and women who love the truth and seek the truth. They say in effect that love for truth is the very basis of the scientific method and that scientists have their dark nights when they are 'tired and disappointed by their vain search'. The Council writes:

> A very special greeting to you, seekers after truth, to you, men and women of thought and science, explorers of the human, of

the universe, and of history, to all of you who are pilgrims en route to the light . . . Your road is ours. Your paths are never foreign to ours. We are the friends of your vocation as searchers, companions in your fatigues, admirers of your success, and, if necessary, consolers in your discouragement and your failures.[18]

Here there is no hint that science is natural and theology supernatural, no hint that the theologian has grace and the scientist has no grace. 'Your road is ours.' All are drawn by the gift of God's love to seek the truth.

If, then, in accordance with Lonergan's fifth transcendental precept, scientists are moved by God's grace to love the truth and make a total commitment to the truth, they will go beyond this world to the Source without falling into idolatry. Their knowledge, like that of the mystics, will be dark and obscure in a cloud of unknowing but it will never conflict with their other clear-cut knowledge that comes from scientific enquiry and is subject to verification in the laboratory. Who can deny that some scientists may be the mystics of the future?

In short, the scientist no less than the theologian can be a lover — in love with a truth that leads beyond the results of laboratory experiments into a cloud of unknowing where God dwells in light inaccessible or darkness impenetrable. The wisdom the scientist acquires through love is the crowning gift of the complete scientific method, as wisdom is the crowning gift of the theological enterprise.

CONCLUSION

Many scientists have been, and are, totally committed to the search for truth. While following the experimental scientific method, they have continued searching for truth according to the transcendental method. Their being has become being-in-love. This means that in addition to the knowledge garnered through laboratory experiments they have acquired the highest wisdom that comes from love — knowledge of the great mystery that surrounds human life and envelops the universe. They have spoken about God in language that resembles that of the mystics. Here two examples can be given. The first is Isaac Newton.

It is generally said that the scientific method reached perfection with the publication of Newton's *Principia* in 1687. Yet Newton never stopped his thinking at this world and was constantly preoccupied with God. Indeed he looked upon himself as a prophet and wrote much more lengthily about theology and alchemy than about mathematics and physics. At the end of his life he made a comment that is worthy of the mystics. He spoke of himself as a little boy playing by the sea-shore and finding pretty shells 'while the great ocean of Truth lay all undiscovered before me'.[19] The pretty shells are the conclusions of his scientific enquiry. And is not the great ocean of undiscovered truth the mystery of mysteries that underlies all things? Is not this the cloud of unknowing, the dark night, the void, the nothingness?

A second scientist dominated the twentieth century. Albert Einstein had a profound sense of the harmony of the universe and spoke of his 'religious feeling' as one of 'rapturous amazement at the harmony of the natural law'. He had 'a deep conviction of the rationality of the universe',[20] so much so that John Polkinghorne calls him 'the last of the great ancients rather than the first of the great moderns'.[21] It was for this reason that he could not accept the seeming irrationality of quantum mechanics and made his famous statement that God does not play dice.

It is true that Einstein once said that he rejected the notion of a personal God. But many of his statements make it clear that what he rejected was an anthropomorphic God and that he had a profound sense of a supreme and mysterious intelligence that governs all and does not play dice. For he speaks of the 'illimitable spirit' revealed in the incomprehensible universe. There is even something of the Ignatian *Contemplation for Obtaining Divine Love* in his words:

My religion consists of a humble admiration of the illimitable superior spirit who reveals himself in the slight details we are able to perceive with our frail and feeble minds. That deeply emotional conviction of the presence of a superior reasoning power which is revealed in the incomprehensible universe forms my idea of God.[22]

Here is a vision of God working in all things. And Einstein had a sense of vocation, a sense of God working within him. A few days before his death in 1955 he said: 'Here on earth I have done my job.'

We can conclude with the Second Vatican Council that the Spirit of love is at work in the scientist who seeks the truth with a humble mind and that the faithful pursuit of truth through science can lead to the highest wisdom. Mystical theology of the future cannot neglect the scientist.

NOTES

1. *The Tao of Physics*, Fritjof Capra, Berkeley 1975.
2. Ibid., p. 50.
3. *Christianity in Evolution*, Pierre Teilhard de Chardin, New York 1971, p. 96ff.
4. Ibid., p. 97.
5. *Hymn of the Universe*, Pierre Teilhard de Chardin, New York 1965, p. 19.
6. *The Spiritual Canticle*, 27.5.
7. *Method in Theology*, Bernard Lonergan, London 1972.
8. *A Second Collection*, Bernard Lonergan, London 1972.
9. Ibid., p. 107.
10. Ibid.
11. Ibid., p. 133.
12. *Method in Theology*, p. 109.
13. Ibid., p. 105.
14. Ibid., p. 113.
15. Ibid., p. 105.
16. *The Cloud of Unknowing*, C.5.
17. *Gaudium et Spes*, III.36.
18. Closing Messages of the Council 'To people of Thought and Science'. Lonergan was acutely aware of the absence of God in modern culture and stated brilliantly that the road back to God for modern people is through love, which is the climax of his transcendental method. Unfortunately he failed to see that the scientist, no less than the theologian, may be motivated by love for truth. In this way he widens the gap between religion and science. For further development of this subject see chapter 11 of this book which deals with revelation through the cosmos. See also chapter 17 which deals with Lonergan's method.
19. Quoted by Ravi Ravindra in 'Newton, Isaac', *The Encyclopedia of Religion*, ed. Mircea Eliade, New York 1987.
20. Quoted by Ravi Ravindra in 'Einstein, Albert', Op. supra cit.

21. *Science and Providence*, John Polkinghorne, London 1989, p. 78.
22. Quoted by Ravi Ravindra, Op. supra cit.

EIGHT

Asceticism and Asia

ASCETICAL PRACTICE

From the earliest days Christians were aware that mystical prayer and ascetical practice go hand in hand. St Paul was fascinated by the athletes who ran in the Isthmian games. 'Athletes exercise control in all things,' he writes. 'They do it to receive a perishable wreath, but we an imperishable one' (1 Corinthians 9:25). And he urged the Corinthian Christians to train themselves like the athletes in order to win the prize offered by Christ Jesus. Indeed, Paul saw himself as a runner who never looked back: 'I press on toward the goal for the prize of the upward call of God in Christ Jesus' (Philippians 3:14). He had to discipline himself, he tells us, lest having preached to others he himself would be disqualified. Yet this discipline had one more powerful effect: it opened his heart to mystical grace, so that he could boast of a man who was caught up into Paradise and heard things that are not to be told, that no mortal is permitted to repeat.

Following in the footsteps of Paul and learning liberally from the surrounding culture, the desert fathers trained their disciples in the art of asceticism. They must have known that while mystical experience can strike like a bolt from the blue as it struck Paul on the road to Damascus, it is ordinarily the reward of persevering effort. And so they taught their disciples how to eat and how to fast, how to sit, how to breathe and, above all, how to read the Scriptures and to pray. This teaching passed into Eastern monastacism where the monks developed hesychastic ways of prayer that are vibrantly alive today at Mount Athos and throughout the Orthodox world. It also passed into the rule of St Benedict and the Western religious orders where it was developed and refined and moulded into a whole body of doctrine that trained men and women to lead a life of prayer in accordance with the evangelical counsels.

St Ignatius of Loyola (1491-1556) was a great master of asceticism. 'For just as taking a walk, journeying on foot and running are bodily exercises,' he writes, 'so we call spiritual exercises every way of preparing and disposing the soul to rid itself of all inordinate attachments, and, after their removal, of seeking and finding the will of God in the disposition of our life for the salvation of our soul.'¹ Here spiritual exercises or ascetical practices are a preparation for mysticism, for the direct action of God on the soul. And Ignatius wrote about ways of prayer, posture in prayer, breathing in prayer. He stressed examinations of conscience, and he elaborated detailed rules for the discernment of spirits. He gave instructions about food and sleep, about custody of the senses and penitential practices. He wrote rules of modesty. And his teaching dominated Catholic spirituality everywhere until the Second Vatican Council.

In the seventeenth century the accumulated wisdom of centuries was gathered and systematized in a new discipline called ascetical theology.² In conjunction with mystical theology, this new discipline, pastoral in nature, was taught in Catholic seminaries throughout the world. It was concerned principally with practice, with spiritual exercises, with ways of training mind and body. Joseph de Guibert tells us that while mystical theology is concerned with gift, ascetical theology is concerned with human effort. He then goes on to define the terms more strictly:

Strictly: we may term mystical the interior life of those souls who are habitually led by the inspirations of the Holy Spirit, who are made so sensitive and so docile to these inspirations that their whole interior life is lived under this leading by grace. On the other hand, we can find an ascetical state in which personal effort and the methodical performances of spiritual exercises are more evident, while the continual flow of grace into the soul is less apparent and less perceived experientially.³

In this way, ascetical and mystical theology went hand in hand, guiding men and women in the way of prayer.

CRISIS

In the twentieth century Western culture broke down. Through a series of revolutions, traditional religion seemed to collapse. Old customs disappeared. Traditional values were called in question. Confusion reigned.

And in this turmoil it is hardly surprising if traditional ascetical practices were challenged, criticized and put to the test. The old religious training, it was now said, did not suit the new people. Contaminated by Stoicism, Neo-Platonism, rationalism and Jansenism, it had strayed far from the authentic spirit of the Gospel. As Freud and Jung and the rest analysed the human psyche, it became clear to some psychologists that much of the traditional training in noviceships and seminaries was unhealthy, dehumanizing and destructive. There was a call for new wine in new wineskins. But what were the areas that caused dissatisfaction?

First of all, there was dissatisfaction with the traditional ways of praying. Here the Jesuits came under fire for teaching a dull, methodical, discursive prayer which they imposed on the whole Church. No less a person than Aldous Huxley accused the Jesuits of destroying Western mysticism with their plodding emphasis on reasoning and thinking. Where was the vibrant mysticism of medieval Europe? What had happened to Julian of Norwich and Meister Eckhart? Where was *The Cloud of Unknowing*?

Then there was the traditional attitude towards the human body and towards sexuality. It all seemed so negative, and the exaggerated distinction between mind and body, sense and spirit, led to an unhealthy dualism. People learning about the immense potentialities of the human body and the high value of sexuality were loath to accept talk about subduing the flesh and conquering the passions. The medieval self-flagellation no longer made sense. What people wanted (and what they felt was more authentically Christian) was a conversion to the body and to the material world.

Again, in the twentieth century the laity were looking for prayer, even mystical prayer. But the ascetical and mystical literature, monastic in nature, was written by celibates for celibates. It had little esteem for marriage and at time it was offensive to women.

Again, the old doctrine ignored the social problems that plague contemporary society. Hunger, oppression, violation of human rights, racial discrimination, unemployment — these problems, which did not exist for the old ascetical and mystical theologians, could not be overlooked in the twentieth century.

All in all, it was clear that Christianity needed a new ascetical theology.

THE NEW SEARCH

At this time enterprising people, inspired by the Spirit, began to look for new ways within the Western tradition. A revival of biblical studies helped many to pray by savouring and relishing the word of God. Liturgical renewal led others to a deeper appreciation of the eucharistic sacrifice and devotion to Christ in our midst. Charismatic renewal led others to baptism in the Spirit and prayer in tongues. Research in spirituality revealed hitherto unnoticed treasures of mysticism in the Ignatian tradition. There was a great revival of interest in Western mysticism.

And at this time also, imaginative people turned their eyes to an Asia that seemed to offer everything the West lacked. Asia seemed to offer not only treasures of wisdom and mysticism but also simple and practical ways of meditation. Its ascetical practice was holistic, rejecting all body-soul dualism. It promised not only health of mind and body but also longevity and the development of human potential. It led to liberation and enlightenment. To a generation floundering in religious and cultural confusion, all this was very appealing. The key question was: *Is it possible to unite Asian ascetical practice with Christian faith?*

Already in the 1950s an interesting and significant book called *Christian Yoga* came from the pen of a Belgian Benedictine monk.[4] J. M. Déchanet was a child of his times, dissatisfied with the traditional ascetical training; but he was also a loyal son of the pre-Vatican II Catholic Church who felt obliged to dissociate humself from the Hindu religion. Whereas yoga at its deepest level is a way to wisdom, liberation and union with God, Déchanet cut it from its Hindu roots and used the *asanas* as a technique for attaining deep, inner silence. He writes:

> As for the practices of yoga, we shall take them simply for what they are, neither religion nor mysticism, but a discipline, a skill ... For us Yoga shall be a *technique* that allows man — when this is fitting — to establish himself in silence; not merely away from this noise, but effectively in the silence of the senses, desires and worries, accepting above all to remain silent so that the Holy Spirit of God may now and then make its voice heard and the spirit of man be listening.[5]

When this was written, the Catholic Church had not yet made its deep commitment to dialogue with other religions. Consequently Déchanet could see yoga as no more than a technique that prepared for Christian prayer. Yet his book was prophetic. It prepared the way for the dialogue that was to come.

EAST ASIA

Just as in the West an ascetical tradition was built up through many centuries, so also in the East, by a similar process, an ascetical tradition slowly came to birth, manifesting itself in the entire culture of China and Japan. This ascetical training, known as *gyo*, is at the very heart of the tea ceremony, calligraphy, judo, fencing, archery and the other so-called 'ways'.[6] In its religious form, where it is called *shugyo*, it appeared in Zen and other forms of Buddhist meditation where the master seeks to lead the disciple to that wisdom in emptiness that forms the very basis of East Asian culture.

This ascetical training can be summed up in the triple formula:

Training of the body
Training of the breathing
Training of the mind

Let us look at these three points.[7]

The attitude towards the human body in East Asia is greatly influenced by Chinese medicine which speaks of *meridians* or channels through which energy flows, giving life to the whole person. This energy is known as *chi* in Chinese and *ki* in Japanese.

The source of this energy is the belly (in Japanese *hara*) which is called 'the sea of energy'; and of particular importance is the *tanden*, a point located a few centimetres below the navel. This is the source of creativity and the principal locus of religious experience. One is encouraged to be aware of it existentially not only in the time of meditation but in all the affairs of life. In the martial arts, awareness of the *tanden* is vital.

A little known Zen master, Master Torajiro Okada, writes powerfully that the *tanden* is the shrine of the divine: it is here that sacred energy dwells. He divides people into three classes. The first class value the head: they amass vast quantities of knowledge, grow big heads — and topple over like a pyramid standing upside down. The second class throw out the chest. Such persons seem courageous and strong but inwardly they are weak. Then he goes on:

> But those who regard the belly as the most important part and so have built the stronghold where the Divine can grow — these are the people of the highest rank. They develop their minds as well as their bodies in the right way. Strength flows out from them and produces a spiritual condition of ease and equanimity. They do what seems good to them without violating any law.[8]

The master goes on to say that the sorrows of humanity are caused by loss of balance, and the way to balance — to a healthy body and an upright heart — is to sit correctly.

Correct posture, then, in which one is aware of the *tanden* and remains centred in the *tanden*, is of primary importance. This can be the lotus posture or the Japanese *seiza* (Confucianist in origin) in which one sits back on one's heels — or one can sit on a chair with back straight and eyes slightly open. And then, whether standing or sitting or walking or sleeping one remains centred in the *hara*. Now one has great stability and inner strength. The important change is interior, as Master Okada stresses when he says: 'Even if the body is changed in *seiza*, the deepest inner state does not change so easily.'[9]

It is interesting to recall that Zen Master Dogen, founder of the Japanese Soto sect, said that correct sitting or *zazen* is already enlightenment.

Next comes training of the breathing.

Here again abdominal breathing is the key. One breathes from the *tanden*, slowly and rhythmically. And just as the very sitting is a religious experience, so also is the breathing. Energy now flows through the body.

It should be noted that we are here speaking not just of the breath and energy in my little body but of the breath and energy of the cosmos. Zen masters, with characteristic bluntness, say that the energy must flow down through the anus, through the cushion to the very centre of the earth, and then upwards through the top of the head to the outermost regions of the universe.

Tanden breathing, then, makes one balanced and brings one into harmony with the whole universe. Master Okada again gives simple and practical advice: 'Sit quite still, breathe gently giving out long breaths, the strength in the lower belly.'[10] When *tanden* breathing becomes habitual, one acquires a wonderful physical and spiritual stability.

The third point is training of the mind.

The human mind is wild and restless, wandering here and there, going anxiously into the future or nostalgically into the past. The great art is to bring the mind to rest on a single point. This is one-pointedness — in Japanese *seishin toitsu*. It is done through the breathing and the sitting. Though the mind is now in the present moment, it does not rest in one part of the body but flows through the whole body in a state that is known as *no-mind* (in Japanese *mushin*) or *no-self* (in Japanese *muga*).

Distractions come. But one does not fight them. One lets them come and lets them go. 'Let go; let flow' is the advice one hears. Master Okada's advice is simple and clear: 'Do not try to free yourself from all thoughts. Simply be aware and keep your strength in your belly.'[11] In this way thoughts flow in and out, while one remains centred at a deeper level.

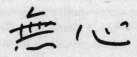

For the sake of clarity the process has been divided into three; but in fact it is all one holistic action.

FAITH AND SALVATION

While training of the body, the breathing and the mind is important in the martial arts and all the 'ways', when one comes to religious meditation another element of the greatest importance enters in: namely, faith. For in Buddhism, ascetical practice is wedded to a great faith in the three-fold treasure — the Buddha, the *dharma* and the *sangha*. One who practises meditation in the temple begins with the proclamation:

I take refuge in the Buddha
I take refuge in the *dharma*
I take refuge in the *sangha*

This act of faith is a total commitment and it echoes through the whole process of meditation that follows. Buddhist meditation is penetrated through and through with silent faith. Moreover one must be ready to die for that faith. 'Even if I die . . .' In fact one passes through the great doubt and the great death. Abandoning the security that comes from clinging to anything, one clings to nothing — to nothing whatever — and one breaks through to enlightenment.

Faith in the *dharma* means faith in the Buddhist teaching, particularly as it is enshrined in the Heart Sutra, the Lotus Sutra and the Kegon Sutra. These sutras are constantly chanted by monks; and then, when one enters the silent meditation, abandoning words and letters, the naked faith of pure commitment carries on. Silent, wordless and thoughtless meditation is nothing other than an act of pure faith.

In another context the saintly founder of the Pure Land sect held that faith alone was necessary — faith was the only *shugyo* or ascetical practice. Shinran (1173-1262) abandoned all ascetical practices, proclaiming that it was enough to call on the name of Amida. Even the greatest sinner, if he or she recites the name with faith, will be reborn in the Pure Land.[12]

For it must be remembered that Buddhism is a religion of salvation. Through reliance on one's deepest self or on the mercy of Another, one is liberated from illusion, freed from the cycle of birth and death, and reborn as a Buddha. The Zen monk, vowing to save not only himself but all sentient beings chants with great determination:

> Living beings are innumerable — I vow to save them all.
> Illusive desires and lusts are inexhaustible — I vow to
> extinguish them all
> Gates to the Truth are numberless — I vow to learn and
> master then all.
> The way of enlightenment is peerless — I vow to realize it.

These vows are a great act of selfless compassion. One sacrifices everything in order to bring to salvation the whole universe. One walks the way of the Buddha.

ASIA AND THE WEST

At the end of the nineteenth century large numbers of religious seekers in Europe and America looked nostalgically towards the mystic East. At the World Parliament of Religions held in Chicago in 1893 the youthful and charming Vivekananda (1863-1902), disciple of the great mystic Ramakrishna, held spellbound hundreds of sophisticated Western intellectuals with his mellifluous words of Asian wisdom; and in the ensuing years Hinduism gave birth to people of genius like the mystic Ramana Maharishi, the poet Rabindranath Tagore and the religious activist Mahatma Gandhi. All this could not fail to impress the religious world of the West.

At Chicago Zen Buddhism was also represented by the Rinzai monk Shaku Soen (1858-1919).[13] Less impressive than Vivekananda and less fluent in English, he nevertheless introduced to the West a young Japanese disciple who was to become one of the most brilliant religious writers of the twentieth century. Dr D. T. Suzuki, sage and scholar, wrote prolifically; and 'Suzuki Zen' swept through the Western world. Soon it became fashionable to talk about the sound of one hand clapping and to ask if a dog possessed the Buddha nature. Suzuki's melodramatic descriptions of the earthshaking experience of *satori* appealed to great writers like the eclectic Aldous Huxley and the adventurous Alan Watts who were looking for extraordinary experiences, caring little whether they came from Zen or mescalin or ecstatic love.

In the sixties thousands of young hippies flocked to India in search of mystical experience, while Indian gurus and Zen masters made their way to California which soon became the home of beat Zen and all kinds of esoteric experience. This movement of Asian religious experience still lives in the West in the trancendental meditation of the Maharishi Mahesh Yogi and in the influential New Age.

Though Eastern religions were taught in the universities and great scholars like Carl Jung and Mircea Eliade studied the Asian classics, most orthodox Christians distanced themselves from this movement. It did, however, fire the fertile imagination of a very creative Trappist monk. Thomas Merton (1915-68) wrote enthusiastically about mystics and Zen masters and entered into dialogue with the great Suzuki. He died symbolically, if tragically, at a conference on interreligious dialogue in Bangkok.

Meanwhile, another group of Christians, Orthodox Christians, was quietly carrying on a profound and significant dialogue with the ascetical and mystical traditions of Asia. Missionaries deemed it a sacred duty to listen to the Spirit working in Asian culture; and eventually their time came to speak to the religious seekers in the West.

MISSION AND INCULTURATION

In the sixteenth century when the missionaries sailed from Lisbon to India, South East Asia and Japan, one of their first priorities was inculturation. That is to say, they wanted to unite Christian faith with Asian culture in a blessed and fruitful marriage. The far-sighted Italian, Alessandro Vilagnano (1539-1606) had a vision of a thoroughly Asian Christianity with religious leaders born and bred in Asia. In China, Matteo Ricci (1552-1610) first adopted the garb of a Buddhist monk and then that of a scholar, writing more than twenty volumes in Chinese on mathematics, apologetics, literature and astronomy. In India, Robert de Nobili (1577-1656), impressed by the religiosity of the people, lived as a *sannyasi* or holy man. He wore saffron robes, walked in wooden clogs, adopted the vegetarian diet and marked his brow with a rectangular shape of paste to signify that he was a religious teacher. He lived the ascetical life of a Brahman to lead people to the Gospel.

Seventeenth-century theology, it is true, was not prepared for esoteric dialogue with the so-called pagan religions, and de Nobili and Ricci never found favour with the establishment. Nevertheless their example of inculturation lived on in Christian *sannyasis* and ascetics who followed the poor Christ in ashrams and centres of prayer throughout Asia. And as the era of the foreign missionaries came to an end, Indian, Chinese and Japanese Christians undertook the work of inculturation, studying and assimilating the ascetical and mystical traditions of their ancestors.[14]

And the Second Vatican Council made its mark. Speaking about the necessity of bringing the rich treasures of Christian mysticism to the world, the Council — in words that recall the memory of Ricci and de Nobili — has this advice for missionaries:

Let them reflect attentively on how Christian religious life may be able to assimilate the ascetical and contemplative traditions whose seeds were sometimes already planted by God in ancient cultures prior to the preaching of the Gospel.[15]

Can this be taken as an exhortation to assimilate the ascetical and mystical traditions of Hinduism, Buddhism, Taoism and the other Asian religions? Challenging words indeed.

ZEN AND CHRISTIAN CONTEMPLATION

Already before the Second Vatican Council a German Jesuit, following in the footsteps of Ricci and de Nobili, was practising Zen in Japan. Hugo Lassalle (1898-1990), who became Enomiya Makibi after taking Japanese citizenship and is frequently known as Enomiya-Lasalle, started to practise Zen in 1943 with a view to understanding Japanese culture and adapting the Christian message to the Asian mentality. And so he practised Zen in temples throughout Japan, taking direction first from the famous Master Sogaku Harada and later from Master Koun Yamada in Kamakura.

The approach of Lassalle was quite different from that of Déchanet who wrote *Christian Yoga*. Whereas Déchanet took the externals of yoga and dissociated himself from the underlying wisdom, Lassalle was fascinated by the underlying wisdom — the *satori* or enlightenment — and made it his aim to attain to this enlightenment and to lead others in the same path. His first book, *Zen: The Way to Enlightenment* spoke about enlightenment for Christians and his subsequent books centred around the same theme.[16] He believed that *satori*, a beautiful jewel of Asian culture and religion, could be integrated into Christianity. Not only *could* it be integrated: it *must* be integrated. And so Lassalle wanted to introduce Zen practice into noviceships and seminaries as part of the religious training. But he could convince neither his colleagues nor church authorities that this was a good idea.

At first Lassalle was interested in building a Japanese Christianity and in finding a Japanese way of prayer — this was part of his vision of inculturation — but as time went on, he felt that he had a mission to the universal Church. And so he gave retreats in Europe, introducing hundreds of Christians to Zen practice. It need hardly be said that he met with opposition. The Zen enlightenment, it was said, was monistic and irreconcilable with the Gospel. To this Lasalle, always practical, replied that he and other Christians had had a glimpse of *satori* and that, far from distancing them from the Gospel, the experience deepened their commitment to Jesus Christ. And so he continued with his work.

And yet, while no one questioned Lassalle's sincerity and deep piety, his approach raised, and continues to raise, theological and pastoral problems that cannot be sidestepped. Some of these questions come from Buddhists.

For the fact is that Zen, as practised in the temple, is primarily an act of faith. It has already been said that the true Zen person puts his or her faith in the Buddha, the *dharma* and the *sangha*, and that this faith lives on as pure faith or naked faith when one enters the silence of *zazen*. The Zen practitioner must be willing to pass through the great doubt and to die the great death; and only a deep faith-commitment gives the strength to do this.

But Lassalle did not put his faith in the Buddha, the *dharma* and the *sangha*. All who lived with him and loved him (and this includes the present writer) know that he was a rather traditional Catholic priest who celebrated the Eucharist with great devotion and lived the Spiritual Exercises of St Ignatius. Besides, he constantly read the Christian mystics, and his own writings are full of quotations from the Rhineland mystics, Richard of St Victor, St John of the Cross and others in whom, he claimed, he found the *satori* he sought. About the Lotus Sutra, the Kegon Sutra, the Heart Sutra he writes almost nothing. As for salvation, he did not doubt that Jesus was his Saviour and the Saviour of the world. What, then, was the nature of his Zen? And what was the nature of his *satori*?

Lassalle was aware of this criticism. He replied by distinguishing between Zen and Zen Buddhism, a distinction which, he claimed, was recognized by his Buddhist teacher. Zen, he held, could be separated from Zen Buddhism (that is to say, from the Buddha, the *dharma* and the *sangha*) and integrated into a Christianity wherein one is devoted to Jesus, the Gospel and the Church. Indeed, it could be integrated into Judaism, Islam or any religion. The long hours of sitting or *zazen* would remain; enlightenment would remain; but the commitment would be different. The greatest Zen Buddhists, he maintained, insisted that one must transcend Zen Buddhism in order to reach the fullness of enlightenment.

Yet this way of thinking was, and remains, controversial. For some Buddhists, Lassalle Zen is heretical Zen (*gedo Zen*) and they do not accept it. For some historians, Zen and Zen Buddhism are indissolubly linked — to tear Zen from its Buddhist roots, they claim, is to do violence both to Zen and to Buddhism.[17] This controversy is not likely to go away in the near future.

Some Christians prefer to *dialogue with Zen and to learn from Zen*. They sit with straight back, their strength in the lower abdomen. They practice *tanden* breathing. They attain to one-pointedness. But they are sitting silently in the presence of God or with the Pauline 'I live, now not I, but Christ lives in me' or with the Jesus prayer or with a biblical *koan*. These Christians are friendly with Buddhists and many meditate with them; but they make no claim to a *satori* like that of Buddhists since they have their own enlightenment based on the Gospel. And they do not call their practice Zen. They are in the tradition of Ricci and de Nobili as developed in the Second Vatican Council. This surely is the way of the future.

THE NEW MYSTICISM

It has already been said that the twentieth century witnessed a breakdown in the ascetical practice of the Christian West. And now it becomes clear that the apparent breakdown was a time of growth. It was a time when Christian people began to search for new ways of praying, for new ways of training their minds and bodies in the service of God. It was a time when Western Christians turned their eyes towards Asia and when Asian Christians became aware of the riches of their own ascetical and mystical tradition.

It all reminds us of those early days when the Gospel moved into the Greek world and the Gentiles, realizing that they could not live like Jews, created their own Christian culture and found their own ways of praying. St John and St Paul were great mystics; but when their teaching met Greek thought, something new was born.

Gregory, Basil, Augustine, Dionysius and the rest created a new mysticism. It was not the same as the mysticism of Plotinus; neither was it the same as the mysticism of John and Paul. It was a third way — a *tertium quid*.

And now at the end of the twentieth century we see a similar creative process. Thanks to the endeavours and the prayers of modern prophets and pioneers, a new mysticism is coming to birth. It is not the mysticism of Eckhart, St John of the Cross and St Teresa of Avila; nor is it the mysticism of Chuang Tzu, Hakuin and Ramakrishna. It is a third way, a *tertium quid*. It is the Gospel of Jesus Christ in a new world.

For the fact is that everywhere we see Christians of all ages and cultures sitting quietly in meditation. Some sit before a crucifix or an ikon in one-pointed meditation. Others sit and breathe as they look at the tabernacle. Others practise mindfulness, awareness of God in their surroundings. Others recite a mantra to the rhythm of their breath. Others, influenced by Zen or yoga or *vipassana* open their minds and hearts to the presence of God in the universe. Others just talk to God. We hear of many new approaches to the living God.

Assuredly, these ways of prayer cannot immediately be called mystical. But they are gateways to mysticism. They all lead to silence and to the wordless state that St Teresa calls the prayer of quiet. Here one remains silent or one-pointed in the presence of God while the imagination (she called it 'the fool of the house') romps wildly here and there. This prayer of quiet is in her fourth mansion; and from it one may be called to the higher mansions. Indeed, one who perseveres will soon hear the voice of the Master: 'Friend, move up higher ...' (Luke 14:10) and he or she will be honoured in the presence of all who sit at table.

THEOLOGICAL SIGNIFICANCE

And this popular movement towards mysticism is of the greatest theological significance. For it is precisely through the contemplation of the people of God that the Church grows in wisdom and comes to understand more and more deeply the Word of God. This is the doctrine of the Second Vatican Council. Speaking about what theologians call development of doctrine, the Council says that there is a growth in the understanding of the realities and the words which have been handed down. And then it goes on:

> This happens through the contemplation and study made by believers, who treasure these things in their hearts (cf. Luke 2:19, 51), through the intimate understanding of spiritual things they experience, and through the preaching of those who have received through episcopal succession the sure gift of faith.[18]

Here, treating of the development of doctrine, the Council gives pride of place to the contemplation of the people. Only secondly come the bishops; and the learned theologians are not even mentioned.

Like Mary who pondered these things in her heart, the people of God throughout the world are sitting in meditation. They are coming to an intimate understanding of the Scriptures and the events related therein. And this, the Council says, is the prime factor in the development of dogma and the Church's growth in wisdom. The first will be last and the last first.

NOTES

1. *The Spiritual Exercises of St Ignatius*, Introductory Observations.
2. The discipline called 'Ascetical theology' dates only from the seventeenth century. 'Ascetical' comes from the Greek *askein*. This word was not used in the Pauline letters but is found in one of Paul's speeches in The Acts of the Apostles, cf. Acts 24:16. In the early Church the name 'ascetic' was given to the one who fought against the flesh and made public profession of celibacy. Then the word came to be applied to the exercises of monastic life. The word was not used in ancient Latin except as a transcript of the Greek nor was it used in the Middle Ages.
3. *Theologia spiritualis ascetica et mystica*, Joseph de Guibert, Rome 1946, I.IV.9.
4. *Christian Yoga*, J. M. Déchanet O.S.B., French original 1956, English translation, London 1960.
5. Ibid., p.59.
6. For the historical development of Zen from India through China to Japan, see *Zen Buddhism: A History*, Vols I, II, Heinrich Dumoulin, London, New York, 1988. For the relationship between Buddhist meditation and the 'ways' see: *Zen and the Ways*, Trevor Leggett, London 1978.

7. See *Call to Meditation*, K. Kadowaki, unpublished manuscript.
8. Quoted in *Hara: The Vital Centre of Man*, K. Graf Durckheim, London 1962, p.176.
9. Ibid., p.177.
10. Ibid., p.178.
11. Ibid., p.181.
12. See the classic *Tannisho* written around the year 1290 by Yuiken, a disciple of Shinran.
13. See *Zen Buddhism in the 20th Century*, Heinrich Dumoulin, New York 1992, p.3ff.
14. See *Gurus, Ashrams and Christians*, Vandana, London 1978.
15. *Ad Gentes*, II.18.
16. *Zen — Way to Enlightenment*, Hugo Enomiya-Lassalle, London 1973. See also: *Zen Meditation for Christians*, Illinois 1974.
17. Heinrich Dumoulin writes: 'One might say that without Zen, Buddhism would not be what it is today. Zen represents one of the purest manifestations of the religious essence of Buddhism; it is the fruit and flower of that larger tree.' *Zen Buddhism: a History*, Vol I, p.17.
18. *Dei Verbum*, II.8.

NINE

✳

Mysticism and Vital Energy

ENERGY IN THE CHRISTIAN TRADITION

An Asian person reading the gospels for the first time was impressed by the energy that radiates from the person of Jesus. It all reminded her of the *ki*, the *chi*, the *prana*, the energy that forms the very basis of Asian culture and religion. For energy goes out from Jesus when he heals the sick and casts out demons. Light, blinding light, radiates from his body and clothing when he is transfigured on Mount Thabor. Then there is the time when he says, 'I am,' and the crowd steps back and falls to the ground, overawed by his spiritual power and magnetic presence. With a burst of energy he dies: 'And crying with a loud voice he yielded up the spirit' (Mark 15:37).

After he was taken up, he continues to work in the world. This is the teaching of the Second Vatican Council which writes that 'Christ is now at work in the hearts of men and women through the energy of his Spirit.'[1] This energy appears clearly in The Acts of the Apostles and the Pauline letters where the Spirit is manifested in gifts of healing and prophecy and wisdom which flow forth from charismatic people. But the greatest energy and the greatest gift is love. 'If I speak in the tongues of mortals and of angels, but do not have love, I am a noisy gong or a clanging cymbal' (1 Corinthians 13:1). For, as St John tells us, 'God is love' (1 John 4:8).

And the energy of the New Testament passed into the mystical tradition which interpreted literally the words of the Gospel that Jesus came to cast fire upon the earth — spiritual fire, powerful energy. The same mystical tradition saw flaming energy in those love poems that make up The Song of Songs. 'You have ravished my heart, my sister, my bride, you have ravished my heart with a glance of your eyes . . .' (Song of Songs 4:9); and the Eastern tradition wrote about the uncreated energies of God, elaborating a theology of light and of fire that gave birth to deep mystical experience. Moreover, the Eucharist, the bread of life, the food of the soul, was, and continues to be, the great source of Christian energy.

Yet the Christian tradition, following the New Testament, always acknowledged the existence of an evil energy also. The Second Vatican Council paints a vivid picture of the perennial struggle: 'For a monumental struggle against the powers of darkness pervades the whole of human history. The battle was joined from the very origins of the world and will continue until the last day, as the Lord has attested.'[2] For 'there is a spirit of vanity and malice which transforms into an instrument of sin those human energies intended for the service of God and humans'.[3] That is why human energy must be purified and perfected by the power of Christ's cross and Resurrection. Such is the struggle as seen by the Second Vatican Council.

And there is cosmic energy in the Bible. It is powerfully mirrored in the apocalyptic literature where we read that 'the sun will be darkened and the moon will not give its light, and the stars will be falling from heaven, and the powers in the heavens will be shaken' (Mark 13:24).

With creation fire entered the universe and it will continue until the end of time. 'For as the lightning flashes and lights up the sky from one side to the other, so will the Son of Man be in his day' (Luke 17:24).

SHAMANISM

In a remarkable study of shamanism Mircea Eliade points out that this 'technique of ecstasy' was the religious experience par excellence of the vast area of Siberia and central Asia.[4] The shaman was the chosen person who succeeded in having mystical experiences. He was, above all, the great master of ecstasy, specializing in the trance state during which he could communicate with the dead, with demons and with nature spirits. He was also the great master of energy, performing extraordinary feats such as swallowing fire, levitating from the earth and flying through the air. But his principal function was that of healing in the community. Eliade points out that the one who has this special vocation necessarily undergoes a deep spiritual crisis that sometimes borders on madness but 'once healed of his initiatory crisis, the new shaman displays a strong and healthy constitution, powerful intelligence, and more energy than others of the male group'.[5]

While shamanism in the strict sense is a phenomenon of inner Asia, similar phenomena have been observed in North and South America, Indonesia, Oceania, Australia and elsewhere. Shamanism is alive today and coexists with established religions, as in the Philippines where some shamans are devout, if unconventional, Christians. Eliade's overall evaluation is positive. 'In a general way', he writes, 'it can be said that shamanism defends life, health, fertility and the world of "light" against death, disease, sterility, disasters and the world of "darkness".'[6]

More sophisticated but not unconnected with shamanism is the psychic energy called *chi* or *ki* about which we spoke in the last chapter.[7] This energy forms the very ground of the martial arts and the Chinese 'ways', just as it is central to Chinese medicine and the practice of meditation. The Chinese masters taught control of the energy through posture and breathing and various exercises. They knew well that *chi* could get out of control, causing psychological havoc or debilitating illness. This was particularly true in the case of people who devoted long hours to meditation. Here the danger of breakdown was very real. While a great upsurge of vital energy can bring enlightenment and overwhelming joy, the same vital energy can cause zen sickness and nervous exhaustion.

One great mystic who passed through physical and psychological tempests on his way to enlightenment is Zen Master Hakuin (1685–1769). Known as the second founder of Rinzai Zen, Hakuin is one of Japan's most beloved Buddhist saints.

ZEN MASTER HAKUIN

From the beginning Hakuin's life was tempestuous. At the age of seven or eight, while listening to a Buddhist priest talk about the torments of hell, he was shocked to the core; and at the age of fifteen

he forsook the world. Enlightenment came to him with a characteristic shock when, after practising zen at night, he heard the sound of
the temple bell — 'It was as if a sheet of ice had been smashed or a jade
tower had fallen with a crash.'[8] Shortly after this he became desperately ill with a nervous condition later diagnosed as zen sickness:

> My ears were filled with ringing as of rushing waters of a swift
> river in a deep canyon. My inward organs felt weak and my
> whole body trembled with apprehensions and fears. My Spirit
> was distressed and weary, and whether sleeping or waking I used
> continually to see all sorts of imaginary things . . . Both sides of
> my body were continually bathed in sweat, and my eyes were
> perpetually filled with tears.[9]

At this point he visited a wise old hermit called Haku-yu who gave
him advice that was to dominate his whole subsequent life. His sickness, he was told, came from excessive meditation practice. The
energy — the *ki* — was unbalanced in such wise that the heat had
gone to the upper part of his body and to the head. 'Sir,' Haku-yu
said, 'your fire heat has been going the wrong way, upwards, hence
your chronic sickness. Unless you bring it down again . . . you will
not be able to stand.'[10] In short, the secret of good health and of
sound meditation lies in bringing the heat and energy down to the
navel, down to the soles of the feet, so that the upper part of the body
is cool while the lower part is filled with fire.

This became a central point in Hakuin's teaching. 'Buddha said:
"A hundred and one diseases are healed by putting your heart under
your feet",' he was to say.[11] And concretely he advised people to sit
and breathe with the strength in the lower abdomen which is the
storehouse of energy:

> This space below my navel,
> my loins and my legs down to the soles of my feet,
> are in truth my original face.
> There is no need of any nostrils.
> This space below my navel
> is in truth my original home.[12]

This space below the navel is the *tanden*, the shrine of the divine. Elsewhere he writes of fields where jewels are produced, and he goes on:

> So, too, in human beings there is what we call the space below the abdomen and this is the treasure room where the energy is stored and preserved . . . so that life may be preserved for long years.[13]

Hakuin gave concrete instructions on how to bring down the energy. He recommended what he called 'the butter method' wherein one imagines that a deliciously scented blob of soft butter the size of a duck's egg is placed on one's head. It melts, and the moist feeling penetrates through shoulders, arms, breast, diaphragm, lungs, liver, stomach, buttocks, loins, to the very soles of the feet. In this way energy is made to pass through the whole body.

Yet there was more to Hakuin than visualization techniques for the control and direction of troublesome energy. Well versed in the Buddhist scriptures he was a master of the highest calibre, who knew from personal experience about the spiritual energy that leads to great enlightenment. He was, moreover, an artist whose enlightened calligraphy is much admired today and whose great poem, *The Song of Zazen*, still echoes through Zen temples in Japan. Above all, he was a man of radical poverty and immense compassion, a man who lived as a simple parish priest with the downtrodden peasants whom he loved and defended while he excoriated the rich and powerful. His most mystical writings, gathered in his *Sermons to Peasant Parishioners*, are precisely for the oppressed people to whom he taught his favourite *koan* — *sekishu* or 'the sound of one hand' — assuring them that in solving this *koan* they would come to the highest enlightenment. What wisdom fills his exhortation: 'So I urge you to listen to that wonderful, voiceless sound or voice of one hand — to hear the sound of the music of non-existence echoing down the valley of the utter void!'[14] These words could only be written by one who lived in the utter void, listening to the music of non-existence.

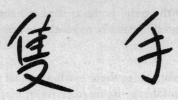

It was precisely because he was poor and detached that Hakuin was filled with the energy of wisdom, creativity and compassion. This is the lesson we must learn from his extraordinary life.

KUNDALINI

The art of awakening, controlling and guiding vital energy is highly developed in the Tantric tradition, particularly in Laya Yoga which speaks of *kundalini*, the serpent power.[15] The sanskrit word *kundala* means circular or coiled; and *kundalini* is 'she who is coiled'. The coiled serpent is indeed a powerful symbol of the explosive energy that lies dormant at the base of the human spine.

Once awakened this energy flows upward along the spinal column, the central axis of the human body, until it reaches the crown of the head where it engenders profound enlightenment, intense joy and non-dual consciousness. While the *kundalini* experience is very precious, leading as it does to transformation and rebirth, it is also fraught with psychological and physiological danger.

To understand *kundalini* it should be remembered that in Hindu thought human beings are composed of three elements: the gross or physical body; the subtle or astral body; and the self or the spirit where the human is one with the divine. In the subtle body are channels (*nadis*) or pathways of which the most important is the *susumna* extending along the spinal column. Along this the energy must flow if all is to go well. There are also *chakras* or wheels, centres of psychic energy which the *kundalini* pierces and awakens; and as each *chakra* is awakened the yogi finds new powers and new wisdom. And so the serpent power flows from the lowest *chakra*, the *mulhadara chakra* situated at the base of the spine, through *chakras* at the genital area, at the navel, at the heart, at the throat, between the eyebrows until finally at the crown of the head the union between the feminine *shakti* and the masculine *shiva* brings supreme enlightenment.

In its journey to the topmost *chakra* the *kundalini* will encounter blocks or impurities that must be burned out. This causes great suffering — suffering that is necessarily bound up with the process. Yet even greater suffering — and perhaps psychological collapse — can come about if the energy is misdirected and fails to travel along the *susumna*.

In studying this process some modern people may have problems with the so-called subtle body. After all it cannot be detected scientifically. Neither is there scientific evidence for the existence of *chakras* and *nadis* and *kundalini*. Can modern people, then, accept them?

It seems to the present writer that *kundalini* is one model for explaining a certain process and that something like this has to be postulated when one speaks about mystical experience. Does not Teresa of Avila speak about interior or spiritual senses? There is a seeing, a real seeing — but not with these eyes of the flesh. There is a hearing, a real hearing — but not with these ears of the flesh. There is a touching, a real touching — but not with these hands of the flesh. Teresa had no doubt about the existence of these inner senses (to deny them would be to contradict her most precious experience); yet no scientific instrument can locate or measure them. And in the same way Hinduism postulates a subtle body with *chakras* or centres of religious experience which cannot be scientifically observed in laboratory experiments.

Kundalini was popularized by an Indian yogi from Srinigar in Kashmir. Gopi Krishna (1903–86) had practised silent meditation for many years when he was suddenly awakened by a *kundalini* arousal that brought him into such nervous crisis that he thought he was becoming insane.[16] But he survived magnificently and found himself so transformed, so enlightened, so integrated, that he became an apostle of *kundalini* and wrote extensively about its wonderful benefits, claiming that it was nothing less than the evolutionary energy within the human person.

Gopi Krishna further argued that the *kundalini* awakening is a deeply human experience that occurs everywhere — in Christian mystics, in Sufi masters and in yoga adepts. If his way of thinking is correct, it can be said that just as shamanism, a phenomenon of Siberia and inner Asia, can be found throughout the world, so *kundalini*, carefully studied and developed in India, can be found among Tibetan Buddhists, Chinese Taoists, American Indians and elsewhere. Obviously the symbolism will be different in different places — the serpent and the *shiva-shakti* need not be universal — but the experience itself may be somehow archetypal.

Studies of *kundalini* have indeed burgeoned and claims are made that 'spiritual emergence' is no rare phenomenon. Of special importance for the renewal of mystical theology is the experience of a devout Catholic. Philip St Romain spent many hours in silent prayer before the Eucharist entering into deep, Christian contemplation. And then strange and unsettling things began to happen in his body and psyche. In vain he looked for help until finally, discovering literature about *kundalini*, he began to understand what was happening in his life. Only now did he understand the *physiological dimension* of his contemplative experience. His autobiographical book attempting to integrate *kundalini* into Christian spirituality is a fine example of dialogue at the level of mystical experience.[17]

FIRE OF LOVE

Christian prayer ordinarily begins with reflection on the Scriptures, particularly on scenes from the Gospel. At first one may use words and form mental pictures; but as time goes on prayer simplifies until one uses few words or only one word. The author of *The Cloud* suggests that one repeat a short word like 'love' or 'sin'; and other authors recommend the famous Jesus prayer. In time there arises a sense of God's presence or what St John of the Cross calls 'loving awareness' and an inner movement of love that impedes thinking. This is the beginning of contemplative prayer.

The author of *The Cloud* speaks of 'the blind stirring of love' — blind because, surrounded by a cloud of unknowing, one does not see. He also speaks of 'a naked intent of the will' — naked because it is not clothed in thought. One is silent, unable to think, caught by a movement of love which, scarcely noticeable at first, eventually becomes an inner fire.

This inner fire is the very core of Christian mysticism. It is dynamic, moving the contemplative to choose what is right in the circumstances of life. The disciple asks the author of *The Cloud* when to eat and when to fast, when to sleep and when to watch, when to speak and when to be silent; and the master, instead of giving him rules, tells him to follow the inner movement of love:

> Then that same thing that thou feelest shall tell thee when thou shalt speak and when thou shalt be still. And it shall govern thee discreetly in all thy living without any error and teach thee mystically . . .[18]

The inner fire constantly guides the contemplative and if he or she tries to disobey — 'it shall smite as sore as a prick on thine heart and pain thee full sore, and let thee have no peace but if thou do it'.[19]

Moreover the blind stirring of love is with the disciple always. It rises with him in the morning; it goes with him to bed at night. It is present while he works and while he plays. It penetrates his whole personality, making him loving and gracious and attractive to everyone. Such is the sweet energy of contemplative prayer.

Now if one asks theologically what precisely is this inner fire, St John of the Cross replies that it is the Holy Spirit.[20] Elsewhere he says that contemplation is 'an inflow of God into the soul'.[21] In the same vein Eastern Christianity speaks of the uncreated energy or of the divine energy. In short, contemplation is the work of God; it is the work of the Blessed Trinity in the human person.

And the divine fire causes suffering; for (as we have seen earlier in this book) the human person by reason of impurities is like a block of wet wood. When the fire is first applied, ugly smoke belches forth — and this is the dark night — but eventually the wood catches fire, and how powerful is the energy that then rises up! 'Thus we have raptures and transports and dislocation of the bones', writes St John of the Cross; and he further says that people 'suffer many infirmities, injuries and weaknesses of stomach.'[22]

But it was most of all his saintly colleague, the commonsensical yet ecstatic Teresa, who was torn asunder by human and divine energy.

That Teresa had her bouts of something like Zen sickness is clear from the opening pages of *The Interior Castle* where she complains that she cannot concentrate because of noises and weakness in the head. Later she writes:

> While writing this, I'm thinking about what's going on in my head with the great noise that I mentioned at the beginning. It makes it almost impossible for me to write what I was ordered to. It seems as if there are in my head many rushing rivers and that these waters are hurtling downwards, and many little birds and whistling sounds, not in the ears but in the upper part of the head . . .[23]

And yet she adds astonishingly that 'all this turmoil in my head doesn't hinder prayer or what I am saying, but the soul is completely taken up in its quiet, love, desires, and clear knowledge'.[24] Deep quiet and painful turmoil coexist.

But more important than her sickness are her ecstasies, raptures, flights of the spirit. Her whole body was raised from the ground by an energy that she could not resist. At one time she writes that she stretched out on the floor and the nuns held her down; for she was acutely embarrassed when such things happened in public. And she writes:

> Sometimes my pulse almost stops, according to what a number of sisters say who are near me . . . and my hands so stiff that occasionally I cannot join them. As a result, even the next day I feel pain in the pulse and in the body, as if the bones were disjoined.[25]

In this way she was overwhelmed by a divine energy that sometimes left her helpless.

Yet for St John of the Cross this kind of experience is not significant. He explains ecstasy by saying that a powerful spiritual communication overflows on the senses; and when the senses are purified, these extraordinary phenomena cease. 'For in the perfect', he writes, 'these raptures and bodily torments cease and they enjoy freedom of spirit without a detriment to, or transport of, their senses.'[26] And the sanjuanist teaching passed into traditional mystical theology. Joseph de Guibert writes that ecstasy is no special gift but 'is only a consequence arising from the weakness of the human organism which cannot bear the force of the divine action'.[27]

He goes on:

> Therefore when ecstasy is present it does not always and necessarily presuppose that the divine action is more intense than when it is lacking; it is dependent on other factors, both psychological and physiological. In fact, the common opinion is that in the highest degree of infused contemplation, the transforming union, ecstasies either cease altogether or become less frequent and less profound.[28]

In support of this thesis de Guibert quotes St Teresa, Auguste Poulain and Garrigou-Lagrange. Raptures and ecstasies, however significant for the masses, are no more than side effects.

As the contemplative is purified, however, a spiritual fire comes to possess the whole personality which develops into a living flame of love. St John of the Cross writes:

> Although the fire has penetrated the wood, transformed it, and united it with itself, yet as this fire grows hotter and continues to burn, the wood becomes much more incandescent and inflamed, even to the point of flaming up and shooting out flames from itself.[29]

Now the Spanish mystic writes in paradoxes of joy and suffering, speaking of the sweet cautery and the delightful wound:

> *¡O cauterio suave!*
> *¡O regalada llaga!*

This violent flame kills him, only to awaken him to eternal life:

> *Matando, muerte en vida la has trocado*

And the last stage is quiet and serene, when the flame consumes and gives no pain:

> *En la noche serena*

One is reminded of Elijah. God was not in the wind, not in the earth-quake, not in the lightning but in the sound of the gentle breeze.

EXTRAORDINARY ENERGIES

It has already been said that mystical experience is a way to the highest wisdom and that this wisdom is very simple, very ordinary, like the gentle breeze wherein Elijah discerned the presence of God. St Ignatius saw this clearly when he wrote that authentic religious experience is like a drop of water falling into a sponge. The Zen tradition also sees it clearly when it speaks of wisdom as one's ordinary, everyday mind. 'Before enlightenment, chopping wood and carrying water; after enlightenment, chopping wood and carrying water.' Sublime wisdom is simple and ordinary.

But on the way extraordinary things may happen. As has been said, those who walk this path may have raptures and ecstasies; they may see visions and hear voices. Or they may develop extraordinary psychic powers of telepathy, clairvoyance, prophecy, mind-reading, levitation or out-of-the-body experience. St Joseph of Cupertino (1603–63) was known as 'the flying friar' because of his ecstatic flights into the air. Similar stories are told of the extraordinary and saintly stigmatist Padre Pio Forgione (1887–1968) whose bilocations are well authenticated. Innumerable instances of visions, ecstasies, levitations and the rest can be found not only in the history of Catholic Christianity but also in shamanism, Hinduism and Tibetan Buddhism.

While such extraordinary phenomena have played an important part in popular Catholic devotion, particularly in the Middle Ages, they have not always been greeted enthusiastically by the institutional Church. Both Joseph of Cupertino and Padre Pio suffered grievously from the establishment; visionaries and wonderworkers have always met with a cool reception. As for the canonization process, it looks for heroic virtue and deep wisdom, down-playing visions and voices and psychic powers.

Yet the thirst for the extraordinary persists and is alive today. As the second millennium draws to a close, we are faced with a worldwide search for extraordinary phenomena. In the morning paper we read about weeping statues, heavenly visions, miraculous cures. We even hear about cosmic phenomena like the spinning sun and falling stars. Privileged visionaries, we are told, have ominous secrets about coming catastrophes; and pilgrims flock to their side to hear their wise words.[30]

Together with this there is great interest in the occult. Bookstores prominently display literature about Satanism, witchcraft and astrology. For here, too, there is powerful energy that influences today's world.

Clearly ours is an age of prophets and false prophets, of good spirits and evil spirits. How are we to distinguish one from the other?

TESTING THE SPIRITS

It has already been said that the Christian tradition recognizes a monumental struggle between the powers of light and the powers of darkness. The First Letter of St John pleads with the beloved not to believe every spirit but to test the spirits to see whether they are from God; for many false prophets have gone into the world.

And the norm by which one can test the spirits is Jesus. 'Every spirit that confesses that Jesus Christ has come in the flesh is from God' (1 John 4:2). St Paul uses a similar criterion when he tells the Corinthians to follow any spirit that cries out: 'Jesus is Lord!' and to reject any spirit that says: 'Cursed be Jesus'. In short, any power or energy that leads to the Jesus of the gospels, to Jesus of the Eucharist, to Jesus dwelling in the poor, the sick, the oppressed, the dying — any such energy is truly from God.

As for the prophets, the New Testament norm is clear: 'By their fruits you will know them' (Matthew 7:16). Look at the life of the so-called prophet. See where his or her teaching is leading. Look at the fruits. Are grapes gathered from thorns, or figs from thistles?

This wise teaching entered into the Christian tradition where a whole science of discernment, closely associated with mystical theology, gradually came to birth. More will be said about discernment as this book progresses. Here it will be enough to mention some basic principles that concern good and evil energies.

The Christian community has always taught that the forces of evil are impotent and ineffective against one who seeks God with a simple heart. Greater is the one who is in us than the one who is in the world. The devil is like a chained dog that barks and howls. If you do not get involved the dog cannot hurt you.

But people do get involved. This is particularly true of people with strong attachments or addictions. We hear much about chemical addiction; but in religious people addiction to experience and recognition can be even more consuming. Religious people can be addicted to enlightenment or consolation or visions or voices or recognition or the gift of prophecy or (most dangerous of all) to the possession of psychic powers. And addicts will do anything, or almost anything, to get what they want.

Now in the Middle Ages the tragic Dr Faustus was an archetypal figure. Addicted to occult powers and esoteric knowledge he made a pact with the devil. 'The clock will strike; the devil will come; and Faustus must be damned.' Exit Faustus with Mephistopheles. Assuredly this is Marlowe's melodrama. But is it totally irrelevant in the twentieth century? Can such things happen today? And if so, can we automatically presume that men and women with extraordinary powers and extraordinary knowledge speak in the name of God?

In judging the presence of good or evil, holy men and women of the past often acted intuitively; for discernment is a charismatic gift whereby one sees the heart. Yet certain guidelines were spelled out by St John of the Cross who is the master in discerning mystical phenomena. Let us consider what he says.

Cautious and even sceptical though he is, St John of the Cross never denies that God communicates with people through voices and visions and that these phenomena may be of the greatest significance in the mystical life. But he does insist that one must not be *attached* to such experiences. Furthermore he insists that the communications of God do their work without effort on the part of human beings. So one need not ask questions or pronounce judgment. One need not ask if the experience was from God or from Satan. Just let it be. If it was from God, it will have its effect. If it was from Satan, it can do you no harm if you do not get involved. Only do not glory in your experiences but, like St Paul, glory in your infirmity.

For the danger of deceit is very real. Satan, transforming himself into an angel of light, can cause voices and visions. By reason of his superior intellect he can at times read the future and communicate prophetic messages. Satan can meddle in the work of God.[31] Besides, there is human weakness. One must distinguish between a communication of God and its interpretation. Saintly people have made mistakes when they came to conceptualize and verbalize the imageless experience in the depths of their being.

Yet St John of the Cross is not negative. He insists that private revelations, however soul-stirring, are incomplete and imperfect. Much more important are the truths of faith. So fix your eyes on Jesus Christ in whom you will find the fullness of wisdom. In him 'are hidden all the treasures of wisdom and knowledge' (Colossians 2:3). 'In him the whole fullness of deity dwells bodily' (Colossians 2:9). To the foolish person who asks for visions and revelations God could respond:

> If I have already told you all things in my Word, my Son, and if I have no other word, what answer or revelation can I now make that would surpass this? Fasten your eyes on him alone, because in him I have spoken and revealed all, and in him you shall discover even more than you ask for and desire. You are making an appeal for locutions and revelations that are incomplete, but if you turn your eyes to him you will find them complete. For he is my entire locution and response, vision and revelation, which I have already, spoken, answered, manifested, and revealed to you, by giving him to you as a brother, companion, master, ransom and reward.[32]

Here St John of the Cross places all the emphasis on faith — pure faith, naked faith, without signs. And his doctrine is profoundly scriptural. 'An evil and adulterous generation asks for a sign, but no sign will be given to it except the sign of Jonah' (Matthew 16:4). Again we are told to be content with the words of Moses and the prophets. 'If they do not listen to Moses and the prophets, neither will they be convinced even if someone rises from the dead' (Luke 16:31). And does not Paul say that Jews demand signs and Greeks desire wisdom but he proclaims Christ crucified?

The conclusion is that what matters is faith. Blessed are those who have not seen visions nor heard voices but have believed. Such a conclusion does not do away with the age-old custom of visiting shrines and going on pilgrimage to holy places. It simply rejects any quest for the sensational and the extraordinary, asking that pious pilgrims proceed with humility, praying for world peace, for forgiveness of sins, for healing of mind and body, and for conversion of heart.

And one final consideration is important in the twentieth century. As parapsychology advances and becomes a reputable science, we come to see that many of the healers and so-called miracle workers are simply tuning in to human energies that are latent in every human being. We must, then, distinguish between the psychic and the mystic. While it is true that some mystics had extraordinary psychic powers, it is also true that some great mystics had no extraordinary powers whatever. And conversely some psychics of international repute have not been mystics, nor even religiously inclined. In short, mysticism is concerned with wisdom. Psychic powers, if present, are an inessential by-product.

CONCLUSION

An understanding of human and divine energy is of the greatest importance for the new mystical theology that is now evolving. As the dialogue goes on, Christians are learning from Asia the art of awakening and nourishing the vital energy that leads to health and to wisdom. Christians are learning about breathing and posture, about the *chakras* and the subtle body, about cosmic energy and the sublime, mystical wisdom that has accumulated through the centuries in Asia. At the same time Christians share with Asia the love of Jesus, Word Incarnate, and the wisdom of the Gospel together with the prudent teaching on discernment that has accumulated within the Christian community. Here lies the mystical path of the future.

NOTES

1. *Gaudium et Spes*, III.38.
2. Ibid., III.37.
3. Ibid.
4. *Shamanism: Archaic Techniques of Ecstasy*, Mircea Eliade, Princeton University Press (Second Printing) 1974. See also the articles on shamanism in *The Encyclopedia of Religion*, ed. Mircea Eliade, New York 1978, Vol 13.
5. *Encyclopedia of Religion*, Vol 13. 203.
6. Ibid., p. 207.
7. Eliade points to a probable link between shamanism and Taoism. 'As for the Taoists, it is probable that they elaborated and systematized the shamanic technique and ideology of protohistorical China' (*Shamanism* p. 450).

8. *Zen Buddhism: a History*, Heinrich Dumoulin, New York and London 1990, Vol. 2, p. 370.
9. *The Embossed Tea Kettle and other works of Hakuin Zenji*, trans. R. Shaw, London 1963, p. 33.
10. Ibid., p. 40.
11. Ibid., p. 41.
12. Dumoulin, p. 377.
13. Shaw, p. 67.
14. Ibid., p. 148.
15. See *Kundalinis and Chakras*, Andre Padoux in *Encyclopedia of Religion* supra cit. See also *Layayoga*, Shyam Goswawmi, Routledge and Kegan Paul, London 1980.
16. *Kundalini: the evolutionary energy in man*, Gopi Krishna, Boston and London 1967 (Revised Edition 1985). See also *The Kundalini Experience*, Lee Sannella, California 1987.
17. *Kundalini Energy and Christian Spirituality*, Philip St Romain, New York 1991.
18. *The Mysticism of 'The Cloud of Unknowing'*, William Johnston, New York 1967 (Reprinted London and California 1992), p. 122.
19. Ibid., p. 123.
20. 'This flame of love is the Spirit of its Bridegroom, which is the Holy Spirit.' *Living Flame*, 1.3.
21. *The Dark Night*, II.5.1.
22. Ibid., II.1.2.
23. *The Interior Castle*, IV.1.10.
24. Ibid.
25. *Life*, 20.12.
26. *The Dark Night*, II.1.2. St John of the Cross applies the same principle to the stigmata of St Francis: 'When the soul is wounded with love by the five wounds, the effect extends to the body and these wounds are impressed on the body and it is wounded just as the soul is wounded with love. God usually does not bestow a favour upon the body without bestowing it first and principally upon the soul' (*Living Flame*, 2.13).
27. *Theologia spiritualis ascetica et mystica*, Joseph de Guibert, Rome 1946, VII.4.439.
28. Ibid.
29. *Living Flame*, Prologue.
30. See *Powers of Darkness: Powers of Light*, John Cornwell, Penguin 1991.
31. Speaking of secrets St John of the Cross writes: 'The devil can be a great meddler with this kind of revelation' (*Ascent*, II.27.3).
32. *Ascent*, II.22.5.

TEN

Wisdom and Emptiness

CHRISTIAN AND BUDDHIST WISDOM

From what has been said it will be clear that the Christian mystic goes beyond reasoning and thinking into a realm of supra-conceptual silence — the *silentium mysticum* — where he or she no longer needs words or concepts because God is immediately present in a non-dualism of love. God is no longer 'out there' but dwells within one's self, within all created things in the vast universe. And at this time there arises in the mind and heart an inner fire, a living flame of love, that leads to the most sublime wisdom. Dark, obscure and filled with mystery, this wisdom cannot be formulated in clear and distinct Cartesian ideas. It is formless and ineffable.

As time goes on, God who was lovingly present becomes distressingly absent. Then the mystics of the apophatic tradition speak of the dark night, the cloud of unknowing, the void, the emptiness, the nothingness — they use all kinds of symbols to describe the state of one who is baffled by the immense mystery in which he or she is plunged.

Yet the apophatic mystics, usually in hindsight, state clearly that this emptiness or nothingness is supreme wisdom. The nothing is all; the darkness is light; the emptiness is fullness. On this point St John of the Cross is clear:

> God is all in himself but nothing to us
> God is light in himself but darkness to us
> God is plenitude in himself but emptiness to us

Just as the bat is blinded by the excessive light of the sun, so we are plunged into darkness by the intense light of God. Paul on the road to Damascus was blinded by such light. In short, the darkness, the nothingness, the emptiness are filled with sublime wisdom. 'Oh, guiding night, O night more lovely than the dawn!'

And in Buddhism we find a strikingly similar doctrine. The *prajna paramita* literature composed in India between 100 B.C. and A.D. 600 and consisting of thirty-eight different books, extols the wonders of wisdom in emptiness. The word *prajna* means wisdom. The word *paramita* is variously translated as perfect, transcendental, liberating: it is wisdom that leads to salvation, carrying us from the conflict and turmoil of this transient world to the other shore which is the realm of enlightenment. What is important is that this wisdom is formless, obscure, ineffable, empty. It finds expression in total silence or in an enigmatic smile like that of the Buddha of whom it is said that he preached forty-nine years and yet his broad tongue never moved. He preached by silence; he preached through emptiness.

Emptiness here is the English translation of the sanskrit *sunyata* which is translated into Chinese as *ku* or *mu*:

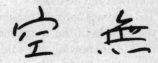

Emptiness, then, is the characteristic of Buddhist wisdom just as darkness is the characteristic of Christian wisdom in the apophatic mystics.

And Buddhist emptiness is filled with compassion. The great wisdom is rooted in the great compassion. There is even an ancient saying that emptiness equals compassion. One who falls into the void falls into a bottomless well of warm and welcoming compassion.

Toward the end of his life the wise Dr D. T. Suzuki was drawn more and more towards the compassionate one. He emphasized the affinity between Amidism and Zen Buddhism saying that without compassion 'there is no religion, no Buddhism, and accordingly, no

Zen'. To make the point he quotes a typical Zen story:

> Somebody asked Joshu, 'Buddha is the enlightened one and teacher of us all. He is naturally free of all passions (*klesa*), is he not?
>
> Joshu said, 'No, he is the one who cherishes the greatest of all passions.'
>
> 'How is that possible?'
>
> 'His greatest passion is to save all sentient beings!' Joshu answered.[1]

Such is the great compassion of the enlightened one.

And while Christian wisdom culminates in the vision of God, a union in love that gives unending beatitude, Buddhist wisdom culminates in nirvana, the ultimate state of enlightenment attained by Sakyamuni.

THE HEART SUTRA

Of special importance in China, Japan, Tibet and Mongolia is the Heart Sutra.[2] Composed probably in the fourth century of our era and formulating the heart or essence or core of perfect wisdom, this short sutra (it can be printed on a single page) is a hymn to wisdom in emptiness. It is chanted constantly in Zen temples throughout Japan, as it is studied in the lamaseries of Tibet. Originally in Sanskrit we now have seven Chinese translations, the poetic renderings of Kumarajiva (344-413) and Hsuan-Chang (600-664) being the most frequently chanted and studied.

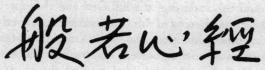

HAN   NYA   SHIN   GYO

While the Heart Sutra extols wisdom, it is not a metaphysical treatise but an exhortation or call to the compassionate emptiness and nothingness of one who has gone to the other shore. Its power lies not just in its meaning but also in the liturgical chanting (in this it resembles the Gregorian chant of medieval Europe); and the rhythmical vibrations draw one inexorably into the void, even when one does not reflect on the content. To hear this sutra recited in a Zen temple is an unforgettable experience.

The sutra opens with a picture of the Bodhisattva Avalokitesvara (in Chinese Kuan-yin and in Japanese Kannon) sitting in deep meditation:

The Bodhisattva Avalokitesvara, when practising deeply the *prajna paramita*, perceives that all five *skandhas* are empty, and is saved from all suffering and distress.[3]

Avalokitesvara, sometimes portrayed as a man and sometimes as a woman, like every bodhisattva is searching for wisdom; but her chief characteristic is that she is the compassionate one. For this reason she is much loved all over Asia where statues of the smiling, compassionate Kannon abound. Her name in Japanese means literally the one who listens to every sound:

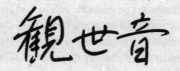

Filled with tender compassion for all sentient beings, she listens not only to the sounds of the whole world but especially to the cries of the poor and the suffering, the afflicted and the oppressed. Her appearance at the opening of this sutra makes the point that wisdom is rooted in compassion. One who would attain to supreme wisdom or enlightenment must embrace a compassion that leads to total emptiness. Only through compassion towards the whole world does one become truly wise.

Kannon is frequently portrayed with innumerable hands and faces, looking compassionately in all directions and stretching out helping hands to all who suffer:

Three aspects of Kannon's compassion should be noted.

The first is that although she is listening to the poor and suffering, her features are not twisted in anguish. On the contrary, a tiny and exquisite smile plays around her lips.

The second is that her compassion is not only directed to the welfare of the suffering in this world. More importantly, she longs for the salvation of all sentient beings and refuses to enter into nirvana until all are saved.

The third is that Kannon does not do anything. She is not an activist. She listens. And by her compassionate emptiness she becomes one with the suffering world and saves it. 'Living beings are innumerable — I vow to save them all.'

THE ENLIGHTENMENT

Immersed in deep, meditative search for wisdom — *prajna paramita* — Kannon perceives within herself a great emptiness. The five *skandhas* — that is to say, the five levels of consciousness — are totally empty; and Kannon is gazing into the void of nothingness. This is the great enlightenment, the lofty wisdom that liberates the bodhisattva from suffering and distress. And now Kannon turns to Shariputra, the favourite disciple, and says:

O shariputra, form is emptiness
and emptiness is form.

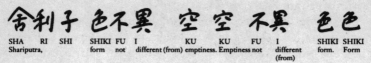

These enigmatic words are of the greatest importance for the understanding both of this sutra and of the basic Buddhist enlightenment.
To the unenlightened, form and emptiness are diametrically
opposed. The character translated as 'form' also means color (色)
and to equate it with emptiness sounds like a contradiction. Yet
Kannon, looking into the *void* sees *form*.

The point is this. To enter the void of transcendental wisdom is not
to escape from everyday life. One need not, must not, escape from the
world of forms. *One does not enter the void by blotting out all forms but by
being detached from all forms.* It is precisely by clinging to nothing that
one enters the emptiness. One stays in the world. One stays with
forms. And the process reaches a climax when one enters nirvana. For
nirvana equals samsara. That is to say, the great emptiness which is
nirvana is no different from the multiplicity of forms that constitute
samsara. Here is the central paradox of the Buddhist way.

Understanding this, one can see how Kannon listens to the cries of
the poor and yet maintains her inner peace, always holding that gentle
smile of compassion. She is aware of the forms but she is not *attached* to
the forms. Freed from anguish she is filled with compassionate love.

Having asserted that form is emptiness and emptiness is form the
sutra goes on to show in a concrete way how this can be so. All the
dharmas — all things, including the Buddhist teachings — are empty.
They do not appear nor do they disappear; they do not increase or
decrease. In short, they neither are or are not because they follow the
middle way (*madhyamika*) of Nagarjuna.[4] In emptiness there is no

form (and this contradicts the initial statement that form is emptiness and emptiness is form) and the sutra continues with its 'no, no, no' in a series of extraordinary paradoxes.

'No feelings, no perceptions, no impulses, no consciousness, no eyes, no ears. . .' Everything that Buddhism holds sacred is denied. The Four Noble Truths are negated — for there is no wisdom, no attainment, no suffering, no liberation from suffering.

If one attempts to understand these paradoxes logically one is up against a brick wall. One must recall that this sutra issues from a *deep experience of non-dualism*. Philosophers, not only Buddhist philosophers but philosophers of all persuasions, sometimes claim that they have experienced the oneness of all things. Indeed it was the experience of the oneness of reality together with the multiplicity of reality that led to the central problem of Greek philosophy: the one and the many. And Buddhism facing the same problem finds a mystical solution. Deep in meditation, liberated from fear and anxiety and illusion, the bodhisattva attains to perfect enlightenment.

The sutra ends with an encomium of perfect wisdom. *Prajna paramita* is great, holy, supreme as is the mantram in which it is expressed. Recitation of this sutra will bring liberation from suffering and distress to the millions of believers everywhere who recite it with devotion. The great transcendent mantram, the supreme mantram, the perfect mantram will carry them across the river to the other shore where they will find true peace.

Gone, gone to the other shore.
Gone to perfect enlightenment.

Even if this sutra faces a problem similar to that of Aristotle, the approach is quite different. Avalokitesvara does not reason from effect to cause; she makes no use of the discriminating intellect; her knowing is not a compound of experiencing, understanding and judging. Instead, she sits in silent meditation, losing the ego and finding true wisdom at the very core of her being. She at the same time finds the true self, the universal self which embraces the whole world. Indeed, through compassion she *becomes* the whole world in an experience of non-dualism.

THE EMPTINESS OF JESUS

In the Epistle to the Philippians Paul composes a hymn to the self-emptying Jesus. Perhaps an adaptation of a hymn that already existed in the Christian community, it is not a philosophical reflection on emptiness and nothingness but an exhortation to the Philippians, urging them to be humble and empty as Jesus was humble and empty. The pre-existent Jesus was in the form of God; but he did not cling to equality with God but emptied himself, taking the form of a slave:

$$\text{ἑαυτὸν ἐκένωσεν}$$

He emptied himself. It is interesting to note that a Japanese translation of the Bible renders emptied himself as 'he made himself nothing'[5]:

自分を無にして

Yet the humiliation of making himself nothing through the Incarnation was not enough. He embraced the crowning humiliation of human existence: death. Nor was it any death, but the most humiliating death any Jew could imagine: rejection by his own people and crucifixion at the hands of the Gentiles.

But God raised him up. He ascended into heaven and now the whole universe adores him. Every knee bends and every tongue confesses that Jesus Christ is Lord. The radical emptiness of Incarnation is followed by an equally radical glorification. And all is an expression of the greatest generosity and compassion. 'For you know the generous act of our Lord Jesus Christ, that though he was rich, yet for your sakes he became poor, so that by his poverty you might become rich' (2 Corinthians 8:9).

In this way Paul exhorts the Philippians to imitate the humility of Jesus. Indeed he exhorts them to put on the very mind of Jesus. 'Let the same mind be in you that was in Christ Jesus' (Philippians 2:5). They are to be empty with the very emptiness of Jesus.

Assuredly the emptiness of Jesus is not based on this text alone. The theme of Jesus rejected and forsaken runs all through the New Testament. The Word made flesh was rejected from the beginning. He was in the world and the world knew him not; he came unto his own and his own received him not. There was no room for him in the inn. The people chose Barabbas and cried out: 'Crucify him.' The disciples fled and left him alone. At first he was not alone because the Father was with him; but later came the heart-rending 'Lama Sabacthani' when he was abandoned by the Father. He gave his mother to the beloved disciple; and finally, when his side was pierced with a lance, there came forth blood and water. Such was the radical emptiness of the Incarnate Word who lost every drop of his blood. His total nothingness is symbolized by the cross.

And death is followed by Resurrection and glorification. 'Was it not necessary that the Christ should suffer these things and thus enter into his glory?' (Luke 24:26). Death and glorification. Emptiness and plenitude. The grain of wheat dies and bears much fruit. This is the life of Jesus.

Moreover, emptiness and fullness is the pattern of religious experience throughout the Bible. Abraham, ready to sacrifice his only son, is filled with joy as he hears the promise that his offspring will be more numerous than the stars of heaven or the sands of the seashore. Mary cries out that God has regarded the emptiness of his handmaid; so all generations will call her blessed. Blessed are the poor — the radically empty — for they shall be glorified. The merciful, the hungry and the mourners will inherit the kingdom. Just as Buddha's emptiness brings joyful enlightenment, so Christian emptiness brings the kingdom. The empty, the little children, are precisely those who inherit the kingdom.

And this emptiness fills the pages of Christian mystical writing. That there is no progress in prayer without humility is the incessant teaching of Bernard, Francis, Ignatius, Teresa and the rest. Humility is the cornerstone without which there is no Christian charity. The greatest love is shown by the total emptiness and humiliation which is death: 'No one has greater love than this, to lay down one's life for one's friends' (John 15:13).

DIALOGUE

The distinguished Buddhist scholar Masao Abe claims that the *kenosis* of Philippians is for him one of the most impressive and touching passages in the Bible, manifesting God's love in a remarkable way. 'Through the incarnation or *kenosis*, the death of Christ,' he writes, 'God the Father reveals himself in terms of unconditional love beyond discriminatory justice. The unfathomable depths of God's love is clearly realized when we come to know or believe that Christ as the Son of God emptied himself and became obedient to the point of death on the cross.'[6] He goes on to say that if the Son of God empties himself, we should also consider the self-emptying of God the Father, the *kenosis* of God himself. 'Is it not that the *kenosis* or self-emptying of the Son of God has its origins in God the Father himself, that is, the kenosis of God? Without the self-emptying of God the Father, the self-emptying of the Son of God is inconceivable.'[7] In short, the kenotic God is the foundation of the kenotic Christ.

And this, Abe continues, opens the way for dialogue with Buddhism. For the ultimate ground of reality in Buddhism is a *sunyata* that is compassionate and dynamic. 'I have suggested', he concludes, 'that in Christianity the notion of the kenotic God is essential as the root-source of the kenotic Christ, if God is truly God of love. I have also suggested that in Buddhism *sunyata* must be grasped dynamically not statically, since *sunyata* indicates not only wisdom but also compassion. Then when we realize the notion of kenotic God in Christianity and the notion of dynamic *sunyata* in Buddhism — without eliminating the distinctiveness of either religion but rather by deepening their respective uniqueness — we find a significant common basis at a more profound level.'[8] In this way, Abe prepares the ground for a stimulating dialogue between Buddhist *sunyata* and Christian *kenosis*.

For an understanding of this thesis it is important to remember that Abe, a Japanese, spent the greater part of his life in Kyoto, receiving profound influence from the Kyoto school of philosophy. He is particularly familiar with the work of the well-known philosopher Keiji Nishitani (1900–90).[9] Abe, moreover, is not just an academic. He has practised Zen assiduously (the present writer sat beside him at a *sesshin* in Kyoto) and he has assimilated the Heart Sutra not only through study but also through life — through many hours of silent *zazen* in the meditation hall. Consequently, when he speaks of emptiness he is talking about something that he has experienced at the depths of his own being.

When he enters into dialogue with the West, however, Abe sometimes indulges in Zen language that might puzzle the unenlightened. 'The Son of God', he writes, 'is not the Son of God (for he is essentially and fundamentally self-emptying).[10] Precisely because he is not the Son of God he truly is the Son of God (for he originally and always works as Christ, the Messiah, in his salvational function of self-emptying).' No doubt this impresses some Western intellectuals, but others are mystified.

Abe has developed his thesis on several occasions, inviting a response from eminent theologians.[11] Here it will be sufficient to refer briefly to the response of Hans Küng.

Küng speaks as a Western academic with a solid basis in biblical scholarship, German philosophy and traditional Christian theology. Somewhat dismayed and bewildered by Abe's Buddhist exegesis of Christian texts he asks incredulously: 'Can this ingenious Buddhist interpretation also be the Christian interpretation?'[12] Nowhere in the Bible, he maintains, is there mention of a renunciation (*kenosis*) of God himself. The Philippians hymn speaks only of the *kenosis* of Jesus Christ, the Son of God. Moreover the *kenosis* is not a permanent state but a humiliation occurring in a unique historical life and death on the cross. He concludes that Abe's thesis is unbiblical. 'As a Buddhist he discovers his own world, even on foreign Christian soil.'[13]

And yet a great Spanish mystic, a theologian of towering stature, uses language like that of Masao Abe. Without referring explicitly to the Philippians hymn, St John of the Cross speaks of the self-emptying of God the Father. Obviously writing from the depths of his own mystical experience he describes the immense love of God who communicates himself to the soul with such genuine love that no mother's affection in which she tenderly caresses her child, nor brother's love, nor friendship is comparable to it. Then he continues with astonishing words that could only come from the pen of a consummate mystic:

The tenderness and truth of love by which the immense Father favours and exalts this humble and loving soul reaches such a degree — O wonderful thing, worthy of all our awe and admiration! — that the Father himself becomes subject to her for her exaltation, as though he were her servant and she his Lord. And he is as solicitous in favouring her as he would be if he were her slave and she his God. So profound is the humility and sweetness of God.[14]

Coming from the pen of another, these words might be considered blasphemy. God is like a servant, like a slave, becoming subject to the soul for her exaltation. What shocking words! Eckhart got into trouble for less. But this is the hyperbolic language of one who, acutely aware of his own unworthiness, understood with St Paul that true love is foolishness and that the love of God is madness to human eyes.

Such is the loving *kenosis* of the Father. But to grasp the notion of emptiness in St John of the Cross it is necessary to say more.

SANJUANIST EMPTINESS

For St John of the Cross the mystical journey is an ascent to the summit of Mount Carmel. At first one may reason and reflect on passages from the gospels or from pious texts, but the time comes when one sits silently like Avalokitesvara in deep contemplation and emptiness, relishing the truth of the gospels in a supraconceptual way. St John of the Cross tells the contemplative to 'desire to enter for Christ into complete nudity, emptiness and poverty in everything in the world.' This is the way of emptiness, the way of darkness, the way of nothing. It is the immortal *todo y nada*:

> To reach satisfaction in all
> desire its possession in nothing
> To come to the knowledge of all
> desire the knowledge of nothing
> To come to possess all
> desire the possession of nothing
> To arrive at being all
> desire to be nothing.[15]

The way is nothing but the goal is all; that is to say, supreme wisdom.

The *nada* of St John of the Cross has become proverbial and he has been called 'doctor de la nada', which could be rendered 'doctor of emptiness'. Yet it is important to remember that his *nada* can never be separated from Jesus crucified. The path of nothingness is the path of Jesus himself as the saint makes clear when, after exhorting his reader to total emptiness, he adds: 'Do this out of love for Jesus Christ. In his life he had no other gratification, nor desired any other, than the fulfillment of his Father's will, which he called his meat and food.'[16] Indeed his whole doctrine is dominated by the counsel: 'Have a habitual desire to imitate Christ in all your deeds, by bringing your life into conformity with his.'[17] The sanjuanist *nada* is an interpretation of the words of the gospels: 'So, therefore, none of you can become my disciple if you do not give up all your possessions' (Luke 14:33).

And for St John of the Cross 'possessions' means not only material goods but all the things, both material and spiritual, to which human beings cling for security. In the utmost poverty of spirit one lets go of imagining and reasoning and thinking; one lets go of sensible and spiritual consolation; one lets go of the craving for enlightenment. 'Nothing, nothing, nothing. And even on the mountain, nothing.'

> *nada, nada, nada*
> *nada, nada, nada*
> *aún en el monte*
> *nada*

And one becomes nothing. 'To arrive at being all, desire to be nothing.' St John of the Cross explains these words with Thomistic metaphysics. Apart from God all things are nothing, just as they were created from nothing. Apart from God I am nothing. And when I realize deeply the nothingness of my separate being, I can in a moment of enlightenment realize that God is all. And so I must never turn toward separate being but must fix my attention on the all. The sanjuanist language is no less mysterious than that of the Heart Sutra:

When you turn toward something
You cease to cast yourself upon the all
for to go from the all to the all
you must leave yourself in all
And when you come to the possession of all
You must possess it without wanting anything.[18]

God is all: the creature is nothing.

We have seen that Avalokitesvara, rapt in deep meditation, saw that all things were empty. It is interesting to compare her vision of emptiness with that which St John of the Cross attributed to Jeremiah:

> All the creatures of heaven and earth are nothing when compared with God, as Jeremiah points out: 'I looked at the earth and it was empty and nothing; and at the heavens, and I saw they had no light' (Jeremiah 4:23). By saying that he saw an empty earth, he meant that all its creatures were nothing and that the earth too was nothing. In stating that he looked up to the heavens and beheld no light, he meant that all the heavenly luminaries were pure darkness in comparison with God. All creatures in contrast to God are nothing, and a person's attachments to them are less than nothing . . . just as darkness is nothing, and less than nothing, since it is a privation of light . . .[19]

Note that St John of the Cross here says that created things are nothing *when compared with God*. Scripture scholars would probably quarrel with his exegesis of Jeremiah but no Thomist would quarrel with his metaphysics. Separated from God all things are nothing, just as they were created from nothing. The Jeremiah of St John of the Cross had a vision of the emptiness and nothingness of separate being.

But is God himself nothing?

We have already seen that while God is all, the human experience of God can be like nothing or like darkness or like emptiness because of the excessive light of the divinity. But it must also be said that when we speak of the nothingness of God we are back with the *kenosis*. 'He emptied himself. . .' Once again we return to the Japanese translator who wrote that Christ Jesus, being in the form of God made himself nothing. Jesus, made nothing through the Crucifixion, is the supreme wisdom, as Paul states clearly in his letter to the Corinthians where he says that Christ is 'the wisdom of God' (1 Corinthians 1:24) and adds: 'For I decided to know nothing among you except Jesus Christ and him crucified' (1 Corinthians 2:2). In short, Jesus made empty and nothing on the cross is the wisdom of God.

St John of the Cross, we have seen, urges the contemplative to become nothing — 'To arrive at being all, desire to be nothing'[20] — and this is done through union with Jesus crucified, a union that comes from love and is enacted in the spiritual marriage wherein the bride and the bridegroom, the soul and the Word Incarnate, fall into a single stream of life. The human person is now divinized and, says St John of the Cross, the soul seems to be God rather than a soul and it *is* God by participation. Just as one cannot distinguish between the light and the purified pane of glass, so one cannot distinguish between the soul and God. Yet just as the pane of glass remains a pane of glass, so the soul retains its individuality.

Supreme wisdom, then, is found in a non-dualism which comes from love for, and union with, the Word Incarnate. At the top of the mountain St John of the Cross writes:

> Here there is no longer any way
> For the just person there is no way
> He is a law unto himself.[21]

Here there is non-dualism vis-à-vis the law. The law is no longer 'out there'. The mystic has *become* the law. He is a law unto himself. St John of the Cross echoes the cry of Augustine: 'Love and do what you want.'

But crucifixion is not the end. God has raised him up. If we are emptied with Christ we will be filled with Christ. If we are naked of self, we will be clothed with Christ. 'For if we have been united with him in a death like his, we will certainly be united with him in a resurrection like his' (Romans 6:5). The sanjuanist spiritual marriage is the summit of the mystical life in this world; but it reaches perfection only through entrance into eternal life. Then it is an entrance into the Trinitarian life of God. For Jesus Christ is Lord 'to the glory of God the Father' (Philippians 2:11). One with the Incarnate Word, the divinized human person calls out: 'Abba, Father!'

CONCLUSION

Masao Abe has said that when we clearly realize the notion of the kenotic God in Christianity and the notion of the dynamic *sunyata* in Buddhism — without eliminating the distinctiveness of either religion but rather by deepening their respective uniqueness — we find a significant common basis at a more profound level. This common basis finds expression in a symbol that is common to Christian and Buddhist mysticism.

At the end of *The Spiritual Canticle* St John of the Cross, writing about 'the fresh juice of the pomegranates' which the lovers will joyously drink, refers to the circular or spherical shape of the pomegranate and goes on to say that God himself 'is represented by the circular and spherical figure because He has no beginning or end'.[22]

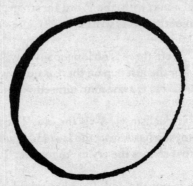

The circle is a symbol of God and a symbol of nothing. It is a symbol of the *todo y nada*.

And it is well known that the circle is an important Buddhist symbol. It symbolizes zero and infinity; it symbolizes the reconciliation of opposites; it symbolizes the emptiness that is *sunyata*. It symbolizes enlightenment.

At the same time, as Abe says so well, the uniqueness of each religion must be preserved. And the uniqueness of Christianity lies in its belief in a personal God and in a personal, historical Saviour, Jesus Christ. From this follows the practical conclusion that wisdom is personal (Christ is the 'wisdom of God') and that emptiness is personal and that nothing is personal — for the Son of God emptied himself and became nothing. And the circle is personal.

Can we, then, see a beautiful similiarity between compassionate, dynamic *sunyata* and a Father who so loved the world as to give his only son? Can the Buddhist and the Christian join hands and lead one another to transcendental wisdom?

NOTES

1. Quoted by Masao Abe in *Zen and Western Thought*, University of Hawaii Press, Honolulu 1985, p.79.
2. *The Heart Sutra* is quoted in full in the Appendix. For a translation from the Sanskrit together with the commentary see: *Buddhist Wisdom Books*, trans. Edward Conze, London 1975. See also *The Buddhist Teaching of Totality*, Garma C. C. Chang, Pennsylvania State University Press, 1974, and *Total Liberation*, Ruben Habito, New York 1989.
3. See Appendix.
4. Nagarjuna, the great Buddhist philosopher, lived in South India in the second or third century A.D. He was the founder of several Mahayana sects.
5. See *Shinkyodo Yaku*, Japan Bible Society, Tokyo 1990. Commenting on this hymn William Barclay writes: 'Every word is chosen by Paul with meticulous care to show two things — the reality of the manhood and the reality of the godhead of Jesus Christ.' (*The Letters to the Philippians*, Edinburgh, 1975). On the self-emptying of Jesus see also: *A Taste of Water*, Chwen Lee and Thomas Hand, New York 1990.
6. See *Buddhist Emptiness and Christian Trinity*, ed. Roger Corless and Paul Knitter, New York 1990, p.12. Also, *Religion and Emptiness*, Donald W. Mitchell, New York 1991.
7. Ibid., p. 16.
8. Ibid., p. 24.
9. See especially *Religion and Nothingness*, Keiji Nishitani, trans. Jan van Bragt, University of California Press, 1982.
10. *Buddhist Emptiness and Christian Trinity*, p. 13.
11. See *The Emptying God*, ed. John Cobb and Christopher Ives, New York 1990.

12. *Buddhist Emptiness and Christian Trinity*, p. 33.
13. Ibid., p. 34.
14. *The Spiritual Canticle*, 27, Introduction.
15. *The Ascent*, 1.13.11.
16. Ibid., 1.13.14.
17. Ibid., 1.13.3.
18. Ibid., 1.13.11.
19. Ibid., 1.4.3.
20. Ibid., 1.13.11.
21. See 'The Sketch of Mount Carmel'.
22. *The Spiritual Canticle*, Stanza 37, 7.

PART III

The Mystical Journey Today

ELEVEN

✳

Journey of Faith

ABRAHAM THE MYSTIC

The mystical life is a journey of radical and living faith. It is the journey of Abraham who went out from his country and his kindred and his father's house to the land that God showed him. 'Abraham believed in God, and it was reckoned to him as righteousness' (Romans 4:3). He believed in God and in him all the nations of the earth have been blessed.

Believing in the promise, Abraham left everything. So great was his faith that he was ready to offer up his only son of whom he had been told 'It is through Isaac that descendants shall be named to you' (Hebrews 11:18). How could he be the father of many nations if his only son was to die? Yet he continued to believe just as earlier 'he did not weaken in faith when he considered his own body, which was already as good as dead (for he was about a hundred years old), or when he considered the barrenness of Sarah's womb. No distrust made him waver concerning the promise . . .' (Romans 4:19). And this radical faith makes him an inspiring model for one who would practise the *nada, nada, nada* of St John of the Cross or the *mu, mu, mu* of Zen.

But why did Abraham believe? What philosophical or theological reasoning, what clear-cut evidence lay behind his abandonment of all things to surrender totally to God?

Abraham believed in God and it was reckoned to him as righteousness. He believed in God for God, just as he hoped in God for God. He believed because he believed, just as he hoped because he hoped. 'Hoping against hope, he believed that he would become the father of many nations' (Romans 4:18). Here St John of the Cross

175

points out characteristically that Abraham's faith had to undergo purification. At first he took the promise literally, thinking it would be fulfilled in his lifetime; and in this he was deceived. 'Consequently,' writes St John of the Cross, 'Abraham was misled in his understanding of the prophecy. If he had acted according to his understanding he would have erred decidedly, since the possession of the land was not to come about during his life.'[1] In other words, Abraham had to abandon *understanding* in order to walk by *faith*. And in this way he becomes a model of the pure faith, the naked faith that fills the pages of the apophatic mystics.[2]

And Abraham's faith was rewarded with an overwhelming enlightenment. At the very moment of losing all, he found all. The *nada* led to *todo*. The *mu* led to *satori*. Abraham was inundated with joy as he heard the angel repeat the extraordinary promise:

> By myself I have sworn says the Lord. Because you have done this, and have not withheld your son, your only son, I will indeed bless you, and I will make your offspring as numerous as the stars of heaven and as the sand that is on the seashore (Genesis 22:16, 17).

Here we have the pattern of all mystical experience. One loses all to find all. One dies the great death to live the great life. One is totally emptied to be gloriously filled. With great literary beauty and moving pathos the story of Abraham calls to mind the mystery of human life and the shattering paradoxes of the mystics.

Abraham is indeed a model of faith. But as we move into the third millennium we also need a theological definition of faith to guide us in the mystical path. This we find in the Second Vatican Council.

FAITH DEFINED

Following sacred Scripture and ancient tradition, the Second Vatican Council gives a definition of faith that serves as a basis for a modern mystical theology:

'The obedience of faith' (Romans 16:26; cf. 1:5; 2 Corinthians

10:5–6) must be given to God who reveals, an obedience by which one entrusts one's whole self freely to God, offering 'the full submission of intellect and will to God who reveals', and freely assenting to the truth revealed by God. If this faith is to be shown, the grace of God and the interior help of the Holy Spirit must precede and assist, moving the heart and turning it to God, opening the eyes of the mind, and giving 'joy and ease to everyone in assenting to the truth and believing it'. To bring about an ever deepening understanding of revelation, the same Holy Spirit constantly brings faith to completion by his gifts.[3]

Here every word is important. Faith is not just an intellectual assent to a number of propositions. It is an act of obedience or surrender, a commitment of the whole person; and it leads to a personal relationship with God. All-important is the clause that declares that 'the grace of God and the interior help of the Holy Spirit must precede and assist'. In other words, the act of faith is an answer to a call. 'We love because he first loved us' (1 John 4:19). No one sits down and decides to make an act of faith. 'You have not chosen me but I have chosen you' (John 15:16). Now all this is vitally important for the mystical journey, the journey of radical faith. First comes the call to abandon all things for the beloved whom one does not see. And how humbly one must wait for this call! 'Do not awaken love before its time' says The Song of Songs. 'Do not enter the sheepfold until the Good Shepherd invites you,' say the mystics. One who embarks prematurely on a journey of total renunciation may end up in broken pieces or in a psychiatric institution. How important it is to wait for the call! How important is discernment!

Having discerned the call of the Spirit, one makes a mighty resolution to overcome all obstacles and to leave no stone unturned. 'Seeking my Love', writes St John of the Cross, 'I will head for the mountains . . . I will gather no flowers; I will fear no wild beasts.'[4]

Ni cogeré las flores
Ni temeré las fieres

In the single-minded search for the one she loves, the bride pays no attention to the gorgeous flowers and the ravening beasts.

And though the cultural context is quite different, a similar resolve is found in Zen where one who has seen the footprints is ready to abandon all and die the great death in pursuit of the mysterious ox that symbolizes wisdom.

Without divine call and human commitment, then, there can be no mystical journey. But this immediately raises another question: to whom or what is the mystic committed?

And here again the Council comes to our assistance, telling us that Christian faith is obedience to *God who reveals*.

This brings up the question of revelation.

REVELATION

Speaking of revelation, the Council tells us that God 'out of the abundance of his love speaks to mortals as to friends . . . and lives among them'.[5] The key to all is the overflowing love of God.

When the Council comes to the practical communication of God it speaks first of what the scholastics called natural revelation wherein God 'gives an enduring witness to himself in created realities'.[6] Here the Council refers to The Epistle to the Romans where Paul states forthrightly that what can be known about God is plain to the Gentiles because God has shown it to them. 'Ever since the creation of the world God's eternal power and divine nature, invisible though they are, have been understood and seen through the things He has made' (Romans 1:20). In short, there is a revelation of God in nature.

Now this natural revelation through the cosmos is of the greatest significance today. Earlier in this book there was some discussion about modern science and mysticism. 'Can one go to God through science?'[7] was the question. And here the Council gives an answer. Scientists who engage in a sincere search for truth may see the revelation of God in the vast and mysterious universe or in the baffling complexities of the subatomic world; and they may cry out with the psalmist, 'The heavens are telling the glory of God; and the firmament proclaims his handiwork' (Psalm 19). This is because 'whoever labours to penetrate the secrets of reality with a humble and steady mind, is even unawares being led by the hand of God, who holds all things in existence, and gives them their identity'.[8]

But the Council speaks of another revelation that is much more significant. This is found in the history of salvation, beginning with the manifestation of God to our first parents and reaching a climax in the death and Resurrection of Jesus:

> God, after speaking in many places and varied ways through the prophets 'last of all in these days has spoken to us by his Son' (Hebrews 1:1–2). '. . . To see Jesus is to see the Father' (John 14:9). For this reason Jesus perfected revelation by fulfilling it through his whole work of making himself present and manifesting himself: through his words and deeds, his signs and wonders, but especially through his death and glorious Resurrection from the dead and final sending of the Spirit of truth.[9]

God reveals himself, then, through created realities and in a special way through the Incarnation, death, Resurrection and glorification of his Son.

St John of the Cross refers mystically and poetically to these two modes of revelation. Seeking her beloved, the bride cries out in anguish to the woods and thickets and the green meadows, asking where is the one she loves. And the creatures reply that he passed through these groves 'in haste'. Then St John of the Cross in his commentary explains these words: 'She declares that this passing was made in haste. Creatures are the lesser works of God, because he made them as though in passing. The greater works in which he manifested himself more and to which he gave greater attention, were those of the Incarnation of the Word and the mysteries of the Christian faith.'[10]

The great revelation, then, is the Incarnation of the Word by which God 'elevated human nature in the beauty of God and consequently all creatures, since in human nature he was united with them all'.[11] Here we have a sanjuanist vision of the cosmic Christ, which is particularly vivid when the saint quotes the fourth gospel: 'If I be lifted up from the earth I will draw all things to myself' (John 12:32).

While we can speak of two modes of revelation, it would be contrary to the mind of the Second Vatican Council to separate them. For the Council makes it clear that the revelation resulting from the death and Resurrection and glorification of Jesus is not just for Christians but for all men and women 'in whose hearts grace works in an unseen way'.[12] The Council continues:

> For since Christ died for all, and since the ultimate human vocation is in fact one and divine, we ought to believe that the Holy Spirit, in a manner known only to God, offers to everyone the possibility of being associated with this paschal mystery.[13]

All, then, in a manner known only to God, are called to see the cosmic Christ in the beauty of the universe.

FAITH AND UNDERSTANDING

From what has been said it will be clear that faith is no blind commitment. It has intellectual content. However, to come to an understanding of the truths of faith it is not sufficient to study the documents of revelation and give assent to what is said. The great precept of Augustine and Anselm echoes through the corridors of the Western theological tradition: *Believe that you may understand.*

Crede ut intelligas

In other words, grace, commitment, submission to God come first, and understanding follows. That is why believers can accept with ease things that sound like madness to the unbeliever. 'Paul, you are mad,' cried Porcius Festus. 'Your great learning is driving you mad.' And Paul replied: 'I am not mad, most excellent Festus, but I am speaking the sober truth' (Acts 26:24, 25). What was sober truth to the fanatical Jew was madness to the cultivated Roman. The wisdom of God is foolishness to human understanding. All this fits with the Council's teaching that 'the grace of God must precede and assist, moving the heart and turning it to God, opening the eye of the mind, and giving "joy and ease to everyone in assenting to the truth and believing it".[14] Or again the Council says: 'To bring about an ever deeper understanding of revelation, the same Holy Spirit constantly brings faith to completion by his gifts.'[15]

In short, faith is a gift which we, poor mortals, try to understand, knowing that we are confronted with mystery and that our understanding will for ever be miserable and inadequate.

PURE FAITH

At the beginning of the journey of prayer one's faith is ordinarily clothed in words and images. One may use the so-called discursive prayer of reasoning and thinking and imagining; one may reflect on scenes from the gospels. As time goes on, however, growth takes place and everything simplifies. One may repeat a word or phrase (the name of Jesus is repeated with love by millions) in an effortless way; and finally one enters into silence, a silence that is filled with the presence of God. This is the *silentium mysticum* also called infused contemplation because it is an inflow of God into the soul. Now one no longer thinks (indeed the contemplative *cannot think* or finds great difficulty in doing so) but remains in a cloud of unknowing, 'doing nothing'.

As one progresses, the sense of presence may give way to a sense of absence. Whereas one previously experienced joy and consolation, one may now experience oppressive darkness and heaviness. Whereas one was aware of the presence of God, one may now be *aware of nothing*. And this is pure faith, dark faith, naked faith. 'Blessed are those who have not seen but have believed' (John 20:29).

What a gift is pure faith! But how painful! In fact one has abandoned words and letters and distinct ideas to contemplate the great and mysterious reality toward which these words and letters and distinct ideas point. That is why St John of the Cross can paradoxically call pure faith a dark vision of God. A great grace indeed; but it does not seem like grace to the poor contemplative who now feels that she is in a dark night, in a mass of doubt, abandoned by God. 'Eli, Eli, lama sabachthani?'

Now pure faith is the ground of sanjuanist mystical theology. It is a powerful light, so bright that it blinds the soul, plunging her into profound and painful darkness just as the light plunged Paul into darkness on the road to Damascus. It is the most sublime wisdom yet it seems like ignorance because, as St John of the Cross says, 'the light of faith in its abundance suppresses and overwhelms the intellect'.[16] Hence the mystics' talk about unknowing and darkness and emptiness. Hence their insistence that the unknowing is knowing, that the darkness is light and the emptiness is fullness.

This unknowing, let us never forget, is a supraconceptual and dark grasp of the truths of faith. It would be quite erroneous to say (as some have said) that the mystics jettison the truths of Scripture and tradition in favour of a higher wisdom. For in fact they enter into a dark and supraconceptual understanding of those very truths. It would also be erroneous (or, at least, highly questionable) to say that the silence and emptiness and nothingness of Zen are the same as the silence, the emptiness and the nothingness of St John of the Cross. For the Zen mystic is entering into a supraconceptual grasp of the Buddhist sutras just as the Christian mystic is entering into a supraconceptual grasp of the truths of Christian faith.

This dark supraconceptual knowledge, then, is called 'unknowing' or 'ignorance'. Since one must put aside the ordinary rational thinking to be open to the sublime light, it is often called 'knowing by unknowing'. St John of the Cross is in the full stream of the Dionysian tradition when he writes that 'a person must advance to union with God's wisdom by unknowing rather than by knowing'[17] and he also writes:

> Hence when the divine light strikes a soul not yet entirely illumined, it causes spiritual darkness, for it not only surpasses the act of natural understanding but it also deprives the soul of this act and darkens it. This is why St Dionysius and other mystical theologians call this infused contemplation a 'ray of darkness' — that is, for the soul not yet illumined and purged. For this great supernatural light overwhelms the intellect and deprives it of its natural vigour.[18]

Note here the sanjuanist teaching that the pain and heaviness are caused not by the light of faith but by the impurity of the person receiving it. The soul, he says, is not yet illumined. Again, note that he values this darkness because it unites the contemplative with God in a way that distinct ideas and images can never do. Never can human beings have clear and distinct concepts of God, who is the mystery of mysteries. St John of the Cross gives a clear example:

> If a person were informed that on a certain island there was an animal whose like or kind he had never seen, that person would have no more idea or image of that animal in his mind than previously, no matter how much he was told.[19]

And so it is with faith. It is a powerful light which gives no *idea* or *image*. But that does not mean it gives no knowledge. Far from it. It gives sublime knowledge of another kind. One knows by unknowing. That is to say, one abandons ordinary clear knowledge for a superior dark knowledge.

St John of the Cross distinguishes again and again between *distinct and particular knowledge* on the one hand and *vague, dark and general knowledge* on the other. This latter is pure faith, and the skilled director will guide the contemplative away from distinct and particular knowledge to the vague, dark and general knowledge of pure faith.

And one more sanjuanist point must be stressed. We are to be wary not only of the distinct knowledge that is found in rational discourse but also of the distinct knowledge found in voices and visions and other mystical phenomena. St John of the Cross does not deny that such voices and visions may come from God; but he is acutely aware of the danger of deceit and he knows that even when true, this knowledge is very imperfect — inadequate to express the reality of God who is mystery.

To sum up: St John of the Cross, faithful to the apophatic tradition, tells the contemplative to *leave behind all distinct knowledge in order to enter into the vague, obscure and loving knowledge that is the cloud of unknowing*. This vague, general and loving knowledge is nothing less than a dark vision of God. It is the happy night of faith.

All this the saint expresses movingly in poetry, telling us that he entered into unknowing and, lo and behold, he understood great things (*grandes cosas entendi*); for he transcended rational knowledge (*toda ciencia transcendiendo*) and came to perfect wisdom (*la ciencia perfecta*):[20]

> *Entréme donde no supe,*
> *Y quedéme no sabiendo*
> *Toda ciencia transcendiendo*

There is a Buddhist saying that words and letters are like a finger pointing to the moon. One might change the metaphor and say that words and letters are like a finger pointing to the sun. Alas, one who looks at the sun may be blinded — plunged into profound and sometimes agonizing darkness. But the agonizing darkness is transitional. Gradually one's eyes become accustomed to the bright light and one moves towards enlightenment which comes to a climax at death and passes on into eternity.

THE GREAT DEATH

One who embarks on the journey of faith must be prepared to die the great death. This is particularly stressed in Zen. One who would come to *satori* must die. That is to say, one who would come to *satori* must be prepared to lose everything and have nothing. Hence the relentless sitting and the *mu . . . mu . . . mu*.

And at the beginning of the journey one makes a great act of faith together with a mighty resolution to go through, even if one dies. 'Even if I die . . . Even if I die . . .' Readiness to die the great death is the first thing:

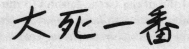

Needless to say, this is a spiritual death. Nevertheless, the thought of biological death is clearly in the background. One must sit with death. One must sit as though confronting a fierce samurai whose upraised sword might fall at any moment. In this way one is ready to die — to lose all. And dying the great death one comes to the great life.

In all this, Zen is psychologically healthy. It is an ordinary finding of psychology that fear of death lies deep in the human psyche and that most people do not advert to it — or deny it. This denial of death, we are told, is responsible for all kinds of paralysing neuroses and psychological disorders. And Zen may help some people to solve their problems. While sitting in silence, the upper layers of the mind are swept bare, and then the hidden fear comes to the surface. If one can face it, accept it, go through it, one may be truly liberated. For, Zen maintains, clinging to life and fear of death are vicious attachments that bind the human person like chains. Once liberated through spiritual death, one can accept biological death. Indeed, only one who had died a spiritual death can face biological death with equanimity.

Now Zen speaks in vivid and picturesque language of something that is common to all forms of mysticism. Abraham died the great death when he raised the knife to plunge it into the heart of his only son; and he lived the great life when he heard the voice of the angel. Then there is the beautiful and infatuated bride of the canticle. Secretly she rises from her bed and goes out into the night, her heart burning with love for him she knows so well — the lover who waits in a place where no one else appears. Truly a romantic story. But one who reads the poem mystically sees that she has a rendezvous with death. Only through the great death can she be united with her lover in a marriage that has no end. 'Unless the grain of wheat falling into the ground dies, itself alone remains. If it dies, it bears much fruit' (John 12:24).

And Jesus died the great death. His eyes were always fixed on Jerusalem where he would be handed over to the Gentiles to be humiliated and killed — and on the third day he would rise again. When the goodhearted Peter protested, Jesus rebuked him sternly: 'Get behind me, Satan! For you are setting your mind not on divine things but on human things; (Mark 8:33). How vulnerable was Jesus!

He could be tempted by his closest friend. But through the agony of Gethsemane he came to profound acceptance of the Father's will. 'The chalice which my Father has given me, shall I not drink it?' (John 18:11). Before death on the cross, Jesus died and rose spiritually.

'Before he was given up to death, a death he freely accepted, he took bread and gave you thanks. He broke the bread gave it to his disciples and said: "Take this, all of you, and eat it: this is my body which will be given up for you." When supper was ended, he took the cup. Again he gave you thanks and praise, gave the cup to his disciples and said: "Take this, all of you and drink from it: this is the cup of my blood, the blood of the new and everlasting covenant. It will be shed for you and for all so that sins may be forgiven. Do this in memory of me."'[21]

And throughout the ages in all places from the rising of the sun even to the going down thereof, the followers of Jesus have been faithful to this command. The offering is made and the people proclaim the mystery of faith:

> When we eat this bread and drink this cup
> We proclaim your death, Lord Jesus,
> Until you come in glory

Death and Resurrection are the most important events in the life of Jesus.

Some years ago a Zen master from Japan gave a *sesshin* (that is, a Zen retreat) to a group of Trappist monks in the United States. The monks duly 'sat' as well as their aching limbs permitted; and as the central *koan*, around which the whole retreat revolved, the Zen master took the death and Resurrection of Jesus. With this *koan* the monks wrestled for seven days. What a mystical theologian that Zen master was! For one who solves this *koan* enters into the heart of the Christian revelation. One who solves this *koan* comes to live the Eucharist. One sees the death and Resurrection of Jesus not just as an event that occurred far back in history two thousand years ago, but as something that is happening today, vibrantly alive in our tumultuous world. One moreover comes to make sense of the enig-matic words of Paul who speaks about carrying in his body the death of Jesus so that the life of Jesus may also be visible in his body. 'For while we live', he exclaims, 'we are always being given up to death for Jesus' sake so that the life of Jesus may be made visible in our mortal flesh' (2 Corinthians 4:11). What a *koan*! When it is solved one can cry out ecstatically with Paul: 'O grave, where is thy victory? O death, where is thy sting?' (1 Corinthians 15:55). One is truly liber-ated and enlightened.

AWAKENING

The journey of faith, then, is filled with paradox. It is a journey of bright darkness, of rich poverty and of wise ignorance. There are times when one walks in agony as though completely blind. But there are other times of light and awakening, when one knows that all is well, when, like Abraham, one is joyfully confident that the promise will be fulfilled. 'There are many kinds of awakening', writes St John of the Cross, 'which God effects in the soul, so many that we would never finish explaining them all.'[22] And all these awak-enings are foretastes of the great awakening which is the vision of God, a vision accorded to no one in this valley of tears where all walk by faith. St John of the Cross, so cautious and wary about distinct voices and visions, waxes eloquent and poetic when speaking about the awakenings that are part of the journey of faith. What, then, are these awakenings?

Just as there are two modes of revelation, one through nature and the cosmos and the other through the manifestation of God in history, reaching a climax with the sending of his only Son, so there are two kinds of awakenings. One is an acute realization of the unity of all things. A person stands, as it were, at the still point and realizes that zero equals infinity, that all is nothing and (as the Greek philoso-pher put it) that the way up is the way down. Now one grasps what is traditionally called the reconciliation of opposites and sees that the paradox of human life is altogether meaningful. In Zen this is called *kensho* or seeing into the essence of things. Awakened from illusion, liberated from anxiety one is filled with overflowing joy. Many philosophers and scientists have had this experience; others have been led to it by a wise and experienced master. It is a wonderful illumination that witnesses to the power of the human mind.

However, there are other awakenings that are more directly concerned with Christian revelation, awakenings to which no human being can lead. These concern truths about God that are ordinarily hidden. God, say the mystics, reveals some of his 'secrets' just as Paul 'was caught up into Paradise and heard things that are not to be told, that no mortal is permitted to repeat' (2 Corinthians 12:4).

The Cloud of Unknowing, speaking about the agonizing struggles, assures the contemplative that there are times when things are easy because God works all by himself — 'but not always, nor yet a long time together, but when he liketh and as he liketh; and then wilt thou think it merry to let him alone'.[23] And then he speaks of a flash of light that pierces the soul and reveals God's secrets:

> Then will he sometimes peradventure send out a beam of spiritual light, piercing the cloud of unknowing that is betwixt thee and him, and show thee some of his secrets, the which humans may not and cannot speak. Then shalt thou feel thine affection inflamed with the fire of his love, far more than I can tell thee, or may or will at this time.[24]

Here, in a flash, God reveals to the human person some of his secrets. But what are these secrets? To this question the English author gives no answer:

> For of that work that pertaineth only to God dare I not take upon me to speak with my blabbering fleshly tongue: and shortly to say, although I durst I would not.[25]

Here all is mystery.

St John of the Cross, however, is more explicit concerning the secrets. In the state of spiritual marriage 'the bridegroom reveals his wonderful secrets to the soul, as to his faithful consort, with remarkable ease and frequency, for true and perfect love knows not how to keep anything hidden from the beloved'.[26] He then goes on to speak more explicitly about these secrets:

> He communicates to her, mainly, sweet mysteries of his Incarnation and of the ways of Redemption of humankind, which is one of the loftiest of his works, and thus more delightful to the soul.[27]

Here the secrets are formulated: they are the mysteries of the Incarnation and Redemption.

And yet an element of secrecy remains; for this awakening is not vision. As death draws near, the saint still living by faith longs for clear understanding of the mysteries of which he has had a fleeting glimpse. 'The first thing a person desires to do after having come a long distance', he writes, 'is to see and converse with the one he deeply loves; similarly, the first thing the soul desires upon coming to the vision of God is to know and enjoy the deep secrets and mysteries of the Incarnation and the ancient ways of God dependent upon it.'[28]

Here the saint looks forward to the time when faith will give way to vision. Indeed, for one who has passed through the dark night and entered the spiritual marriage, death is the great awakening — for now one is slain by love. 'If the death of other people is caused by sickness or old age, the death of these persons is not so induced, in spite of their being sick or old; their soul is not wrested from them unless by some impetus and encounter of love, far more sublime than previous ones, of greater power and more valiant, since it tears through the veil and carries off the jewel which is the soul.'[29] He then goes on with a beautiful description of such a death:

> The death of such persons is very gentle and very sweet, sweeter and more gentle than was their whole spiritual life on earth. For they die with the most sublime impulses and delightful encounters of love, resembling the swan whose song is much sweeter at the moment of death . . . The soul's riches gather together here, and its rivers of love move on to enter the sea, for these rivers, because they are blocked, become so vast that they themselves resemble seas.[30]

As he himself lay dying, he asked the surrounding friars to recite The Song of Songs. 'May the vision of thy beauty be my death.' If death is the great *koan*, death is also the great awakening.

CRISIS OF FAITH

It need hardly be said that there is a great crisis of faith in the modern world. This is particularly evident in Europe and America where whole countries or whole segments of the population seem to have abandoned all religious practice. The Second Vatican Council was stating the obvious when it said that 'atheism must be accounted among the most serious problems of this age, and is deserving of closer examination'.[31]

Thinking people realize that at the root of the crisis of faith is a cultural problem. Modern culture does not support faith. Whereas the poetry of Dante and Shakespeare, the art of da Vinci and Michelangelo, the music of Mozart and Beethoven supported and nourished faith, modern drama, modern novels, modern scientific culture have little place for an irrelevant and outdated God. The death of God is still in the air.

Now the Second Vatican Council saw that its task was to evangelize the culture and to help construct a more human world. Pope John, convoking the Council spoke of the gravity of the situation. 'It is a question', he added, 'of bringing the modern world into contact with the vivifying and perennial energies of the Gospel.'[32] This became one of the chief aims of the Council which called particularly lay men and women to humanize the temporal order, 'to permeate the whole of society with the spirit of the Gospel'[33] and 'to see that the divine law is inscribed in the life of the earthly city'.[34]

However, as the twentieth century draws to a close we see that this noble objective has not yet been accomplished. It may take centuries. And it can only be done through dialogue and collaboration with people of other faiths and with scientists — people who are anxious to ensure that the divine law is inscribed in the life of the earthly city.

In the meantime, what can we say except that contemporary men and women are called to pure faith, naked faith, dark faith? This is the modern religious challenge. Without the support of culture, modern people are called to believe in God for God, to believe because they believe. In short, they are called to mystical faith. Karl Rahner was not wrong when he said that the Christian of the future would be a mystic or nothing. We might add that the inspiring model for Jew and Gentile alike is Abraham the mystic.

NOTES

1. *Ascent*, II.19.
2. Of the contemplative St John of the Cross writes: 'Like a blind man he must lean on dark faith, accept it for his guide and light, and rest on nothing of what he understands, feels or imagines' (*Ascent* II.4). Abraham finally comes to such faith.
3. *Dei Verbum*, 1.5.
4. *Spiritual Canticle*, 3.
5. *Dei Verbum*, 1.2.
6. Ibid., 1.3.
7. See chapter 7.
8. *Gaudium et Spes*, 1.3.36.
9. *Dei Verbum*, 1.5.
10. *Spiritual Canticle*, 5.3.
11. Ibid., 5.4.
12. *Gaudium et Spes*, 1.1.22.
13. Ibid.
14. *Dei Verbum*, 1.5.
15. Ibid.
16. *Ascent*, II.3.1.
17. *Ascent*, 1.4.5.
18. *The Dark Night*, II.5.3.
19. *Ascent*, II.3.2.
20. *I entered into Unknowing*, Stanza 1.
21. From the Second Canon of the Roman Liturgy.
22. *The Living Flame*, 4.4.
23. *The Cloud of Unknowing*, C. 26.
24. Ibid.
25. Ibid.
26. *Spiritual Canticle*, 23.
27. Ibid.
28. *Spiritual Canticle*, 37.
29. *The Living Flame of Love*, 1.30.
30. Ibid.
31. *Gaudium et Spes*, 1.19.
32. *Humanae Salutatis*, December 25, 1961.
33. *Ad Gentes*, 11.15.
34. *Gaudium et Spes*, IV.43.

TWELVE

Via Purgativa

THE THREEFOLD PATH

Ancient mystical tradition speaks of a threefold path to God:

> *Via Purgative — the way of beginners*
> *Via Illuminativa — the way of proficients*
> *Via Unitiva — the way of the perfect*

These three ways of following Christ, who is the Way, culminate in a Trinitarian experience wherein, identified with the Son and filled with the Spirit, one cries out: 'Abba, Father!'

In human living, the three ways are not separate paths. They merge, overlap, intertwine — none can be taken in isolation from the others. While the *via purgativa* or way of purification is the path of beginners, ancient tradition was aware that it lasts until death and beyond. 'For no human being will be justified in his sight' writes Paul (Romans 3:20). 'How can mortal be just before God?' asks Job (Job 9:2). No human being comes into the presence of the all-holy God without passing through the fire of purification.

CONVERSION OF HEART

The *via purgativa* begins with conversion of heart. Recognizing one's weakness and moved by divine grace one turns from sin which is evil to God who is love. The practical author of *The Cloud of Unknowing* describes two stages on the road of conversion; and he does so with the following down-to-earth metaphor.

A man looks in the mirror and sees an ugly smudge on his face. What does he do? He immediately runs to the well to wash himself. And the English author goes on: 'If this smudge be a particular sin, the well is Holy Church and the water is confession, with the circumstances thereof.'[1] In other words, the man runs to the Church, confesses his sins with contrite heart, receives absolution and is thoroughly cleansed. Clearly the author believes that reconciliation comes to the repentant sinner through the sacrament of the Church; and, interestingly enough, he finds a place for the sacrament of cleansing at the very pinnacle of the mystical life. In this he is like Teresa of Avila. For the great Carmelite there could be no substitute for the wise and learned confessor who absolves from sin (for even the holiest mystic can fall face down in the mud), who helps discern the Spirit and who guides the contemplative in a perilous path that is filled with pitfalls and hidden traps.

However, the author of *The Cloud* continues, the ugly smudge may not be any particular sin; it may be an inclination to sin, a root of sin, a stirring or inner movement towards evil. Again the man runs to the well; but this time 'the well is merciful God and the water is prayer and the circumstances thereof'.[2] For confession will not remove the roots of sin whereas contemplation will. This the author states clearly when he says: 'For in this work (i.e. contemplation) a soul drieth up in itself all the root and ground of sin that always remains in it after confession, be it never so busy.'[3] Note that he says 'drieth up'; for he also says clearly that all the contemplation in the world will not remove the roots of sin completely.

Now underlying this simple metaphor lies an important theology of sin and purification. The English author, like Eckhart, Tauler and St John of the Cross, was a devoted disciple of St Thomas Aquinas. He follows the Thomistic teaching that, while sin is washed away in the blood of Christ, *concupiscence remains, the inclination to sin remains, the appalling disorder remains.* Through the sacrament received with contrite heart, sin is forgiven and the image of God restored so that the person truly becomes a temple of the Holy Spirit. But the debilitating effects of sin — both original sin and personal sin — remain and will remain until death.

Consequently, when one who has received the sacrament turns to prayer and embarks on the way of purification, the person does not do so in order that sins may be forgiven (for they are already forgiven) but in order that he or she may be liberated from the shackles of concupiscence — that is to say, from the inclination towards evil, the inordinate affections, the uncontrollable appetites, the craving, the clinging, the attachments and all those debilitating tendencies that we moderns call compulsive addictions, infantile fixations and ungovernable drives. In short, the path of purification is a path of liberation.

And the realistic author of *The Cloud* knows that the *via purgativa* lasts until the grave. In his inimitable and picturesque way he tells his disciple that all the fasting, all the watching, all the self-discipline in the world will not remove the human inclination to sin:

> Fast thou never so much, watch thou never so long, rise thou never so early, lie thou never so hard, wear thou never so sharp; yea, and if it were lawful to do — as it is not — though thou put out thy eyes, cut thy tongue out of thy mouth, stop up thine ears and thy nose never so fast, shear away thy privy parts, and do all the pain to thy body thou couldst think; all this would help thee right nought. Yet will stirring and rising of sin be in thee.[4]

Here the English author teaches graphically the traditional doctine that human weakness remains until death: men and women are capable of sin until their last breath. The scholastics, it is true, taught that certain privileged people, such as the Virgin Mary and the apostles, were 'confirmed in grace' and incapable of sin; but they maintained that such an unmerited grace was rarely granted to weak humanity. The English author stands on solid ground. Such is the human condition.

THE JOURNEY

Anyone familiar with Asian thought will immediately see the parallels between the Christian way of purification and the Hindu and Buddhist ways of liberation. The Second Vatican Council, telling us that Hinduism seeks release from the anguish of the human condition, speaks respectfully of Hindu ascetical practices, deep meditation and loving flight towards God. The Council also describes how Buddhism 'teaches a path by which men and women, in a devout and confident spirit, can either reach a state of absolute freedom or attain supreme enlightenment by their own efforts or by higher assistance'.[5] It then exhorts the faithful to enter into dialogue with the followers of other religions and to cooperate with them.

At the same time we must never overlook the differences and the unique characteristics of each religion. And the whole Christian tradition proclaims that the *via purgativa* is primarily a following of Christ who said, 'If any will come after me, let them deny themselves and take up their cross and follow me' (Matthew 16:24). Jesus walked the path of purification, not for his own sins (for he was without sin) but for the sins of humankind. He is the lamb who takes away the sins of the world. He is the suffering servant of Isaiah: 'But he was wounded for our transgressions, crushed for our iniquities. . . and by his bruises we are healed' (Isaiah 53:5). And Paul startles us by saying: 'For our sake he made him to be sin who had no sin, so that in him we might become the righteousness of God' (2 Corinthians 5:21).

And as Jesus walked the path of purification for the sins of the world, so the Christian mystics, cooperating in his work of redemption, have walked the path of purification not just for their own sins but for the sin of the world. They have made their own the words of Paul: 'I make up what is wanting to the sufferings of Christ for his body which is the church' (Colossians 1:24). This cosmic dimension of purification radiates from the lives of some mystics of our time. Thérèse of Lisieux, Padre Pio, Edith Stein — all had a sense of the world and its need of redemption. Then there is the saintly Takashi Nagai of Nagasaki, who united in himself the way of purification and the way of sacrifice. He offered himself with Jesus to the Father for peace in the whole world.

But to understand the *via purgativa* we must consider, however briefly, the scriptural and theological background.

SIN AND REDEMPTION

For the two short millennia of Christian history, the story of sin and redemption has given rise to innumerable theological controversies. Heated debates have raged, and continue to rage, over questions of original sin, justification, grace, free will, good works, predestination and almost every facet of this vital story. Nor are there any indications that the debate is coming to an end.

Mystical theology, however, being a practical or pastoral science that aims primarily at directing people in the ways of prayer, has not found it necessary to enter deeply into these controversies. Since the fourteenth century it has simply followed St Thomas Aquinas, while appealing to certain basic scriptural texts. And the Second Vatican Council has further developed the traditional doctrine.

Of central importance is the story of the Fall.

Created in the image of God who is their friend, our first parents walk naked and unashamed in the garden of delight. They are unified within themselves and live in harmony with the birds of the air and the beasts of the fields. Above all, they are united with God; and they are good, very good. The scholastics called their condition the state of innocence or the state of integrity or the state of original justice. St Thomas said that Adam was truly contemplative.

Then came the crash. Deceived by the wily serpent they eat the forbidden fruit, only to find that they are naked, ashamed, afraid, broken and scattered. They have lost union within themselves, with one another and with God. They have lost their contemplation. Now they know evil — very soon their son Cain will rise up in anger and murder his brother — and, expelled from paradise, they must live a life of suffering. Eve will have intolerable pains in childbirth; she will long for her man — and he will rule over her. Adam will toil and sweat as he tills the earth. And both will die. They will return to the dust from which they came.

Nor is this the whole story. The universe has fallen with the man and the woman. The serpent is cursed; the ground is cursed: 'Thorns and thistles it shall bring forth for you' (Genesis 3:18). The garden of Eden is no more than a nostalgic dream. This condition the scholastics called the state of fallen nature or the state of original sin. And into this state we, poor banished children of Eve, are born. 'Human beings', writes the Second Vatican Council, 'are split within themselves. As a result, all of human life, whether individual or collective, shows itself to be a dramatic struggle between good and evil.'[6]

But all is not lost. A redeemer will come. 'I will put enmity between you and the woman, and between your offspring and hers. . .' (Genesis 3:15). Early Christian tradition saw the woman as Mary, the mother of Jesus, and statues of Mary crushing the serpent with her heel abound. But however one interprets the text, it tells us that a Messiah will come and save his people from their sins.

The Genesis story is central to the theology of St Paul, who speaks of sin through Adam and redemption through Jesus Christ — a theme that is taken up by the author of *The Cloud* who insists that Adam fell from contemplation through sin and we are restored to contemplation through the grace of Jesus Christ. Paul had indeed a deep sense of sin — both the sin that reigned in his own members and the sin that reigned in the surrounding world. 'For I do not do the good I want' he cries, 'but the evil I do not want is what I do' (Romans 7:19). Who will rescue him? 'Thanks be to God through Jesus Christ Our Lord' (Romans 7:25). And the whole society — the Roman Empire in which he lived — was corrupt. 'They were filled with every kind of wickedness, evil, covetousness, malice . . .' (Romans 1:29). But again, all is not lost. 'For while we were weak, at the right time Christ died for the ungodly' (Romans 5:6). And in this the love of God appeared. We are purified, washed clean in the blood of Christ.

CONCILIAR OPTIMISM

The Second Vatican Council repeats the same story. It speaks of 'the world which the Christian sees as created and sustained by its Maker's love, fallen indeed into the bondage of sin, yet now emancipated by Christ'.[7] And the Council continues:

He was crucified and rose again to break the stranglehold of personified evil, so that the world might be fashioned anew according to God's design and reach fulfilment.[8]

Through the death and Resurrection of Christ the human race is redeemed.

The Council, remarkably optimistic about the human condition and the achievements of the modern world, is nevertheless acutely conscious of the ravages of sin. It speaks of the dramatic struggle between good and evil, reminding us that 'the call to grandeur and the depths of misery are both part of human experience'.[9] It also speaks of the monumental struggle against the powers of darkness, in words that remind us of the Pauline teaching that our struggle is 'against the cosmic powers of this present darkness, against the spiritual forces of evil in the heavenly places' (Ephesians 6:12).

At the same time the Council, radiant with the virtue of hope, stresses the fact that human beings, created in holiness, are now redeemed and restored to a genuine, if imperfect, holiness:

> The final age of the world has already come upon us (cf. 1 Corinthians 10:11). The renovation of the world has been irrevocably decreed and in this age is already anticipated in some real way. For even now on earth the Church is marked with a genuine though imperfect holiness.[10]

When the Council says 'the Church' it means the people of God — 'and there belong to it or are related to it in various ways, the Catholic faithful as well as all who believe in Christ, and indeed the whole of humankind'.[11] In short, the whole of humankind is marked with a genuine if imperfect holiness. Does this mean that our modern world with all its grisly episodes and inhuman wars is basically holy? This is an extraordinarily optimistic claim.

When it comes to the practical path of purification, the Council is again very clear:

> Hence if anyone wants to know how the unhappy situation can be overcome, Christians will say that all human activity, constantly imperilled by human pride and deranged self-love, must be purified and perfected by the power of Christ's cross and Resurrection.[12]

This is an accurate description of the *via purgativa*.

Now two points of the conciliar doctrine are of the greatest practical importance for one who would walk the mystical path.

The first is the Council's teaching that the human race is already redeemed. We are good; we are holy — even if imperfectly so. The Christian sense of sin is far removed from the gnawing guilt that tortures so many modern people and keeps psychiatrists in business. The authentically Christian sense of sin is like the sentiment of Peter who, overwhelmed by the holiness of Jesus, cried out: 'Depart from me, O Lord, for I am a sinful man' (Luke 5:8) or like the statement of the Russian pilgrim who with overflowing joy prayed, 'Jesus, be merciful to me, a sinner!' Or like Paul himself who shouted triumphantly, 'When I am weak, then I am strong' (2 Corinthians 12:10).

The second point is that all is well and all will be well. One who travels the mystical path experiences storm and tempest and earthquake. Such a one needs to be reminded of the words of Juliana of Norwich that all will be well and all will be well and all manner of thing will be well. 'For the one who is in you is greater than the one who is in the world' (1 John 4:4).

THE FOLLOWING OF CHRIST

Giving instructions to beginners about entering the night of the senses, St John of the Cross stresses the imitation of Christ:

> First, have a habitual desire to imitate Christ in all your deeds by bringing your life into conformity with his. You must then study his life in order to know how to imitate him and behave in all events as he would.[13]

Here it is interesting to note that St John of the Cross does not begin by advocating long hours of silent prayer nor does he tell the would-be contemplative to spend many years in solitude. More important is the imitation of Jesus in daily life — 'behave in all events as he would'. This point is made even more forcefully by his saintly collaborator Teresa of Avila. For all her ecstasies and flights of the spirit, Teresa always insists that imitation of Jesus and love of neighbour are more important than sublime experiences in prayer. She would tell her sisters not to bother about the mystic heights but to sweep the corridors, clean the windows and wash the dishes. 'Not everyone who says to me, "Lord, Lord," will enter the kingdom of heaven, but only the one who does the will of my Father in heaven' (Matthew 7:21). And this commonsense teaching entered into subsequent mystical theology which held that Christian perfection consists in charity, listing among the adversaries those who held that perfection consists in sublime contemplation.[14]

At the beginning, then, St John of the Cross tells contemplatives to look at the Jesus of the gospels and bring their lives into conformity with his; and he expects them to study and practise some discursive prayer. When, however, he speaks to proficients who are entering the second night, he advocates a different approach to the imitation of Jesus. Now instead of looking at Jesus outside, one allows the life of Jesus to well up from within in accordance with the Pauline text: 'I live, now not I, but Christ lives in me' (Galatians 2:20). Now one forms no pictures of Jesus nor does one reason and think; one remains in contemplative silence allowing God, who dwells within, to act. Here the eucharistic texts of the fourth gospel are very meaningful. 'Those who eat my flesh and drink my blood dwell in me, and I in them' (John 6:56).

In this way one lives the life of Jesus who sweated blood in Gethsemane and cried out, 'Lama Sabacthani.' St John of the Cross had an acute sense of the passion of Jesus – indeed love for the cross of Jesus is the key to understanding his life, his poetry and his *nada, nada, nada*. And he asserts that mystical death is patterned on the death of Jesus who accomplished the most marvellous works of his whole life by dying:

At the moment of his death he was certainly annihilated in his soul, without any consolation or relief, since the Father left him that way in innermost aridity ... He was thereby compelled to cry out: 'My God, my God, why have you forsaken me?' (Matthew 27:46). This was the most supreme abandonment, sensitively, that he had suffered in his life ... He was most annihilated in all things: in his reputation before men, since in beholding him die they mocked him instead of esteeming him; in his human nature, by dying; and in spiritual help and consolation from the Father, for he was forsaken by his Father at that time. . .[15]

This is the *nada* of Jesus. And it is proposed as the *nada* of one who would follow Jesus. 'Accordingly,' writes St John of the Cross, 'I should not consider any spirituality worthwhile that would walk in sweetness and ease and run from the imitation of Christ.'[16]

BLESSED ARE THE POOR

For the desert father, as for the mystics, the first step in the journey is poverty of spirit. 'How happy are the poor in spirit' (Matthew 5:3).

$$\mu\alpha\kappa\acute{\alpha}\rho\iota\omega\iota\ o\acute{\iota}\ \pi\tau\omega\chi\omega\acute{\iota}\ \tau\tilde{\omega}\ \pi\nu\varepsilon\acute{\nu}\mu\alpha\tau\iota$$

And active purification is based on this central teaching of the Gospel. Poverty of spirit means total poverty — destitution. It is the *kenosis* of Jesus, who emptied himself in the most radical way. It is the *mu* of Zen. It is the *nada* of St John of the Cross. How happy are the poor! The road to happiness is that of self-emptying, of losing everything, of dying the great death. This poverty runs all through the Sermon on the Mount which speaks of the poverty of those who are meek and merciful, those who are insulted and rejected, those who have nothing and become nothing. Blessed are the poor for they shall be enlightened. Blessed are those who have nothing for they shall have everything. 'Sell all you have and give to the poor and . . . come follow me' said Jesus; and here all means all. 'So therefore none of you can become my disciple if you do not give up all your possessions' (Luke 14:33). In this journey, be it noted, one gives up the clinging, the craving, the attachment, the possessiveness — not the thing itself. For all the things that God made are good and beautiful and true. That is why at the summit St John of the Cross can cry out: 'Now that I least desire them, I have them all without desire.' That is why St Francis of Assisi could glory in nakedness of spirit. That is why innumerable Zen monks have laughed uproariously and talked atrocious paradox when they had nothing.

As one gives up all clinging, one gives up all anxiety. 'Do not be anxious!' echoes through the pages of the gospels and through the writings of the mystics. For anxiety is a subtle form of attachment. We cling to our anxieties for security. We cling to our anxieties so as not to fall into the void. But the Gospel, like the *dharma*, tells us to let go of anxieties — when we fall into the void we will be liberated.

Moreover, poverty of spirit in the mystical life demands that one let go of reasoning and thinking and imagining. It demands that one let go of spiritual consolations and ecstasies. It demands that one let go of voices and visions and beautiful experiences. It demands above all that one renounce the fascination of psychic powers. *Nada, nada, nada, mu, mu, mu.* All this leads to great liberation, profound enlightenment and authentic joy.

At the beginning of his great work on active purification, *The Ascent of Mount Carmel* where he describes in detail the path of renunciation, St John of the Cross tells us that inordinate desires torment us, darken and blind us, defile us, weaken us and make us lukewarm in the practice of virtue. And then he goes on with his relentless nothing, nothing, nothing which leads to spiritual death. So radical is the doctrine that even the bravest might tremble and ask: Is not the whole thing depressing? Is it not psychologically absurd?

Yet one who perseveres to the end finds sweet reasonableness. For the saint says clearly that it is only possible to give up attachment to created things if one has another, better love — love for one's heavenly bridegroom:

> A more intense enkindling of another, better love (love of one's heavenly bridegroom) is necessary for the vanquishing of the appetites and denial of all the pleasure. By finding satisfaction and strength in this love, a person will have courage and constancy to deny readily all other appetites.[17]

Here, then, in the midst of appalling asceticism, the beautiful and lovesick bride appears again. Searching for her lover she gladly sacrifices everything and makes light of the *nada, nada, nada.* St John of the Cross goes on to explain the love affair in cold, scholastic language:

For the sensory appetites are moved and attracted toward sensory objects with such craving that if the spiritual part of the soul is not fired with other more urgent longings for spiritual things, the soul will be able neither to overcome the yoke of nature nor enter into the night of sense; nor will it have the courage to live in the darkness of all things by denying its appetite for them.[18]

From this we can see that the key to understanding the radical sanjuanist asceticism is love of the bride for her heavenly bridegroom — the love that makes her go out into the night, leaving all things, with no other love than the one that burns in her heart.

This love accomplishes the passive purification. It is not acquired but infused. It is the gift of God poured into the human heart. It is the living flame of love. It is The Cloud of Unknowing. It is the dark night.

Yet St John of the Cross, aware that his doctrine may sound negative and destructive, returns several times to the theme of death and new life.

DEATH AND NEW LIFE

As has been said, St John of the Cross sounds negative, and even destructive, to those who do not get his total message. The saint himself sees this problem and faces it squarely. 'Observing how we annihilate the faculties in their operations', he writes, 'it will perhaps seem that we are tearing down rather than building up the way of spiritual exercise.'[19] And he goes on: 'This would be true if our doctrine here were destined for beginners who have to prepare themselves through these discursive apprehensions.'[20]

In other words, the work of purification is a process. At the beginning one must reason and think and use one's faculties until the time comes to let go of all natural activity to *make room for the inflow and illumination of the supernatural.*[21] It is very important (and this is stressed by all mystical writers) to stay with reasoning and thinking until the time comes to open one's heart to the silent inflow of the Spirit. One who abandons use of the faculties before the gift of love has come is like one who sells everything before having seen the treasure in the field. Such a one is greatly to be pitied.

St John of the Cross further develops this doctrine. Speaking about the memory and what another author calls the cloud of Forgetting, he writes: 'The annihilation of the memory in regard to all forms is an absolute requirement for union with God.' The word 'annihilation' is indeed disturbing; and the saint, recognizing this, continues:

> Someone may object that this doctrine seems good, but that it results in the destruction of the natural activity and use of the faculties, and that man then lives in oblivion like an animal and, even worse, without remembrance of natural necessities and operations. The objection will be made that God does not destroy, but perfects, nature, and that the destruction of nature is a necessary consequence of this doctrine.[22]

St John of the Cross concedes that a person who walks this path may for a time be somewhat absentminded and eccentric. 'He will forget to eat and drink, or fail to remember whether or not he performed some task, or saw a particular object, or said something — all because of the absorption of the memory in God.' But all this is temporary. In fact, the old way of thinking is dying and a new way of thinking is coming to birth. When the process is complete, these people remember what they should remember and forget what they should forget. 'For God's Spirit makes them know what must be known and ignore what must be ignored, remember what ought to be remembered . . . and forget what ought to be forgotten, and makes them love what they ought to love and helps them from loving what is not God. Accordingly, all the first movements of these faculties are divine. And it is no wonder that the movements and operations of these faculties are divine, for they are transformed into divine being.'[23] In this way there is death and resurrection. 'Was it not necessary that the Messiah should suffer these things and then enter into his glory?' (Luke 24:26). There is a terrible inevitability, a terrible necessity, about death for one who would enter into glory. And the pattern of religious experience in Zen is quite similar. The great Zen masters asked their disciples to die. Sometimes they even killed them spiritually. They asked for nothing short of total annihilation — *mu, mu, mu.* And this death leads to the glory of enlightenment. It also leads to a state where one's true self acts spontaneously without thinking and reasoning and planning. One eats because one eats, walks because one walks, talks because one talks, remains silent because one remains silent. All is done in fidelity to the core of one's being.

One more passage is worth mentioning. St John of the Cross is speaking about the lofty wisdom of God which makes the bride forget all things. 'And it seems that her previous knowledge, and even all the knowledge of the world, in comparison with this knowledge is pure ignorance,' he says, as though downgrading scientific knowledge.[24] Yet he immediately corrects himself, saying that acquired knowledge is not destroyed but perfected. 'When a faint light is mingled with a bright one, the bright light prevails and is that which illumines. Yet the faint light is not lost, but rather perfected, even though it is not the light which illumines principally.'[25]

From all this it will be clear that the way of purification is dynamic and creative. It is not just a question of pulling up the roots of sin but of creating a new person and of going towards a goal. What, then, is the goal of the mystical life?

THE GOAL

To understand the goal of the *via purgativa* one must return to Genesis. After the sin, Adam and Eve lost their contemplation and inner unity. Divided, scattered, anguished, they were driven from paradise to live in exile. And we, their children, live in this state of fallen nature.

Now the mystical tradition taught that contemplation was a 'one-ing' exercise (the terminology is from *The Cloud of Unknowing*) whereby the contemplative becomes one, returning to the state of innocence of the Garden of Eden. Of the soul approaching mystical marriage St John of the Cross writes that she has no knowledge of good and evil, like our first parents before they ate the forbidden fruit:

> In a way the soul in this state resembles Adam in the state of innocence, who did not know evil. For she is so innocent that she does not understand evil, nor does she judge anything in a bad light. And she will hear very evil things and see them with her own eyes and be unable to understand that they are so, since she does not have within herself the habit of evil by which to judge them; for God, by means of the perfect habit of true wisdom, has destroyed her habitual imperfections and ignorances which include the evil of sin.[26]

In this way the contemplative comes to a deep state of inner peace, innocence and integrity.

However, modern people probably prefer to see the contemplative life as a journey forward rather than a journey back. All the more so since the happy fault of Adam brought a redeemer who would merit an even greater grace than a return to paradise. Jesus invites the human race, whether individually or collectively to divinization — to the *theosis* (θέωσις) of the Greek Fathers and the eastern mystics. He invites men and women to be 'participators in the divine nature' (2 Peter 1:4).

St John of the Cross speaks of a union of love whereby one lives the life of God. 'When there is union of love', he writes, 'it is true to say that the Beloved lives in the lover and lover in the Beloved. Love produces such likeness in this transformation of lovers that one can say that each is in the other and both are one.'[27] He then quotes St Paul and comments:

> In saying, I live, now not I, he meant that even though he had life it was not his because he was transformed in Christ, and that it was divine more than human. He consequently asserts that he does not live, but that Christ lives in him. In accordance with this likeness and transformation, we can say that his life and Christ's life were one life through union of love.[28]

The climax of the process is the Trinitarian experience already mentioned, whereby identified with the Son and filled with the Spirit, one cries out: 'Abba, Father!'

St John of the Cross goes on to point out that the Pauline transformation reaches a climax after death. 'Transformed in God,' he writes, 'these blessed souls will live the life of God and not their own life — although, indeed, it will be their own life, because God's life will be theirs. Then they will truly proclaim: "We live, now not we, but God lives in us."'[29]

Mystical purification, then, begins with the imitation of Jesus and develops into living the life of Jesus. It is an emptying of one's self — the *kenosis* of St Paul — to be identified with Jesus and filled with the Spirit who then cries, 'Abba, Father!' But this is a long, long journey, and one who undertakes it is like the lovesick bride. Lost in the night and wounded by the guards, she cries out in agony as she searches for her lover. She needs wise guidance and tender help; she needs encouragement. And mystical theology attempts to give such guidance through careful study of the tortuous ways of this perilous, if sublime, journey.

THE BRIDE

It is night. The bride is in bed. She is asleep — yet she is not asleep. Deep down, at the very core of her being, lies a silent love that makes her aware, and she can sing: 'I slept, but my heart was awake' (Song of Songs 5:2). It is as though she said: 'I was not reasoning or thinking or imagining. My faculties were asleep. But at the centre of my being I was mystically aware because I was in love.'

And then comes the knocking on the door. Her lover has come. Knock! Knock! Knock! 'Open to me, my sister, my love, my dove, my perfect one.' He will take no refusal — 'my head is wet with dew, my locks with the drops of the night.' And the persistent knocking goes on.

Within the breast of the bride rages an anguishing conflict. What is she to do? 'I had put off my garment,' she laments, 'how could I put it on again? I had bathed my feet; how could I soil them?' Torn between desire to stay in bed and longing to meet the beloved she lies silent and still.

Knock! Knock! 'My beloved thrust his hand into the opening, and my inmost being yearned for him' (5:4). And love conquers.

Infatuated, sick with love, she rises from her bed, goes to the door, her hand trembling and dripping with liquid myrrh upon the handles of the bolt. She will open the door. She will invite him in. 'O that his left hand were under my head, and that his right hand embraced me' (2:6). She opens the door. But — the tragedy of it all — her beloved has turned and gone. Now she is faced with a black night of nothingness. Where has her lover hidden? Where can she find him? Out she goes in search of him — quietly and stealthily while everyone in the house is asleep. Out she goes with no other light than the one that burns in her heart. Love alone is her guide. Her distress calls to mind that other bride who, with abundant tears, searched in the garden for the body of the one she loved and begged the gardener to tell her where he had laid him that she might take him away. 'And Jesus said, 'Mary.' She turned and said to him in Hebrew, 'Rabboni' (which means Teacher). Jesus said to her, 'Do not cling to me. . .' (John 20:17).

In the same way the bride asks tearfully where is the one she loves. But the sentinels laugh and mock her. 'They beat me, they wounded me, they took away my mantle, those sentinels of the walls' (Song of Songs 5:7). Stripped naked, deprived of everything, lost in the pitch blackness of the night, she calls piteously to the daughters of Jerusalem:

> I adjure you, O daughters of Jerusalem, if you find my beloved,
> Tell him I am sick with love.

What a story of love and suffering! Yet it is no tragedy. It ends in triumph. 'I found him whom my soul loves. I held him, and would not let him go until I brought him into my mother's house, and into the chamber of her that conceived me' (3:4). Winter is past, the rain is over and gone, the time of singing has come, the voice of the turtle dove is heard in the land.

Of course there is a mystical interpretation of the canticle.

The bride is the human soul — not the soul dualistically separated from the body, but the true self, the core and centre of the person — the innermost being that longs for God as the hart longs for flowing streams and as the bride longs for the bridegroom.

The knocking at the door is an archetypal symbol that sometimes appears in dreams. It symbolizes awakening, the entrance of a new person into one's life, the invitation to begin a new stage in the human journey. The intruder is not always a lover (how Macbeth trembled when he heard the knocking on the door after the murder of Duncan!) but it may be a demanding lover, a lover who asks for all. 'Behold I stand at the door and knock' says a great lover (Revelation 3:20) who wants to enter the innermost sanctuary and dine with the beloved.

We human beings are asleep. We live in a dream world of illusion — in the Buddhist *samsara* — and we need to be awakened called to face the great realities of life and death and eternity. We need to hear the knocking on the door, even when it makes us tremble with fear. 'Hark, my beloved is knocking.' But questions arise immediately.

Why did the lover, after knocking persistently on the door, turn and disappear into the night? Why did he not enter to consummate the union for which both longed? Why did he cause such suffering to the woman he loved? Was it a cruel betrayal?

And to this there can only be one answer. He did not go in because he wanted her to come out. He wanted her to leave her house and the comfort of her bed to follow him into the dark night. He wanted her to leave her customary way of thinking and acting and feeling with all its pettiness and anxieties and fears. He wanted her to leave the house of her little ego with its selfish love of comfort and security, to enter the vast, mysterious night of faith where he was hiding. However painful it was, she must go out in ecstasy — to true freedom. 'Forth unobserved I went' writes St John of the Cross as he identifies with the bride; and he insists that the contemplative must not remain in that comfortable bed if she would find the one she loves: 'Whoever refuses to go out at night in search of the Beloved and to divest and mortify the will, but rather seeks the Beloved in bed and comfort as did the bride, will not succeed in finding him; as the soul declares it found him when it departed in darkness and with longing of love.'[30]

The soul must go forth and lose everything in that night of love. *Nada, nada, nada.* She must be mocked by the guards and stripped naked. So great will be her suffering that no words can describe it.

Yet she enters a glorious night of freedom and of love. For all the time she knows that her lover is faithful and that he also is wounded, as he was pierced on Calvary. She knows with Juliana of Norwich that all will be well, and all will be well and all manner of things will be well. For she will be united with the one she loves in a marriage banquet that lasts for ever.

Such is the journey of love through the dark night to the beloved.

NOTES

1. *The Cloud of Unknowing*, C. 35.
2. Ibid.
3. Ibid., C. 28.
4. Ibid., C. 12.
5. *Nostra Aetate*, 2.
6. *Gaudium et Spes*, 1.13.
7. Ibid., Preface 2.
8. Ibid.
9. *Gaudium et Spes*, 1.13.
10. *Lumen Gentium*, VII. 48.
11. Ibid, II. 13.
12. *Gaudium et Spes*, III. 37.
13. *The Ascent*, 1. 13.3.
14. See chapter 4.
15. *The Ascent*, II. 7.11.
16. Ibid., II. 7. 8.
17. *The Ascent*, 1.14.2.
18. Ibid.
19. *The Ascent*, II.2.1.
20. Ibid.
21. Ibid.
22. Ibid., II. 2. 2.
23. Ibid., II. 2. 7.
24. *The Spiritual Canticle*, 26.13.
25. Ibid., 26. 16.
26. *The Spiritual Canticle*, 26.14.
27. *The Spiritual Canticle*, 12.7.
28. Ibid., 12.8.
29. Ibid.
30. *The Dark Night*, 11.24.4.

THIRTEEN

The Dark Night

SOCIAL SIN

It has already been said that the *via purgativa* is one aspect of a mystical path, a path of love, that leads to the true self — the self that is one with God, that shares in the very life of God, that is divinized by the inflow of divine grace. This is a joyful path of glorious liberation. Freed from the shackles of concupiscence and from the tyranny of inordinate desire one cries out: 'Abba, Father!' But, alas, the liberation is never complete in this life. One can always fall back into the mire of sin. And there is the additional fact that this is a path of great suffering in imitation of one who carried his cross to Calvary before entering into his glory.

Now an outstanding characteristic of our age is that people become increasingly aware of the social dimension of sin. We are aware of the sin of corrupt governments that wage cruel wars that annihilate or cripple entire nations. We are aware of the sin of terrorist organizations that kill and maim innocent children. Then there are mammoth multinational companies that plunder the environment, butcher the wildlife, pollute the atmosphere, exploit helpless people and manufacture lethal weapons — all for filthy lucre and unrighteous mammon. Is not the parable of the rich Dives and the poor Lazarus enacted today on an international scale? And in addition to all this we are made aware of the institutional sin of seemingly holy religions — of the church, the synagogue, the mosque and the temple. These sins are all the more heinous because frequently accompanied by hypocrisy and arrogance. And we are aware that we are all collectively responsible for the sins of the world. No one can point the finger at others or shift the responsibility to the people on top. We are in it together.

And this gives rise to the greatest religious problem of our day. How can purification of society come about?

The Second Vatican Council asked for a collective conversion. Pope John spoke of a second Pentecost as he prayed, 'Renew your wonders in our times, as though for a new Pentecost.'[1] Indeed, the Council opened with a reference to the apostles gathered in prayer with Mary the Mother of Jesus, undergoing a profound change of heart. Was it possible, people asked, for the whole Church of the twentieth century to undergo such a communal conversion? Is it now possible for communities of men and women to undergo a collective change of heart like that of the apostles in the upper room?

It may be possible. But more often one person or a few persons are chosen to suffer and undergo purification for the group, as Caiaphas predicted when he said that it was better that one die for the people than that the whole nation should perish. And frequently those who die for the people are the mystics. They undergo a purification that is far deeper than their personal sins warrant, because they suffer for the human family. Such are those who pass through the dark night of the soul with Jesus in Gethsemane. Sometimes they return to the market place as leaders or activists or prophets or builders of a new more human culture. At other times they die in obscurity. In either case they play a key role in the reform of society. Without them the whole people might perish.

But before speaking about the dark night, it is necessary to examine the psychological background.

PSYCHOLOGICAL BACKGROUND

Traditional mystical theology took its psychology from the Greeks. Dionysius and the Greek Fathers were profoundly influenced by Neoplatonism; and this Neoplatonic influence is still alive today. Later mystical theology, however, was dominated by St Thomas Aquinas who took his psychology principally from Aristotle, though he did quote Dionysius liberally, interpreting the Neoplatonism in his own way. All was carefully systematized by the scholastics. The human person, they taught, is composed of body and soul, sense and spirit. There are exterior senses and interior senses leading to the spiritual power of memory, understanding and will, known as 'the three powers of the soul'. Sense is for spirit (*sensus est propter intellectum*) and there is nothing in the intellect that was not previously in the senses (*nihil est in intellectum quod non fuit prius in sensu*). While the scholastics distinguished clearly between sense and spirit, they were deeply convinced of the unity of the human person. This was the basic psychology used by traditional mystical theology.

When it came to speak about the essence of mystical experience, however, mystical theology, again following St Thomas, went beyond the Greeks to speak of the great Trinitarian mystery that lies hidden at the centre of the human person. 'It should be known', writes St John of the Cross, 'that the Son of God, together with the Father and the Holy Spirit, is hidden by his essence and his presence, in the innermost being of the soul.'[2] He then goes on to quote Augustine: 'I did not find you without, Lord, because I wrongly sought you without, who were within.'[3] And he addresses the soul, telling her of the wonderful riches that are within where the Beloved dwells:

> What more do you want, O soul! And what else do you search for outside, when within yourself you possess your riches, delights, satisfactions, fullness and kingdom — your Beloved whom you desire and seek? Be joyful and gladdened in your interior recollection with him, for you have him so close to you. Desire him there, adore him there. Do not go in pursuit of him outside yourself. You will only become distracted and wearied thereby, and you shall not find him, or enjoy him more securely, or sooner, or more intimately than by seeking him within you.[4]

Needless to say, this doctrine is found throughout the fourth gospel as in the words of Jesus: 'Those who love me will keep my word, and my Father will love them, and we will come to them and make our home with them' (John 14:23).

Now mystical experience is primarily the work of God who dwells within and communicates his love and his light to the human person. While ordinary knowledge, as Aristotle said, is acquired through the senses, mystical knowledge is infused: it is a gratuitous gift of God who now communicates himself 'by pure spirit' to the core of the being without any mediation of the senses. That is why the contemplative is always told to stop thinking, to stop making efforts, to 'do nothing' so as to receive in the depths of her being the dark, formless, infused wisdom of God. This divine wisdom will bring a wonderful transformation. The senses, obedient to spirit, will give light to the beloved who dwells within, and the new, divinized person will have faith in the intellect, hope in the memory and love in the will.

While the framework, then, was Aristotelian and sometimes Neo-Platonic, the deeper understanding of the mystery of the human person came from revelation — from sacred Scripture and tradition.

MODERN PSYCHOLOGY

Our century has witnessed great psychological revolutions that cannot but influence mystical theology. Freud and Jung, both physicians, saw that the Western psyche was sick and desperately in need of healing; and Jung, who believed deeply in the therapeutic dimension of religion, became increasingly interested in religious experience East and West. He wrote about Zen and Yoga, about alchemy and Gnosticism, about the Eucharist and mysticism. Later, transpersonal psychology followed the same path.

We now see the psyche as multilayered. Beneath the waking, conscious mind lies the personal unconscious with its memories going back to childhood, to birth and even to life in the womb. Then there is the collective unconscious with its archetypal figures and its roots back in history. As the depths of the ocean contain precious and beautiful treasures, so the unconscious mind contains beautiful treasures of wisdom and enlightenment. It is an enchanting world.

But the unconscious world is not all beauty. It also has its darkness. It has its fears, anxieties, half-forgotten shocks and childhood traumas. It has, moreover, unconscious or half-conscious drives, addictions and impulses that cannot be controlled by 'I will' and 'I won't' because they are outside the control of the conscious mind. Again, hidden in the unconscious mind is a deep fear of death and a clinging to life. All this constitutes what Jung called the shadow or dark side of the personality. As every human being is a sinner, so every human being has a shadow. Indeed, every group or community, every religion has its shadow; and the whole human race has a shadow that is lodged in the unconscious of each one of us.

Now the great healing process is growth. Jung himself said that problems are never solved: they are outgrown. And growth takes place as the unconscious becomes conscious. This can be a joyful process; but it can also be very painful as ugly or frightening material from the dark side of the personality flows into the conscious mind and is brought to light. Now one is confronted with one's dark side that was previously hidden — with one's capacity for evil and one's inner demons.

And the great challenge is to face one's shadow, to integrate it and to accept it. Put in religious terms, the challenge is to accept that one is a sinner and to rejoice. Paul did this when he cried, 'When I am weak, then I am strong' (2 Corinthians 12:10). Jung observes brilliantly that the accepted shadow is our friend; and the gospel confirms this insight when it says that the tax collector who acknowledged his sinfulness was justified rather than the Pharisee who did not see his shadow at all.

However, it is important to remember that human beings are more than conscious and unconscious. Deeper than the personal or collective unconscious lies an area of mystery. Buddhists speak of the Buddha nature; Hindus speak of Brahman and Atman; Hebrews speak of the image of God; Christians speak of the indwelling Blessed Trinity; Eastern Christianity speaks of the uncreated energies; mystics of all persuasions speak of the ground of being, the centre of the soul, the true self, the void, the emptiness, the cosmic energies.

And about this great mystery that lies hidden in the depths of the human person, psychology cannot speak. This is because psychology, being a science, needs observable data — sensible data or data of consciousness; and about this mystery there is no data. While psychologists can speak scientifically about the personal and collective unconscious, appealing to data that comes from dreams, half-forgotten memories and even from myths and legends, anyone who speaks about the Buddha nature or the Indwelling Trinity must turn from science to faith. For here, as has been said, there is no data. Even the mystics are silent.

All this is of the greatest significance for guiding people in the mystical journey — a journey through darkness to light, a journey in which one is necessarily confronted with one's inner demons. This process never begins with the little ego. It is the work of the great mystery that lies at the depths of one's being. It is an inflow of God into the soul, says St John of the Cross, and he might equally well have said that it is a welling up or rising of God in the soul. A theme that echoes through the whole mystical tradition is: *the initiative does not come from human beings but from God.* 'We love because God first loved us' (1 John 4:19). Mystical experience is an awakening of God, a birth of God, a movement of the uncreated energies.

But now it is time to describe the mystical process in greater detail, following St John of the Cross and the Christian mystical tradition.

NIGHT OF THE SENSES

Prayer, it has been said, ordinarily begins with reasoning and thinking and reflection on the gospels or on some truth of Christian faith. As time goes on, however, it simplifies to the repetition of a word or phrase; and finally it enters into a rich silence. Now one experiences the presence of God in an existential way; one is filled with consolation. God, says St John of the Cross, is like a loving mother who warms her child with the heat of her bosom, nurses it with good milk and tender food and caresses it in her arms. 'But,' the saint goes on, 'as the child grows older, the mother withholds her caresses and hides her tender love; she rubs bitter aloes on her sweet breasts and sets the child down from her arms, letting it walk on its own feet.'[5] Losing its mother and walking alone, however painful and distressing for the child, is a necessary step in growth; and the loss of consolation is a great grace. For now God is communicating himself in a new way — not through the senses but through the spirit. Flowing into the very core of one's being (or welling up from the core of one's being) God is weaning the soul from the delicate and sweet food of infants, making it eat coarse bread which is the food of the strong. 'This dark night', writes St John of the Cross, 'is a privation of all sensible appetites for the external things of the world, the delights of the flesh and the gratifications of the will.'⁶ This process is called passive purification because it is principally the action of God while the human person is receptive.

In addition to the passive purification, however, one enters the night of sense by an active purification whereby one renounces all sensible pleasures of seeing, hearing, touching and smelling. 'Renounce and remain empty of any sensory satisfaction that is not purely for the honour and glory of God,'⁷ writes St John of the Cross to one who would enter the night; and he goes on with his '*nada, nada, nada*'. 'You should endeavour then', he continues, 'to leave the senses as though in darkness, mortified, and empty of pleasure.'

And so, through an active and a passive purification, the senses are emptied and lie fallow for some time.

It is not surprising that this privation of sensible pleasure should have its repercussions on the unconscious life which sometimes rises in revolt. Zen speaks of a hallucinatory stage called *makyo*, literally 'the world of the devil', when unconscious material flows to the surface of consciousness, causing disturbance to the meditator. St John of the Cross seems to speak of something similar when he writes:

> He (the devil) often purveys objects to the sense of sight images of saints and most beautiful lights, and to hearing dissembled words, and to the sense of smell, fragrant odours; and he puts sweetness in one's mouth and delight in the sense of touch. He does this so that by enticing persons through these sensory objects he may induce them into many evils.⁸

It is interesting to note that Zen and the Christian mystical tradition give similar counsel: Pay no attention to these images or lights or words or fragrances. Let them go. Remain quietly with the imageless wisdom that lies hidden in the inner depths.

But, St John of the Cross tells us there can be even more unsettling storms in those called to the summit. There can be a revolt of sexuality:

An angel of Satan (2 Corinthians 12:7) which is the spirit of fornication is sometimes given to some to buffet their senses with strong and abominable temptations and afflict their spirit with foul thoughts and very vivid images, which sometimes is a pain worse than death for them.'

Here St John of the Cross, following the scriptural exegesis of his day, is referring to the experience of St Paul.

Again, there can be a temptation to hate God when 'the blasphemous spirit . . . commingles intolerable blasphemies with all their thoughts and ideas'.[10]

Again, there can be 'a loathsome spirit' that causes 'a thousand scruples and perplexities'[11] and this is one of the most burdensome goads and horrors of this night.

What is one to do? Obviously this is a time when most modern people need counselling in order to face and understand the shadow side of the personality that is now coming to light. They need encouragement and reassurance that all will be well. They must simply ignore these storms and distractions, preserving interior peace. 'They must be content simply with a loving and peaceful attentiveness to God, and live without the concern, without the effort and without the desire to taste or feel Him.'[12]

BETWEEN THE NIGHTS

The night passes, and dawn comes. The contemplative now enters into the state of proficients. 'In this new state', writes St John of the Cross, 'as one liberated from a cramped prison cell, the soul goes about the things of God with much more freedom and satisfaction of spirit and with more abundant interior delight . . . The soul readily finds in its spirit, without the work of meditation, a very serene, loving contemplation and spiritual delight.'[13]

Moreover, the spiritual communication of God overflows on the senses which have been emptied. So powerful is this sensory communication that 'proficients, because of such communication experienced in the sensitive part, suffer many infirmities, injuries, and weaknesses of stomach, and as a result of fatigue of spirit'.[14] Of these communications St John of the Cross further writes:

> Thus we have raptures and transports and the dislocation of bones, which always occur when the communications are not purely spiritual . . . as those of the perfect, who are already purified in the night of the spirit. For in the perfect, these raptures and bodily torments cease, and they enjoy freedom of spirit without a detriment to or transport of their senses.[15]

Here, it is important to note, the sensible delight is not caused by exterior sensible experience of seeing, hearing, smelling or touching. It is caused by the overflow of a spiritual communication of God. Now the interior senses are awakened so that one has a new and rich way of seeing, hearing, touching and smelling. Now the purified senses glorify God as St John of the Cross says poetically: 'The deep caverns of sense, once obscure and blind, Now give forth, so rarely, so exquisitely, Both warmth and light to their Beloved.'[16]

> *Las profundas cavernas del sentido*
> *Que estaba oscuro y ciego*
> *Con extraños primores*
> *Calor y luz dan junto a su Querido!*

Now that sensible purification has taken place, exterior and interior senses unite to give warmth and light to the bridegroom. In his systematic treatises (*The Ascent* and *The Dark Night*) St John of the Cross separates the two nights and describes each in some detail. However, he is aware that the mystic process is not simple and clear cut. 'Not everyone undergoes this in the same way,' he writes, 'neither are the temptations identical. All is meted out according to God's will and the greater or lesser amount of imperfection that must be purged from each one.'[17] Moreover, some are never wholly in the night nor wholly out of it. And yet, writing out of experience, he says:

> Yet, as is evident through experience, souls who will pass on to

so happy and lofty a state as is the union of love must usually remain in these aridities and temptations for a long while no matter how quickly God leads them.[18]

This long time seems to be several years.

THE SECOND NIGHT

The night of the senses is preliminary and is only night in a transferred sense of the word. 'The purgation of the senses', writes St John of the Cross, 'is only the gateway, and beginning of, the contemplation which leads to the purgation of the spirit'[19] and 'it serves more for accommodation of the senses to the spirit than for the union of the spirit with God.'[20] The difference between the two nights is like the difference between pulling up roots and cutting off a branch, or rubbing out a fresh stain and an old, deeply embedded one. Indeed, deep purification of the senses is only achieved in the night of the spirit wherein sense and spirit are together purified and healed in preparation for the spiritual marriage.

When he comes to the theology of the dark night, St John of the Cross is clear:

> This dark night is an inflow of God into the soul, which purges it of its habitual ignorances and imperfections, both natural and supernatural, and which contemplatives call infused contemplation or mystical theology. Through this contemplation God teaches the soul secretly and instructs it in the perfection of love without its doing anything or understanding how this happens.[21]

Here every word is important.

'An inflow of God into the soul.' That is to say, a direct communication of God at the very core of one's being. The divine meets the human in an unmediated way. There are times, says the author of *The Cloud*, when God works all by himself. St Ignatius speaks of 'consolation without previous cause'. All are speaking of the direct, dynamic action of God which is called infused (as opposed to acquired) contemplation or mystical wisdom.

St John of the Cross speaks of an inflow. As has already been said, he might equally well have spoken of a welling up of God in the soul. For God who dwells secretly in the hidden depths of one's being seems to awaken or rise up. This can happen in a gradual way or it can be a sudden eruption of the uncreated energies of which the Eastern Christian mystics speak. These uncreated energies, Orthodox theology insists, are nothing other than God himself. What an earth-shaking event is the rising of God in the depths of the human person!

And in this process, God who is the Inner Teacher — the *Magister Internus* of Augustine — instructs the contemplative in the art of love. 'In contemplation', writes St John of the Cross, 'God teaches the soul very quietly and secretly, without its knowing how, without the sound of words, and without the help of any bodily or spiritual faculty, in silence and quietude, in darkness to all sensory and natural things.'[22] This is the secret or hidden knowledge that is mystical theology. This is the knowing by unknowing.

But the soul does nothing and cannot understand. 'What is happening to me?' is the cry of the mystic in the dark night. She is losing control; she is like the bride lost in the darkness; she knows not where she is going.

SUFFERING OF THE NIGHT

God is light and love. Why, then, does the mystic speak of darkness and torment? St John of the Cross asks the question and provides the answer:

There are two reasons why this divine wisdom is not only night and darkness for the soul, but also affliction and torment. First, because of the height of divine wisdom which exceeds the capacity of the soul. Second, because of the soul's baseness and impurity; and on this account it is painful, afflictive, and also dark for the soul.[23]

Here there are two reasons. The first is the height of divine wisdom which exceeds the capacity of the soul. God is infinite — the mystery of mysteries, the light of lights. The wisdom of God is far beyond anything that human beings can imagine or endure. The inflow of this infinite and eternal light can shake the human person to the very roots, even with a certain violence, as St John of the Cross says:

> Since this divine contemplation assails him somewhat forcibly in order to subdue and strengthen his soul, he suffers so much in his weakness that he almost dies, particularly at times when the light is more powerful. Both sense and spirit, as though under an immense and dark load undergo such agony and pain that the soul would consider death a relief.[24]

No one shall see God and live. In another context, St John of the Cross, acutely aware that the light of God will kill him, longs for death and cries out: 'Reveal thy presence and may the vision of thy beauty be my death!'[25]

Descubre tu presencia
Y mateme tu vista y hermosura

He will be killed by the terrible beauty of God. And then in an interesting passage he goes on to speak almost amusingly about two visions that can kill:

> It is known that there are two visions which will kill because of the inability of human nature to suffer their force and vigour: one is that of the basilisk, from which it is said one dies immediately; the other is the vision of God. Yet the causes are very different, for the sight of one kills with a terrible poison, and that of God by an immense health and glorious good.[26]

In all this, St John of the Cross follows the scholastic tradition which held that human beings cannot endure the vision of God. Even the blessed in heaven, the scholastics held, could not see God face to face without 'the light of glory' (*lumen gloriae*) which sustains and fortifies weak human nature for ever. However, there is a second cause of suffering; namely, the meeting of sinful human beings and the all-holy God. For the true light that enlightens everyone, rising up in the depths of the contemplative's being, brings to light the ugly side of the human personality that ordinarily lies hidden. Alas, there is a lot of darkness in the human psyche, as has already been said — there is a lot of unacceptable crud, a lot of ugliness that we refuse to accept, a lot of shadow. St John of the Cross speaks of the seven deadly sins rooted in the human psyche as a result of original sin. He devotes a chapter of *The Dark Night* to each of these sins — pride, covetousness, lust, gluttony, envy, anger and sloth — showing how these vices can masquerade as virtues and lead to destruction; and he asks the contemplative to face his or her shadow. This is all the more painful since in the collective unconscious lies archetypal evil and a sense of the sin of humanity — the evil that Jesus faced in Gethsemane.

This darkness now pours into the conscious mind. St John of the Cross describes vividly the torment of the soul that sees its own sinfulness:

> The soul at the sight of its miseries feels that it is melting away and being undone by a cruel, spiritual death; it feels as if it were swallowed by a beast and being digested in the dark belly, and it suffers an anguish comparable to Jonah's when in the belly of the whale.[27]

And he writes frighteningly about the sense of rejection by God:

> When this contemplation oppresses a man, he feels very vividly the shadow of death, the sighs of death, and the sorrows of hell, all of which reflect the feeling of God's absence, of being chastened and rejected by him, of being unworthy of him . . .[28]

Reading the sanjuanist descriptions of the dark night, one can understand the agony of the Capuchin mystic Padre Pio, who was constantly tortured by fear of damnation for his own wickedness and sinfulness. One can understand Thérèse of Lisieux who feared she was losing her mind. Mystical experience is paradoxically filled with joy and suffering.

Yet St John of the Cross returns to his important theme that the suffering is not caused by the contemplation itself but by the ugliness and weakness that is brought to light. 'There is nothing in contemplation or the divine inflow which of itself can give pain,' he writes. 'Contemplation rather bestows sweetness and delight. The cause for not experiencing these agreeable effects is the soul's weakness and imperfection at the time, its inadequate preparation, and the qualities it possesses which are contrary to the light. Because of these the soul has to suffer when the divine light shines upon it.'[29]

FIRE OF PURIFICATION

From what has been said it will be clear that the great suffering of the dark night is caused by love. As Jesus came to cast fire upon the earth, so mystical love is a devouring fire that consumes everything that might oppose it. St John of the Cross, appealing to a metaphor widely used in the mystical tradition, speaks of fire applied to the sodden log. 'The fire dispels the moisture, gradually turns the wood black, makes it dark and ugly and even makes it emit a foul odour; but finally, by heating and enkindling it from without, the fire transforms the wood into itself and makes it as beautiful as it is itself.' And then he continues:

> And similarly we should philosophize about the divine loving fire of contemplation. Before transforming the soul, it purges it of all contrary qualities. It produces blackness and darkness and brings to the fore the soul's ugliness; thus the soul seems worse than before and unsightly and abominable. This divine purge stirs up all the foul and vicious humours of which the soul was never before aware; never did it realize there was so much evil in itself, since these humours were so deeply rooted.[30]

With this vision of its own darkness and ugliness the soul feels rejected by God. Yet the painful experience is altogether necessary for 'without this purgation it cannot receive the divine light, sweetness and delight of wisdom, just as the log of wood until prepared cannot be transformed by the fire'.[31]

The dark night, then, is a journey of love in which the bride goes forth from all things in liberty of spirit to meet the bridegroom and to be united with him. 'For love is like a fire,' writes St John of the Cross, 'which always rises upwards as though longing to be engulfed in its centre.'[32]

The concluding chapters of *The Dark Night* speak only of love. There are ten stages of love, leading to the vision of God. The eighth step impels the soul to lay hold of the Beloved without letting him go, as the bride proclaims: 'I found him whom my heart and soul loves, I held him and did not let him go' (Song of Songs 3:4). 'The ninth step of love causes the soul to burn gently. It is the step of the perfect who burn gently in God. The Holy Spirit produces the gentle and delightful ardour by reason of the soul's union with God.'[33]

The tenth step is the vision of God in eternal life. The soul becomes like God. 'We know that we shall be like him' (1 John 3:2). 'Thus it will be called, and shall be, God through participation.'[34]

PURGATORY

St John of the Cross compares the night to purgatory, saying that 'the same loving wisdom that purges and illumines the blessed spirits purges and illumines the soul here on earth'.[35] For this night is a loving and purifying fire of wisdom. 'Just as the spirits suffer purgation there,' he writes, 'so as to be able to see God through clear vision in the next life, souls in their own way suffer purgation here on earth so as to be transformed in him through love in this life.'[36] All mortals must be purified before coming to the vision of God; and this purification is brought about by the fire of divine love, either in this life or in the next.

The comparison with purgatory is particularly apt for two reasons.

First, traditional theology, East and West, teaches that the pain of purgatory is principally that of separation from God; and, as we have seen, the contemplative suffers acutely from the sense of rejection by God, experiencing a deep loneliness or sense of isolation. '*Eli, Eli, lama sabachthani.*' This sense of the separate ego can be almost unbearable.

Again, the scholastics held that the blessed souls are outside time in a state called *aevum* which is intermediary between time and eternity.[37] And the contemplative also, moving through states of consciousness that belong to the next life rather than this, has a different sense of time. Such is the teaching of St John of the Cross:

> It seems to the soul in this night that it is being carried out of itself by afflictions. At other times a man wonders if he is not being charmed, and he goes about in wonderment over what he sees and hears. Everything seems so strange even though he is the same as always. The reason is that he is being made a stranger to his usual knowledge and experience of things so that annihilated in this respect he may be informed with the divine, which belongs more to the next life than to this.[38]

Passing through these states of consciousness the contemplative sometimes loses the sense of time and is constantly disorientated. 'He frequently experiences such absorption and profound forgetfulness in the memory that long periods pass without his knowing what he did or thought about and he knows not what he is doing or about to do, nor can he concentrate on the task at hand, even though he desires to.'[39]

To be outside time in loving union with God and with all things is a beautiful and joyful experience. But to be outside time without God — alone, isolated for ever — this is the great suffering of the contemplative in the dark night. He or she cannot believe that the isolation and loneliness will come to an end; and assurances from friend or confessor that the agony will pass are of no avail. That is why St John of the Cross can say of contemplatives in the dark night: 'These are the ones who go down to hell alive (Psalm 55:15) since their purgation on earth is similar to that of purgatory'[40]; and again he says that 'it seems to the soul that it sees hell and perdition opened before it'.[41] Of the souls in purgatory he claims that one of their greatest sufferings is the doubt about whether they will ever leave and whether their affliction will come to an end. To be isolated, alone and outside time is the agony of the mystics. Eli, Eli, lama sabacthani.

This suffering can be all the greater if one is confronted with archetypal evil, as sometimes happens. St John of the Cross speaks of a meeting with the spirit of evil in the dark night:

> The torment and pain he then causes it is immense, and sometimes it is ineffable. For since it proceeds nakedly from spirit to spirit, the horror the evil spirit causes with the good spirit (in that of the soul) if he reaches the spiritual part is unbearable.[42]

And what is the contemplative to do? The only answer is to be patient and wait upon God who is faithful. One cannot practise vocal prayer; one cannot even petition God for help. One can only put one's mouth in the dust with hope and trust:

> Indeed this is not the time to speak with God, but the time to put one's mouth in the dust, as Jeremiah says, that perhaps there might come some actual hope (Lamentations 3:29) and the time to suffer the purgation patiently. God it is who is working in the soul, and for this reason the soul can do nothing. Consequently, a person can neither pray vocally nor be attentive to spiritual matters, nor still less attend to temporal affairs and business.[43]

The end will come. Gradually the contemplative experiences the inner fire of love. A new energy and vitality has arisen, and one's whole being is filled with a strangely unfamiliar love. The oppressive night has come to an end. Not that suffering comes to an end — for the new love causes suffering of a different kind — but the cruel agony is replaced by joy. One realizes that the agony and the ecstasy come from the same source.

O happy night! O night more lovely than the dawn! What seemed like cruel darkness was really the intense light of God, imparting the most profound wisdom. This is the night that has transformed the beloved in her lover. It ends with ecstasy: 'I abandoned and forgot myself, laying my face on my Beloved.'

Quedéme y olvidéme
El rostro recliné sobre el Amado

TRANSFORMATION OF SEXUALITY

In the garden of delight, Adam and Eve lived in what the scholastics called the state of innocence or the state of integrity. That is to say, their passions, including their sexuality, were integrated so that they lived in harmony with one another, with the universe and with God. They were naked and unashamed.

After the Fall, however, they fell into a profound disharmony and, filled with shame, they hid from God. 'Who told you that you were naked?' (Genesis 3:11). Now they were in the state of fallen nature. 'And the Lord God made garments of skins for the man and for his wife, and clothed them' (Genesis 3:21).

Now it has already been said that the mystical path is a return to the state of integrity or the state of innocence, a slow process in which the passions are integrated and the person becomes whole. One is purified from compulsive addictions, unbridled passions and inordinate affections. Yet the process is necessarily accompanied by falls (the Church defined that no one is without venial sin) and even the greatest mystic is a sinner until death.

It has also been said that this process of integration demands such rigorous detachment that St John of the Cross felt obliged to defend himself against the charge of inhumanity and destructiveness. 'Observing how we annihilate the faculties in their operations', he writes, 'it will perhaps seem that we are tearing down rather than building up the way of spiritual exercise.'[44] And then he goes on to defend himself, speaking of death and rebirth and the transformation of the whole person. Now this is very relevant to the question of sexuality. At first it might seem that St John of the Cross is out to annihilate all sexual desire; but a careful reading of the text shows that he is leading to an integration and transformation of sexuality. Even more, he is leading to a divinization of sexuality in the spiritual marriage which is 'the exchange of love between the soul and Christ, its bridegroom'.[45] But this transformation and divinization only takes place through the rigours and the immense suffering of the dark night. The complete purification of sexuality (in so far as it is ever complete) takes place not in the night of the senses but in the night of the soul since sexuality is rooted in spirit.

It has already been said that in describing the human person in the state of fallen nature, St John of the Cross speaks of the seven deadly sins rooted in what we now call the unconscious. Among these is the vice of lust; that is to say, unintegrated and uncontrolled sexual desire. In beginners this lust rises up even in times of prayer:

> It happens frequently that in one's spiritual exercises, without one's being able to avoid it, impure movements will be experienced in the sensory part of the soul, and even sometimes when the spirit is deep in prayer or when receiving the sacrament of penance or the Eucharist.[46]

Here the sexuality is not integrated; it is not under control of the will. The saint even indicates that some people may lose self control.

'Sometimes', he writes, 'these individuals are aware that certain impure and rebellious acts have taken place . . .'[47] In the case of people who will go into the second night he speaks of even more violent revolts of sexuality.

However, with the process of contemplative prayer experienced as a quiet inner flame of love or (in the words of the author of *The Cloud*) a blind stirring of love, the sexual energy is transformed and gathered up into contemplative energy. That is why, before venturing out into the dark night, the bride sings that her house is now all stilled, meaning that all her sensible faculties are silenced, integrated and at peace:

Estando ya mi casa sosegada

Transformed sexual energy, however, can only be understood in the light of the interior or spiritual senses which have played an important role in mystical theology since the time of Origen. About these a word must now be said.

In the mystical life there is a whole rich area of experience that few modern psychologists know about. There is an inner hearing (a real word is heard clearly and distinctly but not with these ears); there is an inner seeing, an inner smelling, an inner touching. There is experience of inner light and inner fire. Some of the mystics, reading The

Song of Songs speak of an inner kiss; and there is an inner sexual drive leading to union with God in the spiritual marriage. It is important to note that these inner senses are not activated by an exterior stimulating object. They are brought into play as the overflow of a deeply spiritual experience.

To anyone who reads the poetry of St John of the Cross it is evident that the saint did not crush or repress his sexuality. He lived it out in a new way, at the level of the interior senses, in his prayer and in his poetry. But it is equally evident to the discerning reader that the saint could only live it out at this level because he had passed through the purifying terrors of the dark night in which his sexuality was annihilated and reborn. Only through this deep purification could he enter into the spiritual marriage with the all-holy God. Only through this deep purification could he include his sexuality in that triumphant cry about all created things: 'Now that I least desire them, I have them all without desire.'[48]

The journey of love leads to the spiritual marriage — 'which is a total transformation in the Beloved in which each surrenders the entire possession of self to the other with a certain consummation of the union of love. The soul thereby becomes divine, becomes God through participation, in so far as is possible in this life'.[49] And St John of the Cross goes on to speak of a marriage in which the human spirit meets, and is united with, the spirit of God:

> Just as in the consummation of carnal marriage there are two in one flesh, as sacred Scripture points out (Genesis 2:24), so also when the spiritual marriage between God and the soul is consummated, there are two natures in one spirit and love, as St Paul says in making the same comparison: 'He who is joined to the Lord is one spirit with him' (1 Corinthians 6:17).[50]

The spiritual marriage may be enacted in this life. It leads to the glorious marriage that is celebrated in eternity.

BIRTH OF THE CHILD

This chapter began with a reference to social and institutional sin, saying that the mystic who passes through the terrors of the dark night does so, not just for self-purification but for the purification of humankind. With Paul he or she makes up what is wanting to the suffering of Christ for his body which is the Church. From the time of Origen, mystical theologians have seen an ecclesial dimension to The Song of Songs. They have seen the bride not just as the individual person but as the whole Church. In the post-Vatican II era we can see this bride as the people of God linked in various ways with the whole human family.

The mystic, then, plays a central role in the life of the world. He or she resonates with that great conciliar sentence: 'The joys and the hopes, the griefs and anxieties of the men and women of this age, especially those who are poor or in any way afflicted, these too are the joys and hopes, the griefs and anxieties of the followers of Christ.'[51] The mystic is at the centre of the people of God and of the whole human race, with a special love for those who are poor or in any way afflicted.

And mystics are creative. Not all mystics are active, since some live and die in solitude; but all are creative. They give birth to a child who cooperates with Jesus in the salvation of the world. This child is the kingdom of God, the tiny mustard seed that becomes a great tree, the beloved bride of Christ.

On the night before he died, Jesus spoke to those eleven men about their coming dark night. 'When a woman is in labour', he said, 'she has pain, because her hour has come. But when the child is born, she no longer remembers the anguish because of the joy of having brought a human being into the world' (John 16:21). Like that woman, the apostles went through the pains of travail until with great joy they gave birth to their child; and their joy no one could take from them. And what a child that was! Its voice was heard throughout the world, singing the praises of the Creator.

And all the mystics have borne their child. Teresa and John, Eckhart and Juliana, Thérèse and Edith Stein have radiated an influence that will never die. Yet equally or more influential are the silent voices of hidden mystics who die unwept, unhonoured and unsung. These are the people who revolutionize the world. Today they are hand in hand with mystics of India, China and Tibet. All these suffer the pains of travail that a new world may be born.

CONCLUSION

To some students of mystical theology the dark night of St John of the Cross seems esoteric and far removed from ordinary human experience. Was the great Spanish poet exaggerating, they ask. Does he use the language of hyperbole? Was his artistic temperament leading him into melodrama?

Such questions are not unreasonable. Yet other considerations lead the thoughtful person to conclude that while some chosen people undergo a particularly deep purification for the salvation of the world, the experience itself is profoundly human and not even extraordinary.

The first consideration is that throughout his vivid and sometimes terrible description of the dark night, the eyes of the saint are forever fixed on Jesus who emptied himself, died an ignominious death and rose to enter into glory. At the moment of his death Jesus was utterly annihilated in his soul without any consolation or relief. And St John of the Cross continues: 'He was therefore compelled to cry out: "My God, my God, why have you forsaken me?" (Matthew 27:46). This was the most extreme abandonment, sensitively, that he had suffered in his life. And by it he accomplished the most marvellous work of his whole life . . .'[52] This, moreover, was a profoundly human experience; for Jesus was the Son of man, the archetypal human being. And for St John of the Cross the dark night is the path of those who radically follow Jesus to bring salvation to the world. The *nada, nada, nada* is nothing but the cry of one who renounces all things to share in the suffering of the crucified whom he or she loves passionately and mystically. Is anything more human than this?

A second consideration is that in their description of deep religious experience Buddhists speak of the great death, the great doubt, the nothingness, the emptiness, the loss of all things. In short, the Buddhist mystic also passes through a dark night before attaining to enlightenment and supreme wisdom; and he or she uses language that is not far removed from that of St John of the Cross. One distinguished Christian mystic who is committed to dialogue, maintains that the link between Buddhism and Christianity is Jesus forsaken.[53]

A third consideration is that recent psychology tells us of men and women who pass through a dark night of great anguish prior to profound spiritual enlightenment. Not infrequently such persons are misunderstood and badly directed by ignorant psychiatrists who, knowing nothing of the mystical life, can only think in terms of chemical imbalance. Though such misunderstanding enhances the mystic's suffering, it is an important part of the purification.

Again it seems that at the time of death some people utter their *lama sabachthani* before entering into glory. Buddhists also speak of a great death prior to biological death.

All this leads to the conclusion that the dark night is relevant for modern people, that it is a herald of profound enlightenment, and that the creative people who find themselves isolated in impenetrable darkness are the truly privileged ones who share in the redemption of the world. O night more lovely than the dawn!

NOTES

1. *Humanae Salutis*, December 25, 1961.
2. *Spiritual Canticle*, 1.6.
3. Ibid.
4. Ibid., 1.8.
5. *The Dark Night*, 1.1.2.
6. *Ascent*, 1.1.4.
7. Ibid., 1.13.4.
8. Ibid., II.2.5.
9. *The Dark Night*, 1.14.1
10. Ibid., 1.14.2
11. Ibid., 1.14.3
12. Ibid., 1.10.4.
13. Ibid., II.1.1.
14. Ibid., II.1.2.
15. Ibid.
16. *Living Flame*, 3.
17. *The Dark Night*, 1.14.5
18. Ibid., 14.6.
19. *The Dark Night*, II.2.1.

20. Ibid.
21. Ibid., II.5.1.
22. Ibid.
23. Ibid., II.5.2.
24. Ibid., II.5.6.
25. *Spiritual Canticle*, Stanza XI.
26. *Spiritual Canticle*, II.7.
27. *The Dark Night*, II.6.1.
28. Ibid., II.6.2.
29. Ibid., II.9.11.
30. Ibid., II.10.1.
31. Ibid., II.10.4.
32. Ibid., II.20.6.
33. Ibid., II.20.4.
34. Ibid., II.20.5.
35. Ibid., II.5.1.
36. *Living Flame*, 1.24.
37. The notion of *aevum* is attributed to Boethius.
38. *The Dark Night*, II.9.5.
39. Ibid., II.8.1.
40. Ibid., II.6.
41. Ibid.
42. *The Dark Night*, II.23.5.
43. Ibid., II.8.1.
44. *Ascent*, II.2.1.
45. *Spiritual Canticle*, Prologue.
46. *The Dark Night*, 1.4.1.
47. Ibid., 1.4.5.
48. Sketch of Mount Carmel.
49. *Spiritual Canticle*, 22.3.
50. Ibid.
51. *Gaudium et Spes*, Preface 1.
52. *Ascent*, II.7.11.
53. See *Unity and Jesus Forsaken*, Chiara Lubich, New City Press, Philippines 1985.

*

FOURTEEN

Being-in-Love

THEOLOGY OF LOVE

Mystical theology, it has already been said, is the secret wisdom that is communicated and infused into the soul through love.[1] Precisely because it comes from love it is very delightful. 'This knowledge is very delightful,' writes St John of the Cross, 'because it is knowledge through love. Love is the master of this knowledge and what makes it wholly agreeable.[2] He further describes mystical theology as 'the science of love'.[3]

In developing this mystical and loving theology St John of the Cross quotes extensively from sacred Scripture and reflects on mystical experience, both his own experience and that of others. Furthermore, following a mystical tradition that flows from the fourteenth century, he makes use of scholastic theology. 'I hope that, although some scholastic theology is used here in reference to the soul's interior converse with God,' he writes almost apologetically to Mother Ann of Jesus, 'it will not prove vain to speak in such a manner to the pure of spirit.'[4] Clearly he is aware of the limits of scholastic theology when approaching so sublime a subject as mystical wisdom.

Now scholasticism spoke of the three powers of the soul: the memory, the understanding and the will. And when St John of the Cross comes to treat of union with God in a scholastic context, he speaks of faith in the intellect, hope in the memory and love in the will; and in this way he describes the human person filled with the presence of God. However, this scholastic approach is far from satisfactory. A glance at the sanjuanistic poetry and less scholastic writings lets us see that love, far from residing in one faculty, consumes the whole person: the wound created by the living flame of love is in the core and centre of one's being.

It would seem better, then, to approach mystical theology through a methodology that speaks of levels of consciousness, reaching a climax when one's being becomes being-in-love. Such is the method of Bernard Lonergan who, abandoning a faculty theology, writes about falling in love with God. 'The love into which we fall,' he writes, 'is not some series of acts, but a dynamic state that prompts and moulds all our thoughts and feelings, all our judgments and decisions.'[5] Could not a theology which speaks of the state of being-in-love become the basis and starting point for a renewed mystical theology in our day?

But before reflecting on being-in-love it is necessary to consider the prior love of God and some of the powerful symbols used by the mystics in describing the love that is poured into their hearts.

THE PRIOR LOVE OF GOD

'We love,' writes St John, 'because he first loved us' (1 John 4:19); and these wise words echo through all subsequent mystical theology. It is not that we loved God but that God loved us; and the proof of this love is that God sent his only Son to be the atoning sacrifice for our sins. St Paul, too, writes vibrantly about the prior love of God, telling us that God's love is poured into our hearts by the Holy Spirit who is given to us. 'He loved me and gave himself for me!' he exclaims (Galatians 2:20), convinced that nothing in heaven or on earth can separate him from the love of God that is in Christ Jesus. And from the sense of being loved springs his energy, his vitality, his burning love for the cross of Christ and his ecstatic mystical experiences.

But why speak of Paul? Jesus himself was deeply convinced that the Father loved him before the foundation of the world, and he prayed 'that the love with which you have loved me be in them and I in them' (John 17:26). Small wonder if a key text in all mystical theology says that 'God so loved the world that he gave his only Son . . .' (John 3:16).

Now in the mystical life, knowledge that one is loved is not just theory. It is real, lived experience, for the mystical life begins when a blind stirring of love (the terminology is from *The Cloud*) rises in the heart. It never arises as a result of human effort but comes from one-knows-not-where. 'This is something I could never have caused. It is a gift; it is grace; it is undeserved.' Such is the quiet conviction of the contemplative person.

And it is worth observing that a similar conviction arises in the hearts of mystics everywhere, be they Buddhist, Hindu or whatever. The mystic feels that he or she is the unworthy recipient of a treasure that is undeserved and could never be earned. Christian mystical theology sees this as the gift of God's love.

FIRE OF LOVE

At first the blind stirring of love is very gentle, so gentle that one scarcely notices it, so gentle that it could be crushed by anxiety or overactivity. But one who is quietly attentive to its presence feels that he or she wants to be alone, without reasoning or thinking or anxiety or preoccupation, simply relishing the mysterious presence of God who dwells within — God in whom we live and move and have our being. As time goes on, one is filled with consolation and with the sense of being loved with an everlasting love.

But the sense of presence does not last for ever. The sense of presence gives way to sense of absence. Consolation gives way to desolation, dryness and a sense of abandonment. Assuredly the blind stirring of love is still there; but now it is performing the work of purgation, burning out the impurities in that damp and black log which is the human person. Eventually it becomes a cruel fire (though it may not yet be recognized as fire) that causes great suffering and acute anguish. This is the dark night.

However, the night passes. Those who advance in the mystical life begin to experience the inner fire in a new and more mysterious way. Now it rises up as a powerful fountain of energy that envelops one's whole being. This is a time when one needs counsel and direction and encouragement; for one cannot understand what is happening. Some perplexed mystics have even felt that the inner fire would kill them or drive them mad.

The wise director tells the suffering contemplative to remain quiet and at peace, to let the fire rise up, to let the process take place and never to fight against God, for the time of deliverance will come. 'All will be well, and all will be well and all manner of thing will be well.'

Gradually one comes to realize that the inner fire, however painful, is one's friend — that it is giving strength and energy to love in such a radical way that one would die for others and sacrifice one's all for God. Now at last one begins to resonate with those texts of Scripture that speak of love and fire. There is that text of The Song of Songs which says of love:

> Its flashes are flashes of fire,
> a raging flame
> Many waters cannot quench love
> neither can floods drown it (Song of Songs 8:6, 7)

This inner love is nothing other than a flashing fire that all the waters of the world cannot put out. Now one sees new meaning in the pillar of fire in *Exodus* and in the words of Jesus that he came to cast fire upon the earth. One reads anew about the Holy Spirit descending upon the apostles in tongues of fire. One reads with new eyes *The Epistle to the Hebrews* which says that 'our God is the consuming fire' (Hebrews 12:29).

The Eastern mystical tradition speaks eloquently of this inner fire. The story is told of the disciple who came to Abba Joseph asking for direction in prayer, whereupon the Master spread his hands towards heaven and his fingers were like ten lamps of fire as he said, 'Why not become totally fire?'[6] In other words, 'Why not allow the inner fire to encompass your entire being?' And then there is Simeon the New Theologian who speaks of blazing fire and swirling light, saying unabashedly that he is talking out of his own experience. Simeon even maintained that one who has not experienced the fire and the light is still a beginner in the journey to God.

If it be asked what is this inner fire, the Orthodox tradition speaks of the uncreated energies of God. One student of this subject writes:

The doctrine of the energies, as distinct from the essence, is the basis of all mystical experience. God who is inaccessible in his essence is present in his energies. He is wholly unknowable in his essence, yet revealed in his energies.[7]

These uncreated energies, then, are nothing other than the Triune God in his dynamic and loving action. God who is love dwells within and generates a tremendous energy (or, more correctly, God *is* a tremendous energy) which overflows on the senses, paradoxically causing intense delight and acute suffering. This fits the experience of many mystics.

FLAME OF LOVE

In the Western tradition, it need hardly be said, the blazing fire plays a central role in the experience and teaching of St John of the Cross, whose most passionate poetry centres around the delightful yet cruel fire which he calls the living flame of love. This fire passes through many stages. At first gentle and consoling, it eventually causes the terrible suffering of the dark night. Then, when the purification is over, it flares up with immense energy, bringing great delight and overwhelming joy. And what a fire this is! 'God is the principal lover,' writes the saint, 'who in the omnipotence of his fathomless love absorbs the soul in himself more efficaciously and forcibly than a torrent of fire would devour a drop of morning dew.'[8] This is spiritual fire, which penetrates the depth of the human person more fully than anything that touches the senses.

There are times, moreover, when the experience of love is like the momentary touch of a spark that flies out from the fire setting the soul all aflame. 'When he wills to touch somewhat vehemently, the soul's burning reaches such a high degree of love that it seems to surpass that of all the fires in the world, for he is an infinite fire of love.'[9] And the saint describes vividly the mystical experience resulting from the touch of a spark:

The touch of a spark is a rather subtle touch that the Beloved sometimes produces in the soul, even when least expected, and which inflames her in the fire of love, as if a hot spark were to leap from the fire and set her ablaze. Then with remarkable speed, as when one suddenly remembers, the will is enkindled in loving, desiring, praising and thanking God, and reverencing, esteeming and praying to him in the savour of love.[10]

The fire, then, is not my love for God but God's love for me. It divinizes the human person who is set ablaze with a love that makes him or her praise God with overflowing delight. His or her being has become being-in-love.

In the *Living Flame of Love* St John of the Cross distinguishes two stages in the growth of contemplative fire. In the first stage, embers of fire are quietly glowing, giving forth warmth and light. In the second stage, the embers have become so hot that they shoot forth a living flame. This living flame is nothing other than the Holy Spirit consuming and divinizing the human person who surrenders to his transforming action. Here are the saint's words:

> The flame of love is the Spirit of its Bridegroom, who is the Holy Spirit. The soul feels him within itself not only as a fire that has consumed and transformed it but as a fire that burns and flares within it.[11]

The divine fire, then, is the Holy Spirit. But St John of the Cross is theologian enough to know that the Spirit does not act independently, and he goes on to speak of the experience as a Trinitarian foretaste of eternal life, saying that 'the soul is so close to God that it is transformed into a flame of love in which the Father, the Son and the Holy Spirit are communicated to it'.[12]

At the summit of the mystical life the flame is once again peaceful and calm. Now the dark night has become the serene night; the flame consumes but gives no pain:

> *En la noche serena*
> *con llama que consume y no da pena*

The experience reaches completion when night becomes day

through the vision of God in eternity.

As fire consumes, so wine inebriates. It is time, then, to consider yet another symbol of mystical love.

WINE OF LOVE

'Your love is better than wine,' sings the bride (Song of Songs 1:2); and the bridegroom replies that her kisses are 'like the best wine that goes down smoothly, gliding over lips and teeth' (Song of Songs 7:9).

The spiced wine is another symbol dear to the heart of St John of the Cross. Those who receive into their hearts God's overwhelming love are intoxicated 'with a wine of sweet, delightful and fortified love'.[13] While the spark that flies from the fire gives a momentary experience like a sudden enlightenment, inebriation with the love of God lasts for a long time:

> It should be known that this favour of sweet inebriation, because it has more permanence, does not pass away as quickly as the spark. The spark touches and then passes, although its effect lasts for a while, and sometimes for a long while; but the spiced wine — which, as I say, is sweet love in the soul — usually lasts, together with its effect, a long while, and sometimes a day or two, or many days, though not always in the same degree of intensity, because its lessening and increasing are beyond the soul's power. Sometimes without doing anything on their own, persons feel in their intimate substance that their spirit is being sweetly inebriated and inflamed by the divine wine.[14]

Here, then, is the picture of the mystic spending some days sweetly inebriated with the divine wine of love.

Moreover, just as there is new wine and old wine, so there are new lovers and old lovers. The new wine, still in process of fermentation, can be harmful to the person who drinks it in abundance; but the good old wine is settled and fermented. In the same way, new lovers are caught up in the sensible consolation of unfermented wine while the old lovers, deep in the substance of their being and far beyond the fascination of sense, taste the wisdom of wine that is fermented and settled.

And then, in an audacious phrase, St John of the Cross exclaims: 'I drank of my Beloved.'[15]

de mi Amado bebí

Through this deep draught he is penetrated through and through with the Beloved who is the wine of love, and he writes:

> As the drink is diffused through all the members and veins of the body, so this communication is diffused substantially in the whole soul, or better, the soul is transformed in God. In this transformation she drinks of God in her substance and in her spiritual faculties.[16]

In this way her being becomes being-in-love.

And an anonymous medieval poet also writes mystically about intoxication with the wine of love. The context is eucharistic. And the author of the *Anima Christi* prays: Blood of Christ inebriate me.

Sanguis Christi Inebria me

It is as though he would be intoxicated by the eucharistic blood of Christ.

WOUND OF LOVE

From the dawn of history the wound of love has been celebrated in song and in story. The fair maiden, wounded with love, languishes for her lover. 'O Romeo, Romeo, wherefore art thou Romeo?' And the lover in turn is suddenly wounded by the maiden. 'It is my lady; O, it is my love!'

The same theme runs through The Song of Songs. 'My inmost being yearned for him,' sings the bride (Song of Songs 5:4) as she rises anxiously to open the door to her lover. And in her enamoured search she is cruelly beaten and wounded, and her mantle is torn off. 'They beat me, they wounded me, they took away my mantle, those sentinels of the walls' (5:7).

But this is a mutual love affair in which the bridegroom, too, is wounded. The very glance of her eyes and the sight of her necklace pierce him through and through, and he cries out in agony:

> You have wounded my heart, my sister, my bride,
> You have wounded my heart with a glance of your eyes,
> With one jewel of your necklace (4:9).

Such is one of the great love stories of all time.

And St John of the Cross, identifying with the bride and deeply wounded by the divine bridegroom, cries: 'Where have you hidden, Beloved, and left me moaning? You fled like the stag after wounding me.'

> *Como el ciervo huiste*
> *habièndome hevido*

A deep experience of God, the divine Lover, has wounded him in the core of his being. He has fallen in love with God. And now he must go out in search of the beloved, plucking no flowers and fearing no wild beasts 'for he has a kind of immense torment and yearning to see God'.[17] Just as the sentinels of the night beat and wounded the bride, so all creatures beat and wound the saint because they tell him about a God whom he cannot see. 'Henceforth send me no more messengers,' he exclaims, as if to say, 'I want no messengers. I want you alone.' Only the clear vision of God will satisfy him.

And as the bridegroom of The Song of Songs is wounded by the eyes of the bride, so the saint is wounded by the eyes of God. Unable to endure the gaze of the divine eyes he cries out: 'Withdraw them, Beloved. My Soul has taken flight!'

> *¡Avantalos, Amado*
> *que voy de vuelo!*

And he explains these words: 'Unable in her weakness to endure such excess, she proclaims in this stanza: "Withdraw them, Beloved, that is, your divine eyes, for they cause me to take flight and go out of myself to lofty contemplation, which is beyond what human nature can endure.'"[18]

And as the love of bride and bridegroom is mutual, so (*mirabile dictu*) is the love of God and the soul. The divine Bridegroom, the Word Incarnate, is wounded. He is the wounded stag. 'Beholding that the bride is wounded he is wounded with love for her. Among lovers, the wound of one is a wound for both, and the two have but one feeling.'[19]

Sweet and delightful are these wounds and 'the soul would desire to be ever dying a thousand deaths from these thrusts of the lance, for they make her go out of herself and enter into God'.[20]

Sometimes the mystical life is indeed dramatic. At an advanced stage of the journey the soul feels that a seraph is assailing her by means of an arrow or dart that is all afire with love and 'being wounded by this fiery dart, the soul feels the wound with unsurpassable delight'.[21] No doubt St John of the Cross heard about this from his saintly colleague St Teresa who describes such an experience vividly. Close to her side she saw an angel in bodily form. 'He was very beautiful, and his face was so aflame that he seemed to be one of those very sublime angels that appear to be all afire.'[22] And Teresa continues:

> I saw in his hands a large golden dart and at the end of the iron tip there appeared to be a little fire. It seemed to me this angel plunged the dart several times into my heart and it reached deep within me. When he drew it out, I thought he was carrying off with him the deepest part of me; and he left me all on fire with great love of God. The pain was so great that it made me moan, and the sweetness this greatest pain caused me was so superabundant that there is no desire capable of taking it away; nor is the soul content with less than God.[23]

Teresa goes on to say that the pain is not bodily but spiritual, although the body shares in it.

Such is the wound of one who has had a glimpse of God and longs for clear vision. The only cure is the possession of God. 'Until this possession the soul is like an empty vessel waiting to be filled, or a hungry person craving for food, or someone sick moaning for health, or like one suspended in the air with nothing to lean on. Such is the truly loving heart.'[24]

SPIRIT, MATTER, ENERGY

From all that has been said it will be clear that mystical experience has profound repercussions on the human body. This is particularly evident in the case of the ecstatic St Teresa who describes vividly the changes in her breathing, the movement of her eyes, the elevation of her body and the strange phenomena that caused her acute embarrassment when ecstasy came upon her in public places. 'Sometimes,' she writes, 'my pulse almost stops according to what a number of sisters say who at times are near me . . . and my arms are straight and my hands so stiff that occasionally I cannot join them. As a result, even the next day I feel pain in the pulse and in the body, as if the bones were disjoined.'[25] She further goes on to say that in rapture her body is as though dead.

St John of the Cross, too, well acquainted with the experiences of his saintly colleague speaks of a time when the person seems dead for 'the body remains frozen and the flesh stiff'.[26] Perhaps he speaks from personal experience when he writes:

The torment experienced in these rapturous visits is such that no other so disjoins the bones and endangers human nature. Were God not to provide, she would die. And, indeed, it seems so to the soul in which this happens, that she is being loosed from the flesh and abandoning the body.[27]

All this happens when, in the passage already quoted, he is asking God to withdraw his divine eyes lest they drive his spirit away in death.

In his theological explanation of these phenomena St John of the Cross relies on the physiology and psychology of his day. When he speaks of body and soul, sense and spirit, he turns quite naturally to scholasticism. A spiritual experience overflows on the body; for 'God usually does not bestow a favour on the body without bestowing it first and principally on the soul.'[28] In this way he explains the stigmata of St Francis — the wound and sore appeared *outwardly* when he was wounded *spiritually* by the seraph. 'When his soul was wounded with love by the five wounds,' he writes, 'their effect extended to the body and these wounds were impressed on the body which was wounded just as the soul was wounded.'[29] And he explains the mystical experience of St Paul in the same way: 'This happened with St Paul whose immense compassion for the suffering of Christ redounded on his body as he explains to the Galatians: "I bear the wounds of the Lord Jesus in my body"' (Galatians 6:17).[30]

For a further understanding of these phenomena it is important to recall the doctrine of the inner or spiritual senses which runs through the Christian mystical tradition from the time of Origen and was dear to the heart of St Teresa. Just as there is an inner seeing, an inner hearing, an inner touching, an inner smelling which is very real, so there is an inner fire, an inner wound, an inner inebriation with wine and so on. All of this inner experience is somehow connected with the outer senses but is not identical with them.

As has already been said, the Orthodox tradition goes further to speak of the uncreated energy — the divine fire of love — that rises within the human person. The hesychasts were particularly interested in the uncreated light that radiated from the clothes and body of Jesus at the time of the Transfiguration, and they claimed that they, too, saw the divine light that emanated from the body of Jesus.

The Orthodox doctrine of uncreated energies could be very significant today when we attempt to explain mystical experience to the modern world and this for several reasons.

Firstly, to anyone who studies St Teresa it is obvious that an overwhelming energy was surging uncontrollably through her whole system. Only in this way can one come close to understanding her raptures and ecstasies. And the same can be said of St John of the Cross. Are not the blazing fire, the intoxicating wine and piercing wound best explained in terms of divine energy? This was a spiritual energy — an uncreated energy — that overflowed on the senses sometimes leaving the contemplative stiff as though dead.

Furthermore, explanation of mystical phenomena in terms of

energy may open the way to dialogue with modern scientific thinking, which is increasingly evolutionary and dynamic. Since the time of Einstein, physics has been preoccupied with energy and the speed of light; and every schoolboy knows that

$$E = mc^2$$

Teilhard de Chardin, trying to unite physics and theology, spoke of love as human energy. Cannot theology, then, come to see God as Supreme Energy, the source of all energy in the evolving universe?

Again, explanation of mystical experience through energy may open Christianity to further dialogue with Asia. For the fact is that energy is a key to understanding the culture of Asia which centres around the life force, the vital energy — *chi* or *ki*.

Chinese medicine aims at balancing the energies in the body, claiming that sickness is caused by imbalance of these energies. Again, the flow of energy is of crucial importance in the tea ceremony and in the martial arts. Most important of all, the flow of energy is a central thing in meditation. Through abdominal breathing and correct posture one regulates the energy, allowing it to flow through the body and bring enlightenment. The lotus posture and abdominal breathing are at the very heart of Buddhist meditation.

Even more significant is the Tantric tradition of India and Tibet which distinguishes between the gross body with its exterior senses and the subtle body with the *chakras* or energy points through which the life force flows. The notion of a subtle body has much in common with the spiritual or interior senses of the Christian mystics. But one who is interested in mystical experience must note that besides the ordinary energy of *prana* there is another, extremely powerful dormant energy — a divine energy — that can be awakened or aroused. This is the *kundalini* or serpent power which played a vital role in the mystical experience of Ramakrishna and other great mystics of India.[31]

Dialogue with Tibetan Buddhism and Tantra is still in its infancy, and little can yet be said. Nevertheless it is possible that Asian psychology and physiology will play an important role in the mystical theology of the future, and the Orthodox doctrine of the uncreated energies will form an invaluable bridge between Christianity and the religions of the East.

BEING-IN-LOVE

Men and women become authentically human by transcending themselves. That is to say, they become authentic by leaving the self in order to find the self in accordance with the text of the gospel which says that 'those who want to save their life will lose it and those who lose their life for my sake will find it' (Luke 9:24). This leaving self is the *going forth* or the ecstasy of the mystics who leave all to go out into the night of faith where they find all.

Lonergan claims that self-transcendence is achieved through fidelity to the transcendental precepts which are an expression of the basic thrust of the human person and are: Be attentive; be intelligent; be reasonable; be in love. Fidelity to these precepts leads in turn to a series of conversions. By intellectual conversion one transcends self intellectually; by ethical conversion one transcends self ethically; but the real self-transcendence only comes through love which leads to religious conversion. One's capacity for self-transcendence becomes an actuality, says Lonergan, when one falls in love. He then continues:

> Then one's being becomes being-in-love. Such being-in-love has its antecedents, its causes, its conditions, its occasions. But once it has blossomed forth and as long as it lasts, it takes over. It is the first principle. From it flow one's desires and fears, one's joys and sorrows, one's discernment of values, one's decisions and deeds.[32]

Here Lonergan speaks of a love that possesses one's whole being. It is not just a question of loving this person or that but of a love which is so total that it can truly be called infatuation. One's being becomes being-in-love. And while such love shines through the pages of literature as in the tragic love of Romeo and Juliet, it appears at another level in a religious context. Lonergan goes on to speak about grades of love:

> Being-in-love is of different kinds. There is the love of intimacy, of husband and wife, of parents and children. There is the love of one's fellow men with its fruit in the achievement of human welfare.[33]

Here he speaks of romantic love, filial love, patriotic love, love for society and so on. But there is another love which transcends all these, even when it includes them in its embrace:

> There is the love of God with one's whole heart and whole soul, with all one's mind and all one's strength (Mark 12:30). It is God's love flooding our hearts through the Holy Spirit given to us (Romans 5:5). It grounds the conviction of St Paul that 'there is nothing in death or life, in the realm of spirits or superhuman powers, in the world as it is or the world as it shall be, in the forces of the universe, in the heights or depths — nothing in all creation can separate us from the love of God in Christ Jesus Our Lord' (Romans 8:38-9).[34]

Lonergan here quotes St Paul, as a lover whose being became being-in-love; but he might equally well have mentioned the lovers in The Song of Songs or Francis of Assisi or John of the Cross or Edith Stein or a host of others whose being became being-in-love as they were consumed by the fire that was a living flame.

If it be asked how this love differs from the romantic love of Romeo and Juliet, Lonergan replies, 'All love is self-surrender but being in love with God is being in love without limits or qualifications or conditions or reservations.'[35] Just as the human mind can ask questions, questions, questions, so the human heart can go on loving, loving, loving. 'Just as unrestricted questioning is our capacity for self-transcendence, so being in love in an unrestricted fashion is the proper fulfilment of that capacity.'[36]

What then can be said about this love?

It is primarily a gift and only secondarily a precept. We love because he first loved us. It is something we do not understand and cannot understand; for it is mystery. It is existential love, love at the level of being. It is love of the finite for the infinite, love of the limited for the unlimited, love of the contingent for the necessary, love of the creature for the creator. This is a spiritual passion that consumes one's whole person. It is the wound of separate being longing for completion, a wound that will only be healed when one's being is united with God who is love. It is the longing of the psalmist who cries passionately: 'O God, you are my God, I seek you, my soul thirsts for you; my flesh faints for you, as in a dry and weary land where there is no water' (Psalm 63). And again the psalmist writes: 'As a deer longs for flowing streams, so my soul longs for you, O God. My soul thirsts for God, for the living God . . .'(Psalm 42). When one's being becomes being-in-love with God one is totally fire, one is intoxicated with the wine of divine love, one enters the spiritual marriage.

Let us never forget, however, that just as God alone is Being in the full sense of the word, God alone is Being-in-love in the full sense of these words. We human beings struggling against our tendency to reject love, to hate ourselves and others, to destroy ourselves and others — we can only become being-in-love in a very restricted sense. We can be being-in-love only in so far as we are united with the Supreme Being-in-love who is God. And to reach this union is a slow and painful process; it is a journey in which one goes out from self into the darkness of the night, suffering the loss of all things, being wounded and beaten and stripped naked like the bride in The Song of Songs. And journey's end is beyond the grave when through death one sees God face to face and is divinized, becoming God by participation. 'What we know is this: when he is revealed, we will be like him, for we will see him as he is' (1 John 3:2).

Yet the bride enters into a spiritual marriage even in this life and some measure of divinization is possible. And this is what the mystical path is all about. As union with God grows in intensity one's being becomes being-in-love in a real, if imperfect, sense. One radiates love to all men and women and to the whole cosmos. Now the precept to be perfect as our Heavenly Father is perfect becomes meaningful. As our Heavenly Father 'makes his sun to rise on the evil and on the good, and sends his rain on the righteous and unrighteous' (Matthew 5:45), so the person whose being is becoming being-in-love radiates a universal love to all people and all things.

In his quaint and attractive way the author of *The Cloud* speaks of the contemplative who radiates love to everyone but especially towards his enemies:

> For why, in this work a perfect worker has no special regard unto any man by himself, whether he be kin or stranger, friend or foe. For all men and women seem like kin to him, and no one is a stranger. All, he thinks, are his friends and none his foes. Indeed he thinks that all who give him pain and do him hurt in this life are his full and special friends; and he thinks that he is moved to wish them as much good as he would to the dearest friend he has.[37]

Such is the contemplative whose being is becoming being-in-love. But let us return to Lonergan.

When he comes to speak about the object of religious love — to asking who or what one is in love with — Lonergan writes:

> To be in love is to be in love with someone. To be in love without qualifications or conditions or limits is to be in love with someone transcendent. When someone transcendent is my beloved, he is in my heart, real to me from within me, supreme in intelligence, truth, goodness. Since he chooses to come to me by a gift of love, he himself must be love.[38]

The object of one's love is a living person, transcendent goodness, love. Who is this person? Can we say more about this person whom Lonergan, with a touch of mystical insight, then calls 'the unknown beloved'?

To do so we must turn to the mystical tradition which from the time of Origen states unequivocally that the object of mystical love is the Word Incarnate. This is the doctrine of St Bernard. This is the doctrine of St John of the Cross who describes his *Spiritual Canticle* as 'stanzas that deal with the exchange of love between the soul and Christ, its Bridegroom'.[39]

Christ the Incarnate Word, then, is the Bridegroom and the one with whom the mystic falls in love. Since Christ is at once human and divine, love for him is both human love and divine love. But to say more about this love it is necessary to consider briefly the mystery of the Incarnation and its role in mystical theology.

INCARNATION

This century, dominated by the historical critical approach to the Bible, has fixed our eyes on the earthly Jesus. Who was this Jesus of Nazareth? Can we come to know the actual words that issued from his lips? What can we say about his miracles and his teaching? These are the questions of the twentieth century.

Needless to say, the historical research of eminent scholars is of the greatest value and has helped innumerable people to read the Bible. But it would be catastrophic for Christian faith if our eyes were so fixed on the historical Jesus as to forget the Jesus who rose from the dead, entered into his glory and even now pleads for us at the right hand of the Father. This Jesus also walks through the pages of the New Testament. His presence is particularly evident in the fourth gospel, in the writings of St Paul and in The Book of Revelation. Jesus is the Lamb who was slain. Jesus can say: 'I am the Alpha and the Omega, the first and the last, the beginning and the end' (Revelation 22:13). The Second Vatican Council speaks in profoundly scriptural language of the Jesus who is alive today:

The Head of the body is Christ. He is the image of the invisible God and in him all things come into being. He has priority over everyone and in him all things hold together. He is the head of that body which is the Church. He is the beginning, the first-born from the dead, so that in all things he might have the first place (cf. Colossians 1:15-18). By the greatness of his power he rules the things of heaven and the things of earth, and with his all-surpassing perfection and activity he fills the whole body with the riches of his glory (cf. Ephesians 1:18-23).[40]

This is the cosmic Christ who is alive in the world today. This is the Christ who is present in the Eucharist 'where natural elements refined by human beings are changed into his glorified body and blood'.[41] This is the Jesus whom the mystics love. This is the Jesus with whom they enter into spiritual marriage. United with him their being becomes being-in-love.

One of the great mystical experiences of the New Testament is that of Stephen the first martyr who, filled with the Holy Spirit, gazed into heaven and saw the glory of God and Jesus standing at the right hand of God. 'Look,' he cried. 'I see the heavens opened and the Son of Man standing at the right hand of God' (Acts 7:56). And while they were stoning him, he prayed, 'Lord Jesus, receive my spirit.'

Evidently, Stephen saw the Jesus who had entered into his glory. But now Jesus was so transfigured and his body so glorified that Stephen could no longer see him with the eyes of the flesh but only with the inner eyes of the spiritual senses. For no human being can have an adequate image or sensible picture of the glorified body of Jesus.

But what is the glorified body? What is the glorified body of Jesus and of those who rise from the dead?

This indeed is a great mystery of Christian faith, and little can be said. Nevertheless, Paul, addressing the Corinthians, some of whom denied the Resurrection, speaks forcefully and clearly. To those who ask this question he first says, 'Fool! What you sow does not come to life unless it dies' (1 Corinthians 15:36). It is as though he were to say, 'Don't ask foolish questions!' And then he goes on to say that not all flesh is alike, but that there is one flesh for human beings, another for animals, another for birds and another for fish. There are heavenly bodies and earthly bodies and star differs from star in glory. So it is with the resurrection of the dead.

However, mystical theology is a pastoral or practical discipline. It does not aim at unravelling the mysteries of the glorified body but at guiding people in an incarnational path wherein they will shun the fascination of pure spirit and turn their minds and hearts to the Incarnate Word. Furthermore, mystical theology teaches them to love but one Jesus — the earthly Jesus of Nazareth who became the heavenly Jesus and is Lord of the Universe. This may sound like a daunting challenge; but in the practical lives of the greatest Christian mystics it has been a non-problem. This is because their eyes were forever fixed on the Crucified. For them the death and glorification of Jesus were inseparable. Such was the case with Paul who gloried in the cross of Our Lord Jesus Christ. Such was the case with the author of *The Apocalypse* who knelt before the Lamb *who was slain*. Such was the mentality of Francis of Assisi who loved the cosmos and loved the Crucified; and such was the case of Julian of Norwich, John of the Cross, Teresa and the rest. Like the apostles in the fourth gospel, they saw the wounds in the glorified body of Jesus. 'Was it not necessary that the Christ should suffer these things and then enter into his glory?' (Luke 24:26).

But union with the Incarnate Word is not the last stage in the mystical journey. For the Incarnate Word is one with the Father in the Holy Spirit. 'I and the Father are one,' said Jesus (John 10:30); and the contemplative who is united with Jesus can also say, 'I and the Father are one.' Indeed, all the members of Jesus — all the people of God; that is to say 'the Catholic faithful as well as all who believe in Christ, and indeed the whole of human kind'[42] are called to the state of being-in-love with the Incarnate Word and through him with the Father.

And so the mystical journey reaches its climax in a Trinitarian experience of love. The human person — and, indeed, the human race — is united with the Son and in the Spirit cries out, 'Abba, Father!'

CONCLUSION

Mystical Theology is the theology of love, concerned primarily with God's love which is poured into the human heart. In describing their experience of love, the mystics make use of colourful symbols and outrageous paradoxes, speaking of cruel fire, blinding light, intoxicating wine and joyful wounds. Mystical theologians, however, who were concerned with spiritual direction and practical guidance, felt the need for sound philosophy and psychology. For this they turned first to the Greeks and later to the scholastics.

Today, as we enter a new age, we feel it necessary to update our mystical theology and to find a new methodology. The method of Bernard Lonergan which speaks of transcendental precepts that lead to human authenticity in the state of being-in-love is of great value.

Now when Lonergan claims that his method is transcendental, he means that it is universal — it enshrines the basic, dynamic thrust of the human person and is applicable to all men and women everywhere and at all times. If one accepts this and its application to mysticism, it follows that all human beings are called to mysticism.

While this may sound astonishing and even revolutionary, it is in fact quite traditional. At the beginning of this century a number of theologians spoke of 'the universal vocation to mysticism'.[43] For them, it is true, universal meant that all Christians are called — the call to mysticism was included in the grace of baptism. This leads to the interesting conclusion that mysticism is not for an elite but is for everyone. Needless to say, this does not mean that everyone is called to the sixth or seventh mansion of Teresa, but it does mean that all are called to be in love with God in an experiential way and that the being of the human family is called to become being-in-love. Assuredly this gives great hope for the future.

NOTES

1. See *The Dark Night*, 2.17.2.
2. *The Spiritual Canticle*, 7.5.
3. *The Dark Night*, 2.17.6.
4. *The Spiritual Canticle*, Prologue 3.
5. *A Second Collection*, Bernard Lonergan, London 1974, p.153.
6. *Why Not Become Totally Fire?*, George Maloney, Paulist Press, New Jersey 1989, p.5.
7. *Uncreated Energy*, George Maloney, New York 1987. For more about uncreated energy see also 'Eastern Christianity', ch. 5 of the present book.
8. *The Spiritual Canticle*, 31.2.
9. *The Living Flame of Love*, 2.2.

10. *The Spiritual Canticle*, 25.5.
11. *The Living Flame of Love*, 1.3.
12. Ibid., 1.6.
13. *The Spiritual Canticle*, 25.7.
14. Ibid., 25.8.
15. Ibid., 26.4.
16. Ibid., 26.5.
17. Ibid., 1.18.
18. Ibid., 13.22.
19. Ibid., 13.9.
20. Ibid., 1.19.
21. *The Living Flame of Love*, 2.9.
22. *Life*, 29.13.
23. Ibid.
24. *The Spiritual Canticle*, 10.6.
25. *Life*, 29.13.
26. *The Spiritual Canticle*, 14 & 15.20.
27. Ibid., 13.4.
28. *The Living Flame of Love*, 2.13.
29. Ibid.
30. Ibid., 2.14.
31. On the relationship between Tantric yoga and hesychasm see *Yoga and the Jesus Prayer Tradition*, Thomas Matus, Paulist Press, New Jersey 1984. See also chapter 9 of this book, 'Mysticism and Vital Energy'.
32. *Method in Theology*, Bernard Lonergan, London 1972, p.105.
33. Ibid.
34. Ibid.
35. Ibid.
36. Ibid., p.106.
37. *The Cloud of Unknowing*, C. 24.
38. *Method*, p.109.
39. *The Spiritual Canticle*, Subtitle.
40. *Lumen Gentium*, 1.7.
41. *Gaudium et Spes*, 1.3.38.
42. *Gaudium et Spes*, 2.13.
43. Réginald Garrigou-Lagrange (1877-1964) and his disciples insisted on the universal call to mysticism. For them mystical experience (which he called infused contemplation) was the normal way to Christian perfection.

—————— ✳ ——————

FIFTEEN

Bride and Bridegroom

YIN AND YANG

The Yin and Yang of Chinese philosophy continue to fascinate the West. Psychologists like Carl Jung and scientists like Niels Bohr have seen profound meaning in this cosmic drama — in the interplay of two principles that represent shadow and light, earth and heaven, passive and active, belly and head, female and male.[1] These are cyclic principles. The Yin of darkness moves to the Yang of light and back again, each containing the germ of the other, as represented in the ancient Chinese symbol *T'ai-chi T'u* or Diagram of the Supreme Ultimate:

Here we find a movement away from Western dualism towards complementarity and the union of opposites, away from 'either or' to 'both and'.

Influenced by the Yin and Yang, Jung developed his theory of the feminine principle in the man, which he called the *anima*, and the masculine principle in the woman which he called the *animus*. Human beings, he held, come to individuation as they struggle to integrate the contrasexual dimension of their personality and consummate the interior marriage. This is the work of a lifetime. Yet once the interior marriage has taken place, however imperfectly, men and women can begin to love deeply and truly without projection and without self-seeking.

THE BIBLICAL TRADITION

The biblical tradition speaks of yet another cosmic drama: the marriage between Israel and Yahweh. Through the bride-bridegroom theme, running all through the history of Israel, the Jewish people spoke of the covenant that embodies God's steadfast love. Alas, the bride is not always faithful to her lover who cries out:

Return, O Israel, to the Lord your God, for you have stumbled because of your iniquity (Hosea 14:1).

Through Isaiah, Jeremiah and Ezekiel, Yahweh threatens Israel and speaks of dire punishment, yet his steadfast love remains unchanged — 'For the mountains may depart and the hills be removed, but my steadfast love shall not depart from you, and my covenant shall not be removed, says the Lord who has compassion on you' (Isaiah 54:10). So the history of Israel can be viewed as a gigantic romance, a gigantic love affair in which bride and bridegroom alike suffer all the joy and all the pain, all the comedy and all the tragedy that is the warp and woof of the stormy man-woman relationship.

And central to this love affair is The Song of Songs with its ravishing and ecstatic love wherein the bridegroom delights in the beauty of the bride while she delights in his loveliness. 'Ah, you are beautiful, my love; ah you are beautiful: your eyes are doves' (Song of Songs 1:15). The being of both bride and bridegroom becomes being-in-love.

In the New Testament Jesus is the bridegroom and his disciples are the bride. 'Can the wedding guests fast while the bridegroom is with them? As long as they have the bridegroom with them, they cannot fast' (Mark 2:19). Yet the day will come when the bridegroom is taken away. Indeed, he is taken away of his own free will, for he proves his love by laying down his life; and Paul who felt this love so deeply ('He loved me and gave himself for me' (Galatians 2:20)) tells human bridegrooms to imitate Jesus in laying down their lives for their wives. 'Husbands, love your wives as Christ loved the church and gave himself up for her . . .' (Ephesians 5:25). It is precisely in dying that the bridegroom shows his radical commitment to the woman he loves.

For Paul the Christian community was the chaste virgin betrothed to Christ. 'I feel a divine jealousy for you,' he writes, 'for I promised you in marriage to one husband, to present you as a chaste virgin to Christ' (2 Corinthians 11:2). But, alas, just as Eve was deceived by the cunning serpent and as the Virgin Israel wandered away from Yahweh, so the community could be led astray from a sincere and pure devotion to Christ. Hence Paul's divine jealousy.

The Pauline version of the community as the faithful yet fickle bride of Christ continued in history, echoing through the sacred writings and sacred liturgies of the Church; and it is alive today when 'God, who spoke of old, uninterruptedly converses with the Bride of his beloved Son'.[2] It is a vision that will be perfectly realized in the *eschaton* when the bride, no longer fickle, is clothed in great beauty and 'the voice of a great multitude, like the sound of many waters and like the sound of mighty thunderpeals cries out: "Hallelujah! ... for the marriage of the Lamb has come and the bride has made herself ready"' (Revelation 19:6, 7). And John can say: 'And I saw the holy city, the new Jerusalem, coming down out of heaven from God, prepared as a bride adorned for her husband' (Revelation 21:2). This is the eschatological marriage, the fulfilment of the covenant between Yahweh and the new Israel. To this marriage all human relationships point: in it they find meaning.

It was the Greek, Origen of Alexandria, who saw that Christ was married not only to the community but also to the individual person. Origen poetically describes the bride, about to wed and burning with love toward the bridegroom, who is the word of God. 'And deeply indeed did she love him, whether we take her as the soul made in his image or as the church . . .'[3] And so from the early centuries of

Christian history there arose a mystical tradition that describes yet another gigantic love affair. Now it is the marriage between the human person and the Incarnate Word. So central is this theme that the mystical theology of Origen, Bernard of Clairvaux, Ambrose of Milan, John of the Cross and Teresa of Jesus can truly be called a theology of marriage. All leads to the spiritual marriage, the highest degree of divine union to which a human being can attain in this life. Yet even this is not the end.

Through death and entrance into glory there comes an even more intimate union which can be called the glorious marriage. This is nothing less than the vision of God.

But what is the nature of this marriage and what is its relationship to human love and intimacy and sexuality? In order to reflect on this theologically it is necessary first to speak about interpersonal relationships.

PERSON TO PERSON

'For mental prayer in my opinion,' writes St Teresa, 'is nothing else than an intimate sharing between friends; it means taking time frequently to be alone with Him who we know loves us.'[4] And this interpersonal dimension of prayer lies at the very heart of the mystical traditions of Judaism, Islam and Christianity. Holy familiarity with Yahweh characterizes the saints of the Hebrew scriptures. Moses is the great mystic precisely because God spoke to him face to face as a man might speak to his friend, while Job and Jonah call out to God as to a person with whom they have an intimate relationship. 'I love you, O Lord, my strength' cries the psalmist (Psalm 18); and his words have echoed in the hearts of countless mystics through the centuries.

In the case of St Teresa the friend 'who we know loves us' is the Incarnate Word, Jesus who died on the cross and entered into his glory. This is the Jesus who said, 'no longer do I call you servants . . . but I call you friends because everything I heard from my father I have made known to you' (John 15:15). And intimacy with the glorified Jesus runs through the entire Christian mystical tradition. It appears in Origen who writes movingly that no one can understand the fourth gospel who has not lain on the breast of Jesus as did the beloved disciple. It appears in the hesychasts who unceasingly recited the Jesus prayer. It appears in Bernard of Clairvaux whose mysticism centres on Jesus, in à Kempis who writes delicately about familiar friendship with Jesus, in Ignatius of Loyola who wanted his disciples to be companions of Jesus. It all fits with Lonergan's falling in love and being in love without restriction.

It need hardly be said that this falling in love is not just a question of words. As intimacy grows, there are periods of silence, of union or communion — there are times when self seems to be lost. All is leading to an experience of indwelling like that of Paul who cried, 'I live, now not I, but Christ lives in me' (Galatians 2:20). This indwelling fills the pages of the fourth gospel where Jesus says to his disciples: 'Dwell in me as I in you' (John 15:4) and tells them to abide in his love. The climax is transformation when one 'becomes' Christ. This is closely associated with the Eucharist of which St Leo the Great says, 'the partaking of the Body and Blood of Christ does nothing other than transform us into that which we consume'.[5] Here we are at the apex of the mystical life.

Furthermore, this interpersonal dimension of prayer overflows into ordinary life with its relationships between people. The Second Vatican Council notes this when it writes: 'Indeed, the Lord Jesus, when he prayed to the Father "that all may be one . . . as we are one"' (John 17:21, 22) opened up vistas closed to human reason. For he implied a certain likeness between the union of the divine persons and the union of God's children in truth and charity. This likeness reveals that the human person who is the only creature on earth which God willed for itself, cannot fully find self except through a sincere gift of self.'[6]

In this simple statement the Council makes three points of immense theological significance. One is that union between human beings is modelled on union between the persons of the Blessed Trinity. The second is that while all things are created for human beings, human beings are created for themselves. The third is that only in death (the gift of oneself) can human beings find themselves.

Finally, it must never be forgotten that love for the Word overflows on the whole universe in which the Word has become incarnate. This is particularly evident in the mysticism of St Francis of Assisi who talked familiarly with the birds and animals, who joyfully loved brother sun and sister moon. The same spirit pervades Mahayana Buddhism whose saints go out to all sentient beings in the most radical compassion.

MAN AND WOMAN

The primary form of interpersonal communion is the man-woman relationship. Such is the teaching of the Second Vatican Council which, commenting on the first chapters of Genesis, says that God did not create man as a solitary since from the beginning 'male and female he created them' and goes on to say that 'their companion-ship produces the primary form of interpersonal communion'.[7] All the animals were brought to Adam and he named them one by one; but only Eve was his equal, only she was flesh of his flesh and bone of his bone. With her he could have a friendship and an intimacy that was far beyond his relationship with the flowers of the field and the birds of the air.

Now the mystics claim that they find a new dimension of love in this man-woman relationship. Identifying with the bride (and it is significant that both men and women mystics identify with the bride) they claim to experience a profound love of the divine bride-groom who communicates himself to the soul by pure spirit. This is a love that goes far beyond anything that human beings can imagine, far beyond anything that eye has seen or ear heard or the human mind conceived. It is an eminently human love, bringing great joy and intense suffering. Beginning as a tiny, scarcely perceptible stirring, it grows to become a mighty fire or a living flame of such power that, says St John of the Cross, its violent onslaught could cause death if God did not intervene.

The mystics find this love in Hosea, Isaiah and Ezekiel. They find it in the torrid verses of The Song of Songs where 'love is strong as death and passion fierce as the grave' (Song of Songs 8:6). The love they discover goes beyond the romantic, beyond the sexual to a dimension in which they can claim that their very being becomes being-in-love.

In the New Testament the mystics find this divine love embodied above all in Mary Magdalene who is the bride of The Song of Songs, searching tearfully in the garden for the one she loves. 'Tell me where you have laid him and I will take him away' (John 20:15). The anonymous author of *The Cloud of Unknowing* writes movingly of the tender love between Jesus and Mary Magdalene:

> Sweet was the love between Our Lord and Mary. Much love had she to him. Much more had he to her. For whoso would utterly behold all that passed between him and her . . . will find that nothing beneath him might comfort her, nor yet hold her heart from him.[8]

So great was the love of Jesus for Mary that 'he blamed Simon the Leper in his own house, because he thought against her. This was great love: this was surpassing love.'[9]

This mystical love is a great mystery which no human mind can fathom. Yet it does have expressions and fruits by which it can be known. The first of these is a willingness to die for the beloved. There is no greater love than that of the person who will sacrifice life for a friend. Such love is found in literature as in life, as in the Dickensian character, heroic and dissolute, who went to the guillotine for his friend. 'It is a far, far better thing I do than I have ever done.' The willingness to go to prison, to suffer, to take up the cross in daily life — these are the proofs and the expressions of the divine love that awakens deep in the human heart. It is a love that 'bears all things, believes all things, hopes all things, endures all things' (1 Corinthians 13:7).

This love may also be expressed in a word, a look, a gesture, a smile, a small act of kindness, a tender embrace. Most importantly it can be expressed in sexual intercourse, the physical love wherein a man and woman surrender radically to one another and become one flesh. It need hardly be said that millions of hidden and forgotten mystics in all generations and in all religions have expressed their love for their spouse in this way and have reached spiritual marriage by the route of human marriage. They have expressed their love not only in their unwavering, if demanding, fidelity to their marriage partner but also in the daily life of sacrifice for their children and society at large. These are the mystics who save the world.

At the same time no one can forget the millions of mystics of all religious traditions who have expressed this divine love by refraining from sexual intercourse and leading a life of continence. These are the celibates who have forgone sexual intercourse, believing that for them (though not for the whole human race) abstinence from sexual activity allows the inner flame of love to grow and flourish. Such people love very deeply; and sometimes they have celibate friendships of unparalleled intimacy. Often they live lives of radical service to humanity and are prophetic voices in a tumultuous world. The Council hints that such celibates enter into another kind of marriage. Speaking of the celibacy of priests it observes that 'by their celibacy they invoke the mysterious marriage which was established by God and will be manifested in the future and by which the church has Christ as her only spouse'.[10] Celibates know that while celibacy is a charismatic gift granted to a few for lives of love and service, marriage is the vocation through which the majority serve the world and come to the eschatological marriage with the divine bridegroom.

Whether one is married or celibate, divine, mystical love is the same gift of God. Indeed it is the greatest gift, surpassing all the most wonderful charisms, as Paul said so well when he told the Corinthians that 'the greatest of these is love' (1 Corinthians 13:13).

Let us then consider some characteristics of this love.

LOVE AND BEAUTY

'How beautiful you are, my love, how very beautiful!' (Song of Songs 4:1). Bride and bridegroom are fascinated by the blinding beauty they see in one another. 'You are altogether beautiful my love; there is no flaw in you' (Song of Songs 4:7). And Origen reads into these lines a love for transcendental beauty, a love for uncreated beauty and he writes:

> The soul is moved by heavenly love and longing when, having clearly beheld the beauty and the fairness of the Word of God, it falls deeply in love with his loveliness . . .[11]

The scholastics, following Plato and Aristotle, spoke of the transcendentals: the one, the true, the good and the beautiful

Unum Verum Bonum Pulchrum

And it is transcendental beauty, the source of all earthly beauty, that the mystics see when they look ecstatically at their beloved. So overwhelming is this transcendental beauty that it kills any mortal who behold it. 'May the vision of thy beauty be my death!' cries St John of the Cross; and he tells us that the bride 'knows that the instant she sees this beauty she will be carried away by it, and absorbed in this very beauty, and transformed in this beauty, and made beautiful like this beauty itself, and enriched and provided for like this very beauty'.[12]

It should be noted that a great number of the mystics of East and West were poets, artists, lovers of beauty. One could mention the psalmist and the prophet Isaiah. One could speak of God's troubadour, St Francis. One could speak of the poet who composed the Heart Sutra, and of Basho and Ryokan. One could speak of innumerable Zen teachers who mastered the art of calligraphy and artistically practised the tea ceremony. All these were lovers of natural beauty. But did they not also have a glimpse of transcendental beauty, of uncreated beauty? If the world around us is so beautiful, and if men and women can live lives of such beauty, what is one to say of the divine artist who is the source of all?

St John of the Cross had already composed the greater part of his renowned *Spiritual Canticle* when he met a Carmelite nun and asked her to describe her prayer. Francesca de la Madre de Dios replied that she prayed by looking at the beauty of God and rejoicing that he has it. This answer delighted the saint who began to speak ecstatically about the beauty of God and finally composed the last five stanzas of his great poem, beginning with the words, 'Let us rejoice, Beloved, and go forth to behold ourselves in your beauty.'

> *Gocémonos, Amado,*
> *y vámanos a ver en tu hermosura*

Commenting on these lines and intoxicated by the blinding fascination of uncreated beauty, he burst into song, asking the bridegroom 'that we may attain to the vision of ourselves in your beauty in eternal life'.[13] He continues with a startling hymn to personified beauty:

> That is: that I be so transformed in your beauty, that we may be alike in beauty, and both behold ourselves in your beauty, possessing then your very beauty; this, in such a way that each looking at the other may see in the other their own beauty, since both are your beauty alone, I being absorbed in your beauty; hence I shall see you in your beauty, and you will see yourself in me in your beauty; that I may resemble you in your beauty, and you resemble me in your beauty, and my beauty be your beauty and your beauty my beauty; wherefore I shall be you in your beauty, and you will be me in your beauty, because your very beauty will be my beauty; and thus we shall behold each other in your beauty.[14]

In this extraordinary prayer to the Word Incarnate who is transcendental beauty the saint combines poetic hyperbole with theological accuracy. He is using the mirror image, common to mystics of East and West. The bridegroom is the mirror into which the bride gazes with all-consuming love. And what does she see? She sees the bridegroom, the Word of God who is uncreated beauty; and she also sees herself now participating in that uncreated beauty — 'and I shall be you in your beauty, and you will be me in your beauty'. This is ecstasy. This is transforming union. This is a foretaste of eternal life.

BETROTHAL

The house is now all stilled. Everyone is asleep. The bride steals out into the night: she has a rendezvous with her lover, the one she knows so well, the one who waits secretly in a place where no one else appears. And when she finds him she promises to be his bride:

allí le prometí de ser su esposa

Later comes the union when she abandons herself, laying her head on the breast of her beloved, leaving her cares forgotten among the lilies:

> *Quedéme ye olvidéme*
> *el rostro recliné sobre el Amado*
> *cesó todo y dejéme*
> *dejando me Cuidado*
> *entre las azucenas olbidado*

Such is the story of the bride of the Incarnate Word. The spiritual marriage into which she enters is the climax of divine love in this life; yet it is only a shadow of that other glorious and eschatological marriage which through death takes place in eternity. 'However sublime may be the knowledge God gives the soul in this life,' writes St John of the Cross, 'it is but a glimpse of him from a great distance.'[15] Vision comes only through death.

In his prose commentary St John of the Cross interprets the romantic story of the bride in cold, scholastic terms. The house is all stilled (*mi casa sosegada*) because the rebellious passions and unruly faculties have been put to sleep in the dark night; and now the soul goes out of itself with great ease and tranquillity:

> The enamoured soul must leave its house, then, in order to reach its desired goal. It must go out at night when all the members of the house are asleep, that is, when the lower opera-tions, passions and appetites of its soul are put to sleep by means of the night. These are the people of its household who when awake are a continual hindrance to the reception of any good.[16]

After the struggle and suffering of the dark night a great stillness descends upon the bride and she goes forth silently and securely. The going forth, the ecstasy, is only the beginning of a long, long journey that leads to union.

Bride and bridegroom kiss and embrace. 'The kiss is the union . . .

in which the soul is made equal to God through love.'[17] The bride who has always longed to see the face of God without the mediation of human beings or angels or any created thing prays 'that my nature now alone and denuded of all temporal, natural and spiritual impurity may be united with you alone, with your nature alone, through no intermediary'.[18] This is the sanjuanist interpretation of the opening lines of The Song of Songs, 'Let him kiss me with the kisses of his mouth!' (Song of Songs 1:1).

The embrace is 'as though she were placed in the arms of her bridegroom'.[19] St John of the Cross sees this as akin to the experience of St Paul, and he writes: 'As a result she usually experiences an intimate spiritual embrace, which is a veritable embrace, by means of which she lives the life of God. The words of St Paul are verified in this soul: "I live, now not I, but Christ lives in me"' (Galatians 2:20).[20]

In this romance it is important to remember that the bridegroom takes the initiative and searches for the bride with whom he is in love. 'In the first place it should be known', writes St John of the Cross, 'that if anyone is seeking God, the Beloved is seeking that person much more.'[21] The prior love of God who passionately loves the human family and the individual person is the key to the whole drama. St John of the Cross emphasizes this by quoting at length the vivid sixteenth chapter of Ezekiel where Yahweh, seeing the infant Israel derelict, abandoned and floundering in her blood, loves her deeply and takes her into his care to rear her and make her his beloved bride and queen:

> As for your birth, on the day you were born your navel cord was not cut, nor were you washed with water to cleanse you, nor rubbed with salt, nor wrapped in cloths. No eye pitied you, to do any of these things for you out of compassion for you; but you were thrown out in the open field, for you were abhorred on the day you were born (Ezekiel 16:4, 5).

Such was the infant Israel. Such is the human race. Such is the individual soul. We are all helpless, abandoned, abhorred, cast out in the field.

But Yahweh saw us and was moved to compassion:

I passed by you, and saw you flailing about in your blood. As you lay in your blood, I said to you, 'Live! and grow up like a plant of the field.' You grew up and became tall and arrived at full womanhood, your breasts were formed, and your hair had grown; yet you were naked and bare (Ezekiel 16:6, 7).

But when the virgin Israel grew tall and beautiful, Yahweh entered into a covenant with her, taking her as his bride:

I passed by you again and looked on you; you were at the age for love. I spread the edge of my cloak over you and entered into a covenant with you, says the Lord God, and you became mine. Then I bathed you with water and washed off the blood from you, and anointed you with oil (Ezekiel 16:8, 9).

Now she is to become the privileged and glorious queen. Yahweh adorns her with ornaments, putting a bracelet on her arms, a chain on her neck, a ring on her nose, earrings in her ears and a beautiful crown on her head. She is clothed with garments of gold and silver; she eats flour and honey and oil. Yahweh continues:

You grew exceedingly beautiful, fit to be a queen. Your fame spread among the nations on account of your beauty, for it was perfect because of my splendour that I had bestowed on you, says the Lord God (Ezekiel 16:13, 14).

St John of the Cross quotes Ezekiel in full and quietly remarks, 'And so it happens with the soul of which we are speaking.'[22] The point is that the loving initiative comes from God and that everything in the mystical path is gift. And what a gift! The helpless, abandoned infant is to become the ravishingly beautiful bride of the Word Incarnate.

SPIRITUAL MARRIAGE

An important aspect of the marital relationship is that bride and bridegroom are equal with an equality that comes from love. This is a point to which St John of the Cross constantly returns. The Son of

God, he writes, wishes to exalt the soul and maker her equal to himself; and he continues:

> For the property of love is to make the lover equal to the object loved. Since the soul in this state possesses perfect love, she is called the bride of the Son of God, which signifies equality with him. In this equality of friendship the possessions of both are held in common, as the Bridegroom himself said to his disciples: 'I have now called you my friends, because all that I have heard from my Father I have manifested to you' (John 15:15).[23]

In this way the bridegroom loves the bride so much that he makes her his equal. For her part the bride has a great longing to be equal to the Son of God:

> The soul's aim is a love equal to God's. She always desired this equality, naturally and supernaturally, for lovers cannot be satisfied without feeling that they love as much as they are loved.[24]

Nor is this just poetic hyperbole. The saint justifies his extraordinary thesis with a Thomistic theology which states that God who does not love anything outside himself somehow puts the soul inside himself and makes her his equal:

> It should be noted . . . that just as God loves nothing outside himself, he bears no love for anything lower than the love he has for himself. He loves all things for himself; thus love becomes the purpose for which he loves. He therefore does not love things because of what they are in themselves. With God, to love the soul is to put her somehow inside himself and make her his equal. Thus he loves the soul within himself, with himself, that is, with the very love by which he loves himself.[25]

God loves because he loves. He loves himself and all things within himself. In this way St John of the Cross explains the sublime vocation of the human person, which is nothing less than a call to divinization and equality with God through love.

The marriage is consummated. 'Just as in the consummation of carnal marriage there are two in one flesh, as sacred Scripture points out (Genesis 2:24), so also when the spiritual marriage between God and the soul is consummated, there are two natures in one spirit and love, as St Paul says in making this same comparison: "Whoever is joined to the Lord is one spirit with him"' (1 Corinthians 6:17).[26] Here it is important to note that while in this marriage there is one spirit and one love, there are still two natures. The soul is divinized through love, but human nature never becomes divine nature. St John of the Cross is careful to avoid any taint of pantheism.

Yet the union is extraordinary; and the saint can write:

This spiritual marriage . . . is a total transformation in the Beloved, in which each surrenders the entire possession of self to the other with a certain consummation of the union of love. The soul thereby becomes divine, God through participation, insofar as is possible in this life.[27]

Elsewhere the saint uses other comparisons, saying that the two become one as the window unites with the ray of sunlight or the coal with the fire or the starlight with the light of the sun. Yet in the end no words can describe this union, just as no words can describe the being of God.

MYSTICISM AND SEXUALITY

It is generally agreed that from the early centuries of our era the Christian approach to human sexuality has been negative. This is sometimes attributed to the Neoplatonic influence on the Church Fathers, an influence that is all too evident in the mystical tradition. Origen, who violently rejected his own sexuality and opted for a totally spiritual interpretation of The Song of Songs, stands like a giant at the springs of the mystical stream. His Neoplatonic influence is still with us. Yet side by side with this negative approach to sexuality was a positive love for celibacy and virginity with a realization that continence for the kingdom is a privileged path to God. Undoubtedly this is one of the glories of the Christian mystical tradition.

Marriage was considered second best. There were, of course, married mystics; but it was never clear how they integrated sexual experience with mystical prayer. As for the celibates, while the ideal was transformation of sexual energy — and great mystics like Francis of Assisi and Teresa of Avila and others did transform their sexual energy into extraordinary spiritual power — many thought they must crush or reject their sexuality in order to walk the mystical path to God.

St Teresa, speaking about spiritual marriage, is somewhat typical:

And even though the comparison may be a coarse one, I cannot find another that would better explain what I mean than the sacrament of marriage. This spiritual espousal is different in kind from marriage, for in these matters that we are dealing with there is never anything that is not spiritual. Corporal things are far distant from them, and the spiritual joy the Lord gives when compared to the delights married people must experience are a thousand leagues distant. For it is all a matter of love united with love, and the actions of love are most pure and so extremely delicate and gentle that there is no way of explaining them . . .[28]

St Teresa here says something important: that the joys of the spirit are far greater than the pleasures of the flesh. But she fails to see that these spiritual joys can also be given to married people. Elsewhere she concedes that married people may walk the path of sanctity, but their speed will be that of a hen.

In an article on mysticism and sexuality Bernard McGinn observes that the Christian mystical tradition has seen little connection between sexuality and sanctity.[29] While Christian mystics from the time of Origen use sexual imagery abundantly — so much so, that there is a link between mysticism and erotic language — they eschew sexual practice as incompatible with the mystical path to God. This is in sharp contrast with Judaism and Islam where sexual practice, as well as sexual imagery, play their part in the mystical life. 'Jews and Muslims', writes Bernard McGinn, 'were able to develop types of mysticism that made use of transformed sexual activity; that is, marital intercourse practised within, and as part of, a spiritual discipline.'[30] In

Judaism God's command to procreate played its part in the mystical life. In Islam the majority of mystics were married; and according to Ibn Arabi, the 'Supreme Master' of the sufis, the sexual activity of the true mystic is the favoured way to achieve union with God.

Professor McGinn has the greatest esteem for the celibacy and virginity that have played a vital role in the Christian mystical tradition; but he asks if this is the only viable form of Christian mysticism. We are at the threshold of a new stage in Christian mysticism and he asks the significant question:

> If the present interest in spirituality and mysticism indicates the possibility of the beginning of what might become a new layer, or stratum, in the long story of Christian mysticism, one that does not cancel what went before, but rather both learns from it and yet still creates its own new possibilities for deeper life in God, then the issue of what to do with sexuality forms . . . one of the most serious problems to be addressed.[31]

What to do with sexuality? The answer is clear. Sexuality must be integrated and transformed — never annihilated but integrated and transformed both by married and celibate people. But how does this integration and transformation come about?

St John of the Cross, as has already been said, insists that it comes about only through the dark night, which is an inflow of God into the soul, a deep and harrowing purification of the whole person. But St John of the Cross was a celibate, writing for celibates; and we may legitimately ask if there is another path or if the dark night can take another form for married people.

In approaching this challenging problem Professor McGinn wisely suggests dialogue with Judaism and Islam. Here we might add one more suggestion: dialogue with Asia.

Chinese and Japanese cultures have found ways of directing and guiding and balancing the psychic energy that flows through the human body. This is central to Chinese medicine as well as to the martial arts. But it is principally in meditation that the transformation of energy is achieved — through breathing and posture and above all through the living out of the total commitment of faith.

Even more important than dialogue with China and Japan is dialogue with India and Tibet where the transformation of sexual energy through *kundalini* yoga is highly developed. Obviously dialogue does not mean total acceptance and assimilation. It simply means prudent study with good will and fidelity to truth.

Such dialogue will demand both great scholarship and great mystical experience. It is beyond the scope of this present work. Here it will be sufficient to reflect on what the Christian mystical tradition is saying today.

COMMUNITY OF LOVE

Speaking of the universal vocation to sanctity the Second Vatican Council points out that married people have their own distinctive path to God. The Council then outlines a spirituality of marriage that could well become the basis for a mysticism no less powerful, no less earthshaking, no less demanding than that of Origen, Bernard, Teresa of Jesus and the rest.

The Council reminds us that God is the author of marriage and that the intimate partnership of married life is rooted in the conjugal covenant of irrevocable personal consent. For marriage is modelled on the covenant between Israel and Yahweh. It gives birth to a community of love; it is a path in which the spouses love one another and their children with a love like that of Christ who gave himself up for his bride the Church:

> For as God of old made himself present to his people through a covenant of love and fidelity, so now the Saviour of men and the Spouse of the Church comes into the lives of married Christians. He abides with them thereafter so that just as he loved the Church and handed himself over on her behalf, the spouses may love each other with perpetual fidelity through spiritual self-bestowal.[32]

In this way Christ the saviour enters into this community of love and walks with the family. There may be a presence of Christ similar to the sense of presence experienced by the mystics. Even more importantly there is a progressive divinization of the family when 'human love is caught up into divine love'[33] and 'there is a merging of the human with the divine'.[34] Now we move towards spiritual marriage which is the crown of the mystical life.

Here, it should be noted, there could be an evolution or a development in mystical theology. Whereas the earliest Christian tradition, following Judaism, saw the spiritual marriage as union between God and Israel, and Origen saw it as union between God and the individual person, now we can see spiritual marriage as a union between Yahweh and the married couple. Now we can see the couple hand in hand climbing Mount Carmel and passing through the dark night of the soul. They have all the joy and all the suffering, all the ecstasy and all the agony — but in a new context.

Without separating sexual intercourse from the overall context of conjugal love, the Council says that the marital act expresses and perfects the covenantal love existing between the spouses:

> This love is uniquely expressed and perfected through the marital act. The actions within marriage by which the couple are united intimately and chastely are noble and worthy ones. Expressed in a manner which is truly human, these actions signify and promote that mutual self-giving by which spouses enrich each other with a joyful and thankful will.[35]

This self-giving recalls how Christ gave himself to death for his bride the Church. Total self-giving is indeed an integral part of a mystical life which centres on *todo y nada* — and sexual intercourse signifies and promotes such self-giving.

That sexual intercourse should take place in the context of prayer pertains to the biblical tradition. One has only to read the Book of Tobit:

> When the parents had gone out and shut the door of the room, Tobias got out of bed and said to Sarah, 'Sister, get up, and let us pray and implore our Lord that he grant us mercy and safety.' So she got up, and they began to pray and implore that they might be kept safe (Tobit 8:4).

It is then that Tobias prays: 'I now am taking this kinswoman of mine, not because of lust, but with sincerity' (Tobit 8:7). As in the whole Bible, the Book of Tobit idealizes sexual union while calling for sexual restraint.

Professor McGinn is surely right in advocating dialogue with other religious traditions which integrate sexual intercourse into the mystical path. In doing so, however, let us be open to the possibility that these mystical traditions will also teach us the value of refraining from sexual intercourse at certain times — periodic continence — in order to walk more surely the mystical way. This we will learn from Judaism. This we will learn from Islam. This we will learn pre-eminently from authentic Tantric Buddhism which, far from advocating unbridled sexual indulgence, demands the most rigorous asceticism.

But what, it may be asked, is the value of periodic continence or periods of celibacy?

Here, men and women who aspire to mysticism within marriage would do well to reflect on what the old authors called 'the use and non-use of creatures'. There is a time when human beings find love, energy, joy and strength by using created things on their path to God: there is a time when human beings find love, energy, joy and strength by not using these same created things. As wise old Qoheleth said, there is a time for everything under the sun — there is 'a time to embrace and a time to refrain from embracing' (Ecclesiastes 3:5). It is all a question of timing.

That there is a time to embrace is all too clear. There is a time to express authentic love bodily — to surrender oneself to the other, to cooperate with God in the work of creation. But why refrain from embracing?

Here one can recall that just as fasting, the non-use of food, clears the mind for prayer, so refraining from sexual intercourse by mutual agreement can bring a similar clarity. Paul prudently and cautiously writes to the Corinthians: 'Do not deprive one another except perhaps by agreement for a set time to devote yourselves to prayer . . .' (1 Corinthians 7:5). Again, periodic refraining from sexual intercourse by mutual agreement creates the detachment from the outer senses that leads to the awakening of the inner spiritual senses.

Liberated from the tyranny of sense, men and women can love one another with a mystical love that transcends, without excluding, the sensual. Again, particularly in our times, responsible parents, seeing that they must limit their family, may feel called to periodic continence. Needless to say, this presupposes assiduous prayer, honest dialogue, sensitivity to the working of the Spirit in self and the other, prudent discernment and authentic love. All this is part of the mystical path.

Finally it must be said that much of what is written here about marriage is necessarily tentative. The mystical theology of married life is yet to be written. It will no doubt be written by men and women who have together read The Song of Songs, climbed Mount Carmel, passed through the night of the soul and aspire to enter into spiritual marriage with the Incarnate Word.

NOTES

1. The Danish physicist Niels Bohr, his interpretation of quantum theory fully elaborated, visited China in 1937 and was impressed by the Chinese Yin and Yang. In 1947 he was knighted and chose as motif for his coat-of-arms the Chinese symbol *t'ai-chi* together with the inscription *Contraria sunt complementa.*
2. The Second Vatican Council, *Dei Verbum*, II.8.
3. Origen: *The Song of Songs: Commentary and Homilies*, trans. R. P. Lawson, New York 1956, Prologue, p.29.
4. St Teresa: *The Book of Her Life*, 8.4.
5. St Leo the Great, "Serm." 63.7 *Patrologia Latina*, ed. J.B. Migue, Paris, 54, 357 C.
6. *Gaudium et Spes*, I.II.24.
7. Ibid., 1.1.12.
8. *The Cloud of Unknowing*, C.22.
9. Ibid.
10. *Presbyterorum Ordinis*, III.2.16.
11. Origen., Op. supra cit., p. 29.
12. *Spiritual Canticle*, II.10.
13. *Spiritual Canticle*, 36.5
14. Ibid.
15. Ibid., 13.10.
16. *The Dark Night*, II.14.1.
17. *Spiritual Canticle*, 24.5.
18. Ibid., 22.7.
19. Ibid., 22.5.

20. Ibid.
21. *The Living Flame*, 3.28.
22. *Spiritual Canticle*, 23.6.
23. Ibid., 28.1.
24. Ibid., 38.3.
25. Ibid., 32.6.
26. Ibid., 22.3.
27. Ibid.
28. *Interior Castle*, V.4.3.
29. See "Mysticism and Sexuality' by Bernard McGinn in *The Way*, Supplement 77, Summer 1993.
30. Ibid.
31. Ibid.
32. *Gaudium et Spes*, II.1.48.
33. Ibid.
34. Ibid., II.1.49.
35. Ibid.

———————— * ————————

SIXTEEN

Union

ALL THINGS ARE ONE

During this century scientists everywhere have come to an acute realization of the unity of the universe. The old Newtonian world view which saw solid bodies, separate entities, moving in time and space, has given way to a world view which sees the universe as a field of energy pervaded by consciousness. Now we see the interrelatedness and interdependence of all existing things, so much so, that it is no longer possible to separate the observer from the observed. Penetrating into the secrets of the subatomic world, scientists have seen with shock that the old logic no longer seems to apply: they are faced with a universe of uncertainty.

Albert Einstein, convinced that God does not play dice, was greatly concerned with the search for a unified foundation for physics. Many scientists followed in his footsteps. Some turned to Asian thought, claiming that they found a remarkable similarity between their scientific conclusions and the insights of Oriental mystics. Recently a distinguished Japanese physicist joined the search. Mutsuo Yanase, in a book entitled *Meeting God through Science*, maintains that the unifying force is existence and finally the source of all existence; namely, God.[1] Through an attitude which he calls 'hidden realism' Yanase comes to grasp a fundamental existence underlying all existences, an existence which is hidden but very real. One finds this reality, he claims, not through formal logic which gives clear, conceptual knowledge but through fuzzy logic which gives obscure knowledge in a cloud of unknowing. This reality is the God of the Christian mystics.

In all this, Professor Yanase passes from physics to metaphysics.

He is particularly influenced by Aquinas who was at once a consummate mystic and an insightful metaphysician. In both capacities Aquinas had a profound vision of the universe as one in God.

ALL THINGS ARE NOT ONE

If all things are one, common sense tells us that all things are not one. This is the paradox that faced the Greeks; and they formulated the problem of 'the one and the many'. Aquinas inherited this problem and, following Aristotle, he solved it by holding that all things are one by reason of their existence (*that they are*) and many by reason of their essence (*what they are*). In God, who is the source, essence and existence are one. The Being that unifies all beings is God.

But there is yet another way — a tragic way — in which we are separated. Torn asunder by arrogance, covetousness, lust, gluttony, envy, anger and sloth, we have fought one another, plundered the environment, alienated ourselves from the universe in which we live. Even now, political, social, economic, racial and ideological disputes continue; and with these unbridled passions comes the danger of a war that will reduce everything to ashes.

Buddhism is aware of all this. It sees that all is suffering (*dukkha*). It speaks of illusion (*maya*) and of the illusory separate self. It speaks of pernicious dualism and of karma inherited from past lives. And it holds out the hope that all sentient beings, becoming Buddhas, will enter into nirvana. This is the Buddhist mystical path in which the separate little ego is lost and all becomes one.

For St John of the Cross and the traditional mystical theology all goes back to the garden of Eden and the revolt against God. Adam and Eve were contemplative — in harmony with themselves and the environment. Living in communion with God, Adam gave names to the animals while he walked in the garden of delight. But he and the woman fell from grace into a cruel dualism which separated them from God, from one another and from mother earth. And we, poor children of Eve, have inherited their sin.

The mystical path is a return to union. That is to say, it is a return to union with God, union with all men and women, union with the universe and union within ourselves. But what a struggle this is! The journey would be utterly impossible without God's grace.

UNION WITH GOD

St John of the Cross, being a committed Thomist, saw that all things are one by reason of their existence in God. Speaking of the mystical union he writes:

> To understand the nature of this union, one should know that God sustains every soul and dwells in it substantially, even though it be the greatest sinner in the world. This union between God and creatures always exists. By it he conserves their being so that if the union should end, the world would immediately be annihilated and cease to exist.[2]

In this way God is the hidden reality, holding all things in existence.

However, as a mystical theologian, St John of the Cross is concerned primarily with another union that comes from love. 'Consequently', he writes, 'in discussing union with God we are not discussing the substantial union that always exists, but the soul's union with and transformation in God that does not always exist, except when there is likeness of love.'[3]

The union with God that mystical theology speaks of, then, is a union through love and is the fruit of a journey of love. It depends on God's grace and human free will. This journey is the ascent of Mount Carmel with its *nada, nada, nada*; it is the dark night which liberates and purifies from the shackles of sin and inordinate affection, even when it tortures and torments the soul. 'When the soul rids itself completely of what is repugnant and unconformed to the divine will, it rests transformed in God through love.'[4] In other words, when the soul rids itself completely of what is repugnant and unconformed to the divine will, its being becomes being-in-love.

This love can be described in terms of indwelling, as though the bridegroom was asleep in the centre of the soul:

> Oh, how happy is this soul, which ever experiences God resting

and reposing within it! Oh, how fitting it is for it to withdraw from things, flee from business matters and live in immense tranquillity, so that it may not, even with the slightest dust or noise, disturb or trouble its heart where the Beloved dwells.[5]

Just as there are many mansions or dwelling places in the interior castle, so there are many ways in which God can dwell in created beings:

> In some souls he dwells alone, and in others he does not dwell alone. Abiding in some he is pleased, and in others he is displeased. He lives in some as though in his own house, commanding and ruling everything; and in others as though a stranger in a strange house, where they do not permit him to give orders or do anything.[6]

Yet the union can become so powerful that the soul appears to be God:

> When God grants this supernatural favour to the soul, so great a union is caused that all the things of both God and the soul become one in participant transformation, and the soul appears to be God more than a soul. Indeed, it is God by participation. Yet truly, its being (even though transformed) is naturally as distinct from God as it was before, just as the window, although illumined by the ray, has being distinct from the ray's.[7]

In all this, St John of the Cross undoubtedly speaks from experience. He knows that at the beginning of the contemplative life one experiences a sense of presence with the conviction that God is within and around. First there is Teresa's prayer of quiet wherein one is united with God at a deep level while the imagination, the fool of the house, romps wildly here and there. Then comes a deep union wherein one is totally immersed in God like a sponge in the vast ocean. Passing through the dark night one forgets self so completely that 'the soul appears to be God rather than the soul'. Now the soul is God 'by participation'.

With these words St John of the Cross echoes the biblical phrase constantly quoted by the Eastern mystics — 'that we may become participants of the divine nature' (2 Peter 1:4). Furthermore, he follows Aquinas who taught that we share in God's being by analogy. Yet to experience this union profoundly is overwhelming. Left to herself the soul might think she has become God; but by faith she knows she is distinct from God just as the window illumined by the ray has being distinct from the ray's.

In the Christian life, however, all union with God is through Jesus Christ our Lord. It is necessary, then, to consider the role of Christ in the mystical union.

UNION WITH CHRIST

Christ is the bridegroom with whom the soul is united in mystical marriage. To understand the mystics, however, it is of the greatest importance to remember their faith that Christ the bridegroom is the eternal Word of God, consubstantial with the Father. 'In the beginning was the Word and the Word was with God and the Word was God' (John 1:1). Furthermore, the Word enlightens everyone coming into the world and has done so from the beginning of time. The Second Vatican Council, following the Church Fathers, states this clearly:

> Before becoming flesh in order to save all things and to sum them up in himself, he was in the world already as 'the true light that enlightens everyone'.[8]

The Word has been present to every man and woman who has ever been born; and by his Incarnation he united himself with all men and women. This, again, the Second Vatican Council makes clear:

> For by his incarnation the Son of God has united himself in some fashion with every man and woman. He worked with human hands, He thought with a human mind, acted by human choice, and loved with a human heart.[9]

After his death on the cross, the Incarnate Word entered into his glory in accordance with his own prayer: 'So now, Father, glorify me in your presence with the glory that I had in your presence before the world existed' (John 17:5); and he continues to enlighten every man and woman and to bring all into contact with his cross and Resurrection. Again the Council makes this clear:

> For since Christ died for all, and since the ultimate vocation of everyone is in fact one and divine, we ought to believe that the Holy Spirit in a manner known only to God offers to everyone the possibility of being associated with this paschal mystery.[10]

Such is the universality of the grace of Christ, Lord of the Universe, to whom every knee should bend and every tongue confess that Jesus Christ is Lord to the glory of God the Father.

The mystic, then, is united in transforming love with the glorified Jesus. This is the Jesus who said: 'But I, if I be lifted up from the earth, will draw all things to myself' (John 12:32). This is the Jesus of whom Paul says: 'I live, now not I, but Christ lives in me' (Galatians 2:20). So different is this transformed Jesus from the historical Jesus that Paul can write: 'Even though we once knew Christ according to the flesh, we know him no longer in that way' (2 Corinthians 5:16). And yet it is the same Christ, the Jesus who died on the cross, that Paul can speak of — 'always carrying in the body the death of Jesus, so that the life of Jesus may also be made visible in our bodies' (2 Corinthians 4:10).

Shortly before his death in his ashram in South India, Bede Griffiths (1906-93) wrote a short account of his personal prayer. For over fifty years, he tells us, he recited the Jesus prayer like the pilgrim who travelled through Russia reciting the name of Jesus — 'Lord Jesus, Son of God, have mercy on me a sinner.' When he was not otherwise occupied or thinking of something else, the prayer went on quietly, sometimes almost mechanically. And it may be added that someone close to Bede relates that the Jesus prayer was on his lips as he lay dying.

What is important here is his theological understanding of the prayer:

When I say, Lord Jesus Christ, Son of God, I think of Jesus as the Word of God, embracing heaven and earth and revealing himself in different ways and under different names and forms to all humanity. I consider that this Word 'enlightens everyone coming into the world', and though they may not recognize it, it is present to every human being in the depths of their soul. Beyond word and thought, beyond all signs and symbols, this Word is being secretly spoken in every heart in every place and at every time.[11]

These words recall the statement of the Council already quoted that grace is calling all people to the Word: from the beginning of time the Word has been enlightening everyone born into the world. Bede continues: 'I believe that the Word took flesh in Jesus of Nazareth and in him we can find a personal form of the Word to whom we can pray and to whom we can relate in terms of intimacy.'[12] In other words we can pray intimately to the Jesus who walked by the Sea of Galilee and died on the cross, while knowing by faith that the same Jesus, cosmic and glorified, communicates with all men and women who have existed or will exist. Such is the richness of mystical union with Christ, the Word Incarnate.

Nor is this the last step. Through union with Jesus who is the Son, one is united with the Father in a trinitarian experience which will reach a climax in the *eschaton* — 'in that day you will know that I am in my Father and you in me and I in you' (John 14:20).

ECCLESIAL DIMENSION

In the Hebrew scriptures Yahweh is the bridegroom and the people of Israel are his beloved bride. In the New Testament Jesus is the bridegroom and the Church, the New Israel, is his beloved bride. Today the Church, faithless and sinful though she may be, continues to be the beloved bride, as the Second Vatican Council reminds us when it speaks of 'the bride of the incarnate Word and the pupil of the Holy Spirit'[13], telling us that 'God who spoke of old, uninterruptedly converses with the bride of his beloved Son'.[14] In short, the bride is primarily the community.

Though Origen spoke of the individual person as the bride, he never forgot the ecclesial dimension of mystical experience; and subsequent mystical theology, always pastoral and practical, kept warning people drawn to mystical prayer that they must not be isolated escapists. However solitary their life might be in desert or on mountain, they were always part of the mystical body of Christ, with a vocation to pray and suffer and do penance for the salvation of the whole world. Concretely, their lives must be rooted in the sacraments. Their mystical call stemmed from baptism wherein, like St Paul, they died and rose to new life. But even more important was the Eucharist, the bread of life, which nourishes contemplative prayer. And, of course, we are all sinners and need the sacrament of reconciliation.

Again, traditional mystical theology, knowing from experience that the mystical path is full of pitfalls and potential deception, insisted that contemplatives consult and obey a director, since revelations and messages from on high could be a trap and a path to destruction. As for the mystics who wrote experiential or theological treatises, their declarations that they submit in all things to the judgment of the Church have been construed as the fearful protestations of men and women who faced an oppressive establishment or a ruthless and vigilant inquisition; but more likely their words stem from a real diffidence and a genuine belief that the Spirit was acting in the whole body of which they were weak and fallible members, capable of falling into illusion at every step.

For the truth is that many mystics were deeply involved in the institutional Church, even in its ugly politics. Some, like Gregory the Great and Pius X, were popes. Others, like Augustine of Hippo and Anselm of Canterbury, were bishops. Others were founders of religious orders. Others, like St Catherine of Siena, played a prophetic role, rocking the boat of Peter, challenging the establishment and vigorously confronting the authorities.

One of the most glorious and lovable mystics in Christian history had a profoundly ecclesial vocation. Mary Magdalene, sitting lovingly at the feet of Jesus, will for ever be a model of Christian mystical prayer. Standing at the cross she passed through her agonizing dark night. She had a profound awakening (was it spiritual marriage?) when Jesus said, 'Mary' and she answered, 'Rabboni.' Yet her vocation only reached its climax when she was sent. She heard those earth-shaking words: 'But go to my brothers and say to them, "I am ascending to my Father and your Father, to my God and your God"' (John 20:17). Then Mary announced to his disciples, 'I have seen the Lord' (John 20:18). On the testimony of Mary Magdalene the institutional Church was founded.

THE WIDER COMMUNITY

But the Church is broader than the institution, and some hidden and unknown mystics have lived on the periphery of the institutional Church. To understand their ecclesial experience one must call to mind 'the communion of saints'. An ancient tradition speaks of a threefold church:

The Church Militant
The Church Suffering
The Church Triumphant

Without using this terminology the Second Vatican Council spoke of a threefold Church of Christ:

Meanwhile some of his disciples are exiles on earth. Some have finished with this life and are being purified. Others are in glory, beholding God himself triune and one, as he is.[15]

Here are Christ's disciples, living and dead, all united in one enormous community. The Council sees a close relationship between those who are alive and those who are dead:

Therefore the union of the wayfarers with the brethren who have gone to sleep in the peace of Christ is not in the least interrupted. On the contrary, according to the perennial faith of the church, it is strengthened through the exchange of spiritual goods.[16]

This community, consisting of innumerable human beings, living and dead, becomes even more splendid in the light of the Second Vatican Council.

The church militant we now see as the people of God linked in various ways with the whole human family — 'And there belong to it or are related to it in various ways, the Catholic faithful as well as all who believe in Christ, and indeed the whole of humankind.'[17] This church militant is also the sinful Church, hand in hand with sinners everywhere — those who, having separated themselves from God and others, are groping in darkness. And the mystic is at the centre of this vast Church. Like Moses he or she raises hands of intercession asking God for world peace and for the salvation of the whole human family.

Then there is *the church suffering*, consisting of those who have died and are being purified. The souls in purgatory, St John of the Cross maintains, are undergoing the purification that mystics pass through in the dark night on earth. Their closeness to men and women on earth is brought to mind in the eucharistic prayer: 'Remember our brothers and sisters who have gone to their rest in the hope of rising again . . .'[18]

In the Eucharist *the church triumphant* is also present. 'Make us worthy to share eternal life with Mary, the Virgin Mother of God, with the apostles and with all the saints . . .'[19] The great array of saints is present at the altar.

Now the mystical life brings one into communion with this vast assembly of living and dead in a very real way. Sometimes in a moment of enlightenment, contemplatives have felt themselves in contact with the totality of existence and with God who is the source. They have felt at the core of their being the fulfilment of the prayer of Jesus — 'that they may be one, as I, Father, in Thee and Thou in me, that they may be one in us (John 17:21).'

COMMUNAL MYSTICAL EXPERIENCE

But can there be a communal mystical experience? As the individual enters the prayer of quiet or the prayer of union, as the individual in harrowing loneliness passes through the dark night of the soul and enters into mystical marriage, can a community do likewise? If the bride is truly the community, one would expect her to have such a communal experience in which many people, united in mind and heart, suffer together and find enlightenment together.

The classic example of such an experience is the descent of the Holy Spirit on the apostles. That community had passed through a harrowing dark night when Jesus was crucified and the disciples fled ignominiously in terror. Now, gathered together in one place with Mary and the holy women, they heard the rush of a violent wind, saw the tongues of fire and were filled with the Holy Spirit. St John of the Cross sees this as a veritable mystical experience. The sound of the fierce wind, he says, was no more than an exterior manifestation of an intense interior clamour and sound that the apostles heard in the depths of their soul.

All through The Acts of the Apostles we find the Spirit descending on the group, communicating gifts and filling all with his presence. Likewise, the communities founded by Paul prayed together as a body, each with his or her own gift. Often their prayer went beyond the rational consciousness to the mystical consciousness where the Spirit speaks as the Spirit wills.

But it was particularly at the Eucharist that the community prayed as a body. It was here that the deepest union between them and the Lord was enacted. 'Because there is one bread, we who are many are one body, for we all partake of the one bread' (1 Corinthians 10:17). They were to be one in Jesus like the branches and the vine. They were to be perfectly one as the Father in the Son and the Son in the Father. Just as Jesus took bread and blessed and broke, so they together entered into his experience, the experience of his death and Resurrection.

Yet the struggle for unity was a great one. Within the community there were deep divisions. How true this was at Corinth where Paul asked angrily if Christ had been divided! Here the Eucharist was no mystical experience but an excuse for carousing and getting drunk. 'When you come together, it is not really to eat the Lord's supper. For when the time comes to eat, each of you goes ahead with your own supper, and one goes hungry and another becomes drunk . . . In this matter I do not commend you' (1 Corinthians 11:20-2).

From the beginning Christians made great efforts to form community — to share their goods, to have one heart and one soul, to pray together, to help one another, to receive the gifts of the Spirit together, to witness together — 'by this everyone will know that you are my disciples, if you have love for one another' (John 13:35). And as the centuries passed by, great religious families — Benedictines, Franciscans, Dominicans, Jesuits — continued the struggle for a communal contemplative experience based on a common rule and a common way of life, often failing ingloriously like the Corinthians to whom Paul wrote in anger. And the struggle for community continues today, as men and women everywhere strive to meet the needs of the new world we are entering. The gospel ideal will not be fulfilled until the *eschaton*. Then the human family will have a communal mystical experience when the new Jerusalem comes down from God, prepared as a bride adorned for her husband. This is the mystical marriage — not the mystical marriage of millions of separate individuals but the mystical marriage of the whole human family gathered into one. The Son will hand over the kingdom to the Father, says St Paul, 'so that God may be all in all' (1 Corinthians 15:28). Father, Son and Holy Spirit with the whole human family and the entire cosmos will be Being-in-Love.

CONTEMPLATIVE FRIENDSHIP

While the marriage theme is central to mystical theology, the theme of friendship is also of great importance. Here the archetypal figure is Moses to whom God spoke face to face as one might speak to a friend. 'Never since then has there arisen a prophet in Israel like Moses, whom the Lord knew face to face' (Deuteronomy 34:10). The towering figure of Moses the mystic, climbing the mountain and entering the cloud, is central to the whole apophatic tradition from Gregory of Nyssa and Dionysius to the author of *The Cloud* and St John of the Cross. So intimate was the friendship between Yahweh and Moses that some theologians claimed that Moses enjoyed a fleeting vision of God. And while today we need not pay serious attention to this thesis, it points to the reverence with which the great prophet was held in the mystical tradition.[20]

Friendship plays a central role in the gospels. Jesus loved Martha and Mary — and he wept over Lazarus. He also loved Peter and James and John. How profoundly intimate was his relationship with the beloved disciple who symbolizes every Christian! Yet it is only at the last discourse that he speaks powerfully about friendship. Great love is based on sacrifice; and he tells his disciples that there is no greater love than that of the one who lays down life for a friend. 'You are my friends . . .' (John 15:14). The relationship has changed. Previously they were servants: now they are friends. The master may love the servant, but he does not reveal his heart. Jesus has revealed everything he heard from the Father — his whole self — and this has created not only a profound intimacy but also a relationship of equality. He goes on to say, 'You have not chosen me but I have chosen you' (John 15:16) as if to say that his friendship is a gift, not something the disciples acquired by human effort nor something they merited by good works.

The union that comes from this friendship is like the union of the vine and the branches. 'Dwell in me,' says Jesus. And 'Dwell in my love,' (John 15:9) he says. The disciples experience a deep union with Jesus (a foretaste of another communion they will experience in the Eucharist) and they were heartbroken that he was going away. 'But,' he says, 'it is expedient for you that I go. For if I do not go the Holy Spirit will not come; but if I go I will send him' (John 16:7). The separation was necessary. It was purificatory. The Spirit would inspire in them an even deeper love, a new kind of intimacy. They must not cling to him — just as Magdalene was later told not to cling. 'Do not cling to me, for I have not yet ascended to my Father' (John 20:17).

And the union of friendship is intensely creative. As the branch bears fruit, so the disciples will bear fruit; as the mother with much suffering gives birth to her child and is filled with joy, so the disciples with much suffering will give birth to their child and be filled with joy. All leads to dynamic creativity and overwhelming joy.

Now it is of the greatest importance to note that the fourth gospel speaks not only of friendship with Jesus but of friendship between the disciples: 'Love one another as I have loved you' (John 13:34). As Jesus washed their feet, they were to wash one another's feet. As Jesus laid down his life for them, they were to lay down their lives for one another. As he shared everything with them, they were to share everything with one another. As he dwelt in them, they were to dwell in one another. As he was a friend to them, they were to be friends to one another. They were to be one as Father and Son were one. What an ideal! No doubt the disciples did their best; but the New Testament reveals an infant Church beset with bitter infighting and acrimonious quarrels.

Nevertheless, an ideal of friendship passed into tradition, influenced not only by the Bible but also by the *De Amicitia* of Cicero. Of special importance is the English Cistercian abbot, Aelred of Rievaulx (1110-67) who, following Augustine and Bernard, wrote of contemplative friendship in monastic life. One who is contemplative in relating to God will be contemplative in relating to people and even in relating to nature. That is to say, the contemplative relates at a deep level as in the prayer of quiet or the prayer of union; and when such a loving relationship is mutual there will result a silent communion, a deep indwelling from which a spiritual child will be born. The friendship will bear fruit like the branch that dwells in the vine.

Looking at the lives of the mystics it is clear that deep contemplative friendship was almost always an integral part of their spiritual journey. Sometimes the friendship began in the context of spiritual direction. As time went on, however, in a process resembling that of the servant and the master in the fourth gospel, the spiritual child became a mature and equal friend. In other cases the relationship was between parent and child. Such was the case with Monica and Augustine and with Thomas More and his beloved daughter Margaret. Again, such contemplative friendships have sometimes arisen in the ordinary circumstances of life, as with Teilhard de Chardin who claimed that his creative work was inspired by loving relationships that he treasured. And, needless to say, contemplative love can exist between husband and wife. Indeed, it is the crowning gift of marriage, pointing to the eschatological marriage between God and the soul.

But contemplative friendship is the endpoint of a long process. Sometimes, it is true, consummate mystics have met at the core of their being in a moment of enlightenment. But this is the exception. Ordinarily the journey to contemplative love in human relationships is a way of purification like the ascent of Mount Carmel and the dark night of the soul.

ASCENT TO LOVE

In the context of man-woman relationship Jung refers to four symbols that describe the ascent to contemplative love whether in marriage or celibacy.[22] The symbols are:

Eve

Helen

Mary

Sapientia

Eve, associated with *Hawah* or earth, symbolizes biological, instinctive, sexual love. She is a symbol of the instinctive urge to procreate and preserve the species.

Helen of Troy represents the romantic or courtly love of the troubadour. She is the beautiful woman who bewitches Marlowe's Faust as he cries in ecstasy, 'Is this the face that launched a thousand ships and burned the topless towers of Ilium? Sweet Helen, make me immortal with a kiss.'

Mary symbolizes the devotional love of one who prays with deep feeling and with tears.

Sapientia or wisdom is mystical love. She is the Shulamite of The Song of Songs. It is the glory of the human person to love her with unlimited spiritual passion — and for ever.

Called and sustained by grace alone, one passes through the stages of growth symbolized by Eve, Helen and Mary, reaching a climax with the all-consuming love of wisdom. In this ascent, however, it is important to note that the lower is not rejected for the higher. Eve is not rejected by one who loves Helen. Eve and Helen and Mary are not rejected by one who loves Sapientia. Indeed, Eve and Helen and Mary are somehow contained in Sapientia, which is the all-embracing feminine. Unrestricted love goes on and on, transcending but not rejecting.

Clearly the path is very demanding. While one does not reject Eve and Helen and Mary, one does reject *clinging* to Eve and Helen and Mary. There must be no clinging, no inordinate attachment. This is the path of *nada, nada, nada,* the path of *mu, mu, mu*. It is the surrender of all to find all.

At the summit one reaches a love that is both human and divine, valid for both married and celibate. The married person, while being consumed by sapiential love for the other, can still express this love at the level of Eve when it is appropriate to do so. The celibate person is finally so consumed by sapiential love that he or she is able to sacrifice the love of Eve without undue suffering. In the final analysis what matters is not celibacy or marriage but love — the same love is poured into the hearts of all.

A further word must be said about this love of sapientia.

In this book reference has been made to the work of Bernard Lonergan for whom the transcendental precepts to be attentive, intelligent, reasonable, responsible are crowned by the precept to love. Following the Christian tradition, however, Lonergan makes it clear that love is only secondarily a precept. It is primarily a gift poured into the human heart by the Holy Spirit who is given. This love is unrestricted, being without limits or qualifications or conditions or reservations. It is a love that goes on and on and on, as one's being becomes being-in-love. It leads to fulfilment of the commandment to love God with one's whole heart and soul and mind and strength.

The object of this love is God; and Lonergan speaks of being in love with God. Furthermore in the Christian mystical tradition (though Lonergan does not develop his theology in this way) the object of this love is the Word Incarnate. One's being becomes being-in-love-with-the-Word-Incarnate. And since the Word Incarnate is the Son who loves the Father, one's being becomes being-in-love with the Father. In other words, this unrestricted love leads finally to a trinitarian experience.

But who is this Word Incarnate with whom one's being becomes being-in-love?

It is Jesus who has risen from the dead and entered into his glory. It is Jesus who identifies with the poor and the sick, the afflicted and the suffering. It is Jesus who identifies with the whole human family.

While, according to the Sermon on the Mount, human beings are called to a universal love which includes love for one's enemies, the sapiential love of friendship which is here under discussion has special characteristics which are worth mentioning.

The first of these is mutuality. In words that might make one smile St John of the Cross speaks of the intimacy of lovers:

> Strange it is, this property of lovers, that they like to enjoy each other's companionship alone, apart from every creature and all company. If some stranger is present they do not enjoy each other freely, even though they are together and may speak to each other just as much as when the other is absent, and even though the other does not talk to them. The reason they desire to commune with each other alone is that love is a union between two alone.[22]

These words could have been written by the author of a romantic novelette. But just as St John of the Cross uses The Song of Songs in his own way, so he uses this imagery to speak of the deep communion that finally exists between the soul and God. Yet it also reveals his insight into the intimacy of human lovers who want to be alone together.

A second characteristic of love or friendship is that it is from person to person. Precisely because it goes to the divine core of the other it does not change. 'Love never ends,' writes Paul (1 Corinthians 13:8). 'Love's not time's fool,' cries Shakespeare. Rosy lips and cheeks, he adds, fall beneath the sweep of time's cruel scythe, but love itself is unchanging and timeless. It is as though he were to say that Helen will wither and die but Sapientia is timeless, beautiful and for ever young.

A third characteristic is that the climax of this love is a union in which one finds one's true self. Teilhard de Chardin, faced with the problem of union, asked how one could become the other while remaining oneself; and, distinguishing between union and absorption, he came to the paradoxical conclusion that *union differentiates*. Father, Son and Holy Spirit are one in the greatest of all unions, yet the Father is not the Son nor is the Son the Holy Spirit. And in the same way, when the disciples, in accordance with the prayer of Jesus, become completely one as the persons in the Trinity are one, they yet remain themselves. Magdalene is not Peter; John is not Martha; Paul is not Luke. Yet they are one. And so it will be at the *eschaton*: 'That they may be one as I, Father, in you and you in me, that they may be one in us' (John 17:21).

WORLD COMMUNITY

As the world comes together with unprecedented rapidity, as men and women everywhere become conscious of their interdependence, we feel acutely the need of world community. The Second Vatican Council, from its very inception, saw this need and stated clearly that the Church wanted to be a sign or sacrament of unity. In accordance with the prayer of Jesus she wanted to work for unity among all Christians and for deep reconciliation with Jews, Moslems, Hindus and Buddhists. She wanted to work for unity among the nations and to bring peace to the world. She wanted to be the Church of the poor and the sick and the oppressed, excluding no one from her tender embrace. Such was the vision and the ideal of the Council.

When it came to concrete ways of promoting unity, the Council spoke eloquently about dialogue. The Church wanted to enter into conversation with the world about the many critical problems of our time. She wanted to promote dialogue within the Church and to talk with peoples of all religions on terms of equality. In fact she wanted to talk with everyone. 'For our part, the desire for such dialogue . . . excludes no one', wrote the Council, adding that it wanted dialogue with those who persecute the Church — always respecting the full dignity of the human person.[23]

Now dialogue at the level of discursive reasoning, however valuable and necessary, will not achieve much unless the participants are united in mind and heart. In other words, the participants must find unity at a level of consciousness that transcends words and letters and thinking; that is, at the mystical level. Here there will be no controversies or politics or polemics or manipulation but silent communion. If the dialogue arises out of such communion it will be truly fruitful.

At the parliament of religions held in Chicago in 1993, two hundred and fifty religious leaders from around the world signed their approval of 'The Declaration of a Global Ethic' drafted by the Swiss theologian Hans Küng. Pointing to the agony of the world — peace eludes us, the planet is being destroyed, neighbours live in fear, women and men are estranged from one another, children die — the document solemnly declares: 'We affirm that a common set of core values is found in the teaching of the religions and that these form the basis of a global ethic.'

What is important is that the document does not contain a legalistic set of rules and regulations that all must follow. Instead, it advocates a transformation of consciousness and speaks of reflection, meditation, prayer, positive thinking, conversion of heart. 'Together we can move mountains! Without a willingness to take risks and a readiness to sacrifice there can be no fundamental change in our situation.'

This document, it seems to the present writer, while not speaking explicitly about mysticism, is pointing to the mystical dimension in the religions. It is here that we will find the union of minds and hearts that will enable us to confront the grave and critical problems of the world today.

CONCLUSION

The Declaration of a Global Ethic points to the enormous problems with which we are confronted. However, underlying all is a single basic problem that affects millions of men and women; namely, the sense of alienation, loneliness, isolation, separation, rootlessness. Alienated from family, friends and society, alienated from the tender embrace of mother earth, millions seek to escape from the frightening isolation that fills them with dread. They want communion.

And the mysticism of all the religions points to a union and a communion that is part of the journey of life. Assuredly in this journey one passes through periods of loneliness and isolation and apparent separation (for Gethsemane is an inescapable part of the human adventure) but it is a journey of love that brings union with other people, with the universe and with the Ultimate Reality that Christians call God.

NOTES

1. See *Meeting God through Science: Hidden Realism*, Mutsuo Yanase, translated with a preface by William Johnston, Sophia University 1991. Mutsuo Yanase graduated from Tokyo University and studied at Princeton under Robert Oppenheimer with whom he developed a close relationship. He is currently professor emeritus at Sophia University.
2. *The Ascent*, 2.5.3.
3. Ibid.
4. Ibid.
5. *The Living Flame*, 4.15.
6. Ibid., 4.14.
7. *The Ascent*, 2.5.7.
8. *Gaudium et Spes*, 57.
9. Ibid., 22.
10. Ibid.
11. 'In Jesus' name' by Bede Griffiths in *The Tablet*, London, 18 April 1992.
12. Ibid. Elsewhere Bede again emphasizes the uniqueness of Jesus: 'The unique value of Christianity is its profoundly historic structure. That to me is a key point. Christ is not an *avatara*. The Incarnation is a unique historic event and Jesus a unique historic person. In gathering all things, all humanity and all matter, into one in himself, he transforms the world, bringing the cosmos back to its source in the transcendent Reality whom he called Abba, Father. This is unique.' ('The New Consciousness' by Bede Griffiths in *The Tablet*, London 16 Jan. 1993.)
13. *Dei Verbum*, 23.
14. Ibid., 8.
15. *Lumen Gentium*, 49.
16. Ibid.
17. Ibid., 13.
18. The Second Eucharistic Prayer of the Roman Liturgy.
19. Ibid.

20. Cuthbert Butler goes into this question at length and concludes: 'Thus it would seem that the whole conception of Moses, or of St Paul, having had the vision of God's essence, is built upon St Augustine's misinterpretation of a mistranslation of a biblical text.' (*Western Mysticism*, Dom Cuthbert Butler, London 1926, p. lxviii.)

21. See *The Collected Works of C.G. Jung*, 16. 361, London 1954. Here Jung simply refers to these symbols without development. However, some of his disciples did develop them in the context of the growth of the anima. See 'Process of Individuation' by M.L. von Franz in *Man and his symbols*, ed. Carl Jung, London 1964.

22. *Spiritual Canticle*, 36.1.

23. *Gaudium et Spes*, 92.

SEVENTEEN

---*---

Wisdom

THE SEARCH FOR WISDOM

From the dawn of history men and women in every culture have devoted their lives to the search for wisdom. This is particularly evident in Asia where monks travelled from place to place enduring extreme hardship and acute suffering in their quest for the jewel of enlightenment. Frequently their search reached a climax when they met a wise teacher, a profoundly enlightened guide. Yet the teacher did not give them wisdom as a ready-made product. He or she developed a deep relationship with the disciple, teaching ways to enlightenment through meditation, chanting and reading the sutras. 'Even Buddhas do but point the way' is an ancient saying, emphasizing that one must find one's own hidden treasure. It will not come from outside.

The Mahayana tradition emphasizes certain points that deserve mention.

The first is that there is no wisdom without compassion. The one who would attain to enlightenment must have a profound compassion for all sentient beings. He or she must love the poor and the sick and the afflicted and must share in their sorrows. Furthermore, compassion does not end with material help. The compassionate person desires the salvation of all, even refusing to enter into nirvana until all sentient beings are saved. Compassion leads to wisdom just as wisdom leads to compassion.

The second characteristic is emptiness. Through compassion one becomes empty, abandoning any kind of attachment. One becomes so empty as to receive the whole universe into one's belly. One may meditate by repeating *mu* or *ku* with the exhalation of the breath, thus letting go of everything and experiencing total emptiness.

Closely associated with wisdom is Buddhist mindfulness whereby one becomes aware of every breath and every action. One becomes aware of the energy (the *ki*) flowing through one's body. One even becomes aware of the cosmic energy of the vast universe; and in this way one is filled with wisdom.

The wisdom to which one now attains is transcendental — *prajna paramita*. That is to say, it is the wisdom of one who has crossed from the shore of illusion and suffering to the shore of enlightenment — 'gone, gone, gone to the other shore'.

揭諦 揭諦 波羅 揭諦 波羅 僧 揭諦

GYA TE GYA TE HA RA GYA TE HA RA SO GYA TE

gone, gone to the other shore gone, reach enlightenment

Yet one only passes to the other shore through much purification in a series of lives.

The wisdom thus attained is formless and empty: it is knowledge in a cloud of unknowing. The Heart Sutra, which is a hymn to the beauty of enlightenment, says clearly that form is emptiness and emptiness is form.[1] In the enlightened consciousness there is no dualism, no separation between form and formlessness; for form equals formlessness and formlessness equals form.

Finally, since formlessness equals form, the enlightened person is not torn away from the world of suffering and distress but remains in the humdrum world with its daily chores. Before enlightenment, chopping wood and carrying water: after enlightenment, chopping wood and carrying water. The wise person is very ordinary.

LOVE AND WISDOM

In the Hebrew Scriptures wisdom is personalized. Here we have a beautiful lady who was with God at the beginning and now cries out in the streets:

> I love those who love me
> and those who seek me
> diligently find me (Proverbs 8:17)

The quest for wisdom is a love affair with this woman who can be compared to the Shulamite of The Song of Songs. The same lady walks through the pages of the Wisdom literature, and one gets glimpses of her in the New Testament. In the Christian tradition she is sometimes identified with Mary the mother of Jesus, the Seat of Wisdom (*Sedes Sapientiae*) to whom scholars and doctors prayed and to whom they dedicated their work.

Again wisdom is personalized by Paul, for whom the greatest wisdom is to know Christ crucified and risen from the dead. He states his idea forcefully: 'I want to know Christ and the power of his resurrection and the sharing of his sufferings. . .' (Philippians 3:10). But it is in his first letter to the Corinthians that his love for Christ crucified and the ensuing wisdom shine forth most brilliantly. Paul did not want to preach the Gospel with the eloquent wisdom of the Greeks lest the cross of Christ be emptied of its power. 'For I decided to know nothing among you except Jesus Christ, and him crucified' (1 Corinthians 2:2). Jews demand signs and Greeks desire wisdom, but Paul proclaimed Christ crucified, a stumbling block to Jews and foolishness to Gentiles, but to those who were called, both Jews and Greeks, 'Christ the power of God and the wisdom of God' (1 Corinthians 1:24).

Paul's teaching is foolishness. Yet, as though having second thoughts, he reflects paradoxically that this foolishness is real wisdom: 'Yet among the mature we do speak wisdom . . . we speak God's wisdom, secret and hidden' (1 Corinthians 2:6, 7). Secret and hidden! This wisdom, like the formless and empty wisdom of Buddhism, cannot be expressed in clearcut concepts and images and has nothing to do with the senses. As though to emphasize this point Paul adds: 'What no eye has seen, nor ear heard, nor the human heart conceived. . .' (1 Corinthians 2:9). This is wisdom in a cloud of unknowing. No doubt Paul himself experienced this formless wisdom when, raised to the third heaven whether in the body or out of the body, he heard voices that he could not repeat nor put into human words.

Paul's teaching that the highest wisdom is found in love for Christ crucified passed into the Christian mystical tradition where it had immense influence. The highest wisdom is not necessarily found in long periods of silent prayer or meditation but in a deep love for Christ crucified — that is, for Christ who died on the cross and for Christ crucified in the poor, the sick, the afflicted, the oppressed and the dying. As Buddhist compassion is the way to enlightenment, Christian love is the way to mystical vision.

The personification of wisdom reaches a climax with the descent of the Holy Spirit. At the last supper Jesus said he would send the Spirit to those who love him — 'I will ask the Father and he will give you another Advocate and he will be with you for ever. This is the Spirit of truth' (John 14:16, 17). And throughout Christian history innumerable contemplatives have called on the Holy Spirit, repeating the words 'Come, Holy Spirit! Come, Holy Spirit!', asking the Spirit to enkindle in their hearts the light of wisdom and the fire of love. For the Holy Spirit is the divine wisdom (*Divina Sapientia*) who enlightens and guides through the darkness of night and the light of day.

Wisdom, then, is the end and love is the way. This was the doctrine of Aquinas who taught that the goal of the human person and of the human race is the vision of God in accordance with the words of Jesus: 'And this is eternal life, that they may know you, the one true God, and Jesus Christ whom you have sent' (John 17:3). And St John of the Cross, forever a Thomist, follows this teaching, claiming that 'essential glory lies in seeing God and not in loving'.[2] His Spiritual Canticle is the agonized cry of one who loves God but cannot see God. It is the cry of one who longs for death — not because death is good in itself but because only through death can he have the desired vision of God. 'Henceforth send me no more messengers', he cries, as if to say, 'I do not want signs or messages about your presence and work in the world; I want the clear vision of you as you are in yourself.'

Yet St John of the Cross was above all a lover. Asking himself why the goal should be vision rather than love, he replies that the desire to see is included in the desire to love and ends with the comment that 'with love the soul pays God what she owes him; with the intellect, on the contrary, she receives from him'.[3] The fact is that the gift of God is a delightful mingling of wisdom and love. Throughout the writings of St John of the Cross we find the skilful interplay of intellect and will, love and wisdom, light and fire. Sometimes fire predominates and there is little light: at other times light predominates and there is little heat. But wisdom and love are always so closely intertwined as to be inseparable.

THE GIFT OF DIVINE WISDOM

From what has been said it will be clear that in human life there are two types of knowing. One type is clear knowledge in images and concepts. This is the acquired knowledge of common sense, philosophical reasoning and scientific research: it has been carefully studied by Western epistemology for more than two thousand years.

The other type of knowledge, more properly called wisdom, is found not only in Buddhism and Christianity but in the mystical tradition of all the great religions. This wisdom is formless, obscure knowledge in a cloud of unknowing. The Christian tradition spoke of it as gift and called it infused contemplation or mystical theology. Whereas acquired knowledge comes through the senses, infused, imageless knowledge wells up from the dark depths of one's being or flows into these depths like a river from without.

Concretely, the mystical theologians of the twentieth century (Joseph de Guibert, Garrigou-Lagrange and the rest) instructed beginners to use the discursive prayer of reasoning, thinking, reading the Scriptures, meditating on the sacred word and speaking to God. As time goes on, they explained, this discursive prayer simplifies into affective prayer and the repetition of an ejaculation such as the name of Jesus. This can be called acquired contemplation.

In the next stage one enters into silence without words or images, resting only in the presence of God. This is the prayer of quiet, the beginning of infused contemplation. As one enters more and more deeply into the cloud of unknowing, one must abandon reasoning and thinking of all kinds in order to open one's being to the inflow of God. One becomes more and more effortless, entering into what St John of the Cross calls 'idle tranquillity'. The saint describes this wisdom beautifully:

This wisdom is loving, tranquil, peaceful, mild, by which the soul feels tenderly and gently wounded and carried away without knowing by whom or from where or how. The reason is that this wisdom is communicated without the soul's activity.[4]

Without the soul's activity. The soul is 'doing nothing' and wisdom is pure gift. In the same context St John of the Cross insists that one must be detached from all reasoning and thinking and imagining:

It is impossible for the highest wisdom and language of God which is contemplation, to be received in anything less than a spirit that is silent and detached from discursive knowledge and gratification.[5]

This is knowing by unknowing. One abandons the ordinary discursive knowledge (and this is unknowing) in order to relish the sublime wisdom that is infused by God. *The Cloud of Unknowing* describes it picturesquely by saying that there is a cloud of unknowing above (for no one can see God) and a cloud of forgetting below (for one must forget all created things) and one remains in total emptiness with formless knowledge which is wonderful wisdom.

Now the gift that is infused into the silent and tranquil soul is both wisdom and love. St John of the Cross describes it poetically as 'sublime knowledge of God enveloped in divine love'. He again insists that one abandon forms and discursive meditation in order to receive this gift:

For little by little and very soon the divine calm and peace with a wondrous, sublime knowledge of God, enveloped in divine love, will be infused into souls. They should not interfere with forms or discursive meditations and imaginings. Otherwise the soul will be disquieted and drawn out of its peaceful contentment to distaste and repugnance.[6]

The person must have no scruple about remaining inactive, idle and at peace. St John of the Cross quotes the psalmist: 'Be still and know that I am God' (Psalm 46:10) and explains: 'Learn to be empty of all things — interiorly and exteriorly — and you will behold that I am God."

It is precisely when one is empty that God infuses sublime wisdom and love. Indeed, when one is truly empty there may be a touch of the divinity. Whereas ordinary knowledge comes through the senses, this wisdom is directly communicated to the spirit by God. 'This communication', writes St John of the Cross, 'is not brought about through any means but through a certain contact of the soul with the divinity. This contact is something foreign to everything sensory and accidental, since it is a touch of naked substances — the soul and the divinity.'[8] And elsewhere he writes with power and clarity:

> Manifestly, in this high state of union God does not communicate himself to the soul — nor is this possible — through the disguise of any imaginative vision, likeness, or figure, but mouth to mouth: the pure and naked essence of God (the mouth of God in love) with the pure and naked essence of the soul (the mouth of the soul in the love of God).[9]

This sublime wisdom is clearly a wonderful gift, an entrance of God into the world of men and women. Yet in the twentieth and twenty-first centuries when married, working people aspire to mystical prayer, one must ask about its relationship to daily life in factory or kitchen or classroom; and scientists may ask about its relationship to their work in the laboratory. Obviously the ordinary person cannot spend his or her life in a cloud of unknowing, burying all worldly concerns beneath a cloud of forgetting. What, then, is the relationship between sublime wisdom and ordinary life, or between sublime wisdom and the knowledge of the scientist or scholar?

MYSTICAL WISDOM: SCIENTIFIC KNOWLEDGE

The reconciliation of contemplative wisdom with ordinary, common-sense knowledge is a practical problem that confronts the director of contemplatives. For the fact is that the gift of wisdom can be so powerful, so absorbing, so overwhelming that it carries the contemplative into a world of ecstasy and oblivion. Contemplatives can be so forgetful of time and space that they no longer attend to the ordinary affairs of life.

And yet Teresa, constantly swept away by raptures and ecstasies, was an eminently common-sensical and practical woman. She had a shrewd sense of humour, and she knew how to sweep corridors and wash dishes. Other contemplatives were scholars and scientists; some had an acute business sense. How explain this reconciliation of wisdom with practical or scientific knowledge?

St John of the Cross faces the problem theologically and follows the Christian mystical tradition.

The whole mystical tradition is at one in declaring that beside the wonderful, infused wisdom of God the knowledge of the world (whether it be the knowledge of common sense or that of the scholar or theologian) is like a tiny candle held up to the glaring light of the noonday sun. On this point St John of the Cross is clear. He has a charming description of the bride drinking of the highest wisdom and forgetful of all worldly things: 'And it seems that her previous knowledge and even all the knowledge of the world is pure ignorance in comparison with this knowledge.'[10] He even insists that the natural sciences are ignorance:

> . . . in the excess of the lofty wisdom of God, the lowly wisdom of humans is ignorance. The natural sciences themselves and the very word of God, when set beside what it is to know God, are like ignorance. For where God is unknown nothing is known.[11]

He then goes on to quote St Paul that the wisdom of God is foolishness to human beings and he makes a clearcut distinction between divine wisdom and human wisdom:

> Hence the wise people of God and the wise people of the world are foolish in the eyes of each other; one group cannot perceive the wisdom and knowledge of God, and the other cannot perceive the wisdom and knowledge of the world. The wisdom of the world is ignorance to the wisdom of God, and the wisdom of God is ignorance to the wisdom of the world.[12]

This sounds like dualism. It sounds like a radical rejection of natural science. But one who reads further sees that it is no more than the hyperbole of a poet and mystic. Elsewhere, after quoting St Paul and lambasting the vanity of stylish preachers, he corrects himself with the words: 'Indeed, it is neither the Apostle's intention nor mine to condemn good style and rhetoric and effective delivery; these, rather, are most important to the preacher . . .'[13]

In fact, St John of the Cross makes it clear that infused, divine wisdom, far from destroying the acquired knowledge of science, perfects this knowledge. Of the bride he writes:

> It should not be thought that because she remains in the unknowing she loses there her acquired knowledge of the sciences; rather these habits are perfected by the more perfect knowledge infused in her.[14]

In short, scientific knowledge is ignorance *in comparison* with the wisdom of God. *Ordinary knowledge and scientific knowledge are joined to the superior wisdom of God and are perfected by it.*

This is of the greatest importance today. For some scientists, attracted by the mystical vision, are studying Oriental and Occidental mysticism. If they are inspired by a faithful love of truth, they will find a wisdom which, far from being irrelevant for their scientific study, completes and perfects it. The same holds true for people engaged in the study of economics or politics or whatever. As grace perfects nature, so mystical wisdom perfects science and scholarship and common sense.

Yet, having said this, let us remember that this is an area in which Christian mystical theology can learn from Asia. Influenced by Neoplatonism and fascinated by flight from the world, some Christian mystics have despised scientific achievements and the chores of daily life. They need to be reminded that ecstasies and raptures are transitional and that finally what matters is chopping wood and carrying water. Wise old Qoheleth saw this; and, in words that remind us of Zen, he says: 'There is nothing better for mortals than to eat and drink, and find enjoyment in their toil' (Ecclesiastes 2:24).

LONERGAN'S METHOD

Bernard Lonergan, who devoted his life to the study of method, ended with the same problem as St John of the Cross: how to integrate acquired knowledge and infused wisdom.

Lonergan's method has already been outlined in this book. Knowing is a process of experiencing, understanding and judging; and the human being who would be authentic strives to obey the transcendental precepts: Be attentive, be intelligent, be reasonable. One who is faithful to these precepts will come to objective knowledge in the judgment that 'this is so'. Moreover, such a person will transcend self intellectually and come to intellectual conversion.

This method, which is in accord with the deepest thrust of human nature, has been used by science since the scientific revolution that began with Galileo and reached a climax with Newton. Of course scientists do not ordinarily analyze their own method; yet the great pioneers did make a practical discovery that achieved extraordinary things in our planet and in outer space. Lonergan, however, seeing that science could be inhuman, even destructive, if it followed this method alone, formulated another precept, also in accord with the deepest thrust of human nature: Be responsible. Fidelity to this precept leads to ethical conversion.

Later in life, when Lonergan came to reflect on religious experience, he found a new kind of knowledge, the knowledge that comes from love, the wisdom of the mystics. Actual self-transcendence comes when one falls in love with God and one's being becomes being-in-love. However, this falling in love with God is not the result of human effort: it is the gift of wisdom and love poured into human hearts by the Holy Spirit. This is a formless, obscure wisdom that does not come through the senses and is not acquired by experiencing, understanding and judging. 'God's love is poured into our hearts through the Holy Spirit who has been given to us' (Romans 5:5). Furthermore, as the true light enlightens everyone coming into the world, so the love of God is offered to every man and woman born into the world.

Now Lonergan did not live long enough to see how the two kinds of knowledge (acquired knowledge and infused wisdom) can be integrated in one person. Had he lived he might have come to a conclusion similar to that of St John of the Cross. He might have seen that his original method is transformed and perfected by love. Since love and wisdom poured into the depths of one's being influence one's every activity, the transcendental precepts become:

> Be lovingly attentive
> Be lovingly intelligent
> Be lovingly reasonable
> Be lovingly responsible

Love penetrates the whole of human life, including the scientific method, which it perfects and completes. Now we can say that the scientist who devotes himself or herself to research with a deep love of truth, who is lovingly attentive, intelligent, reasonable and responsible will come to the highest wisdom. The Second Vatican Council hints at this when it says succinctly: 'Indeed, whoever labours to penetrate the secrets of reality with a humble and steady mind, is, even unawares, being led by the hand of God, who holds all things in existence and gives them identity.' In short, science pursued with love of truth is a way to God.[15] This is exemplified in the life of Teilhard de Chardin and not a few scientists today.

Let us, then, celebrate the marriage between acquired, scientific knowledge and infused, divine wisdom. This is the way of the future.

WISDOM AND THE WORLD

It has been said that the highest wisdom is the knowledge of God, which reaches a climax when we see God face to face in the beatific vision. However, divine wisdom does not neglect the world with its joys and sufferings and immense social problems. This point is made by the Second Vatican Council which, after extolling the superlative victories of modern science, declares that 'the intellectual nature of the human person is perfected by wisdom and needs to be'.[16] So great is our need of wisdom that the world is in peril unless wiser men and women are forthcoming. The Council issues a sombre warning:

Our era needs such wisdom more than bygone ages if our discoveries are to be further humanized. For the future of the world stands in peril unless wiser men and women are forthcoming.[17]

Characteristically the Council goes on to indicate that these wise men and women may come from the Third World:

It should be pointed out that many nations, poorer in economic goods, are quite rich in wisdom and can offer noteworthy advantages to others.[18]

Indeed, many nations poorer in economic goods have maintained the rich, ancient wisdom that the sophisticated and materialistic West has lost.

But what is the nature of this wisdom that is at the same time worldly and divine?

As people advance in contemplation they sometimes develop extrasensory perception. This is part of a natural process and need not be considered extraordinary. St John of the Cross seems to speak about telepathy or clairvoyance when he says that 'contemplatives possess light and knowledge about events happening in their presence and absence'[19]; and he adds: 'This knowledge derives from their illumined and purified spirit.'[20] Again, he indicates that such people can naturally read minds:

Individuals whose spirit is purified can naturally perceive — some more than others — the inclinations and talents of other persons and what lies in the heart of the interior spirit. They derive this knowledge through exterior indications (even though extremely slight) such as words, gestures and other signs.[21]

Contemplatives whose spirit has been purified through long silence and the suffering of the dark night find that their senses are sharpened and refined so that they become very sensitive to body language. Through the body — a slight gesture or an unthinking word — they read the mind.

This knowledge, acquired through the senses, is quite different from formless, infused, divine wisdom. It is interesting to note that people who spend long hours in *zazen* speak of a similar quickening of the senses. They become extremely alert to colour and to sound; they are sensitive to body language; radical detachment gives them clarity of vision; they acquire 'the illumined and purified spirit' that St John of the Cross speaks of.

Though St John of the Cross himself had remarkable powers of extrasensory perception he was very cautious about the use of such knowledge. Contemplatives can easily be deceived and 'the devil is a notorious and subtle meddler in this area'.[22]

More important than the natural knowledge acquired through a quickening of the senses are the infused gifts of the Holy Spirit which include wisdom, knowledge, faith, prophecy, discernment or recognition of spirits, knowledge of tongues, interpretation of words and so on. These come to people passively without their doing anything on their own. 'For it will happen that, while a person is distracted and inattentive, a keen understanding of what is being heard or read will be implanted in the spirit, an understanding far clearer than that conveyed through the sound of the words.'[23] Moreover, there are times when God 'will reveal to some the number of days they have to live, or the trials they will have to endure, or something that will befall a particular person or kingdom and so on'.[24]

When this knowledge is really a gift of the Spirit, it carries deep conviction:

> When bestowed, this kind of knowledge is so embedded in the soul — without anyone telling it anything — that if someone were to assert the opposite it would be unable to give interior assent even by force, for it has a spiritual knowledge of this truth that resembles clear vision. This knowledge pertains to the spirit of prophecy and to the grace St Paul terms the discernment of spirits (1 Corinthians 12:10).[25]

And yet St John of the Cross insists that even in these circumstances one must obey one's spiritual director.

Now it becomes necessary to consider the wisdom of the prophet.

PROPHECY

Biblical prophecy emerged from a Semitic background of divination and ecstasy, reaching a climax with the great inaugural visions of Isaiah, Jeremiah and Ezekiel. The prophets were filled with wisdom because God spoke to them and through them. When the word of God came to them, they could say with confidence, 'Thus says the Lord. . .' Indeed, one of the distinguishing features of the Semitic religions is the belief that God spoke and continues to speak. 'Long ago God spoke to our fathers in many and various ways by the prophets, but in the last days he has spoken to us by a Son' (Hebrews 1:1, 2).

The Second Vatican Council revived the notion of prophecy which had fallen into the background of Catholic Christianity after the Council of Trent. The Council saw Jesus as the greatest of the prophets (Conciliar Christology centred around Jesus as priest, king and prophet) and said clearly that the faithful of every rank share in the prophetic vocation of Jesus. Of the gifts of the Spirit the Council said: 'Allotting his gifts "to everyone according as he will" (1 Corinthians 12:11), He distributes special graces among the faithful of every rank.'[26] Among these gifts prophecy is so important that Paul can write to his neophytes: 'Pursue love and strive for the spiritual gifts, and especially that you may prophesy' (1 Corinthians 14:1).

When the early Christians assembled for prayer, some spoke in tongues, some prophesied, some exercised gifts of healing or discernment, and in this way they built up the community. So important was prophecy that Paul issued a stern warning to the Thessalonians: 'Do not quench the Spirit, do not despise prophecy' (1 Thessalonians 5:19-20). Old and New Testaments remind us that we must be open to this gift which may appear in surprising people at unexpected times. Peter himself quotes the prophet Joel: 'And in the last days it shall be, God declares, that I will pour out my Spirit upon all flesh, and your sons and your daughters shall prophesy' (Acts 2:17).

While prophecy was greatly weakened by the condemnation of Montanism in the second century, it continued to exist and flowered in the great women mystics — Hildegaard of Bingen in the twelfth century, Brigitta of Sweden in the thirteenth century and Catherine of Siena in the fourteenth century, all of whom were recognized as prophets. Just as in Old Testament times there had to be a healthy, if painful, tension between king and prophet, so within the Church there had to be a similar tension between the establishment and the great prophetic figures. Both were necessary for the household of God which is built 'on the foundation of apostles and prophets' (Ephesians 2:20).

Our era has seen a galaxy of extraordinary prophets who have spoken to the world by their words, by their writings, by their lives and not infrequently by their bloody death. Mahatma Gandhi (1869-1948) spoke of justice, peace, nonviolence. Assassinated on his way to prayer he died with the cry, 'Ram! Ram! — My God! My God!' Edith Stein (1891-1942) died in Auschwitz, reminding us that the world is saved by the blood of innocent people. Dietrich Bonhoeffer (1906-45) martyred by the Nazis, witnessed to the fact that there can be no compromise with evil. Oscar Romero (1917–80), gunned down by an assassin as he celebrated the Eucharist in his church in San Salvador, cries out against injustice and oppression of the poor. Beside these one could list countless names: Martin Luther King, Dorothy Day, Alexander Solzhenitzyn, Thomas Merton, Teilhard de Chardin, Mother Teresa and a host of others whose prophetic word is still alive and will for ever echo through the corridors of history. Moreover, the future will see even more prophets for, as the Council said, our era stands in need of wise people if we are to be saved from destruction.

Since Max Weber's *Sociology of Religion* it has become fashionable to pit the prophet against the priest. Yet we should not forget that the establishment also has produced great prophets. Outstanding among these is Pope John XXIII (1881-1963) who called the Second Vatican Council in response to an inner voice. He describes how he was talking to the assembled cardinals on the feast of St Paul; and just as Paul unexpectedly saw a flash of light on the road to Damascus, so Pope John experienced an unexpected flash of light, 'the first sudden bringing up in our hearts and lips of the simple words "Ecumenical Council",[27] and he goes on:

> It was completely unexpected, like a flash of heavenly light, shedding sweetness in eyes and hearts. At the same time it gave rise to a great fervour throughout the world in expectation of the holding of a Council.[28]

As Pope John was a prophet, so the Council he summoned was one of the great prophetic events of the twentieth century. And yet, if the twentieth century has seen prophets of extraordinary power it has also seen false prophets whose words have brought appalling destruction and horrendous suffering to millions of people. When one reflects on the evils of our era — the prison camps, the gas chambers, the gulags, the death marches, the systematic rape, the oppression of the poor, the torture of the innocent, the destruction of whole cities, the attempts at genocide, the plundering of the environment, the death squads, the racial prejudice, the ruthless child prostitution, the buying and selling of human beings, the massacre of the unborn, the cruel wars in the name of religion, the subtle and diabolical propaganda that has deceived millions of well-intentioned people — when one reflects on this, it is difficult to doubt the existence of false prophets through whom the spirit of evil speaks and acts.

The gospels tell us of those who come in sheep's clothing while inwardly they are ravening wolves. They also give us the norm for distinguishing between the true and the false:

> You will know them by their fruits. Are grapes gathered from thorns or figs from thistles? In the same way, every good tree bears good fruit, but the bad tree bears bad fruit (Matthew 7:16-17).

By their fruits we will know them. Yet one of the greatest and most delicate tasks of mystical theology is to distinguish between the true and the false prophet. In the last analysis discernment is not a rational process performed by scholars but a gift of the Spirit. Nevertheless this is a problem that theology cannot neglect.

THE INNER VOICE

An inner voice echoes in the depths of every human being. This is the teaching of the Second Vatican Council which writes of the voice of conscience: 'Always summoning us to love good and avoid evil, the voice of conscience can when necessary speak to the heart more specifically: do this, shun that.'[29] The Council goes on to say that God himself speaks: 'Conscience is the most secret core and sanctuary of a person. There the person is alone with God whose voice echoes in the depths.'[30] Just as the true light enlightens everyone coming into the world, so this voice speaks in the heart of everyone born into the world.

In the great prophets of antiquity the inner voice spoke with power and clarity. Deutero Isaiah can say: 'A voice says, "Cry out!" And I said, "What shall I cry?"' (Isaiah 40:6). Jeremiah heard the voice that said, 'Before I formed you in the womb I knew you' (Jeremiah 1:4). So also Ezekiel and the Baptist heard a voice that spoke with unmistakable clarity. Jesus tells the disciples that they, too, will hear such a voice in time of great stress. They must not be anxious 'for what you are to say will be given to you at that time; for it is not you who speak but the Spirit of your Father speaking through you' (Matthew 10:19-20).

Some contemplatives hear a substantial word. From the depths of the void there arises, sometimes quite unexpectedly, a voice that immediately produces its effect and revolutionizes their lives. The voice may say, 'Fear not!' and the person is immediately liberated from fear. Or the voice may say, 'Forgive' and the person immediately forgives everyone. 'A locution of this sort', writes St John of the Cross, 'does more good for a person than a whole lifetime of deeds.'[31] And he adds, 'Happy the soul to whom God speaks these substantial words. "Speak, Lord, for your servant is listening"' (1 Samuel 3:10).[32] Such is the word that produces substantially in the soul what is said.

But not all inner words are substantial. Modern psychology reminds us that the complex human psyche contains a chorus of voices that may well be a cacophony. Zen knows this all too well. One who sits for a long time may find that, as the upper layers of the psyche are swept clean, the unconscious surfaces. Then one may hear strange voices or see coloured lights or experience strange sensations. This is *makyo*, meaning 'world of the devil'; and the wise and prudent Zen master tells us to ignore it. One who gets involved in this world of the devil can be sadly deceived.

But voices may come from a deeper area of the psyche. Successive words may emerge from the true self. Or one may hear formal words that seem to be spoken by another person. Whereas the substantial word does its work immediately, here one is free to reject or accept the inner word. Hence the importance of discernment.

Now even if prudent discernment reveals that the voice is good and holy, leading to inner peace and giving glory to God, one must be slow to accept it as an authentic prophecy. For the language of God is quite different from human language. St John of the Cross gives an impressive list of biblical saints who misunderstood the word of God; and he writes:

We see this in every step in Sacred Scripture. With a number of the ancients, many of God's prophecies and locutions did not turn out as had been expected, because they understood them in their own way, in another very literal manner.[33]

Many saints have been misled, understanding God's word according to the outer rind rather than according to the spirit. Joan of Arc's voices told her she would be liberated. She took this to mean liberation from prison whereas it meant the liberation of death. Deceit, however, may come from the devil. Here it is important to remember that for the mystics of all religions the forces of evil are very real, as they were for St Paul who writes that our struggle is not against flesh and blood but 'against the spiritual forces of evil in the heavenly places' (Ephesians 6:12). Cosmic forces of evil are at work in the world. Furthermore, for the mystics the evil spirit is not ordinarily a violent enemy who makes a frontal attack. Rather is he the father of lies, a crafty enemy with a superior intellect, who disguises himself as an angel of light to lead unsuspecting souls to destruction. Yet the spirit of evil, however intelligent, cannot enter the inner sanctuary of the human person where God alone dwells — that is, he cannot enter unless invited to do so. He takes his stand at the gateway between sense and spirit, influencing human beings by suggestion. Such is the traditional doctrine.

Possessing a superior, angelic intellect the evil spirit can sometimes see into the future. 'The devil can learn and foretell that Peter's life will naturally last only a certain number of years,'[34] writes St John of the Cross. Again he writes of the superior intellect of the evil one:

> The devil perceives that when the earth, air, and sun have reached a certain relationship, they will necessarily at that time become corrupted and thereby cause pestilence. He is cognizant of the areas in which the pestilence will be grave and those in which it will be mild. The example, then, is that of a pestilence known in its cause. Is it a wonder, then, that the devil's prediction about a pestilence, due within six months or a year, comes true? Yet it is a prophecy of the devil.[35]

Even authentic prophets are sometimes deceived by forces of evil. They must examine their consciousness, see where they were deceived and take care not to be deceived again.

People with strong addictions, people who are paranoid, people attached to occult knowledge or psychic power or a reputation for sanctity are particularly vulnerable and can even make a pact with the devil to get what they want. The classical example is the legendary Faust who, after selling his soul to the devil, performs astonishing magical feats, flies through the air and conjures up the dead. This may be melodrama but St John of the Cross knows of people who have made a pact with the devil to receive supernatural powers:

> The joy and covetousness they have in these works reaches such a point that if previously their pact with the devil was secret — for often the works are performed through a secret pact — now through their boldness they make an express and open one with him and by an agreement subject themselves to him as his disciples and friends.[36]

Moreover, such people can go to frightening extremes:

> Joy in these works goes so far that some, as Simon Magus, not merely want to buy gifts and graces with money (Acts 8:18) for the service of the devil, but they even try to get hold of sacred and divine objects — which cannot be mentioned without trembling — as has already been witnessed in the theft of the most sacred body of our Lord Jesus Christ for evil practices and abominations. May God extend and show forth his infinite mercy in this matter![37]

St John of the Cross himself was a cautious and common-sensical spiritual director. Nevertheless, he did find cases of diabolical possession, as in Avila where he exorcised a nun who had signed a pact with the devil in her own blood.

To conclude this section it will be sufficient to refer to two points made by St John of the Cross.

The first is that no one should search for revelations, locutions or occult knowledge:

> The reason is that no creature may licitly go beyond the boundaries naturally ordained by God for its governance. He has fixed natural and rational limits by which humans are to be ruled. A desire to transcend them, hence, is unlawful, and to desire to investigate and arrive at knowledge in a supernatural way is to go beyond the natural limits. It is unlawful, consequently, and God who is offended by everything illicit is displeased.[38]

In a modern context, however, the science of parapsychology with its investigation of telepathy, clairvoyance, psychokinesis and the rest is not illicit.

The second point is even more important. One should listen to the advice of another person. He writes:

> It should be kept in mind that individuals must never follow their own opinion about these locutions or do or admit anything told through them without ample advice and counsel

from another. For in this matter of locutions strange and subtle deceits will occur — so much so that I believe a person who is not opposed to experiencing such things cannot help but be deceived in many of them.[39]

And one may legitimately ask if the sanjuanist teaching has relevance today. It may be that underlying the horrendous things we have seen in the twentieth century there lies real evil acting through false prophets.

But now it is necessary to give further consideration to the journey into the mystery of the cloud of unknowing.

FURTHER INTO THE MYSTERY

As one enters the cloud of unknowing, transcending thoughts and images, one enters into the mystery of Christ. 'There is much to fathom in Christ,' writes St John of the Cross, 'for he is like an abundant mine with many recesses of treasures, so that however deep individuals may go they never reach the bottom, but rather in every recess find new veins with new riches everywhere. On this account St Paul said of Christ: "In Christ dwells hidden all treasures of wisdom"' (Colossians:2.3).[40] This is the risen Christ, the Alpha and the Omega, the beginning and the end, who will be with us all days even to the end of the world.

Entering into the mystery of Christ means entering further and further into the spiritual marriage wherein 'the Bridegroom reveals his wonderful secrets to the soul as to his faithful consort. . .'[41] But what are these wonderful secrets?

St Paul was caught up into paradise and heard secret things 'that are not to be told, that no mortal is permitted to repeat' (2 Corinthians 12:4). The voice he heard was not sensible (for he did not know whether he was in the body or out of the body) and it spoke mysterious words he could never repeat — though his great epistles may well be a faltering attempt to put these sublime secrets into words. St John of the Cross speaks more explicitly about the secrets, telling us that they are 'the sublime, exalted and deep mysteries of God's wisdom in Christ, in the hypostatic union of the human nature with the divine Word, and in the corresponding union of human beings with God, and the mystery of the harmony between God's justice and mercy with respect to the manifestations of his judgments in the salvation of the human race'.[42] In other words, in the silence and emptiness of the cloud of unknowing one receives a supraconceptual understanding of the mysteries of Christ. Like the apostles at the Transfiguration, one may hear a voice from the cloud saying, 'This is my Son, my chosen; listen to him!' (Luke 9:35).

For in the cloud 'He communicates to her sweet mysteries of his Incarnation and the ways of redemption of humankind.'[43] Above all, the Incarnation is the mystery that St John of the Cross longs to comprehend. To understand this mystery he longs for death — 'One of the main reasons for the desire to be dissolved and to be with Christ (Philippians 1:23) is to see him face to face and thoroughly understand the profound and eternal mysteries of his Incarnation, which is by no means the lesser part of beatitude.'[44]

The mystical journey reaches a climax when the soul is 'transformed in the three Persons of the Most Holy Trinity in an open and manifest degree'.[45] The Son, who is the wisdom of God and with whom the human person is united through the spiritual marriage, *awakens*. The Spirit, who is the love that exists between the Father and the Son, *breathes*. The human person, united with the Son, has a *face to face vision* of the Father who is the mystery of mysteries. This awakening can never be put into words. St John of the Cross, after making a stumbling attempt to do so, ends in silence.

THE AWAKENING

'There are many kinds of awakening which God effects in the soul, so many that we would never finish explaining them all', writes St John of the Cross.[46] He does not explain them all, but he writes poetically of one of the greatest: 'How gently and lovingly You wake in my heart.'

¡Cuán manso y amoroso
recuerdas en mi seno. . .

And together with this awakening he sings tenderly of the breathing of the Spirit. 'And in your sweet breathing, filled with good and glory, how tenderly you swell my heart with love.'

> *y en tu aspirar sabroso*
> *de bien y gloria lleno*
> *cuán delicamente me*
> *enamoras!*

Here it is interesting to note that the saint never says 'I awaken. . .' or 'I get enlightenment.' *It is the Son of God who awakens in me.* Moreover, it is not an awakening of a God of pure spirit: it is an awakening of the Word Incarnate. 'For the awakening is a movement of the Word in the substance of the soul. . .' Here are his words:

> For this awakening is a movement of the Word in the substance of the soul, containing such grandeur, dominion and glory, and intimate sweetness that it seems to the soul that all the balsams and fragrant spices of the world are commingled, stirred, and shaken so as to yield their sweet odour, and that all the kingdoms and dominions of the world and all the powers and virtues of heaven are moved; and not only this, but it seems that all the virtues and substances and perfections and graces of every created thing glow and make the same movement all at once.[47]

But words are inadequate to describe the movement of this great Emperor (the reference here is to Isaiah 9:6). The remarkable delight of this awakening is that the soul comes to know the creatures through God and not God through creatures. In other words, it comes to know the effects through their cause and not the cause through its effects. 'And the soul sees what God is in Himself and what He is in His creatures in only one view, just as the one who is opening the door of a palace beholds in one act the eminence of the person who dwells inside together with what he is doing.'[48] And then a mighty voice sounds within:

That which a person knows and experiences of God in this awakening is entirely beyond words. Since this awakening is the communication of God's excellence to the substance of the soul, which is its heart. . . an immense, powerful voice sounds in it, the voice of a multitude of excellences, of thousands of virtues in God, infinite in number.[49]

And if such is the experience of man or woman in this life, what must be the experience of the vision of God in glory? 'For if, when He does awaken, scarcely opening His eyes, He has such an effect on the soul, what would it be like were He ordinarily in it fully awake?'[50]

Besides the awakening there is the breathing of the Spirit. But about this St John of the Cross will not speak. 'I do not desire to speak of this spiriation, filled for the soul with good and glory and delicate love of God, for I am aware of being incapable of so doing, and were I to try, it might seem less than it is.'[51]

And so *The Living Flame* ends with silence.

THE VISION OF GOD

If one cannot speak about the greatest awakenings in this life, how can one speak about the vision of God in glory? In treating of the beatific vision, which is the goal of human life, St John of the Cross follows the theology of his day. Towards the end of *The Dark Night*, speaking of the ladder of love by which one ascends to God, he uses an interesting metaphor. He tells us that 'as one climbs a ladder to pillage the fortresses containing goods and treasures, so too, by this secret contemplation, the soul ascends in order to plunder, know and possess the goods and the treasures of heaven'.[52] And so one climbs this ladder, rung by rung, until one comes to the vision of God. After the ninth step the soul departs from the body and undergoes a period of purification (since few are totally purified in this life) before entering into glory where it sees God face to face. This is the glorious marriage, the climax of the mystical life. St John of the Cross writes:

St John says: 'We know that we shall be like Him' (1 John 3:2) not because the soul will have as much capacity as God — this is impossible — but because all that it is will become like God. Thus it will be called, and shall be, God through participation.[53]

But again, in speaking of the vision of God, the greatest mystics are reduced to silence.

Quoting liberally from the New Testament, the Second Vatican Council speaks of the state of glory 'in which we shall be like God, since we shall see Him as He is' (cf. 1 John 3:2). It quotes St Paul that 'the sufferings of this present time are not worthy to be compared with the glory to come that will be revealed to us' (Romans 8:18); and it concludes with an apocalyptic vision:

> For when Christ shall appear and the glorious resurrection of the dead takes place, the splendour of God will brighten the heavenly city and the Lamb will be the lamp thereof (cf. Revelation 21:23). Then in the supreme happiness of charity the whole Church of the saints will adore God and 'the Lamb who was slain' (Revelation 5:12), proclaiming with one voice: 'To him who sits upon the throne, and to the Lamb, blessing and honour and glory and dominion, for ever and ever' (Revelation 5:13).[54]

Such is the vision of God in eternity.

NOTES

1. See Appendix 1.
2. *Spiritual Canticle*, 38.5.
3. Ibid.
4. *Living Flame*, 3.38.
5. Ibid., 3.37.
6. *Ascent*, 2.16.5.
7. Ibid.
8. *Spiritual Canticle*, 20 & 21.4.
9. *Ascent*, 2.16.9.
10. *Spiritual Canticle*, 26.13.
11. Ibid.
12. Ibid.

13. Ascent, 3.45.5.
14. *Spiritual Canticle*, 26.16.
15. See *Gaudium et Spes*, 36. Unfortunately Lonergan did not see this. Not realizing the full implications of his own transcendental method, he failed to see that the scientific method can be perfected by love. He separates the scientific method from God, thus creating an intolerable dualism in the mind of the scientist who would seek God. See chapter 8 of this book.
16. *Gaudium et Spes*, 15.
17. Ibid.
18. Ibid.
19. *Ascent*, 2.26.13.
20. Ibid.
21. Ibid., 2.26.14.
22. Ibid.
23. Ibid., 2.26.16.
24. Ibid., 2.27.2.
25. Ibid., 2.26.11.
26. *Lumen Gentium*, 12.
27. Pope John's Opening Speech to the Council.
28. Ibid.
29. *Gaudium et Spes*, 16.
30. Ibid.
31. *Ascent*, 2.31.1.
32. Ibid., 2.31.2.
33. Ibid., 2.19.1.
34. Ibid., 2.21.11.
35. Ibid., 2.21.8.
36. Ibid., 3.31.5.
37. Ibid.
38. Ibid., 2.21.2.
39. Ibid., 2.30.6.
40. *Spiritual Canticle*, 37.4.
41. Ibid., 23.1.
42. Ibid., 37.3.
43. Ibid., 23.1.
44. Ibid., 37.1.
45. Ibid., 39.3.
46. *Living Flame*, 4.4
47. Ibid.
48. Ibid., 4.7.
49. Ibid., 4.10.
50. Ibid., 4.15.
51. Ibid., 4.17.
52. *Dark Night*, 2.18.1.
53. Ibid., 2.20.5.
54. *Lumen Gentium*, 51.

※

EIGHTEEN

Action

THE MODERN PREDICAMENT

We are entering a new age in which meditation and mysticism are no longer the preserve of monks and nuns and anchorites. Now people who work in offices and factories and laboratories, people who spend their lives washing dishes, teaching classes or working with computers — such people are searching for something deeper that will give meaning to their lives. And they ask: 'Is meditation for me? Is mysticism for me? Will meditation and mysticism help me in my busy life?' They have been told, of course, that meditation helps generate alpha brain waves, that it is restful and relaxing, that it enables one to face life with courage and equanimity. But is there more to it?

The question is not new. Throughout the centuries the story of Martha and Mary has been told and retold with a variety of interpretations. 'Mary has chosen the better part' was used as an excuse for belittling action and extolling contemplation. But there were always people to point out that Paul was an activist — 'in frequent journeys, in danger from rivers, danger from bandits, danger from my own people, danger from Gentiles, danger in the city, danger in the wilderness, danger at sea, danger from false brothers and sisters' (2 Corinthians 11:26). And then one could quote Dominic, Francis, Joan of Arc, Ignatius and a host of others who in the midst of action found the one thing necessary.

Nevertheless, controversy about the primacy of contemplation and the value of activity raged throughout history; and the Christian community, faithful to the Gospel, always reached the same conclusion: what matters is not action or contemplation but love. When love tells us to act, we act; when love tells us to enter into silent contemplation we enter into silent contemplation. In this way we follow God's will.[1]

However, controversy continued to rage in the twentieth century between those who did not trust action and fled to contemplation and those who overvalued action at the expense of contemplation; and the fathers of the Second Vatican Council felt they must say something about human activity.

The Council describes the church as 'eager to act and yet devoted to contemplation, present in the world and yet not at home in it'.[2] It goes on to say that the human is subordinate to the divine, the visible to the invisible, action to contemplation, and this present world to the city to come. And what the Council says of the Church must be true of the individual — he or she must be eager to act, remembering that action is subordinate to contemplation.

Elsewhere, reflecting on the monumental achievements of the human family, the Council states clearly that such human activity accords with God's will since 'man and woman, created in God's image, received a mandate to subject to themselves the earth and all it contains, and to govern the world with justice and holiness'.[3] The Council goes on to describe activity as a spiritual experience:

> For when people work they not only alter things and society, they develop themselves as well. They learn much, they cultivate their resources, they go out of themselves and beyond themselves.[4]

Such going out of oneself and beyond oneself is already contemplation.

Yet the Council was very conscious of the temptations and dangers. Human activity is infected by sin. 'In our day, the magnified power of humanity threatens to destroy the race itself.'[5] Hence human activity needs to be purified; and this purification takes place in a life of contemplation. In short, human activity is of immense value, contributing to the realization of the divine plan in history; but human activity must be purified through contemplation by which one is united with God. The ideal is a life in which action and contemplation are united in a harmonious marriage.

CONTEMPLATIVE ACTION

In early monasticism contemplation and action were not separated. After reciting the divine office, celebrating the Eucharist and spending time in silent prayer, the monks worked in the fields and did the household chores. As they turned over the soil or washed the dishes, they remained in the presence of God who was dwelling in nature and in the depths of their being. They were to seek God in all things and to maintain *purity of intention* so as not to act from selfishness or self-interest. Furthermore, they gave food and drink to the poor and sick and maimed who flocked to the doors of the monastery. In this way they united action and contemplation.

In Asia, also, the union of contemplation and action has always been vibrantly alive. The ideal set before those who meditate as well as those who practise the martial arts (the *dō*) is the perfection of action. 'When walking I am conscious that I am walking. When sitting I am conscious that I am sitting. When lying down I am conscious that I am lying down . . . No matter what position my body is in, I am conscious of that position. Practising thus, I am in direct and constant mindfulness with my body.' Moreover, mindfulness extends to every activity. One is conscious of each breath, each movement, each thought, each feeling. One enters into a state known as no-mind (*mushin*) wherein one is conscious of the mind flowing through every part of the body. One's whole being is unified: one is united with the tea or the sword or the bow or the flower and enters into one-pointedness. Now, having found one's true self, one can act with extraordinary spontaneity — without reasoning or thinking or planning. Zen masters urge their disciples to carry mindfulness into daily life — into work in the kitchen or the office or the laboratory or the classroom. 'Live in the present' is the clear instruction. And in this way one comes to the perfection of action.

A similar contemplative action is described in the *Bhagavad Gita* which speaks of detachment from the fruit of one's labour. The story goes that Gandhi, told that his nonviolence would not succeed, answered that he practised nonviolence not because it would succeed but because it was the right thing to do. He wanted to be detached from success and to aim at the perfection of action.

Action

DECISION-MAKING

One of the most challenging and important aspects of the active life is decision-making. People must decide what to do and what not to do, what to say and what not to say. The Council, for ever insightful, pointed out that modern people consider it part of human dignity to make their own decisions. More than ever before they resent being coerced and pressured from outside:

> A sense of the dignity of the human person has been impressing itself more and more deeply on the consciousness of contemporary men and women. And the demand is increasingly made that people should act on their own judgment, enjoying and making use of responsible freedom, not driven by coercion but motivated by a sense of duty.[6]

The Council was speaking in the context of religious freedom; but the problem extends to every aspect of human life. Young people must make decisions, sometimes anguishing decisions, about their direction in life. Parents must make decisions, sometimes anguishing decisions, about their family. Heads of State and presidents of companies must make decisions that will affect the lives of millions. Alas, we know that in our century millions of people have been sold into slavery through the decisions of irresponsible politicians. We know that the earth has been destroyed by unscrupulous multinational companies.

Yet we also know that we are entering a new age when many married people, working in the world of politics, economics and education, feel called to an authentic mystical experience which will help them make decisions with courageous faith and disinterested love. Such people are committed Christians who want to follow Christ no less than the monks and nuns of old; and they are called to perform a task — perhaps a task on which the very survival of the human race depends — which they alone can perform. And they look for guidance.

Here the mysticism of a sixteenth-century Basque is of special value. Ignatius of Loyola (1491-1556) was a mystic of action who constantly sought God's will and taught others to do likewise. His doctrine is demanding (for mysticism is never sweet and easy) and calls for total commitment to the crucified Christ. It can lead to profound mysticism in a busy life.

MYSTIC IN ACTION

Ignatius' conversion began when he was lying in bed with a broken leg after the siege of Pamplona. Out of sheer boredom he began reading lives of the saints and, in particular, the *Vita Christi* of the Carthusian Ludolf of Saxony. This occasioned his conversion from a life of sin (though how sinful he really was we do not know) which reached new depths at Manresa. Here he devoted days and nights to prayer, passing through a harrowing crisis which passed away when he came to profound enlightenment while watching the flow of the river Cardonner.

The chief characteristic of his conversion was a radical commitment to Christ. He loved the *Anima Christi* with its mystical cry: 'Hide me within thy wounds!'

Intra tua vulnera absconde me

And the first week of his *Spiritual Exercises* closes as the exercitant kneels at the foot of the cross asking, 'What have I done for Christ? What am I doing for Christ? What am I going to do for Christ?"

What have I done for Christ?
What am I doing for Christ?
What ought I to do for Christ?

For Ignatius right action meant following Christ.

His ideal was to follow Christ the King 'bearing all wrongs and abuses and all poverty, both actual and spiritual'." He delineates three stages in this path — poverty with Christ poor, humiliation with Christ humiliated, radical emptiness with Christ who humbled himself taking the form of a slave. This is the path of nothingness and emptiness; it is the *kenosis* of the Son of God. It is the mysticism of St Paul who told the Corinthians that they must become fools if they want to be wise. It is the *nada, nada, nada* and the *mu, mu, mu*. It leads inexorably into the cloud of unknowing and the mystical void.

The young Ignatius followed Christ as a knight in shining armour; but as time went on, his commitment became increasingly Trinitarian. While journeying to Rome at the little village of La Storta 'he was visited very especially by God' and had an experience which was to influence his whole life and activity. He describes it simply:

> One day, a few miles before reaching Rome, he was at prayer in a church and experienced such a change in his soul and saw so clearly that God the Father placed him with Christ His Son that he would not dare doubt it — that God had placed him with his Son.[9]

To be placed with the Son was to enter into the mystery of the Blessed Trinity.

Towards the end of his life he spent long hours in prayer before and after celebrating the Eucharist. His prayer, both Eucharistic and Trinitarian, was accompanied by floods of tears.

His teaching on contemplation and action was clear. One who would act in God's service must be well trained, well educated. However, union with God through charity is more important than natural gifts, however wonderful these may be. Here are his words:

> The means which unite the human instrument with God and so dispose it that it may be wielded dexterously by His divine hand are more effective than those which equip it in relation to people . . . for these are the interior gifts from which force must flow to the exterior for the end proposed to us.[10]

The interior gifts are the most important. Charity is the most important. From inner charity flows the energy which gives efficacy to the exterior work.

True to this commitment to Jesus and to the Father, Ignatius wanted his sons to be men crucified to the world and to whom the world is crucified. His company was to be called 'the company of Jesus' and nothing else. When the Roman cardinals, exasperated because they had to raise their birettas when this new Society was mentioned, demanded that the name be changed, he fought tooth and nail to keep the name as the Society of Jesus. And it has remained the Society of Jesus to this day.

Yet the wounded young soldier had other experiences which were to influence profoundly both his own activity and the activity of the order he founded. These we must now consider.

DISCERNING THE SPIRIT

Lying wounded in bed Ignatius began to listen to himself and to watch his daydreams. Sometimes his thoughts and fantasies turned romantically to beautiful women and deeds of chivalry. This delighted him for a while but eventually left him sad and desolate. At other times he dreamt of serving God like the saints, and such thoughts gradually gave him lasting peace. Unconsciously he was following the advice of St John, 'Beloved, do not believe every spirit but test the spirits to see whether they are from God . . .' (1 John 4:1). And gradually he learnt which thoughts were leading to destruction and should be banished, and which thoughts were leading to authentic joy and should be followed. For the rest of his life much of his prayer was spent in listening to the inner movements, asking which came from the forces of evil, which came from himself and which came from the Holy Spirit. The ideal was to be guided by the Holy Spirit in every action.

One interesting example of Ignatian discernment is worth mentioning. It occurred when he was in Manresa. He describes quite vividly how in broad daylight he saw a beautiful serpent in the air near him:

While in this hospice it often happened that in broad daylight he saw something in the air near him. It gave him great consolation because it was very beautiful — remarkably so. He could not discern very well the kind of thing it was, but in a way it seemed to him to have the form of a serpent with many things that shone like eyes, though they were not. He found great pleasure and consolation in seeing this thing, and the oftener he saw it the more his consolation grew. When it disappeared, he was displeased.[11]

This vision was followed by inner turmoil, desolation, scrupulosity and sadness.

Then came the great awakening as he sat by the river. Filled with joy he went to a nearby cross to give thanks to God. And again he saw the serpent:

There, the vision that had appeared to him many times but which he had never understood, that is, the thing mentioned above which seemed very beautiful with many eyes, now appeared to him. But while before the cross, he saw clearly that the object did not have its usual beautiful colour . . .[12]

Now he knew it was the devil. It continued to appear but he drove it away with a staff that he held in his hand.

What was the significance of this beautiful serpent that Ignatius saw floating in the air?

The serpent is a sexual symbol and we know that at this time Ignatius was still dreaming about beautiful and attractive women. We also know that the serpent is a symbol of primitive life, of life in the womb. And it is possible that Ignatius was at a crossroads in his life. He was faced with the possibility of going forward to embrace the poverty and humiliation of the cross or of going back to embrace the fascinating beauty of the serpent. This was the struggle of Manresa.

After the Manresa experience Ignatius travelled to the Holy Land and to various parts of Europe, always searching for the will of God, always listening to the interior movements of his soul, becoming more and more sensitive to the inner voice of the Spirit. Later in life, a great part of his prayer was devoted to discerning what he should write in the constitutions of his order. Whereas other mystics might rigorously banish such thoughts in order to be alone with God, Ignatius took all his problems and preoccupations into his prayer —

like Mary who pondered the events of her life in her heart — as he celebrated the Eucharist. His abundant tears, his inner locutions or *loquela* were guiding him to make important decisions; and he kept discerning, fearing that the inner movements might be from the powers of evil and might lead him in the wrong direction.

This mysticism of discernment was part of the heritage he bequeathed to his order. He says frankly that he is reluctant to write rules and regulations. What should govern the activity of the fathers and brothers is not the exterior law (how like St Paul!) but 'the interior law of charity and love which the Holy Spirit writes and imprints on the human heart'.[13] Fidelity to the Spirit comes first: fidelity to the law is secondary. 'The letter kills, but the Spirit gives life' (2 Corinthians 3:6).

And can modern men and women learn to follow the Spirit in a mysticism of discernment? Is this a viable way of life for those who live in the secular city? Two Ignatian points are worth mentioning.

The first is that Ignatius was deeply concerned with the fundamental option. One whose fundamental option is for good finds peace and joy in the prompting of the Spirit and anguish in the prompting of the evil one; on the other hand, one whose fundamental option is for evil will find anguish and pain in the prompting of the Spirit and malicious joy in the prompting of the evil one. The fundamental option is all-important. Concretely, the mysticism of discernment is only for those who are totally committed to Christ.

The second point is that this is a learning process and takes time. Ignatius takes it for granted that everyone makes mistakes. Almost humorously he says that such a one should simply look at the serpent's tail (the *cauda serpentina*) and resolve not to make the same mistake again.

But there are times when one must make a major decision that will determine the whole direction of one's life. Ignatius advised such a person to go through his spiritual exercises.

GREAT DECISIONS

Before beginning his public life Jesus spent forty days in the wilderness, alone in prayer. Before choosing his disciples 'he went out to the mountain to pray; and he spent the night in prayer to God' (Luke 5:16). Before his passion and death he prayed in Gethsemane, making his greatest offering — 'not my will but thine be done' (Matthew 26:39). The great events of his life were preceded by prayer.

In the same way Ignatius asks for long and intensive prayer before one makes a decision about one's state in life. One who would make the *Spiritual Exercises* is asked to spend thirty days in silence, praying for at least five hours during the day and sometimes for an hour at midnight. As for the methods of prayer, Ignatius at the beginning teaches a discursive prayer of the memory, the understanding and the will (the so called three powers of the soul) and then a contemplative prayer whereby one pictures scenes from the gospels. These came to be called Ignatian forms of prayer and, unfortunately, some directors insisted that the exercitant pray only in this way, thus robbing the exercises of their mystical content. In fact, in teaching discursive prayer Ignatius was only simplifying the methods of prayer current at the time. And the contemplative prayer of looking at the scene he learned from Ludolf of Saxony. He was open to any kind of prayer that the Spirit prompted, and he tells the exercitant to stop where he or she finds fruit and to rest there — thus preparing the way for the gift of mystical experience. All that was necessary was that one enter progressively into the mystery of Christ, tasting and relishing the inner fruit with sighs or tears or whatever gifts were given.

In order to listen to the indwelling Holy Spirit one must be detached or non-attached, fixing one's eyes on God's glory alone. One who is torn this way and that by inordinate attachment to money, power, health, a long life or a short life — such a one does not have the inner calm to listen to the Spirit and make a good decision. Again, one who is torn by anxiety and fear loses the necessary inner peace. One must have what Ignatius calls 'indifference' towards all created things. But how come to this indifference?

Here Oriental meditation — awareness of breathing and body in order to live in the present moment — is of great value. Again, Oriental detachment from the fruits of one's labour teaches a similar lesson. People who practise mindfulness can come to this inner calm;

and if they follow Ignatius in Christian faith they will orient their whole lives to the promotion of God's glory or (as Ignatius loved to say) God's greater glory.

And needless to say a key role in the whole process is played by the director who accompanies the exercitant. Yet the director must never forget that the real director is the Holy Spirit and no other. Therefore, while listening attentively and asking pertinent questions, the director must never influence the exercitant in one way or the other. Never must the director interfere in the work of God. He or she must be careful to leave the exercitant alone with the Alone.

In the context of discernment Ignatius speaks of consolation without previous cause.[14] 'It belongs to God alone to give consolation without previous cause.' What is this consolation without previous cause which he considers so important?

Earlier in this book a distinction was made between contemplation which is acquired by human effort and contemplation which is pure gift, being infused by God. There may be times in life when people receive a divine gift. They know with great conviction that they do not deserve this gift nor did they do anything to cause it. They are filled with confusion and a sense of unworthiness. This is a mystical grace. Ignatius calls it consolation without previous cause; and his *Exercises* aim at disposing the exercitant to receive this unmerited grace.

The *Exercises* come to a climax when one receives this gift. Paul on the road to Damascus and Matthew who in a moment left all to follow Jesus are examples of such grace. The decision of these two apostles was not made by human effort but was a gift of God. 'You did not choose me but I chose you' (John 15:16).

Such moments of dazzling gift are by no means rare; they have graced the lives of prayerful people everywhere and continue to do so. Nevertheless, Ignatius, aware that gift is gift, proposes other ways of coming to an important decision.

DISCERNMENT ABOUT POVERTY

Ignatius was faced with an important decision concerning the poverty of his infant Society. Fortunately we have the notes he jotted down while deciding whether or not the churches of the Society should have a fixed income. While celebrating the Eucharist, he tells us, he felt inclined to total poverty, and this inclination stayed with him all during the day. A couple of days later he writes: 'I saw Mother and Son disposed to intercede with the Father, and I felt more inclined to perfect poverty at the time and throughout the day.'[15] He continues to pray and to reflect, and after some days he writes again that 'there would be some confusion in having a partial revenue, and a scandal in having a complete revenue, and an occasion for making little of the poverty which Our Lord praises so highly'.[16]

This experience of discernment, far from being rational and calculating, was filled with fire and tears: 'I felt within me an impulse to go and betake myself to the Father, and in doing so my hair stood on end with a most remarkable warmth in my whole body. Following on this, tears and deep devotion.'[17] In this way he made his decision to embrace perfect poverty; and as he offered his decision to God he felt deep peace and inner security:

> I felt an abundance of devotion and tears, and later, making a colloquy with the Holy Spirit before saying His mass, with the same devotion and tears, I thought I saw Him or felt Him, in a dense brightness, or in the colour of a flame of fire. Quite unusual, and with all this, I felt satisfied with the election I made.[18]

Ignatius made much of the interior peace and security that filled his soul after the decision was made. This he took as confirmation that his decision was pleasing to God:

> Later, great peace and security of soul, like a tired man taking a good rest, neither being able nor caring to seek anything, considering the matter finished, except to give thanks, pay some devotion to the Father, and say the mass of the Holy Trinity . . .[19]

Here is the mystical discernment of one who, while celebrating the Eucharist with tears and inner warmth and visions, was listening to the guidance of the Spirit. When all was finished, Ignatius made a rational check, writing out the advantages and the disadvantages, the pros and the cons.

But how is one to explain the tears of Ignatius? No other mystic has wept so much. His intimate friend Laynez tells us that ordinarily he wept six or seven times a day. His eyesight was endangered by the abundance of tears.

Mystics often speak of a deeply spiritual experience that overflows on the senses. They speak of an inner fire, a blind stirring of love, a living flame of love which is so powerful that it causes the stigmata, the five wounds of Jesus, or other physical phenomena such as rapture or ecstasy or dislocation of the bones. Ignatius did not experience such phenomena. Instead he shed tears. In a person of his temperament tears were the outer expression of his deeply spiritual interior experience.

AWAKENING

Dialogue with Eastern mysticism has made us more and more conscious of the phenomenon of awakening or enlightenment or illumination. Mystics East and West have moments when their inner eye is opened and they come to see reality in a new way. Such was the case with Ignatius who came to a new vision of the world as he sat looking at the river Cardonner.

It is interesting to note that the flowing river is often the occasion of enlightenment. 'As I was among exiles by the river Chebar,' writes Ezekiel, 'the heavens were opened and I saw visions of God' (Ezekiel 1:1). In the same way Ignatius, going out of devotion to a church near Manresa, sat down and looked at the river. He relates what happened:

> While he was seated there, the eyes of his understanding began to be opened: not that he saw any vision, but he understood and learnt many things, both spiritual matters and matters of faith *and of scholarship* and with so great an enlightenment that everything seemed new to him.[20]

Ignatius saw no vision — neither corporeal nor imaginative — but he had a new understanding of reality — 'everything seemed new to him' — and he was filled with wonder:

> He experienced a great clarity in his understanding. This was such that in the whole course of his life, after completing sixty-two years, even if he gathered up all the various helps he may have had from God and all the various things he has known, even adding them all together, he does not think he had got as much as at that one time.[21]

This experience of Ignatius is significant and important for mystical theology. For it is an awakening with definite theological content. What the content was Ignatius does not say explicitly; but he does speak of spiritual matters and matters of faith and of scholarship. At the same period in his life he speaks of seeing with his interior eye (that is, with the spiritual senses) the humanity of Jesus in a white form — it may have been a white light — without distinction of members; and he makes the remarkable statement:

> These things he saw strengthened him then and always gave him such strength in his faith that he has often thought to himself: if there were no Scriptures to teach us these matters of faith, he would be resolved to die for them, solely because of what he had seen.[22]

Here again there is clear intellectual content in his experience.

Later in his life he makes a similar comment in his spiritual journal concerning the lights he had received in prayer and their relation to study:

> . . . with many lights and spiritual memories concerning the Most Holy Trinity which served as a great illumination to my mind, so much so that I thought I could never learn so much by hard study, and later, as I examined the matter more closely, I felt and understood, I thought, more than if I had studied all my life.[23]

Here again it is clear that his mystical experience has theological content. Is it quite different from the apophatic experience of those mystics who speak disdainfully of theology as a tiny candle beside the glorious light of the sun? If there was content in the Ignatian experience — theological content or material for discernment — what about the void, the emptiness, the cloud of unknowing and the darkness?

The present writer does not doubt that Ignatius was in the void and in the cloud of unknowing. Indeed, his writings throw precious light on the void. Let us never forget that the void and the cloud do not mean that one has emptied the mind of all content so as to become a blank sheet or a *tabula rasa*. *The void is constituted by detachment*. One can be in the void while being aware of the sound of the waterfall, the singing of the birds and the croaking of the frogs. One can be in the void while wrestling with the *koan*. One can be in the void while struggling with material of discernment. One can be in the void while working in the kitchen, the office, the laboratory or the classroom. One can be in the void and speak to the persons of the Trinity. To be in the void means that one has entered a deep level of consciousness wherein one is detached and free, without clinging and grasping and anxiety.

The fact is that there is always content in authentic mystical experience. Sometimes God himself is so intimately present that he blinds the eyes as the light of the sun blinds the bat: then the content is dark. At other times the inner eye is opened to a new vision of reality: and then the content is bright. At other times God reveals his secrets and one gets a partial glimpse of the mysteries of faith.

And this leads to two conclusions that are important for mystical theology.

The first is that there is an intimate connection between theology and mystical awakening. The theology of the Church Fathers — of Augustine, Gregory, Chrysostom and the rest — came from their mystical experience. Their doctrine of the Trinity did not come simply from books — though they did study assiduously — but more importantly from what they saw. Like Ignatius they could say that if there was no Scripture to teach these matters of faith they would be resolved to die for them solely because of what they had seen. If there is a defect in our theology of the twentieth century it is surely that mystical experience has been downgraded by theologians who work solely with books and computers.

The second important conclusion is that we cannot say that Hindu, Buddhist, Islamic, Jewish and Christian mysticism are all the same. While it is true that all mystics enter into the silence and emptiness of the cloud of unknowing and while it is true that mystical experience is the best locus for interreligious dialogue, it is also true that the content is different. This means that mystics can share and enrich one another as they go on their journey into the mystery. Let us avoid a facile ecumenism.

VISION OF LOVE

Though Ignatius was an incorrigible romantic he never fell under the spell of The Song of Songs. Nevertheless, he did speak about lovers, saying that love should manifest itself in deeds rather than in words and that love consists in a mutual sharing. Lovers share with one another their knowledge, their money, their honour and everything else.

And this mutual sharing is the culmination of the human relationship with God. Just as lovers share their whole being with one another in marriage, so God and the human person share totally with one another. God is love. Through creation and redemption God has shared with us. He is alive in the whole world, giving it existence — in the elements, the plants, the animals, the human beings. God is working for us in the heavens, the elements, the plants, the fruit, the cattle — always giving himself as a great Lover. God's goodness, justice, mercy are flowing down upon us as the rays of light descend from the sun and as waters flow from a fountain. God is love.

And as God shares all with me, so in response I share all with God and pray:

Take, O Lord, and receive all my liberty, my memory, my understanding and my entire will, all that I have and possess.[24]

This is a total offering. It is the *nada*, the *mu*, the all. And it is an act of love. One ends the prayer by saying, 'Give me thy love and thy grace for this is enough for me.'[25] One asks for the gift of love; and the union of the lover and the beloved is consummated. Now there takes place a total transformation of the beloved in the lover.

Moreover, this prayer leads to the perfection of action. For having surrendered all one's powers to God one prays:

Dispose of them in any way according to thy will.[26]

From now the activity will not be mine; it will be the activity of God making use of my powers to move heaven and earth. Now the divine lover is acting through one who has surrendered her all to him.

In this way we have the gigantic love affair of traditional Christian mysticism, translated into action when the beloved asks the lover to use her and all her powers according to his will. Two points are here worth mentioning.

The first is that this offering is eucharistic. It was while celebrating the Eucharist that Ignatius made the total offering of himself and his projects with many tears and sighs and sobs. And he asks the exercitant lover to make this radical offering with great feeling — 'Thus as one would do who is moved by great feeling, I will make the offering of myself.'[27]

The second is that this offering is Trinitarian. It is the offering of one's whole self with the Son to the Father in the Holy Spirit. All through his life Ignatius prayed with childlike simplicity to the Father, the Son and the Holy Spirit. He had visions of three persons in One God, claiming at one time that he saw the essence of God 'under the figure of a sphere, slightly larger than the appearance of the sun'.[28]

In fact the whole Contemplation for Obtaining Divine Love is an attempt to put into words the awakening Ignatius experienced at the river when 'he understood and learned many things, both spiritual matters and matters of faith and scholarship and with so great an enlightenment that everything seemed new to him'. At the end of *The Spiritual Exercises* he wishes to lead others to the same mystical experience.

And the sons of Ignatius did share in that experience. The

Contemplation for Obtaining Divine Love profoundly influenced the poetry of Gerard Manley Hopkins, the theology of Karl Rahner and the mystical vision of Teilhard de Chardin. All these Jesuits saw a world penetrated through and through with the glory of God who is love; and as lovers they responded with the prayer, 'Take, O Lord, and receive . . .' They prayed that their actions be not theirs but the actions of God, 'Dispose of them in any way according to thy will . . .'

TEACHER OF PRAYER

Ignatius was primarily a teacher of prayer. As a layman he went from place to place guiding chosen people through the *Exercises*. Later, as general of the Jesuits, he continued to teach contemplation in action, always with eyes fixed on the world of his day. Though he loved the Carthusians and even thought of joining them, he vigorously opposed any kind of prayer that would withdraw his little group from the activity to which they were called.

After leading his disciples through *The Spiritual Exercises* he sent them to study. During this time he did not prescribe long hours of prayer, but he insisted on short prayer. Participation in the Eucharist and two periods of fifteen minutes were mandatory. He always insisted that one who was striving to live a mortified and unselfish life would progress more in fifteen minutes than the unmortified and selfish person who devoted many hours to prayer. Outside the time of prayer he led people to live in the presence of God and to seek God in all things — in this he was like the hesychasts who followed the gospel teaching on unceasing prayer.

His eyes were fixed on the world of his times and he was constantly discerning its needs, asking what action should next be taken. He sent Xavier to the Indies and Laynez to the Council of Trent. The vocation of his followers was to travel — to travel to places where they could work for God's glory and the help of souls.

Were he alive today, discerning the signs of the times, what would he do? If he saw the social upheaval — the grinding poverty side by side with overflowing luxury, the cruel violence sustained by a flourishing arms industry — what would he say? No doubt he would again realize that prayer and action must not be separated, that we must continue to discern the action of the Spirit and that there is a social dimension to mystical theology.

NOTES

1. See chapter 4 of this book.
2. *Sacrosanctum Concilium*, 2.
3. *Gaudium et Spes*, 34.
4. Ibid., 35.
5. Ibid., 37.
6. *Dignitatis Humanae*, 1.
7. *The Spiritual Exercises of St Ignatius of Loyola*, trans. Louis J. Puhl, Loyola University Press, Chicago 1968, 53. For a description of Ignatian mysticism, see *Ignatius of Loyola the Mystic*, Harvey Egan, Michael Glazie, Delaware 1987.
8. Ibid., 98.
9. *A Pilgrim's Testament: The Memoirs of St Ignatius of Loyola*, trans. Parmananda R. Divarkar, Gregorian University Press, 1983, 96.
10. *The Constitutions of the Society of Jesus*, trans. with an introduction and commentary by George E. Ganss, St. Louis, Institute of Jesuit Sources, 1970.
11. *A Pilgrim's Testament*, 19.
12. Ibid., 31.
13. *Constitutions*, Part I.
14. *Spiritual Exercises*, 330.
15. *Spiritual Journal of Ignatius of Loyola*, trans. William J. Young, Woodstock College Press, 1958, part 1.4.
16. Ibid., 5.
17. Ibid., 7.
18. Ibid., 10.
19. Ibid.
20. *A Pilgrim's Testament*, 30.
21. Ibid.
22. Ibid., 29.
23. Ibid., 18.
24. *Spiritual Exercises*, 234.
25. Ibid.
26. Ibid.
27. Ibid.
28. *Spiritual Journal*, 34.

NINETEEN

Mysticism of Social Action

SOCIAL CONSCIOUSNESS

From its very inception Christianity was a vigorously active religion. 'Go, therefore, make disciples of all the nations. . .' was a clarion call to missionary activity. The gospel injunction to feed the hungry, give drink to the thirsty and clothe the naked was always alive. Wherever there was earthquake, famine or natural disaster, wherever there were lepers or blind or lame, Christians could be found binding wounds and pouring in oil like the good Samaritan of the gospel. And this compassion is alive today when the sisters of Mother Teresa take into their arms the destitute and dying in the streets of the great cities throughout the world.

From the end of the nineteenth century, however, a new development took place. Christians began to look more carefully at the structures of society. They became conscious of social sin. They saw that sin, besides being an individual's offence against God, is built into the very structures of society. Pope Leo XIII (1810-1903) issued an encyclical on the human rights of the worker that came to be called 'the workers' charter'.[1] It was followed by a series of papal encyclicals that challenged established governments. Christians opposed communist governments not simply because they persecuted religion but because they oppressed and dehumanized human beings. Similarly Christians fought against the racial enormities of Nazism; and when communism and Nazism collapsed, Christians continued to fight against an unbridled capitalism that treats people as mere things to be manipulated and used for the pleasure, power and profit of the few.

Meanwhile the Second Vatican Council stressed the social dimension of Christianity, speaking authoritatively about marriage, economics, politics and culture. 'The mission of the Church', said the Council, 'is not only to bring men and women the message and grace of Christ, but also to penetrate and perfect the temporal sphere with the spirit of the gospel.'[2] Christians were faced with the mind-boggling task of penetrating world economy with the spirit of the Gospel.

In 1993 the World Parliament of Religions in Chicago brought to the fore the social dimension of all religions, proposing a global ethic that would stress the inviolable dignity of every human person and would work for social justice, nonviolence, world peace and protection of the environment.

Now it is clear that we are moving towards one world. People everywhere have a sense of the solidarity of the human family, realizing that we must help one another, protect one another and care for mother earth as never before.

THE ROLE OF MYSTICAL THEOLOGY

In the great social revolution that was taking place in the twentieth century the traditional mystical theology taught in seminaries and faculties of theology played no part. Concerned with making people holy as individuals or as groups, it encouraged students to devote themselves to prayer and the reading of Scripture in isolation from the world. Such mystical theology quickly became irrelevant and disappeared from the curriculum.

However, a wave of contemplation, even of mysticism, swept into Christianity from another, unexpected quarter. It all began with a Hindu. Mahatma Gandhi gave a social interpretation to the Sermon on the Mount and his doctrine of nonviolence, forgiveness, love of one's enemy shook the world. What endeared Gandhi to the people of India and to people everywhere was his poverty (Winston Churchill called him a 'half naked fakir'), his prayer, his fasting, his compassion, his readiness to forgive and his down-to-earth holiness.

But was Gandhi a mystic? If by mystic we mean the person who has esoteric experiences then Gandhi does not qualify. But if we mean a person of vision, if (as in this book) we mean one in whose heart the living flame of love burns brightly so that his being becomes being-in-love then Gandhi may rightly be called a mystic. For he was totally committed to truth and spoke frequently about the power of truth which he called *satyagraha*. Furthermore, he genuinely strove to put into practice the words of one who said, 'But I say to you that listen, Love your enemies, do good to those who hate you, bless those who curse you, pray for those who abuse you. If anyone strikes you on the cheek, offer the other also. . .' (Luke 6:27-9). Such a person is inexorably drawn into the nothingness, the emptiness, the loss of self, the void that is the very basis of mystical experience.

Be that as it may, Gandhi's approach to human dignity and freedom was taken up in the United States by Martin Luther King and then by a renowned Cistercian contemplative. As a young monk Thomas Merton, imbued with the spirit of the Carmelite mystics, wrote pious books on contemplation for thousands of enthusiastic readers. But as time went on, he realized that he could no longer be a guilty bystander. Uncompromisingly he wrote controversial books and articles about injustice, discrimination, racial violence, the evils of capitalism and the exploitation of poor countries by rich countries. He was particularly eloquent in his condemnation of the Vietnam war and of any war.

Merton's religious superiors were not always happy with his social and political preoccupations, and he lost some disillusioned readers. Yet Father Louis, as he was called in the monastery, far from abandoning his vocation to contemplation, spoke to the world precisely as a contemplative, proclaiming from his hermitage in Kentucky that social concern was an integral part of contemplative life in the twentieth century.

Furthermore, Merton saw that in the building of a more human society Christians cannot work alone. When a sympathetic monk became abbot, he got permission to travel to Asia where he entered into dialogue with Vietnamese and Thai monks and spoke with the Dalai Lama. After his sudden death in Bangkok, Merton continued to exercise great influence on a peace movement associated with the names of Dorothy Day, Thich Nhat Hanh, Cesar Chavez and many others. His influence extended to the struggle for justice and peace in Latin America. His message was clear: Christianity cannot overlook the contemplative dimension of social revolution.

Yet another contemplative who dedicated himself to social reform was a Basque. Pedro Arrupe (1907-91) spent more than thirty years of his life in Japan. On August 6, 1945 when the fateful bomb fell on Hiroshima, Arrupe, as Jesuit Master of Novices, was living just outside the city. As a young man he had been a medical student, and now he promptly turned the novitiate into a hospital which welcomed the long line of wounded that streamed despairingly out of the atomic wilderness. Later, as Superior of the Society of Jesus, he visited Latin America and, shocked by what he saw and heard, led the Jesuits into a new and controversial path of commitment to justice and peace. This commitment was to bear fruit in 1989 when four Jesuits with their companions were martyred for social justice in El Salvador. Those who knew him well agree that Arrupe was a mystic who spent long hours in prayer, who translated St John of the Cross into Japanese, who lived the Ignatian ideal of seeing God in all things.[3]

The twentieth century, then, that has seen so many revolutions, has also seen the rise of a new mysticism of social involvement. Now we find activists in whose hearts the living flame of love burns brightly, activists whose being has become being-in-love, activists who have passed through the dark night of cruel misunderstanding. These are activists who express their love by demonstrating in the streets, pouring blood on nuclear installations, condemning evil structures, opposing tyrannical governments, going to prison, enduring torture and even death for their convictions. These mystics of social action will surely stand beside Teresa, John of the Cross and Eckhart in the annals of contemplative history. Their experience cannot be overlooked as we create a mystical theology for the future.

SCRIPTURAL BACKGROUND

Social concern prompted scholars and activists to take a new look at the Bible. In the Hebrew Scriptures they found prophets deeply involved in social problems and in politics. The great prophets of the eighth century — Amos, Hosea, Micah and Isaiah — bitterly attacked the establishment, both secular and religious, demanding that the rich and powerful turn away from greed, exploitation of the poor and all manner of injustice. To a worshipper who asks anxiously what sacrifices are pleasing to God the prophet Micah says:

> And what does the Lord require of you but to do justice, and to love kindness and to walk humbly with your God (Micah 6:8).

Of special importance is the prophet Jeremiah whom St John of the Cross repeatedly cites as a consummate mystic and whom Christian tradition has always seen as a type or figure of the suffering Jesus.

Now Jeremiah was deeply involved in the politics of his day. He attacks the prophets who curry favour with the establishment and forget justice — 'for from the prophets of Jerusalem ungodliness has spread throughout the land' (Jeremiah 23:15). So opposed to violence is Jeremiah that he even tells his people to surrender to Nebuchadnezzar — 'Serve the King of Babylon and live' (Jeremiah 27:17). Indeed, he is considered a traitor because he champions the cause of Nebuchadnezzar whom he calls God's servant:

> Thus says the Lord of hosts, the God of Israel . . . I have given all these lands into the hands of King Nebuchadnezzar of Babylon, my servant, and I have given him even the wild animals of the field to serve him (Jeremiah 27:6).

Jeremiah tells the Jews taken into captivity to pray for the peace of Babylon and to serve the king. Small wonder if he was hated by so-called patriots. Probably he was killed by them.

Again, thanks to theology of liberation, we can take a fresh approach to evangelical poverty. Now we see that the grinding poverty of millions who live in squalor is an insult to human dignity, not the plan of God. Jesus came to liberate us not only from the shackles of sin but from the shackles of whatever robs human life of its inherent dignity. It is the will of God that all men and women live with the dignity that befits human beings. No longer can pious Christians tell the destitute and downtrodden that they are God's chosen people who will receive their reward in heaven.

What then is poverty? What do the gospels mean by saying that the poor are blessed?

Here, as has been said earlier in this book, dialogue with Buddhism can help us. The poverty of the gospels is the radical detachment of one who becomes completely empty. It is the *mu*, the *ku*, the *nada*. It means becoming nothing to become all in imitation of Jesus who, being in the likeness of God, emptied himself taking the form of a slave and humbled himself becoming obedient unto death, death on a cross. We become poor in spirit by sharing in the *kenosis* of Jesus.

Now this *kenosis* (as has been said throughout this book) is the very basis of all mystical experience. And today we find men and women who imitate Jesus by emptying themselves totally in order to share the grinding poverty of the people they love. This freely chosen poverty makes the lives of these people both mystical and prophetic.

But as Christians devote themselves to reform of the sinful structures that oppress the downtrodden, an interesting and significant development is taking place: committed men and women throughout the world become increasingly sensitive to the sinful and oppressive structures in their own religious institutions. The Council spoke of the Church's continual need of reformation, saying that 'Christ summons the Church, as she goes on her pilgrim way, to that continual reformation of which she always has need, insofar as she is an institution of men and women here on earth'.[4] And in recent times some courageous Christians, deeply conscious of this need for reformation, have criticized oppressive structures of the institutional Church with an angry love and a prophetic vehemence that remind one of Jeremiah confronting the false prophets or of Paul confronting Peter angrily, telling him that he must not make the Gentiles live like Jews. This new spirit of prophecy has caused turmoil which continues today and is likely to continue for many years to come.

THE ROOTS OF THE PROBLEM

Faced with the enormous social and political problems of today's world many good people are overcome with a feeling of utter helplessness. 'Why should I worry about it? What can I do about it?'

To this question mystical theology might answer that the very feeling of helplessness is the key to the ultimate solution. Did not Paul glory in his helplessness? It was precisely when he was beaten down and helpless that the power of God rose up within him and he cried, 'When I am weak then I am strong' (2 Corinthians 12:10). But before speaking about helplessness it is necessary to uncover the root cause of the turmoil in which we are engulfed.

About the root cause of the cruel Babylonian exile Jeremiah had no doubts. The people had forgotten God. 'You did not listen to me, says the Lord, and so you have provoked me to anger. . .' (Jeremiah 25:7). The same theme runs all through the Bible; and Hosea offers a simple and compassionate solution: 'Return, O Israel, to the Lord your God, for you have stumbled because of your iniquity' (Hosea 14:1). Humble return to a loving God is the answer.

Paul, looking at the corrupt Roman Empire, has a similar reaction. The Empire is filled with every kind of wickedness, evil, covetousness and malice. And how did this come about? Paul is clear:

> They are without excuse. For though they knew God, they did not honour him as God or give thanks to him . . . (Romans 1:20-1).

The root cause of decline was rejection of God.

Yet Paul is no pessimist. A Saviour has come. 'But when the fullness of time had come, God sent his Son, born of a woman, born under the law. . .' (Galatians 4:4). This Son saved the world by laying down his life.

And what a scene meets the eyes of the visionary who wrote the book of Revelation! Terrible yet realistic is his vision of the great whore clothed in fine linen, in purple and scarlet, adorned with gold, with jewels and with pearls, drunk with the blood of the saints. How powerful was the great city of Rome! 'It was given authority over every tribe and people and language and nation, and all the inhabitants of the earth will worship it . . .' (Revelation 13:7-8). Yet ignominiously it will fall. 'Alas, alas, the great city . . . for in one hour all this wealth has been laid waste' (Revelation 18:19).

For the author of this apocalyptic drama, as he looked at the

Roman Empire and listened to the voice that told him to write, saw a deeper meaning to it all. He saw a struggle between Jerusalem and Babylon, between the great red dragon and the innocent lamb who was slain. It was a struggle between good and evil. And John did not doubt that the lamb would conquer 'for he is Lord of lords and King of kings' (Revelation 17:14).

And as we look on the world of today what do we see? Human rights are violated. Men and women are tortured. Empires rise and fall. Rich nations exploit poor nations. Multinational companies pollute the atmosphere, destroy nature and sell deadly arms to the highest bidder. What is the root problem?

Jeremiah and Paul and all the prophets remind us that we must not be so mesmerized by the external horrors as to forget the deeper, underlying problem; namely, the struggle between good and evil. Nor must we forget that through it all shines the triumphant story of salvation.

The task of the Christian together with men and women of all religions, then, is to see the world at two levels. Here and now we see the earthly city in which the enemies are hunger, sickness, oppression, injustice and the sinful structures of human society. At the same time we remember with St Paul that 'our struggle is not against enemies of flesh and blood but against the cosmic powers of the present darkness, against the spiritual forces of evil in the heavenly places' (Ephesians 6:12). And as we work to improve this earthly city we fix our eyes on the city of God in which death will be no more 'for God will wipe every tear from their eyes' (Revelation 21:4).

And how is this battle fought?

Paul is clear. He tells the Ephesians to put on the armour of God — the belt of truth, the shoes of peace, the breastplate of righteousness, the shield of faith, the helmet of salvation and the sword of the Spirit. He then sums up his teaching by saying:

Pray in the Spirit at all times in every prayer and supplication (Ephesians 6:18).

In short, Paul speaks of the power of the Spirit. He is telling us to overcome evil with good.

Yet to this there is an important corollary.

If all the evil were 'out there' and all the good were 'in here' the battle would be simple. If 'they' were the city of Babylon and 'we' were the city of Jerusalem it would be clear. But, alas, we know from revelation and experience that Babylon lives in our hearts and that the great whore flourishes in our religious institutions. This makes the battle more complex. We know, moreover, that wheat and weeds will grow in the field until the end of time. 'Let both of them grow together until the harvest,' said the master.

Such is the world that confronts us today.

THE POWER OF BEING

The mysticism of East Asia is dominated by the Taoist principle of *wu-wei*, usually translated as non-action.

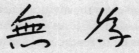

Wu-wei, also translated as non-interference, means that by not acting one allows the forces of the universe to act. Personal effort falls into the background or even disappears as the immense energies of the cosmos surge up, carrying the process forward. Needless to say, *wu-wei* presupposes great confidence in the goodness of the universe and its energies. One does not act, knowing that the universe will bring things to a happy consummation. Puny human effort is unnecessary and superfluous.

Wu-wei is practised principally in meditation where one sits, doing nothing, allowing the inner energies to arise. There is a Zen saying,

Sitting, only sitting, and the grass grows green by itself

It is as though the master were to say: 'Just sit! Let the process take place. Don't be anxious about the grass. Trust the universe.'

And yet just sitting or just being is a great art that can only be mastered through years, even decades, of practice. It is quite different from lounging in a chair or letting the mind run amok. It is quite different from quietism. One must discipline oneself in all things, learning how to breathe, how to sit, how to relax, how to let the energy flow. Above all, one must learn detachment so that one can sit in utter freedom without clinging to anything. When one can do this (and it takes twenty years to learn the art) the forces of the universe are unleashed and true activity is born. It is like the birth of a child or the birth of any great work of art. The mother suffers, undergoes, lets the process take place, and then new life comes into the world.

Parallel to the *wu-wei* is the mysticism of the Byzantine and Orthodox traditions which speak of the uncreated energies and the divine light that come to birth in the heart of one who has recited the Jesus prayer for many decades.

A parallel process is also found in the Latin tradition, which can here be briefly described.

One who is invited to enter the mystical life may begin by actively meditating on the passion of Jesus or on some scene from the gospels. She then goes on to repeat an ejaculation such as the Jesus prayer, until the time comes when she rests in silence at the core of her being, doing nothing, without words, just being. At this time the inner fire rises up, the inner light begins to shine, the uncreated energies are awakened. Her being has become being-in-love.

Now such a person while doing nothing is radiating energy to the whole universe. She is, unknown to herself, a powerful agent of social reform. In *Le Milieu Divin* Teilhard de Chardin speaks of a tiny nun rapt in contemplative prayer and he sees her as the centre of the cosmic powers of the universe. Is she not the one who is conquering the Pauline powers of darkness?

Likewise the author of *The Cloud of Unknowing* speaks of the contemplative in whose heart the meek stirring of love has arisen; and, using the terminology of his day, he describes the cosmic dimension of such prayer:

> This is the work of the soul that most pleases God. All saints and angels have joy of this work and hasten to help it with all their might. All the devils are mad when you do this and try to stop it.

All men and women in the world are wonderfully helped by this work, you know not how. Yea, the souls in purgatory are eased of their pains by virtue of this work.[5]

In just being and 'doing nothing' one pleases God, helps men and women everywhere, relieves the pains of the souls in purgatory. Above all, one works for the salvation of the whole human family. Such is the power of being-in-love.

However, there is one point that must make the modern reader pause. The English author urges his disciple to bury beneath a cloud of forgetting every creature that God ever made so as to be alone with God in a cloud of unknowing. This is certainly a legitimate way of prayer, for the cloud of forgetting is not a rejection of creation but a way to detachment. Nevertheless we now realize that we cannot, and must not, run away from the poverty, the injustice, the oppression, the torture, the violence, the hunger that afflict so many people. Nor can we forget that the Second Vatican Council told us to resonate with the joys and the sufferings of the world. Is there, then, a way of contemplation that helps us to share in the suffering of our fellow men and women and at the same time brings us to the divine core of our being?

One outstanding example of such meditation is the bodhisattva Kannon (in Chinese *Kuan-Yin*) who stands on pedestals throughout Asia. Kannon is the bodhisattva of compassion who listens to the cries of the poor and afflicted. Around her lips plays a gentle smile of compassion as she listens, listens, listens. She is concerned not only with the material suffering of the people but more especially with their salvation. She refuses to enter nirvana until all sentient beings are saved.

Now Kannon does not *do* anything. She is not an activist. Yet through her gentle smile she radiates comfort, joy and hope. Millions are energized by her compassion. The exquisite statues symbolize being-in-compassion. And contemplatives imitate Kannon when they silently and compassionately listen to the suffering of the world. As they listen they may be overcome with the feeling of helplessness. What can I do about it? What can I do? But the good director humbly assures them that they change the world by doing nothing. By being and by suffering they perform a great service to the human family and to the cosmos.

For it must be remembered that Jesus redeemed the world less by what he *did* than by what he *was* and what he *suffered*. It was precisely from the cross that salvific energy flowed to the world, as Jesus himself prophesied when he said: 'And I, when I am lifted up from the earth, will draw all things to myself' (John 12:32).

Contemplatives, then, change the world even when they do nothing. They conquer by being.

THE POWER OF NONVIOLENCE

The *ahimsa* or nonviolence of Gandhi was quite different from the *wu-wei* of the Taoists. Whereas the Taoists believed in doing nothing that the forces of the universe might act, Gandhi was an activist who believed in doing something. He taught *active nonviolence*. He believed in fighting by not fighting. The movement that stems from him advocates prayer, fasting, peace marches, civil disobedience; it makes use of art, poetry, music, mass media and every kind of symbolic action in its search for truth, justice and peace. Above all, it emphasizes the power of suffering — the power of going to prison, accepting all manner of calumny and embracing death.

Gandhi, a fervent Hindu, loved the nonviolent Jesus. A single picture of Jesus hung in his tiny room. At the end of his life he wept at the pietà of Michelangelo in St Peter's. And now that his nonviolence enters into the Christian life, we must learn to centre it more and more on Jesus who came not to be served but to serve and to lay down his life for many.

That Jesus taught nonviolence no one doubts. The very centre of his message is love of one's enemy and forgiveness of everyone. We must forgive not seven times but seventy times seven times (that is, without limit); and then there is the disturbing warning that if we do not forgive our neighbour God will not forgive us.

But even more important than the teaching of Jesus is the example of Jesus who freely accepted death and did not resist evil. The early Christians saw Jesus above all as the suffering servant of Isaiah:

I gave my back to those who struck me and my cheek to those who pulled out the beard. I did not hide my face from insult and spitting (Isaiah 50:6).

This is the nonviolent Jesus who did not cry out or lift up his voice — 'a bruised reed he will not break, and a dimly burning wick he will not quench' (Isaiah 42:3).

The death of Jesus was the greatest mystical event in human history. It was the culminating *kenosis* of one who emptied himself, taking the form of a slave, becoming obedient unto death. This was the time when Jesus became nothing in order to become everything through his Resurrection. Small wonder if every authentically Christian mystical experience is based on this *kenosis* of Jesus. Paul is crucified and dies with Jesus — 'I have been crucified with Christ' (Galatians 2:20) — in order that he may rise with Jesus. The cross of Jesus is the core of the sanjuanist *nada, nada, nada*. The cross is at the heart of the mysticism of Francis of Assisi, Julian of Norwich, Edith Stein. Mystically they lived the death and Resurrection of Jesus.

And awesome power flowed from the death of Jesus. When he cried with a loud voice and yielded up the spirit, a tremendous energy was unleashed in the universe. The veil of the temple was torn in two from top to bottom. The earth shook, and the rocks were split. The tombs also were opened and many bodies of the saints were raised, entered into the holy city and appeared to many. The terrified centurion gasped, 'Truly this was the Son of God.' The death of Jesus swept into the Roman Empire, accomplishing more than the armies of Caesar. It continues to accomplish more than the nuclear explosions of Hiroshima and Nagasaki.

Such is the power of suffering. Such is the power of death. Such is the power of nonviolence.

The first Christians saw that there was a tremendous power not only in the death of Jesus but also in their own death. For them the great ideal, the glorious ideal, was martyrdom in which, like Stephen, they would die praying for their enemies. They also saw that as the death of Jesus was creative and dynamic so their martyrdom was creative and dynamic — for the blood of martyrs was the seed of the Church. As for killing, the Church Fathers, including

Origen and Tertullian, affirmed that Christians must not take life and should not serve in the Roman army. One who participates in the Eucharist must not destroy the bodies and shed the blood of human beings for whom Jesus died. In short, the whole climate was nonviolent until the fourth century when Emperor Constantine made Christianity the state religion. Then, in some perverse way, the cross of the nonviolent Jesus became a symbol of military conquest and remained so for more than a millennium.

The horrific suffering of the twentieth century, however, made its impact. The Second Vatican Council took a firm stand against war. Stating that 'we must strain every muscle for the time when war will be completely outlawed by international consent',[6] the Council urged Christians to cooperate with all men and women in securing a peace based on justice and love. Nevertheless, some Christians were not satisfied. Notable among these was the chaplain who served the U.S. forces on the Island of Tinian in 1945. George Zabelka (1915-90) watched the planes fly to Hiroshima and Nagasaki and subsequently underwent a crisis of faith. Unable to reconcile any kind of violence with the gospels, he claimed that the just war theology was false and must be discarded. George Zabelka joined a group of Christians who pray, fast, make pilgrimage, tirelessly demanding that the institutional Church take a public stand on nonviolence in imitation of the nonviolent Jesus.[7]

Meanwhile the movement for peace in the modern world continues to gather momentum. Nonviolence is a way of life wherein one renounces violence of any kind — violence to human beings, violence to animals, violence to the environment — out of love for God and for the world. It partakes in the foolishness of the cross and the dynamic creativity of the cross. It is the power that will bring social change when war and violence bring only disillusionment, sorrow and destruction. A mystical theology of the future must be prepared to guide those who embrace this challenging way of life. This is especially so, since one who embraces nonviolence must undergo a deep and painful mystical purification in which anger is transformed into love of justice and truth.

PURIFICATION OF ANGER

Traditional mystical theology saw anger as one of the seven deadly sins that lurk in the unconscious of human beings, always ready to erupt ferociously and to destroy. But traditional mystical theology also saw the reality of just anger, a powerful and precious emotion that can bring reform and build up society. The Hebrew prophets, filled with righteous indignation when they saw the waywardness of the faithless people, called angrily for a return to the covenant. Jesus himself was angry when he saw the temple defiled: 'Take these things out of here! Stop making my Father's house a marketplace!' (John 2:16).

The challenge, then, in the mystical life is not to annihilate anger (for in so doing one might annihilate something precious) but to purify and to heal — to channel the underlying emotional energy into a constructive path. The task is no slight one. For we know that anger lies deep in the human psyche. Frequently it is passed from generation to generation in such wise that peoples who have been treated with injustice for centuries are often filled with uncontrollable anger. We know that some of the great revolutionaries of our century have drunk in anger with their mother's milk and have caused intolerable suffering to millions. Yet such terrible anger often has a core of goodness that could have been of immense value in building a just society. The task is to purify; the task is to preserve what is good.

Again anger, like other emotions, can masquerade as something else. People will say they have lost all faith or that they can no longer control their sexuality; and counselling reveals that the real problem is anger. This makes the work of purification all the more difficult.

Concretely, people who walk the path of prayer may ask: 'What am I to do with my anger? What am I to do with this uncontrollable force that rises like a volcano threatening to destroy me and everything around me?'

Mystical theology speaks of an active purification which is the way of human effort, and a passive purification which is the dark night of the soul.

Now we know that human effort, however necessary, will not

alone control human anger. 'I will' and 'I won't' can even be counter-productive, ramming the psychic energy into the unconscious where it festers and erupts in some unrecognizable form. More important is the passive purification which heals the unconscious levels of the psyche. Something has been said about this already, but a further word is not out of place.

At the beginning of the contemplative life the upper levels of the mind are swept clean, as one lets go of attachments, anxieties, reasoning, thinking and clinging of all kinds. When this happens, the unconscious begins to surface. Now the dark side of the personality (the part that has been thrown into the shade) rises up. One is faced with one's anger, just as one is faced with one's covetousness, lust, envy, pride and the rest. Now the good director tells the contempla-tive: 'Stay with your anger. Do not repress it. Go through it to liber-ation.' But why give such advice?

The reason is that at an even deeper level God is surfacing in the soul. The divine, uncreated energy is, so to speak, pushing into consciousness all the crud that has collected in the unconscious through the centuries. Needless to say, this causes great suffering. To be faced with one's darkness is painful. To be faced with the darkness of God is even more painful; for the meeting of the limited human with unlimited divine is necessarily a terrible thing.

Yet salvation comes in this way. As the human person is divinized by the inflow of the divine, so the human energies — the anger, the sexuality, the appetites — are divinized. The person whose anger has been transformed can face society with a divine anger that truly shakes heaven and earth. Nor is this mere theory. Leaders of peaceful revolution have been filled with divine anger. Oscar Romero, while identifying with the poor and downtrodden, casti-gated the ruling class with a passionate anger that led to his death.

MYSTIC OF PEACE

The atomic holocaust in Nagasaki gave birth to a mystic of extraor-dinary depth. Takashi Nagai (1908-51) was a medical doctor, a nuclear physicist and head of the radiology department at the University of Nagasaki. A Nagasaki Christian, Nagai was totally committed to the Japanese war effort and to the victory of his country. Then the bomb fell. Buried beneath a heap of rubble he managed to survive, only to find that his wife was dead, his home destroyed, his country defeated, his dreams shattered. Later he describes it to a friend:

The university has lost everything. The buildings are totally destroyed. Most of the staff and students have died and those of us who have survived are crippled and useless as you see. My wife is dead; my property is lost; my house is destroyed. I have lost everything. I have nothing.[8]

Like the mystics of the apophatic tradition Nagai has become nothing.

Yet from the depths of this nothingness came a deep conversion of heart. As he lay on his tatami mat with a few doctors and nurses, a man appeared asking them to treat a wounded friend. Nagai curtly told the nurse to refuse. 'Japan has lost. Why talk about the wounded? A hundred million people are today in tears. Are we to make a fuss about the life or death of one or two? Japan will never rise again.'[9]

As the man walked lifelessly away, Nagai had a sudden change of heart. Jumping to his feet and scarcely able to stand, he told the nurse to call the man back. In his breast there had arisen a deep love for all men and women and a longing to devote the remainder of his life to peace. Under his leadership the little band of doctors and nurses, crippled and wounded, made their way through the devastated countryside tending the sick, until they themselves collapsed from exhaustion.

As he prayed in his tiny hut, Nagai tried to find meaning in the terrible thing that had happened; and he was torn by two conflicting emotions.

On the one hand, war was a terrible scourge which must never happen again. The militarists had idealized war, enlisting the help of poets; and Nagai exclaims:

But where is the beauty of the atomic bomb? If you had been

here on that day and at that time, if you had seen hell opened up on earth before your eyes, if you had even a glimpse of that, you would never, never entertain the crazy thought of another war.'[10]

He goes on to speak of the innumerable innocent people who would be annihilated in a split second. 'There will be no beautiful stories, no songs, no poems, no paintings, no music, no literature, no research. Only death.'[11]

On the other hand, as his faith deepened, Nagai tried to fit the atomic tragedy into the plan of God. Why did a loving God permit such a catastrophe and so much suffering?

He answers with a question, 'Is there not a profound relationship between the destruction of Nagasaki and the end of the war?'[12] And he comes to the conclusion that the holy city of Nagasaki, the city that ran red with the blood of martyrs 'was chosen as a victim, a pure lamb, to be slaughtered and burned on the altar of sacrifice to expiate the sins committed by humanity in the Second World War'.[13] The victims of Nagasaki were privileged martyrs, chosen by God. 'How noble, how splendid was that holocaust of August 9, when flames soared up from the cathedral, dispelling the darkness of war and bringing the light of peace!'[14]

Nagai's sacrificial theology was, and remains, controversial. Some theologians have argued that a loving God does not exact such bloody sacrifice and that Nagasaki was simply a consequence of human sinfulness. Yet even if this is true, no one can deny that when he came to a practical solution Nagai was profoundly Christian. His formula was simple and evangelical: Love one another. If we can love one another peace will come.

As he lay dying of leukaemia, he was more and more consumed with a love of humanity and a love of peace. The rosary passed through his feeble fingers and he kept repeating the words: 'Grant us peace!'

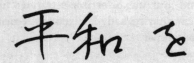

平和を

These characters he wrote on parchment in his inimitable calligraphy, giving them to all who visited his little hut. Peace was a gift of God. It could not be achieved by human effort.

Most striking is the optimism that radiated from the dying Nagai. He listened to the cathedral bells ringing out to the world the message of peace. Those bells were silenced by the bomb: they must never again be silenced. They must for ever ring peace. 'The bells are ringing!', cries the dying man. 'These are the bells of the Angelus ringing out from the ruined cathedral, echoing across the atomic wilderness and telling us that dawn has come.'[15]

Dawn has indeed come. With the bells of peace clanging in the background the dying Nagai makes a last impassioned prayer to God:

Grant that Nagasaki may be the last atomic wilderness in the history of the world.[16]

Nagai's prayer still echoes in the hearts of millions throughout the world.

CONCLUSION

A great development has taken place in the twentieth century as Christians everywhere become aware of the social dimension of their religion. Christians see that to follow Christ they must resonate with the suffering of the world — with the poor and afflicted and distressed. The Second Vatican Council summed it up in the grand opening sentence of *Gaudium et Spes*: 'The joys and hopes, the griefs and the anxieties of the men and women of this age, especially those who are poor or in any way afflicted, these too are the joys and hopes, the griefs and anxieties of the followers of Christ.'[17]

And in feeling this sense of the world Christians are not alone. A sense of solidarity — of union with one another, with the environment and with the whole cosmos — has descended upon the human family. If people in one part of the globe experience love and compassion, people elsewhere rejoice. If people in one part of the globe are massacred, people elsewhere react with concern. Not to do so would be to betray our humanity.

And if men and women are moving toward a sense of solidarity, those called to the mystical life cannot claim exemption. The authentic mystic can never flee from the world. He or she must resonate with the suffering and the agony that is the common legacy of humankind. Even the solitary mystic who retires to mountain or desert must remain in contact with the world — loving the world, suffering with the world, confronting the evil of the world.

And active mystics who live in the hurly-burly enter into the same inner silence as those who live in the desert. They experience the inner fire and the inner light; they experience the living flame of love that makes their being to be being-in-love. Now the inner fire drives them — no longer to the wilderness (though they may spend some time in the wilderness) but to the crowded marketplace and to the inner city. The living flame of love drives them to walk in peace marches, to demonstrate in the streets, to denounce oppressive structures, to confront princes and kings, to go to prison and to die. Like the mystic in the desert they pass through agonizing dark nights and come to profound enlightenment. The mystic in the silent desert and the mystic in the noisy city are alike in following one who emptied himself taking the form of a slave and was given a name that is above all names.

NOTES

1. *Rerum Novarum* (1891). This was followed forty years later by *Quadragesimo Anno* of Pius XI.
2. *Apostolicam Actuositatem*, 5.
3. See *Arrupe, una explosion en la Iglesia*, Pedro Miguel Lamet, Madrid 1989. See also *Justice with Faith Today*, Pedro Arrupe, The Institute of Jesuit Sources, St Louis U.S.A. 1980.
4. *Unitatis Redintegratio*, 6.
5. *The Cloud of Unknowing*, C. 3.
6. *Gaudium et Spes*, 82.
7. George Zabelka had a deep conversion to nonviolence. At the age of 67 he walked 7,500 miles from Washington to Bethlehem, praying for peace. In England a television documentary was made of his life, 'The Reluctant Prophet.' In Australia a popular song 'My name is George Zabelka' is still played on the radio.
8. *The Bells of Nagasaki*, Takashi Nagai, trans. by William Johnston, Kodansha International Tokyo — New York — London, 1984, p. 101.
9. Ibid., p. 81.

10. Ibid., p. 103.
11. Ibid., p. 104.
12. Ibid., p. 107.
13. Ibid.
14. Ibid., p. 108.
15. Ibid., p. 117.
16. Ibid., p. 118.
17. *Gaudium et Spes*, 1.

—————— ❋ ——————

The Heart Sutra

The Bodhisattva Avalokiteshvara,
When practising deeply the *prajna paramita*,
Perceives that all five *skandhas* are empty
And is saved from suffering and distress.

Shariputra, form does not differ from emptiness;
Emptiness does not differ from form.
Form is emptiness;
Emptiness is form.
The same is true of feelings, perceptions, impulses, consciousness.

Shariputra, these *dharmas* are all marked with emptiness;
They neither appear nor disappear,
Are neither tainted nor pure,
Do neither increase nor decrease.

Therefore in emptiness there is no form,
No feelings, no perceptions, no impulses, no consciousness;
No eyes, no ears, no nose, no tongue, no body, no mind;
No colour, no sound, no smell, no taste, no touch, no object of mind;
No realm of eyes and so forth until no realm of mind-
    consciousness;
No ignorance and also no extinction of ignorance, and so forth until
    no-old-age-and-death and also no extinction of them;
No suffering, no origination, no stopping, no path;
No cognition, also no attainment.
With nothing to attain
The Bodhisattva depends on *prajna paramita*

And the mind is no obstacle.
Without any obstacle no fears exist;
Departing from every perverted view he attains Nirvana.

In the three worlds all Buddhas depend on *prajna paramita*
And attain supreme, perfect enlightenment.

Therefore know that *prajna paramita*
Is the great transcendent mantram,
The great bright mantram,
The supreme mantram,
The perfect mantram,
Which is able to relieve all suffering
And is true, not false.
So proclaim the *prajna paramita* mantram,
Proclaim the mantram that says:

Gate, gate, paragate, parasamgate. Bodhi! Svaha!

ACKNOWLEDGMENTS

————————— ✳ —————————

The author wishes to express deep gratitude to Heinrich Dumoulin who read each chapter of this book as it was written, making invaluable comments, always giving encouragement and reassurance. He also wishes to thank James Heisig and the scholars of the Institute of Religion and Culture of Nanzan University with whom this book was discussed as a seminar. Their comments were of great value. The author is also greatly indebted to Shigeko Yano who wrote the Japanese characters and to Renato Ortega who typed and edited the manuscript.

The author also thanks the editors of *The Way* (London), *Studia Missionalia* (Rome) and *Cistercian Studies* (California) for permission to reprint material already published in these periodicals. He is, furthermore, grateful for permission to quote from *The Collected Works of St John of the Cross* and *The Collected Works of St Teresa of Avila* translated by Kieran Kavanaugh and Otilio Rodriguez, published by The Washington Province of Discalced Carmelites, ICS Publications 2131 Lincoln Road, N.E., Washington, D.C. 20002, U.S.A. He also thanks the trustees of the Lonergan Estate for permission to quote from *Method in Theology* and *Second Collection* by Bernard Lonergan.

Index